Mahler & Strauss

Mahler & Strauss

In Dialogue

CHARLES YOUMANS

INDIANA UNIVERSITY PRESS
Bloomington & Indianapolis

This book is a publication of

Indiana University Press
Office of Scholarly Publishing
Herman B Wells Library 350
1320 East 10th Street
Bloomington, Indiana 47405 USA

iupress.indiana.edu

© 2016 by Charles Youmans

All rights reserved
No part of this book may be reproduced or utilized in any form or by any means, electronic or mechanical, including photocopying and recording, or by any information storage and retrieval system, without permission in writing from the publisher. The Association of American University Presses' Resolution on Permissions constitutes the only exception to this prohibition.

The paper used in this publication meets the minimum requirements of the American National Standard for Information Sciences—Permanence of Paper for Printed Library Materials, ANSI Z39.48-1992.

Manufactured in the United States of America

Library of Congress Cataloging-in-Publication Data

Names: Youmans, Charles Dowell, [date]– author.
Title: Mahler and Strauss : in dialogue / Charles Youmans.
Description: Bloomington ; Indianapolis : Indiana University Press, 2016. | Includes bibliographical references and index.
Identifiers: LCCN 2016024305 (print) | LCCN 2016024671 (ebook) | ISBN 9780253021595 (cl : alk. paper) | ISBN 9780253021663 (e-book)
Subjects: LCSH: Mahler, Gustav, 1860–1911. | Strauss, Richard, 1864–1949.
Classification: LCC ML410.M23 Y68 2016 (print) | LCC ML410.M23 (ebook) | DDC 780.92/2 [B] —dc23
LC record available at https://lccn.loc.gov/2016024305

1 2 3 4 5 21 20 19 18 17 16

For Nancy

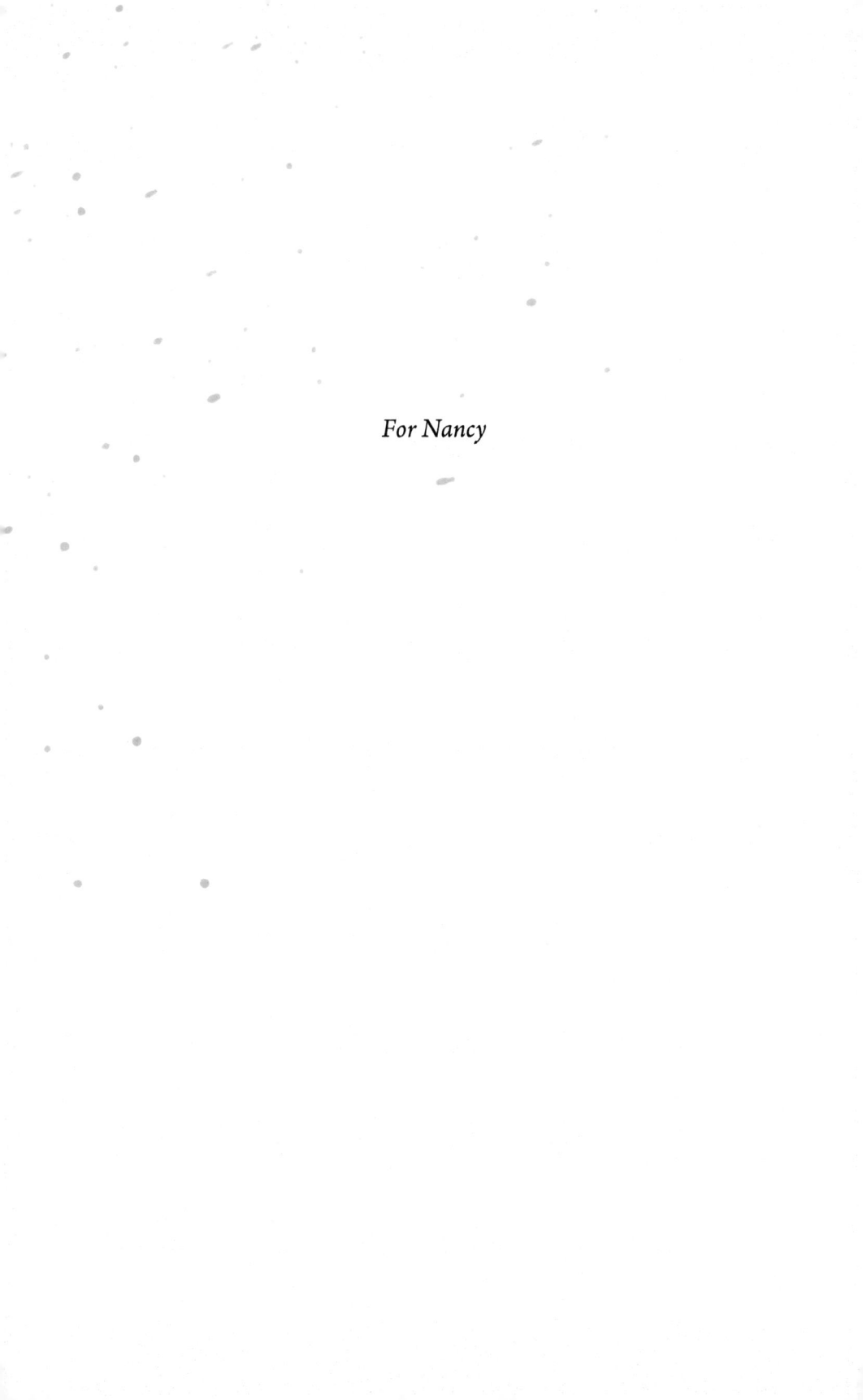

Contents

Preface ix
Acknowledgments xiii
Note on Translation xvii

Introduction: *Friends* 1

1 Children 20

2 Conductors 35

3 Husbands 49

4 Wagnerians 64

5 Businessmen 79

6 Literati 92

7 Autobiographers 107

8 *Programmmusiker* 122

9 Imports 137

10 Allusionists 153

11 Ironists *167*

12 Metaphysicians *182*

Epilogue: *Individuals* *197*

Notes 211
Bibliography 259
Index 277

Preface

⇜ FIFTEEN YEARS AGO, chatting with colleagues in the dependably fruitful setting of a hotel bar, I floated the idea of a conference on Mahler and Strauss. My youthful tenure-track self considered this a sure winner, an idea long overdue. "Forget it," came the instant response of a senior scholar who belonged neither to the Straussians nor the Mahlerians but knew both sides well. "It'll never work."

There was wisdom in this pronouncement. Polite intercourse notwithstanding, the scholars effectively belong to camps, more so than the general enthusiasts. A joint gathering has yet to be seen on either side of the Atlantic, despite growing scholarly interest in both figures. And yet, for a lone wolf the topic holds an irresistible attraction.

Anyone who flips through the correspondence—carefully edited in 1980 by Herta Blaukopf, who wrote what remains the definitive treatment of the topic—can see that these composers got along far better than have their devotees. Strauss, the self-styled "first Mahlerian," was already called an "old friend" by Mahler in 1897, ten years after their introduction in Leipzig. The substantial historical record includes meetings, conversations, study and performance of one another's works—and, yes, sharp, interesting disagreements. There is good reason for someone to forge ahead with a scholarly investigation, then, expecting that others will eventually join in.

I have not set out to write *the* book on this relationship. Particularly in biographical writing, we musicologists tend to produce monographs that double as reference sources, with every scrap of documentary evidence collected and arranged chronologically for easy access. This volume is not such a tool, though it makes fairly thorough use of the surviving evidence and contributes some new material. What I have written instead is a reading, and one that dispenses with linear narrative in favor of a fragmentary, topic-based approach. The details and intent of this methodology are explained in the introduction. Here I would merely suggest that our best chance to catch glimpses of truth in such a complex and contentious area is to look from different angles and allow peripheral vision to fill in what is missing.

The question of which themes to include has cost me as much sleep as the methodological challenges. Certainly other topics could be imagined. Nature, for example, would seem an obvious choice, considering the quasi-religious enthusiasm of both composers in this area. Should it have its own chapter, or can the points be made through discussion of other concerns? I hope the latter, but another writer might choose differently. Likewise, many of the subjects I did select could themselves receive book-length treatments. This reality bothered me particularly in the chapter on Wagner, where my desire to make a specific point (about the composers' distinct receptions of Wagner's musical philosophy) preempted interesting but ultimately overburdening tasks, such as tracing the voluminous allusions to Wagner across the two oeuvres.

The Mahler-Strauss relationship deserves many books, then, not one, and hopefully mine will serve as a stimulus. By training and experience I am a Straussian; perhaps that in itself will be enough to elicit a companion volume in the near future. Nonetheless, I do not believe that this book treats Strauss more gently than it does Mahler, even if at some subconscious level I hold ingrained biases. As will become clear, in certain qualities of personality, spiritual outlook, and even musical taste, I find Mahler easier to identify with than Strauss. Although twenty-five years of research on Strauss have left me feeling that I lived his life along with him,

I would still claim, not at all pejoratively, that Mahler's character is self-evidently less confounding than that of his counterpart.

It is my hope that this book can and will be read by nonmusicians. Obscure musical terminology appears only rarely, and most of what I describe in the music will be audible to lay readers. Interdisciplinary research teaches one all too keenly that every field has its own jargon; I have attempted to forestall the Babel effect wherever possible. Likewise, in the interest of readability I have used English translations (published, if available) for quotations from German sources, though where clarity and/or style demands it I have included the original language, either in the main text or the notes. For quotations from unpublished sources I have provided the German.

Acknowledgments

◈ MANY INDIVIDUALS AND INSTITUTIONS have kindly assisted me in my work. At the beautiful villa on Zoeppritzstraße, the Strauss family once again warmly supported my research. I am grateful to Gabriele Strauss (whose late husband Richard hosted me, as I will always remember, on my first visit in 1994) and to Christian Strauss for permission to study and quote from archival materials. Also in Garmisch-Partenkirchen, Christian Wolf and Jürgen May at the Richard-Strauss-Institut facilitated my work in numerous invaluable ways, as they do for Strauss scholars across the globe. At the Bayerische Staatsbibliothek in Munich, Hartmut Schaefer and Sabine Kurth of the Musikabteilung and Sigrid von Moisy of the Abteilung für Handschriften und Alte Drucke allowed me easy access to materials on both Strauss and Mahler, especially those portions of the splendid Moldenhauer Archives now held at the Stabi. Henry-Louis de La Grange and his efficient staff at the Médiathèque Musicale Mahler in Paris made available a number of unique sources, some unknown to me, and gave me an excuse for picnics in the Parc Monceau. In Vienna, Frank Fanning scrambled to arrange for the offices of the Internationale Gustav Mahler Gesellschaft to be opened for me during a visit in the vacation month of July. Likewise, the librarians of the Musiksammlung of the Österreichische Nationalbibliothek generously accelerated the ordering process and agreed without exception to my requests to see original documents rather than copies. I am grateful also to the staffs of the Morgan Library & Museum and the Music Division of the New York Public Library. For the necessary arrangements and permission to publish images I warmly thank Gilbert Kaplan of The Kaplan Foundation, New York; Jürgen May of the Richard-Strauss-Institut, Garmisch-Partenkirchen; Brian McMillan of the University of Western Ontario; Ann Kersting-Meuleman of the Universitätsbibliothek Johann Christian Senckenberg, Frankfurt am Main; and Irina Graef of the Archiv Berliner Philharmoniker.

I am particularly appreciative of the comments provided to me by Bryan Gilliam and Jürgen Thym, who read the entire manuscript and improved it in countless ways; any errors that remain are my responsibility. Over the years I have read portions of the manuscript at assorted venues and am happy to have heard many useful responses; for these and for enlightening informal conversations I thank especially Walter Werbeck, Morten Kristiansen, David Larkin, Stephen E. Hefling, Morten Solvik, Jim Zychowicz, and Walter Frisch. My colleagues at Penn State—Marica Tacconi, Mark Ferraguto, Maureen Carr, Taylor Greer, Eric McKee, Steve Hopkins, Tom Cody, and Vincent Benitez—create a work environment that could not be more congenial. For ten years now I have had the good fortune to work for Sue Haug, director of the Penn State School of Music, a fine musician and thoughtful administrator who values musicological research and ensures that it is supported. Grants from the College of Arts and Architecture and Penn State's Institute for the Arts and Humanities provided the funding necessary for research trips to Germany, Austria, France, England, and New York City; I would like to thank Barbara Korner, dean of the College, and Marica Tacconi, former director of the Institute, for contributing to my efforts in this meaningful way. I also thank Gunalan Nadarajan, former associate dean for research and graduate studies in the College of Arts and Architecture, for his support early in the process, as well as William Doan and Andrew Schultz, his able successors. At Indiana University Press, Raina Polivka provided invaluable support and guidance throughout the process. I offer my sincere thanks to her, to my keen-eyed copyeditor Adriana Cloud, and to all the staff who worked diligently on my behalf.

The early stages of research for this project gave me the opportunity for an unforgettable summer in Europe with my wife, Nancy, and our daughters, Frances and Hannah. We climbed the Eiffel Tower, we hiked the Zugspitzplatt, we looked out at Vienna from the Upper Belvedere, we played in Munich's English Garden, we ate and drank like royalty—and during business hours, a doting father wrote a book about two doting fathers. With fond memories of those happy months and all the wonderful years since, I dedicate this book to Nancy, in love and gratitude.

Note on Translation

In citing German sources I have used published English translations (occasionally emended) when available. Unless otherwise noted, page numbers in the notes refer to the translations.

Bauer-Lechner	Killian, Herbert, and Knud Martner, eds. *Gustav Mahler in den Erinnerungen von Natalie Bauer-Lechner.* Hamburg: K. D. Wagner, 1984; Bauer-Lechner, Natalie. *Recollections of Gustav Mahler.* Edited by Peter Franklin. Translated by Dika Newlin. Cambridge: Cambridge University Press, 1980.
Chronicle	Willi Schuh. *Richard Strauss. Jugend und frühe Meisterjahre. Lebenschronik 1864–1898.* Zurich: Atlantis, 1976; *Richard Strauss: A Chronicle of the Early Years, 1864–1898.* Translated by Mary Whittall. Cambridge: Cambridge University Press, 1982.
Gustav/Alma	La Grange, Henry-Louis de, and Günther Weiß, eds. *Ein Glück ohne Ruh': Die Briefe Gustav Mahlers an Alma.* Berlin: Wolf Jobst Siedler, 1995; *Gustav Mahler:*

	Letters to His Wife. Edited by Henry-Louis de La Grange and Günther Weiss, in collaboration with Knud Martner. Translated and revised by Antony Beaumont. Ithaca, NY: Cornell University Press, 1995.
La Grange I	La Grange, Henry-Louis de. *Mahler.* Vol. 1. Garden City, NY: Doubleday, 1973.
La Grange II	La Grange, Henry-Louis de. *Gustav Mahler.* Vol. 2, *Vienna: The Years of Challenge.* Oxford: Oxford University Press, 1995.
La Grange III	La Grange, Henry-Louis de. *Gustav Mahler.* Vol. 3, *Vienna: Triumph and Disillusion.* Oxford: Oxford University Press, 1999.
La Grange IV	La Grange, Henry-Louis de. *Gustav Mahler.* Vol. 4, *A New Life Cut Short (1907–1911).* Oxford: Oxford University Press, 2008.
Life, Work and World	Blaukopf, Kurt, and Herta Blaukopf, eds. *Mahler: His Life, Work and World.* Translated by Paul Baker et al. London: Thames & Hudson, 1991.
Mahler Letters	Mahler, Gustav. *Briefe.* 2nd ed. Edited by Herta Blaukopf. Vienna: Zsolnay, 1996; *Selected Letters of Gustav Mahler.* Edited by Knud Martner. Translated by Eithne Wilkins, Ernst Kaiser, and Bill Hopkins. New York: Farrar, Straus and Giroux, 1979.
Mahler/Strauss	Blaukopf, Herta, ed. *Gustav Mahler, Richard Strauss: Briefwechsel 1888–1911.* Munich: R. Piper, 1980; *Gustav Mahler, Richard Strauss: Correspondence 1888–1911.* Translated by Edmund Jephcott. Chicago: University of Chicago Press, 1984.
Memories and Letters	Mahler, Alma. *Gustav Mahler: Erinnerungen und Briefe.* Amsterdam: Allert de Lange, 1949; *Gustav Mahler: Memories and Letters.* Edited by Donald Mitchell. Translated by Basil Creighton. London: Cardinal, 1990.

Recollections   Strauss, Richard. *Betrachtungen und Erinnerungen*. 2nd ed. Edited by Willi Schuh. Zurich: Atlantis, 1957; *Recollections and Reflections*. Translated by L. J. Lawrence. London: Boosey & Hawkes, 1953.

Rivalry   Blaukopf, Herta. "Rivalität und Freundschaft: Die persönlichen Beziehungen zwischen Gustav Mahler und Richard Strauss." In *Mahler/Strauss* (German), 129–220; "Rivalry and Friendship: An Essay on the Mahler-Strauss Relationship." In *Mahler/Strauss* (English), 103–58.

Mahler & Strauss

Introduction

FRIENDS

THIS BOOK ADDRESSES a perplexing lacuna in musical scholarship. For over a century, Gustav Mahler and Richard Strauss have been widely acknowledged as the greatest Austro-German musicians of their generation. They knew each other for twenty-four years, maintaining regular personal contact. Their surviving correspondence includes over ninety items (many of Strauss's letters having been lost). They performed each other's music eagerly and promoted it using every advantage of position and reputation. Yet, somehow, no scholarly treatment of the relationship appeared until nearly seven decades after Mahler's death. That first attempt, an essay appended by Herta Blaukopf to her 1980 edition of the correspondence, made a good start but inspired few followers.[1] Shorter accounts appeared sporadically—mostly on this side of the Atlantic—but none of them built substantially on Blaukopf's work, and authors of the many biographies have continued to dispense with the topic in a few pages.[2]

I shall not waste much time fretting over this deplorable lack of curiosity. For the most part it reflects blatant partisanship on both sides among critics, artists, and scholars, even those as gifted as Arnold Schoenberg and Theodor W. Adorno.[3] (Blaukopf herself was accused, by no smaller an authority than Carl Dahlhaus, of "one-sidedly placing Mahler in the foreground.")[4] Analyzing petty disputes can do little to illuminate composers who, as we shall see, felt much greater affection for each other than would their devotees. Therefore, mindful that the relationship and its reception are different things, I begin with two questions that seem more interesting, one historical and the other historiographical. First, was there really any depth to this relationship? And second, how far can we go in reconstructing it?

Blaukopf certainly made the case for a deep connection, on artistic, philosophical, personal, and emotional planes. Her essay is steeped in primary sources, and they tell an unfamiliar story. We hear Strauss claim the title of "the first 'Mahlerian.'" We smile as Mahler rails against "New German pedantry," then sheepishly calls Strauss "of all the gods my only friend." We find Strauss risking his own reputation to intercede with Hans von Bülow, who had dismissed the young Mahler too hastily. We feel Mahler's pride at sending an autograph to his sister from "one of the most notable composers," someone with "a great future in front of him." The anecdotes abound, extending across half of Mahler's life. Strauss champions his friend's First Symphony while hosting the festival of the Allgemeiner deutscher Musikverein (General German Music Association, henceforth ADMV) in 1894 at Weimar, beginning a long record of advocacy. Mahler accepts a ballet of Strauss for Vienna before he has seen the score, and indeed before the work has been composed; later he fights (quixotically) to establish a place in the Vienna repertoire for Strauss's bizarre second opera, the über-Bavarian conceit *Feuersnot*. Strauss encourages the forty-six-year-old Mahler to try his hand at opera, asserting that he has "great talent for it." Mahler insists to a skeptical Alma Mahler that *Salome* "is one of the greatest masterpieces of our time." Strauss attends Berlin rehearsals of Mahler's Fifth (under Nikisch) and sends earnest constructive criticism, as he would for all the symphonies through the Sixth. Mahler advises Strauss on the dance in *Salome*, after the composer plays and sings the opera to him—minus Salome's yet-to-be-composed seven-veil performance—in a piano shop in Strasbourg. Strauss rearranges a vacation auto tour to visit Mahler in the Dolomites, a meeting Mahler calls "almost as between potentates." Mahler instructs his publisher regarding gratis copies of his Eighth Symphony, putting Strauss at the top of the list. Strauss writes to the dying Mahler of his enjoyment at preparing a new performance of the Third Symphony, a work they both know to be his least favorite; Alma, no ally of Strauss, later tells him that the letter provided "one of Gustav's last joys."

Interest, honesty, concern, annoyance, humor, joy—their association had all the signs of a genuine friendship, notwithstanding the obvious rivalry and a fair share of lively disagreements.[5] For once in the history of western music, we meet a pair of great composers who knew and liked each other. This revelation alone earns Blaukopf our gratitude, all the more because she made it while limiting herself to the presentation of documentary evidence, supplying basic context but steering clear of broader critical interpretation. Her choice here was more conventional than personal; the severe conception of intellectual honesty characteristic of Blaukopf's era and scholarly milieu demanded that she stop the investigation just as it became interesting. And there is no denying that for many interactions between Strauss and Mahler we have only a few shreds of information: when, where, and a hint or two of what was discussed. Faced with yawning gaps and spotty documentation, an empirical musicologist faithful to her training adopted a dignified reticence.

Should that be the final word? Can we advance no further? I would suggest that in fact we know more than we realize. Early modernism has been one of the most studied periods in the history of western music, especially in the last few decades. We now have a wealth of information that, while perhaps not constituting direct evidence, allows us to imagine reliably what might have transpired between the two leading figures in given sets of circumstances.

Consider, for example, the day they met: October 12, 1887. Our factual information is exceedingly limited; we know only that Strauss was visiting Leipzig in order to conduct his F-minor Symphony with the Gewandhaus Orchestra (on October 13), and that he spent time with Mahler, whom he called (in a letter to Bülow of October 29) a "highly intelligent musician and conductor," "one of the few modern conductors who knows about tempo modification," a musician with "excellent views, particularly on Wagner's tempi," who had recently created a new "masterpiece"—the arrangement of Weber's *Die drei Pintos*.[6] No other record of their conversation exists, and indeed we have no indication of whether they met again while Strauss remained in Leipzig. We cannot even say with certainty that Mahler attended Strauss's performance.

From Strauss's few comments, however, we can infer much. First, Bülow himself obviously would have been a topic of conversation, and in particular his idiosyncratic handling of tempi, which Strauss absorbed in Meiningen rehearsals with score in hand (while serving as the conductor's assistant in the fall of 1885). Strauss would for the rest of his life call Bülow the greatest performing musician he had ever known, and the deepest impression had been made by Bülow's flexible approach to tempi, which allowed considerable fluctuation in order to accommodate the fundamental artistic considerations of musical energy and line. While Mahler obviously wanted a detailed report on the experience that had been denied him when Strauss won the Meiningen position, he also would have wanted to demonstrate that he already understood—not least of all so that he could get the word out, through Strauss, that he had kept faith with Bülow and had managed a successful discipleship from afar. (In Hamburg four years later Bülow would finally recognize Mahler for what he was.) The small number of Welte-Mignon recordings left by Mahler, of the *Songs of a Wayfarer* and the first movement of the Fifth Symphony, offer hints of this Bülowian practice: tempo is shaped no less assertively than dynamics, in a manner that can strike the modern ear as "rushing" or "dragging," but that in the school of Bülow was deeply related to the life of a musical line.[7]

Having studied Strauss's symphony and shared his own creative activities as arranger (we know that he played the first act of *Pintos* for Strauss), Mahler likely would have described his own current project, the First Symphony, and inquired about Strauss's recent compositions. Mahler's intense early devotion to program music, and his embrace of the full range of divergent programmatic approaches (tone painting, detailed written programs à la Berlioz, Liszt's practice of distilling a program to what Wagner called the "eternal motive"), would have been reinforced powerfully by this rising New German celebrity. Although the composition that Strauss would perform on this trip was remarkable for its formal strictness, his latest creative activity had taken an entirely different tack: it included a *Tondichtung* (tone poem) based on the shattering and gruesome tale of Macbeth, and an opera libretto building on Wagner's idiom (for better or worse). The story of Mahler's compositional career through the mid-1890s would be one not of opposition to Strauss's new direction but of attempted emulation: the First is at once a panoply of ultramodern tone painting, a Beethovenian *per aspera ad astra* drama, and a mélange of overlapping literary influences. The seeds of such a project were nurtured, if not planted, in this first meeting with the greatest program musician after Liszt.

A conversation between young professionals about performance and composition would have touched on marketing, directly or indirectly—on what they might do for one another, in other words. We know that over the next few years Mahler regularly inquired as to the progress of *Guntram* and volunteered his efforts to promote it, even after he decided that the music was irritatingly pompous. And Strauss would become Mahler's most effective publicist as soon as he had something to promote. There was more to this practical advocacy than crass opportunism; from their earliest years these composers regarded the market as a meaningful and authentic gauge of artistic quality. If the music was good and if it was understood, it would draw a large audience—or so they believed (as good students of Goethe). Thus the pursuit of public success was not separable from the pursuit of authentic artistic success, however strongly their mutual protégé Schoenberg may have argued to the contrary. The same held true in the world of conducting, where a full house did not necessarily indicate a real connection with the audience, but a real connection with the audience always led to full houses—hence the high stakes of Wagnerian conducting, to which Strauss alluded in his letter to Bülow. They both were gearing up for a battle with "accredited" conductors of Wagner who, as agreed by Mahler and Strauss in their first conversation, were putting the legacy in danger. Not to present these works in "authentic" interpretations would mean changing their very nature—it would deprive them of their power to move the listeners who kept them alive.

Aside from these areas there were of course the more immediate personal interactions in the process of sizing up, when a poor impression or an awkward move on either side could have sidetracked the relationship for good. Aborted friendships of this sort were common for both men; by this early date they both had well-developed routines for sniffing out and dismissing mediocrity. Education, knowledge, wit, self-confidence, range of interests, and so on would have been assessed more or less instantly. It is to be expected, for example, that they quickly recognized each other's gymnasium education and, even more important, the living reality of *Bildung* (spiritual education or formation) in each other's personality. A genuine intellectual life constituted one of two requirements for a real bond to form, the other being the demonstration of *Fachkenntnis*, professional competency. And that was naturally the principal root of their esteem. Looking back over the twenty-four-year friendship, one finds that the special attachment of these composers was first of all a musical one: a mutual recognition that the two of them enjoyed a level of ability that no one else alive at that time possessed or could fathom. In that regard, Strauss knew Mahler and Mahler knew Strauss in ways that they could never explain to others. And in the moment when for the first time they sat down at the piano together, talking and playing and listening, they recognized that there at last was the kindred spirit for whom each of them had longed since childhood.

Even this preliminary sketch shows that much is to be gained by fleshing out the context and using a bit of imagination. Extensive research has been done on Mahler in the last thirty years, and Strauss too has had some healthy attention, if from a smaller group of scholars. One can safely say that we know these composers better now than we ever have before. How, then, can we not also have gained a deeper account of their friendship? Certainly we have the means of telling the story in a new way.

For these composers there exist any number of topics or themes that invite comparative analysis. How did they line up as Wagnerians? As program musicians? In their appropriations of other composers' music? On the conducting podium? How did their childhood experiences shape their mature lives? What were they like as husbands? Businessmen? Celebrities? What literature interested them? What philosophical and religious ideals grounded their work? What did they make of the United States, and what did "Americans" make of them? What did they think of themselves? Approaching the matter within these broader frames of reference could reveal a bigger picture than would seem possible given the fragments we possess. It could work, I might say, as the human eye does:

in spite of dreadful peripheral vision, an awkward blind spot, and a tiny focal area, we somehow manage to see what is in front of us, thanks to the constructive power of our brains.

What I propose, then, is to investigate the relationship in thirteen different contexts, in the hope that along the way the familiar becomes new, or in any case richer. For the remainder of this introduction I will briefly discuss the three main phases of the friendship, mentioning the principal events and suggesting how my chosen themes might be relevant. That overview, and the information provided by Blaukopf (whose essay I assume readers of this book will have consulted) should provide a useful jumping-off point for the subsequent chapters.

Because Mahler and Strauss worked for most of their lives in the relatively small circle of elite Austro-German composer/conductors, they had regular occasions for informal contact. Typically they met at least once a year, at the conference of the ADMV, in addition to chance encounters at performances and in hotel lobbies, trains stations, and the like. Beyond this routine, there were three periods during which the contact was particularly intense. The first came in the early to mid-1890s, when they were separating themselves from their competitors—Strauss having more success as a composer, Mahler as a conductor. Just after the turn of the century they again seemed to need each other more than usual, not coincidentally at a crucial moment of transition in their creative careers, when Mahler ostensibly abandoned program music and Strauss shifted from tone poems to operas. Finally, in the second half of the decade their status as senior leaders fostered a new kind of commiseration, first over *Salome*, a work Mahler recognized as a watershed moment in the history of music and championed even though it cost him professionally and personally.

In the first phase they established their interest in and loyalty to each another. Most letters (twenty-one of twenty-eight) come from 1894–95, but the content and tone make it clear that the relationship developed steadily in the years after 1887. (A few bits of corroboration exist; we know, for example, that Mahler visited Munich in the summer of 1888, when Strauss had occasion to read through the third movement of the First Symphony at the piano with Hermann Levi.) The first half of 1894 saw them behave for the first time as confidantes, even intimates, during the decline and death of Bülow. That season they each conducted one concert of Bülow's Hamburg series, and Bernhard Pollini, the clever and ruthless director of the Hamburg Stadttheater, stepped forward as a shared antagonist.[8] Shoring up his negotiating position for Mahler's upcoming contract renewal, Pollini played the two conductors against each other, flirting with Strauss but seemingly intent on keeping Mahler, albeit with the most favorable conditions possible. Their responses to his machinations reveal a strong and warm alliance; they shared intelligence freely and alerted one another to their own strategic moves before making them.[9] In this same period they took great pains to look after each other's new compositions: Strauss would assist Mahler in making a second attempt at introducing his First Symphony (at the 1894 meeting of the ADMV, in a performance arranged by Strauss), and Mahler very nearly brought about a Hamburg premiere of Strauss's ill-fated first opera, *Guntram*. For neither individual did these efforts promise any personal gain; indeed, there is no reason to suspect any motivation other than a sincere belief in the quality of the music, and a desire to learn from anything that was good. Mahler's later disparagement of *Guntram* is belied by his continued programming of excerpts from it in his concert performances, in Vienna and later in New York. For his part, Strauss maintained a real affection for the First long after his musings on the possibility of ending the finale after the aborted breakthrough at mm. 370–75 (five measures before reh. 34)—a suggestion that Mahler found especially vexing.[10]

May and June of that year gave them each a first opportunity to watch the other deal with failure. *Guntram*'s initial production survived four performances only because it was given in Weimar, where the intendant Hans von Bronsart's affection for his difficult but brilliant employee protected the work no matter what the audiences said. (Strauss had by then been hired as kapellmeister at Munich, and was obviously headed for even greater things at Bayreuth and elsewhere.) The First had a downright rowdy reception in Weimar, complete with catcalls—a harsh response indeed, given that the audience consisted mainly of professionals expecting modernist experimentation.[11] These setbacks made both of them ponder their intended directions; as Strauss attempted the transition to operatic composer—to assume the mantle of Wagner, he would have dreamt—Mahler hoped to join Strauss at the forefront of trailblazing programmaticism. In fact, Mahler's career might have been quite different had Strauss not decided to backtrack. Putting aside plans for another opera, Strauss produced a fourth tone poem, *Till Eulenspiegels lustige Streiche* (*Till Eulenspiegel's Merry Pranks*, completed in May 1895), a work whose pyrotechnic intensity and pithy wit set a difficult standard for Mahler to match in his Second. In March 1895, Strauss, after hearing the first three movements in a performance that he arranged in Berlin, announced that he loved the new symphony, and he championed it enthusiastically with Wilhelm Kienzl and Carl Muck (figure 1). But the experience also informed his creative mind as he worked on *Till*, pushing him toward mischief and away from *Erlösung* in the high Wagnerian style. By the end of the year, when the Second would have its first full performance, *Till* was a rising tide, the Second seemed old-fashioned, and Strauss once again stood unchallenged as Europe's outstanding program musician.

For a time the friends went silent, struck dumb by this first competitive encounter. They were never far from one another's thoughts, however. Finding themselves now vying for the leadership of the programmatic avant-garde, they both turned to Nietzsche and thereby brought a private interest into public view. Mahler moved first; the roots of the Third Symphony extend back to 1893, the year in which Strauss himself delved into Nietzsche after realizing that Schopenhauer's metaphysics was a dead end for composers.[12] Having discussed *Guntram* regularly with Strauss since their first meeting, Mahler recognized both that the work had an almost pedantically Schopenhauerian ending and that this ending was meant ironically.[13] (The minstrel Guntram breaks his lyre, renounces music, and heads into the woods for a life of asceticism.) Clearly Strauss's later works would have to turn in a Nietzschean direction; as James Hepokoski has argued at length, *Till Eulenspiegel* made this move without spelling it out.[14]

In the meantime, Mahler recognized an opportunity both to trade on Nietzsche's sensationalist popularity and to offer a critique. The setting of the "Midnight Song" in the fourth movement treats the philosopher with a sentimentality and high seriousness bound to strike philosophically informed listeners as assertively anti-Nietzschean. By following this piece with the "sweet song" of three angels (the "Poor Children's Begging Song" from *Des Knaben Wunderhorn*), the composer's critical intent came as

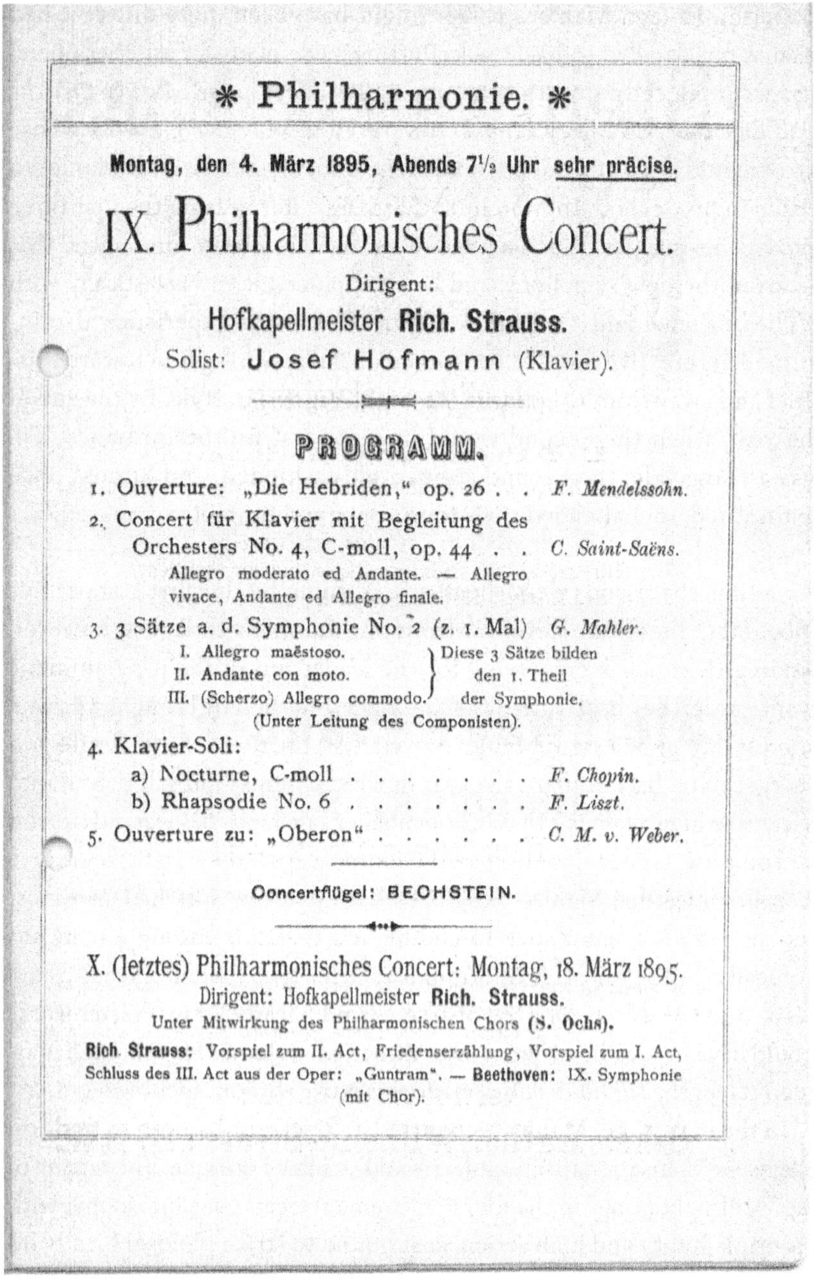

> ✻ Philharmonie. ✻
>
> Montag, den 4. März 1895, Abends 7½ Uhr sehr präcise.
>
> ## IX. Philharmonisches Concert.
>
> Dirigent:
> Hofkapellmeister **Rich. Strauss.**
> Solist: **Josef Hofmann** (Klavier).
>
> ### PROGRAMM.
>
> 1. Ouverture: „Die Hebriden," op. 26 . . *F. Mendelssohn.*
> 2. Concert für Klavier mit Begleitung des
>   Orchesters No. 4, C-moll, op. 44 . . *C. Saint-Saëns.*
>   Allegro moderato ed Andante. — Allegro
>   vivace, Andante ed Allegro finale.
> 3. 3 Sätze a. d. Symphonie No. 2 (z. 1. Mal) *G. Mahler.*
>   I. Allegro maëstoso.   ⎫ Diese 3 Sätze bilden
>   II. Andante con moto.   ⎬ den 1. Theil
>   III. (Scherzo) Allegro commodo. ⎭ der Symphonie.
>   (Unter Leitung des Componisten).
> 4. Klavier-Soli:
>   a) Nocturne, C-moll . . . . *F. Chopin.*
>   b) Rhapsodie No. 6 . . . . *F. Liszt.*
> 5. Ouverture zu: „Oberon" . . . . . . *C. M. v. Weber.*
>
> Concertflügel: **BECHSTEIN.**
>
> X. (letztes) Philharmonisches Concert: Montag, 18. März 1895.
> Dirigent: Hofkapellmeister **Rich. Strauss.**
> Unter Mitwirkung des Philharmonischen Chors (**S. Ochs**).
> **Rich. Strauss:** Vorspiel zum II. Act, Friedenserzählung, Vorspiel zum I. Act,
> Schluss des III. Act aus der Oper: „Guntram". — **Beethoven:** IX. Symphonie
> (mit Chor).

Figure 1. Program, Berlin premiere of Mahler's Second Symphony, movements 1–3. Courtesy of the Berliner Philharmoniker.

close to an explicit disavowal as a sensitive artist could tolerate.[15] But even in the first movement, the scenes with the "rabble" already engage with *Zarathustra*, specifically the protagonist's desire for escape from the "unclean" horde, presented in the chapter called "Of the Rabble," as Peter Franklin points out.[16] (Mahler added the annotation "Das Gesindel!" ["The Rabble!"] at fig. 44 of his manuscript full score.) Franklin argues for a "critical revision or reinterpretation" of Nietzsche in the rabble's ultimate participation in the march; as they join a "community of purpose," Mahler redeems them from Nietzsche's accusation. Thus even as he drew from Nietzsche the publicity value that he sensed Strauss would soon tap, Mahler promoted an alternative vision of the future, as optimistic as Nietzsche's but all-inclusive and based in love (the topic of the last movement).

The fact of Strauss's awareness of this project is only too clear from the speed with which he produced *Also sprach Zarathustra*, a tone poem begun, unusually for him, in February, the heart of the conducting season. Not only did he compose the work in the spring, allowing the orchestration to proceed in the summer in time for a late-autumn premiere (he normally spent the summer composing, not orchestrating), but he fed intelligence to the press in order to build a frenzy of expectation that would outshine other current attempts at musically rendering Nietzsche. In the short term this tactic worked; Strauss's tone poem had brilliant premieres in Frankfurt (November 27, 1896, under Strauss) and Berlin (November 30, conducted by Arthur Nikisch), the latter of which prompted Mahler to write to the critic Max Marschalk five days after the performance and accuse Strauss of "currying favor" with the press—"shallow Corybants" blinded by a "knight of industry."[17] The Third Symphony, conversely, would not have its premiere until 1902, when despite Mahler's suppression of its program it would be heard as the latest and perhaps most radical example of orchestral modernism—that is, as a work of "New German programmaticism of the Straussian kind," in Franklin's words.[18] The immediate outcome of this first real confrontation, then, was that Strauss trumped Mahler, even though the prospects were not good for either piece in the first two decades of their existence.

The foregoing episode cries out for further unpacking. The question is how to do it. What I would observe at this stage is that we require analysis on several levels; numerous subtopics present themselves that could be developed significantly. For example: 1) The business of art was no less messy than any other capitalist enterprise. 2) Success of new compositions depended on how they were conducted; only the composers themselves—or so they believed—could produce compelling interpretations of their new music until it established itself in the repertory. 3) "Program music" meant different things to different people, so that for each new work a composer had to decide which types suited his personality and which were likely to gain a positive response. 4) Both Strauss and Mahler took contemporary philosophical trends seriously, i.e., they felt a need and indeed a responsibility to respond to them artistically. 5) They likewise saw important literary sources as stimuli to creativity, generally on the Lisztian grounds that music could tease out meanings that were otherwise unavailable. 6) Behind all of this stood the imposing figure of Wagner and the question oppressing every composer of this era: what now? 7) And what of the other previous musical greats, especially Beethoven, but also the romantics, and timeless models like Mozart and Bach? By what intertextual steps were their achievements to be taken into account in music suited to the approaching twentieth century? 8) These questions had been on the minds of Mahler and Strauss throughout the time when they learned to take music seriously—childhood, which their own statements require us to consider if we are to make sense of their mature attitudes.

The collection of relevant layers is equally complex when we consider the other phases of the relationship, including periods that seem relatively fallow. Between December 1895 and April 1900 Strauss received only a single letter from Mahler (assuming that none were discarded or lost, which is unlikely as Strauss was a fastidious archivist of incoming correspondence). That lone communication, from August 1897, arose from a practical need for materials related to *Das Rheingold*, and it concluded with a warm request that Strauss not be annoyed "that I don't write anymore."[19] Workload is always a credible excuse for Mahler, particularly during the first year of his Vienna position. Yet it seems important that even Strauss's note of thanks for the score of the Second, sent in February of that year, went without acknowledgement. Strauss had mentioned his regret at their loss of contact—"I was so delighted to receive a sign of life from you after such a long time; indeed I wondered whether you had completely forgotten the first 'Mahlerian!'"—yet Mahler apparently returned not the simplest indication of reassurance.[20] (The need for personal distance from Strauss reminds one of Hugo von Hofmannsthal, who, with a few exceptions, could abide Strauss only in small doses, and declared, when he learned in August 1918 that Strauss might assume the directorship of the Opera in Vienna, that the city was not big enough for both of them.)[21]

Neither Mahler nor Hofmannsthal had the slightest doubt about the value of Strauss's music, however. When in April 1900 Strauss finally took a more aggressive step toward breaking the ice, offering a ballet that he had not yet begun composing, Mahler responded immediately, with the single caveat that there would likely not be a large budget for scenery. We see in this instance the first evidence of a tendency that would define the remainder of the relationship. Mahler followed Strauss's development out of a genuine artistic need, one to which he gave himself wholly in spite of strong personal distaste for certain features of the composer's personality. Strauss, conversely, had strong feelings for Mahler the person and the musician, and for these reasons he promoted works that struck him as interesting and meaningful but not always as great. The famous remark to Fritz Busch—"Mahler, he's really no composer at all, just a very great conductor"—surely overstates his disdain.[22] But what he did for Mahler's music, while enormously valuable, did not necessarily reflect the same level of personal investment in the artistic enterprise that his works would receive from Mahler. This difference was palpable to them, if unspoken.

In preparing *Feuersnot*, for example, Mahler lavished every conceivable attention on the production, even conducting it himself rather than taking a place in a box, so that he could offer the gift of a model performance to the inspired creator who had produced the music. The public's tepid response was as great a disappointment to Mahler as it was to Strauss; indeed, the conductor took it harder than the composer, and he made a fresh attempt in 1905, despite his ever more complicated relations with the Opera administration and the critics. For his part, Strauss felt deeply moved by Mahler's devotion and thanked his friend in unusually expressive and heartfelt terms, particularly for the "magical orchestral sound, the magnificent staging," and the "glorious tone-poetry" of the singers.[23] Strauss would arrange many performances of Mahler's music, and often would prepare works in advance before handing over the performance to the composer. We do not find in these cases, however, evidence of the kind of connection between conductor and music that we see when Mahler conducted Strauss's greatest works—a deep interest and respect in which a fundamentally moral need to do justice to the work exists outside the considerations of a personal relationship.

From Strauss's side, Mahler's Fourth Symphony stands as the exception that proves this rule. It quickly became Strauss's favorite of his friend's works; even before he knew the music he seems to have sensed that it would turn away from the practice of the Second and Third. When attempting to program it in Berlin in 1901, Strauss was rebuffed several times by Mahler, who insisted on the Third being presented first. Eventually the disagreement led to the good-natured but pointed rebuke from Strauss, "What a pig-headed fellow you are! But it does no harm! It's just what is charming about you!"[24] In this extraordinary symphony, an anomaly even for Mahler, Strauss found the one case in which his friend showed him a path to his own future; Adorno would claim, believably, that Strauss could not have conceived *Der Rosenkavalier* without knowing the Fourth.[25] Where the twenty-two-year-old Alma could remark snidely that "Haydn has done that better," Strauss recognized in this symphony an insight that would have a more profound impact on musical modernism than any supposed teleological development toward atonality: the witting reinterpretation of the past, in which anachronism and distance filled the aesthetic need left empty by the obsolescence of traditional expression and originality.[26]

Just at the turn of the century, then, the composers found their way back to one another, both of them searching for artistic inspiration at a difficult moment. In the process they interacted through a variety of connections: musical, literary, philosophical, professional, always fascinated by each other's self-representation, sometimes ironic, within the history and tradition of their art. Strauss would in the end be deeply disappointed to see Mahler turn away from the path suggested by the Fourth. (The Sixth would return to the romantic obsession with the self, following a Fifth that used massive forces to announce a rejection of program music, i.e., a renewal of faith in musical idealism and the autonomy aesthetic.)

Feuersnot, with its Bavarian niche market, nonetheless had something to teach Mahler with its simultaneous homage and parody of Wagner. Even the Fifth would be touched by it; the treatment of Bach and Bruckner in the last movement draws on this practice of affectionate caricature.

More than any other work of Strauss, *Salome* would be an obsession for Mahler, as it was for Schoenberg. The fascination began in a piano store in Strasbourg, where in May 1905 Strauss played and sang the entire work (minus the dance) to Mahler and Alma. Having opposed the project for "a thousand reasons" when Strauss told him of it (as Alma recalled), Mahler now sat dumbfounded as his friend "played and sang to perfection" and proved—"Mahler was won over"—that "a man may dare all if he has the genius to make the incredible credible."[27] No doubt Mahler was remembering the scene eighteen years earlier when Strauss shared portions of *Guntram* and looked for his new friend's reaction; while politeness and politics conditioned the response on that occasion, neither man could or would hide anything from the other any longer. And Mahler found himself granting instinctively that this was a product of genius—an opinion he would reaffirm again and again when he heard the work in the opera house.

Shortly after the Austrian premiere (Graz, May 16, 1906) Mahler would defend the opera to Alma, cautioning her not to "*underestimate* the work" and calling it "a very significant one, though 'virtuosic' in the negative sense" and thus not quite at the level of Wagner.[28] As he came to know it better, he would rescind even that qualification, a complaint that in any case he said had "nothing to do with his talent but with his *character*."[29] Hearing another performance on January 9, 1907, he wrote: "My dear Almschili, you have seriously underestimated the qualities of this score. It's absolutely brilliant, a *very powerful* work and without doubt one of the most significant of our time! Beneath a pile of rubble smolders a living volcano, a subterranean fire—not just a display of fireworks [. . .] I've acquired a profound respect for the man as a whole, and this has confirmed my opinion. I'm absolutely delighted, and I go with him *all the way*" (emphasis in original).[30] From Mahler's side, at least, this was a major turning point in the relationship, for it announced not that the art trumped the personality, but that the art and the personality were inseparable, one dependent on the other. Mahler did not feel, as Alma did, that the work had a weak spot in the "botched-up commonplace" of the dance.[31] Rather he seems to have understood that, as Alex Ross has observed, the dance "is the music that Herod likes," and thus necessarily trivial, tawdry, cheap—a "kitschy foil for the grisliness to come."[32] And, more importantly, Mahler finally recognized in the coolness pervading Strauss's personality and works a feature that made this music representative of its own time. *Feuersnot* had been a necessary preparation here, no less than Mahler's early symphonies are a prerequisite for understanding his middle-period works. Strauss was not simply calling on all means necessary to create an entertaining mélange; he was forging a modernist alternative to nineteenth-century musical monuments, with a skill and seriousness deserving to be called genius. Thus Mahler returned for yet another performance on January 11, and then the next month (thanks to a special arrangement between Strauss and his publisher) dived into the score, studying again the curious form that contemporary genius had chosen for itself—and, if we follow Carl Niekerk, taking the work as inspiration for his own rather different musical orientalism in *Das Lied von der Erde*.[33]

The unrestricted enthusiasm that Mahler felt for *Salome* beginning in Graz did not prevent certain disappointments with Strauss on a personal level, even though Mahler had accepted that somehow Strauss's vexing demeanor was necessary for his work. It is impossible to know how strong a role these played in the fact that between May 1907 and Mahler's death they shared only a handful of letters. Certainly the relationship had suffered difficult moments, especially after the scene at the dress rehearsal for the Sixth (at the May 1906 meeting of the ADMV in Essen). We may well trust Alma's implication that the callous behavior of Strauss, who discovered Mahler in a state of personal despair, made matters worse. ("What's the matter with him?" Strauss asked impatiently in the green room.) The downfall that Mahler dramatized in the Sixth had its tragic root in his failed attempts to communicate artistically. Now in his late forties and well accustomed to artistic incomprehension, he was reduced to thematizing his own failures, in compositions that themselves were likely to meet the same sorry fate. Strauss's oblivious reaction to the scene was not the problem, however. It was his embodiment of a future in which Mahler did not know how to participate. Mahler's present showed signs of obsolescence, and to be confronted in the flesh by a living and vibrant way forward was too much. Even in her disgusted response to Strauss's behavior Alma knew that this archenemy was simply living out the power of confidence and self-awareness; she herself would later describe him as "the greatest master of contemporary music in the first decade of this century."[34] But whereas in *Salome* the self of the composer merged into the glow of an overpowering incandescent modernism, in the Sixth the personality was the work, and it had to be, for Mahler did not know how to compose otherwise. Mahler rejected Strauss personally because Strauss did not need to project personal authenticity in order to succeed as an artist—indeed, he succeeded as an artist because his art concealed his personality, in a way that was nevertheless paradoxically and uniquely Straussian.

The genesis of the Eighth Symphony demonstrates eloquently that despite the trauma of the Sixth, Mahler had no intention of being anything other than himself. With the first work he composed in the post-*Salome* world, Mahler returned to the dramatic mode of the Second: a grand communal symphonic/choral reenactment of creation and apotheosis, drawing equally on Beethoven and Goethe. Summoning the "*creator spiritus*," he martialed the faith necessary to make one final attempt at connecting with his listeners, and at composing music that would embrace the past in a modern revival rather than manipulate it to modernist ends. One cannot imagine that Mahler expected this avenue to lead anywhere after him; he was, even more than Strauss, "the last mountain of a large mountain range."[35] He determined instead to affirm himself and his nature in a kind of historicism that rejected the necessity of cutting oneself off from one's work or from fellow humanity, past or present. In place of the neoclassicism of the Fourth we have here a revived classicism, a re-immersion in it, and perhaps a willing blindness to the aesthetic necessities that so many of his contemporaries took for granted.

This keeping of faith with the past figured prominently in his popularity among the emerging Second Viennese generation. They too hoped to recapture music's idealistic promise, its power to teach the inner truth of the individual and the outer truth of the world. If their tools were new, their ends were the same. Mahler would not have shared the Expressionist view of what one would find through these investigations, but in the end his followers would maintain faith with him—particularly Schoenberg, whose religiosity only intensified with age (as did Mahler's). It is difficult, then, not to see in the end an extension of romanticism in these artists; romanticism is no less true to its own impulses when it is marked by self-doubt. Insecurity amidst the hope for triumph was always a precondition of this worldview, however powerful an individual's heroic drive. The audience's high regard for the Eighth, which meant so much to Mahler as a sign of his acceptance into a human community, was thus not incompatible with a modernist spirit of the Second Viennese sort, because it reinforced the premises on which the enterprise rested: the possibility that music could communicate truth about the human situation in the world.

Strauss attended the first performance of the Eighth, in Munich on September 12, 1910,[36] and two weeks later he completed *Der Rosenkavalier*, picking up the thread of the Fourth where Mahler had abandoned it. Only a lack of interest in the politics of musical modernism prevented Strauss from commenting on the irony that *Rosenkavalier* would earn him the label of musical reactionary, while Mahler's most popular and least forward-thinking effort would cement his reputation as spiritual father of the New Music. (The Eighth would be the last work by Mahler premiered during his lifetime.) It is an enormous loss for music history that we do not know how Mahler might have responded to this new opera. *Elektra* disgusted him, but from that reaction we only know that he did not understand it. (At the last private meeting between the two, in Toblach sometime between September 3 and September 5, 1909, Strauss played passages from *Elektra* to Mahler, later writing in his "blue diary," "My boldest passage harmonically is perhaps Clytemnestra's day-dream narrative where the pedal-note has the function of nightmare. A piece which even Mahler [it was the last thing I played to him] could not accept.")[37] The materials of *Rosenkavalier* surely would have settled him down, and perhaps in this new and unexpected direction Mahler would have found a different kind of link between himself and his friend, one based in an alternate form of musical engagement with the past. But death would intervene, albeit slowly enough that Strauss could offer a sensitive gesture of reconciliation, promising in his last letter to Mahler (May 11, 1911) that he would take up the Third Symphony again and prepare it carefully for a concert to be conducted by Mahler.[38] That kindness would be balanced by a tirade against idealism scribbled in his diary shortly after Mahler's death on May 18:

> Gustav Mahler, after a grave illness, passed away on 19 May [sic].
> The death of this lofty-minded, idealistic and energetic artist is a heavy loss. [I] read the stirring memoirs of Wagner with emotion.
> [I] studied *German History during the Age of Reformation*, Leop. Ranke: this confirmed very clearly for me that all the elements that fostered culture at that time have been a spent force for centuries, just as all great political and religious movements can only have a truly fruitful influence for a limited period.
> The Jew Mahler could still find exaltation in Christianity.
> The hero Rich. Wagner descended again to it as an old man through the influence of Schopenhauer.
> It is absolutely clear to me that the German nation can only attain new vigor by freeing itself from Christianity [...]
> I shall call my Alpensinfonie: the Antichrist, since it embodies: moral purification through one's own strength, liberation through work, worship of eternal, glorious Nature.[39]

Strauss touched here on the heart of their relationship, in a furious indictment of a cultural force that had overwhelmed his greatest predecessor and now his finest contemporary. Sorting out the implications of this outburst will be a central task of my remaining thirteen chapters. For now I would simply observe that, even after twenty-four years, Strauss wanted more time to argue with his friend, more time to show him an alternate path, more time to develop a philosophy of music appropriate to the twentieth century. Those energies would have to be applied in other directions.

CHAPTER I

Children

☙ THOUGH WE KNOW a good deal about the childhoods of Strauss and Mahler, the topic has yet to inspire much serious interest. With the memoirs of relatives and a few early associates, and the inside information of La Grange and Schuh, biographers can choose from a healthy supply of colorful anecdotes and throwaway lines.[1] Putting these to critical use has been mostly an unaccepted challenge, however, which may explain why in comparisons of the two artists almost every commonly held assumption rests on misconception and exaggeration, regarding material circumstances, family relations, early study of music, basic educational development, introduction to religion, social maturation, and so on.

As adults, Strauss and Mahler explicitly requested something different. Both stated categorically that their early lives determined their mature personalities, artistically and otherwise. For Mahler this feeling intensified as he got older: "each day I become more conscious of the degree to which the impressions and the spiritual experiences of that period gave to my future life its form and its content."[2] Strauss focused as always on the practical, calling his adult accomplishments a product of the discipline imposed on him by his parents. (He believed firmly that if a skill had not been mastered by age nineteen, the window had closed.)[3] A fair assessment of the grown artists, then, demands that we reflect on their formative years with some degree of sophistication, asking how the conditions of youth might have determined the course of life and creative activity.

The socioeconomic backgrounds of the young Strauss and the young Mahler have been reduced over the years to a simplistic tale of privilege and deprivation.[4] On one hand, Strauss is seen as a child of plenty: the grandson of Georg Pschorr, Strauss enjoyed the protection of a master brewer in the beer capital of the world. On the other we have Mahler, whose family too made its money from alcohol but on a smaller and less secure scale, leaving one of his grandmothers to scrape out a living as a peddler until the age of eighty, lugging her basket of wares from one house to the next (or so the tale goes).

In fact neither of these accounts tells us much about the circumstances and daily lives of the immediate families. Strauss's father supported his wife and children on the salary of a principal player in the Munich opera, which meant, as the composer later described in painful detail, endless work for a wage that rarely covered the bills without assistance from the in-laws. In a private rant from the 1940s, Strauss laid out the fifteen-hour workday of the average nineteenth-century orchestral musician, calling the salary equivalent to that of streetcar coachmen, stenographers, and uneducated factory workers.[5] The family lived in a small apartment on the fourth floor of the brewery where Strauss was born, a sizeable building on Neuhauserstrasse in the heart of Munich. That accommodation provided no special luxuries. Strauss's younger sister Johanna, who improved her position by marriage to a military officer, remembered growing up in "very modest" circumstances: "to make ends meet was a hard job for father, who was neither paid too well nor cared too much for money."[6] Johanna had one Sunday dress, and she did not own a ball gown until Richard bought one for her after he became an assistant conductor at Meiningen.[7] Not surprisingly it was the mother who kept track of the family ledgers, and who bore the responsibility and psychological burden when they did not balance. Once a year she allowed herself to buy chocolate for the children; when the young Richard broke the family mirror (by flinging his one-year-old sister into it), Franz paid for a replacement by going without a new winter coat.[8]

If, as is widely reported, Bernhard Mahler cared a good deal for money, it was not simply for its own sake but as a means to his family's social and intellectual improvement. His efforts might have yielded a better result had he been the father of two children instead of fourteen. In any case the family did not live in poverty, and, along with the well-known brutality of this apparently fearsome individual, one must bear in mind his devotion to goodness as he understood it. A distiller, and the son of a distiller, he allowed no alcohol in his house; the making and selling of spirits was one of the few financially promising businesses open to Jews in Moravia, and he made what he could of it. When in 1873 after thirteen years of successful business activity in Iglau he was made a citizen of the town, he hung the certificate on his velvet-covered living room wall, where the teenage Gustav could see it as he practiced on the family's grand piano (figure 2).[9] Although destined for a career in music from early childhood (by virtue of a talent obvious to all), the first-born son attended the gymnasium at the insistence of his father (as did Strauss) and had no choice but to fight through his academic difficulties. As La Grange has observed, Mahler never once spoke of his father with affection; he did owe him some important debts, however: an education, a fanatical sense of discipline, and the unfailing support of a large family that organized itself around the collective goal of advancement for its most gifted member.

How different were these families, in the areas that would have mattered for a young musical genius? The father modeled industry, self-reliance, and intolerance of mediocrity. The mother offered love and servitude, and otherwise got out of the way.[10] Devotion to music was encouraged and facilitated, at a level that left open the option of professional activity. The insistence on a strong general education imposed a requirement beyond, and many would have said extraneous to, what a musician needed in order to find employment. In a household with little disposable income, no financial concern interfered with the family's best hope of future achievement. Mahler did not live in a home with a trained musician, but this lack seems to have motivated (as Donald Mitchell has suggested) Bernhard's decision to send Mahler for his ill-fated stay with the Grünfelds in Prague, where he received daily contact with current and future professional musicians but little food and clothing.[11] At bottom, it is evident that in

Figure 2. In a decidedly middle-class setting, the young Mahler (left) poses with an unidentified companion. Courtesy of the Gustav Mahler—Alfred Rosé Collection, University of Western Ontario, London, Ontario.

both cases talent was recognized early and fostered with every means available.

Along with similarities of family background, the gymnasium represents an area of common experience for Mahler and Strauss that must not be undervalued. In the cultural milieu of Munich, as in towns within striking distance of Vienna, *Bildung* reigned supreme in the 1860s and '70s as a bourgeois ideal of education and indeed of existence.[12] It defined the personality as no religious or social experience ever could. The habits formed during the forbidding trial of a gymnasium education became a worldview in adulthood, especially when reinforced by a family atmosphere linking all manner of reward and punishment to disciplined intellectual endeavor. In the school years the various domains of contemplation—spiritual, historical, aesthetic, philosophical, social, comic—were stamped by a consistency of approach, a technique of thought that would unite adult peers in mutual recognition regardless of specific opinions. According to his namesake grandson, the elderly Strauss forthrightly declared this preparation essential for a civilized modern European, "or else he's not a fully qualified human being."[13] Former *Gymnasiasten* could disagree on virtually everything and still feel in one another a common type, a kindred spirit.

Likewise, grasping the meaning of "maturity" in the late nineteenth century requires a healthy dose of historical imagination nowadays. The average bourgeois twelve-year-old living in Austro-German lands ca. 1870 had—was forced to have—a stronger sense of intellectual purpose and self-control than many a present-day college student. Childhood as we understand it was shorter, if in fact it existed at all; Thomas Mann's Hanno Buddenbrook found death through typhus an "escape" from a hated premature adulthood. Complaints of a stolen childhood abound, for example in Stefan Zweig's unvarnished account in *The World of Yesterday*, where he complained that "what every young person secretly longs for was entirely lacking" and declared of the gymnasium in particular that "the one real moment of elation for which I have to thank my school was the day when I closed its doors behind me forever."[14] Mahler echoed the sentiment in a biographical sketch for Max Marschalk in 1896, writing "[I] spent my youth in the gymnasium—nothing learnt."[15] But such comments disregarded a positive side that in the long run the victims obviously treasured. However cruel the existence, it meant that the survivors would acquire in their teenage years a lifetime's worth of learning across the full spectrum of humanistic disciplines—the kind of learning that could allow a Zweig to go from high school student to feuilleton writer for the *Neue freie Presse*. Mahler could thank his broad learning for the ease with which he was folded into the "Pernerstorfer circle" of student intellectuals in Vienna; Strauss's analogous group in Munich included friends who would go on to positions of distinction in the world of letters, and who for the rest of his life remained his most intimate confidantes.[16]

Establishing this basic common ground allows a closer examination of subtle differences that had a real impact on Strauss's and Mahler's artistic personalities. Richard Specht reported, for example, that as a teenager Mahler considered giving up music for a life as a poet.[17] Such a flight of fancy would be unthinkable without Mahler's lifelong attraction to romanticism, already manifesting itself when, as an eighteen-year-old piano tutor to a wealthy family in Hungary, he waxed poetic while climbing a tree:

> When I go out on to the heath and climb a lime tree that stands there all lonely, and when from the topmost branches of this friend of mine I see far out into the world: before my eyes the Danube winds her ancient way, her waves flickering with the glow of the setting sun; from the village behind me the chime of the eventide bells is wafted to me on a kindly breeze, and the branches sway in the wind, rocking me into a slumber like the daughters of the Erlking, and the leaves and blossoms of my favorite tree tenderly caress my cheeks. Stillness everywhere! Most holy stillness![18]

The year of 1879 seems late to be reveling in romantic clichés, even when one finds, in the next sentence, a typically Mahlerian fly in the soup: "Only from far away comes the melancholy croaking of a toad, sitting mournfully among the reeds." Strauss would have scorned effusions of this sort in any of his nine decades. He knew the romantics, obviously, but he sought artistic inspiration in every direction but that one, including some of dubious aesthetic value, such as the vapid sentimentalism of Hermann von Gilm and the quirky modernist socialism of John Henry Mackay.[19] These divergent tendencies of the young composers, which manifested themselves outside of music and long before the arrival at intellectual maturity, speak to a basic difference in what each person sought from art.

Mahler's soft spot for the romantics must have had some connection to his performing background. If not a full-fledged virtuoso as an adult, he nonetheless followed the path to virtuosity as a child; after his first public concert, given at the age of ten, the Iglau newspaper *Der Vermittler* called him a "future virtuoso" whose "success with his audience was great."[20] Two years later he performed Liszt's variations on the Wedding March from Mendelssohn's *A Midsummer Night's Dream* and enjoyed "an interminable and wildly enthusiastic ovation."[21] His entrée to the Vienna Conservatory was Julius Epstein, the city's leading piano pedagogue, who admired Mahler's youthful compositions but accepted him with the understanding that he would study to be a pianist.

Strauss, on the other hand, had no aspirations to the public glory of performance at any time of his life, even if he could play Weber's *Invitation to the Dance* at the tender age of eleven, and notwithstanding his onetime appearance as soloist in Mozart's relatively demanding Piano Concerto in C Minor, K. 491 under Bülow.[22] Thus while Strauss could not have identified with the mindset of a young Liszt or a Thalberg—especially given the strictures of the classicist musical environment imposed by his father—Mahler clearly did, at least until the experience of hearing Liszt play the "Emperor" (on March 16, 1877, in Vienna) caused him to hurl aside his score and declare that he would never play again.[23]

We can also learn much from the contrasts between what drew the two adolescents to the piano. Mahler treated it as a means of intensifying the daydreams in which he so frequently indulged. The "silent reveries" of an introverted child remained the habit of a young man who spent every available hour alone in a room with a piano, and who would rage at anyone who dared listen through the door, including his mother. (Mahler's brother Ernst cleverly won the privilege of occasional listening by agreeing to serve as a valet of sorts.)[24] The "Wagnerian" qualities that Epstein heard in the early compositions recall the *weltfremd* improvisations of Hanno or the adolescent Nietzsche: forays into the beyond, motivated by depression. Here again, one cannot imagine Strauss abandoning himself for even a minute to chromatic pessimism. For him the piano was a tool, for learning about music and for sharing it with others. Curiously, the experience of music during the apprentice years was more "absolute" for Strauss than for Mahler; he appreciated music's expressive capacity in something like a Mendelssohnian way (as an art emotionally specific beyond the capacity of words), but he loved the art for the specifically musical inner workings to which his mind was so exquisitely sensitive. Where Strauss spent his young life rejoicing in his innate musical capacity, and sharing it with anyone who would listen, Mahler used his gift as self-administered therapy for a psyche disposed against rejoicing.

When seeking out musical friends, the young composers understandably looked for people who shared their predilections. Mahler did not have the opportunity of friendship with a Ludwig Thuille—a born theorist with a penchant for doing things by the book and with enough creative talent to produce competent and interesting original works.[25] Interaction with this "more experienced" musician (he was three years older than Strauss, and well trained from earliest youth) offered Strauss not just a model of discipline and knowledge but a generous helping of pedantry. The scandalous antics of Strauss's creative maturity owe something to his experience as a musical younger brother who entertained himself by antagonizing a role model obsessed with correctness. At the same time, friends such as Arthur Seidl and Friedrich Rösch, trained musicians but a future essayist and a future lawyer respectively, encouraged the freer sides of Strauss's nature while keeping him grounded in the real world.[26]

Not until his Conservatory years (1875–78) did Mahler find such friendships; the Grünfeld brothers, in whose home he lived in Prague during the fall of 1871, might have fit the bill but they were interested only in persecuting him. With Rudolf Krzyzanowski and Hugo Wolf, fellow students at the Conservatory, Mahler found companions for a thorough exploration of Wagnerian profundity: in the Vienna Academic Wagner Society (which they joined in 1877), in late-night read-throughs (such as a rendition of the trio for Gunther, Hagen, and Brünnhilde from *Götterdämmerung*, Act II; we do not know who played the Valkyrie), and in personal encounters with Wagner himself (whom Wolf, but not Mahler, dared to approach at the Opera in 1875 and 1876).[27] Wolf eventually served as a cautionary tale of romanticism run amok, but no more so than Hans Rott, who on the evidence of Mahler's own remarks might reasonably be called his artistic soul mate.[28] An organ protégé of Bruckner, and the other leading member of Franz Krenn's composition class, Rott elicited from Mahler a kind of admiration that over the next thirty years only Strauss would duplicate. And that love was not without narcissism: "We felt ourselves to be two fruits from the same tree, growing from the same earth and breathing the same air... We could have done great things together in our new musical epoch."[29] When Mahler took a composition prize at Rott's expense, the former complained vehemently enough that his own mother railed at the injustice. The tragedy of unfulfilled genius played out for Mahler even more vividly in this man than in himself, and later, as Rott languished in an asylum, using his own manuscripts as toilet paper, he suffered the calamity Mahler feared most.

Mahler's choice of friends at the Vienna Conservatory reveals a keen interest in talent, but also an enthusiasm for a kind of student counterculture. Along with Wolf and Krzyzanowski, Mahler served as the principal tormentor of Josef Hellmesberger, Sr., the philistine head of the conservatory, whose "typically light, superficial Viennese nature" and open anti-Semitism drew their attention more than his status as concertmaster of the Vienna Philharmonic. At one point Mahler apparently went so far as to renounce his membership in the conservatory, a choice that he soon regretted and that called forth a brand of apology that one does not often find in his correspondence.[30] Generally Mahler's protests against the establishment were quiet, however, or at least wordless, and thus it is not surprising to find that he had a close relationship with Bruckner—close enough, in fact, that although Mahler denied being Bruckner's pupil, he maintained an intimacy far greater than any of the composer's official students. It was Mahler, for example, whom Bruckner called into a studio to hear the newly composed theme for the Adagio from the Seventh Symphony; after recognizing Mahler's four-hand arrangement of the Third as a masterwork, Bruckner treated the younger musician as a colleague, often spending time with him in cafés and walking with him between the conservatory and the university.[31] Mahler for his part seems to have enjoyed reassuring the ego of a persecuted genius. Some fourteen years after his graduation, Mahler felt obvious joy in reporting on a Hamburg performance of Bruckner's "magnificent and powerful" *Te deum*: "The *players* as well as the entire *public* were moved to their very core by the work's powerful structure and truly sublime musical ideas. At the end of the performance I witnessed what I consider the greatest triumph of an artwork: the audience remained silent, without moving a muscle, and only when the conductor and musicians left their places did the storm of applause break loose" (emphasis in original).[32] Doubtless this letter reminded Bruckner of other such touching demonstrations of esteem, from a great composer whom he had assisted in the transition from apprenticeship to maturity. For Mahler the friendship provided a meaningful way to express his contempt for the Viennese musical establishment, thus adding to the legend that would be worshipped by the next generation of upstarts.

As Adorno grumbled, Strauss took a subtler approach to power (musical and otherwise), challenging it but winking before things got serious.[33] That tendency shows a strong schoolboy influence that we see also in Thuille, Rösch, Seidl, and Max Steinitzer—all "good boys" who styled themselves as iconoclastic. Whatever their later interest in the arch-Wagnerian passion of Alexander Ritter, they did not want to end up impoverished and ranting on the sidelines; as teenagers they heeded their parents and devoted their considerable energy to excelling in the gymnasium (or the Hochschule für Musik in the case of Thuille).[34] Their measured daring offset the conservatism of Strauss's music teachers, principally Carl Niest and Friedrich Wilhelm Meyer, from whom he acquired what we might call "book knowledge" of the strictest sort. (See his early instrumental works, including such mature efforts as the D-minor Symphony.)[35] The artistic midwife for Strauss, however—the figure who did for him what Bruckner did for Mahler—was Hans von Bülow, who taught him the crucial new skill of productively inciting resistance, perhaps the most important lesson of Strauss's entire career.[36] Arguably the most acerbic musical personality of the nineteenth century, Bülow also had a first-rate sense of humor and a cynical wit second to none. He knew how to walk the line between expectation and scandal, using his brilliant and excruciatingly hard-won political sense to manipulate listeners by setting challenges that provoked a response. (Recall that Bülow was known for performing the last five piano sonatas of Beethoven in a single evening, and for encoring the entire Ninth Symphony.) Strauss admitted that the early tone poems benefited immensely from Bülow's sense of what was enough and what was too much. Through a process of calibration, Strauss translated that experience into a strategy for building a musical career.

The attraction to Bülow on one hand and Bruckner on the other suggests a fundamental difference in how the composers instinctively reacted to conflict.[37] Paradoxically, the students learned from their teachers how not to behave, or rather the mentors' examples reinforced something preexistent: on Strauss's side a need for stability and predictability (with a lackadaisical veneer), on Mahler's a use of spiritual retreat as periodic utopian refreshment from the raging battles of everyday life. Mahler's fiery, confrontational moralism may have had roots, one supposes, in long experience of anti-Semitic persecution. But if so, his personal reaction to the challenge did not invite reference to all-too-current stereotypes—at least not from Strauss. It seems telling that while Strauss could occasionally draw on garden-variety anti-Semitism in his comments on fellow musicians (usually in correspondence with authority figures whom he believed would respond positively to casual bigotry, such as Cosima Wagner), he apparently never said such things of Mahler, whom he characterized instead as an incurable idealist.[38] Arthur Schnitzler would respond similarly to Mahler, calling him "a man of mystic rumination" and an "idealist," and observing that "someone who didn't know that Richard Strauss is Aryan and Gustav Mahler is of Jewish descent would undisputedly observe specifically Semitic characteristics in the composer of *Salome*."[39]

The sources of a private spiritual outlook are easily discernible for both composers, at least in their outlines. Strauss openly admitted that his atheism went back to his school days. His family remained committed to the *alt-katholisch* faith common in Bavaria, but not in any way that encumbered his precocious freethinking.[40] In religion, as in every other area of his existence, he outgrew the fairy tales of his childhood eagerly and speedily. Sports, toys, and games held no interest for him (with the exception of skat), the music and literature of childhood quickly gave way to premature adulthood, and no sense of nostalgia for the lost innocence of youth ever troubled his mind. Even when the octogenarian found a creative outlet in revisiting the genres of his early years, the objects were his first attempts at adult genres (the concerto, ensemble works for winds, chamber music for strings); he longed to relive not some ideal vision of uncorrupted ignorance, but the first joys of adult existence. That disposition remained consistent for seven decades, and aside from the musical theme for his son in *Symphonia domestica*, we find precious little evidence in Strauss's works that children even exist, much less that they occupy a position of elevated spiritual significance. (Those in *Die Frau ohne Schatten* are as yet unborn.)

Mahler's career began with such a child-focused composition: *Das klagende Lied* (1880), a Grimm fairy tale in which we look through a child's eyes and witness harsh realities of betrayal, murder, and retribution. Initiating a pattern that would hold at least through *Kindertotenlieder* (1905), Mahler here used the child's worldview as an avenue of approach to basic themes of the sort that Wagner called "eternal."[41] That quality of timelessness, what nineteenth-century philosophy would label "reality," always pushed Mahler toward extremes; he laid bare the greatest agony, or he fantasized a world of everlasting bliss. But more important than the object of contemplation was the manner of expression. To Mahler, childhood was not just a state but a mode of perception, and one that distorted reality in ways that the composer found moving and instructive. The painful became the grotesque; naiveté became bliss.

This distinctive brand of perspectivism seems not unrelated to a personal history of abuse. Strauss, who knew less of physical brutality, was predisposed to underestimate the intensity of experience possible for a child. Indeed, from all indications he felt that children had nothing interesting to add to one's contemplation of anything. But Mahler knew better. Never denying that the child's view of the world is limited in scope, he claimed that in fact this naive perspective held something closer to truth, even if it too was still in the end (philosophically speaking) a kind of metaphor.[42] Children have not learned to lie to themselves, and so the limits of their perceptive faculties—limits that themselves amount to a kind of truth, by clarifying the epistemological condition of all humanity—are still clear.

In the Fourth Symphony, we hear a movement for each of the three realms of existence—the world, hell, and heaven—before realizing through whom we have been listening. As in the Third, we survey all creation, but from rather a different vantage point. The peculiarity of these movements becomes intelligible only when we hear the song "Das himmlische Leben," which is "to be sung with childlike, cheerful expression." This final step, in a movement that serves as capstone but also as foundation, reveals in these earlier movements' images the heightened sensitivity, and the limited range, of a child's vision.[43] Mahler uses a simple means to achieve this effect: the last movement is the source of musical material for the other three (as it was for two movements of the Third).[44] As one listens to the song and recognizes the seeds of what has gone before, those previous impressions of the dreamlike, or the grotesque, or the deeply (excessively?) sentimental assume the character of a child's heightened awareness. And that is how Mahler could use a designation such as "entirely without parody" for a movement that clearly hopes to stand for something other than itself. Symbolic meaning springs to life through a flood of reinterpretations: of the first movement (where the juxtaposition of "unearthly joy" with a traditional/pedantic formal scheme now makes sense), the second (with a devil who suddenly seems childishly real), and the third (through worship of the mother as St. Ursula, "sad and yet laughing, as if through tears").[45] As it becomes a frame of reference for the entire symphony, the character of the song exerts overwhelmingly more power than it could have in the Third, where the vestige of a child's perspective acts as a foil to Nietzsche and a way station before the last movement. In the Fourth, the child's view is a worldview.

The closest thing to an idealized vision of childhood in Strauss is, not surprisingly, a musical rendering of his own son. Over a shimmering string accompaniment, a gentle oboe d'amore melody in D minor throws a spotlight onto the child as we gaze in static admiration (*Symphonia domestica*, m. 157 [reh. 14], "III. Thema").[46] There is no chance that we will adopt the perspective of this person, however; we are kept at a distance and forced to remain still and silent. Who he may be we cannot say, and no sooner do we adjust to the dim lighting than the image is shattered by the child himself, who begins screaming. This moment comes as a relief, by design. Likewise, when "Bubi" returns at the end of the work, now in the brass and a more vigorous D major (he has grown up, not unlike the hero of *Tod und Verklärung*), he poses, we admire, and then he is off. His mobility intensifies the Straussian emphasis on tone painting, which has its own points to make philosophically and firmly refuses to admit us to an interiority. The adults do have inner lives—especially the composer himself, whose reveries we hear briefly at the beginning and then more extensively in the sections labeled privately "Papa composes" ("Papa komponirt," m. 559, reh. 49) and "Creation and Contemplation" ("Schaffen und Schauen," m. 599, reh. 55)—yet as with the child, the music encourages us not to take him too seriously, and certainly not to look for a sophisticated figurative significance behind the apparent meaning.[47] On the topic of childhood, then, we have no choice but to accept the music's claim that nothing worth knowing is to be found within.

The Fourth was Strauss's favorite of Mahler's symphonies, for a host of reasons: the small scale, the ironic naiveté, the thoughtful manipulation of classical models, the eschewal of an overblown redemptive vision.[48] It is probably not an accident that after hearing this work Strauss decided to write a "Symphonia" of his own, his first orchestral work of the twentieth century and one with a child at its center. (The D of Bubi's music is equidistant from Strauss's F and Pauline's B.) We have no documentary evidence that one work influenced the other, however, just as we can establish no specific link between the *Symphonia domestica* (1902–03) and Mahler's next work—and his last child-focused one—the *Kindertotenlieder* (1901–04). Yet despite the sharp contrast in emotional character, Mahler's choices here and there suggest that he was reacting to Strauss. To name a few parallels: the setting is the family home, the subject, the ordinariness of the events that occur within it (all the more tragic for being mundane). The musical perspective is that of the parent, not the child. A static formal plan (beginning and ending in the same key) underlines an absence of emotional trajectory: the mood is the same at the end as at the beginning, aside from the completing touch of conscious resignation. The tonal anchor is D, the *primus tonus* of old, which tells us that we are dealing with something fundamental, universal, and unchangeable. And orchestrational devices serve at once as symbols and formal signposts, preventing us from losing ourselves in the works' emotional current. As Donald Mitchell has observed, the most striking of the timbral markers in the *Kindertotenlieder* is the tolling of the "childlike" Glockenspiel in "Nun wird die Sonn' so hell aufgehen," which announces again the death and awakens us from the consoling D-major reverie (for example at mm. 6–7).[49] The programmaticism in this gesture leans toward tone painting, not quite as severely as Strauss's alarm clock (*Symphonia domestica*, m. 549 [two measures before reh. 48], and m. 821 [seven measures after reh. 85]), but with sufficient denotative clarity to undermine, as in the Strauss, the music's seductive spirituality. The result is a clearer and more intense perception of the "real" child.

Here we enter, if haltingly, the world of the late Mahler. Instead of suffering the pain of the child ourselves, as in the bitter cries of "Das irdische Leben" ("Earthly Life"), we confront our own loss. And it must be said that for Mahler the child is far less a prop than it is for Strauss. The fate of the child is intertwined with Mahler's own destiny in a way that simply is not true in Strauss's self-involved adult world of comfort and creation. For Mahler the loss of the child still means the loss of himself. And that fact indicates a broader theme of Mahlerian significance, one detectable across his oeuvre. Alma remarked after Mahler's death that his response to the affair with Gropius had been to flee into childhood. Such moments are easy to locate in his music; they go back at least as far as the funeral march of the First Symphony, in which memories of the music he heard in the streets of Iglau yield momentarily to the escapist vision of the *Wayfarer* song, a G-major redemptive vision under a linden tree, where youthful innocence and blissful nonexistence blend and offer hope.[50] This is the world to which Mahler watched his siblings depart—especially his beloved Ernst, who died when Gustav was more adult than child—and ultimately his darling Putzi (Maria Anna Mahler, 1902–07), the daughter whose final struggle with death Mahler could not bear to hear. His longing to join these departed souls confirms Alma's claim, whatever the power of that fear of death that manifested itself so frighteningly in other moments in his music. As Strauss never really was a child, so Mahler never really stopped being one.

CHAPTER 2

Conductors

∽ THE RECENT BURGEONING of musicological interest in Strauss and Mahler has yet to produce a serious treatment of their work as conductors—a treatment, that is, integrating this activity with the broader contexts of compositional output and artistic philosophy.[1] Conducting was a day job, says the unspoken consensus, and therefore at best tangentially related to the inner creative life of the composer. To be sure, the topic has drawn some attention, but mainly as a source of amusing anecdotes. We chuckle at Mahler the diminutive tyrant, who could make even Toscanini cringe, and at Strauss the lethargic manager, eager to get to his card game. Deeper study rarely follows, and indeed it might raise awkward questions in a larger context. What transcendent spirit would repeatedly stop a rehearsal to torment an elderly section player who was "just too nervous" to play his part alone?[2] What artist of historical significance would cancel a run-through of his own piece because the orchestra had already played the work?[3] By their very eloquence such anecdotes invite sweeping under the rug.

In fact the conducting careers of Mahler and Strauss reveal important details about almost every aspect of their lives, including the creative dimension. First, they testify to depth of education and breadth of ability.

Professional conducting was the prize at the end of a series of trials survived only by the very best musicians, people whose talent and skills could have led to any number of musical careers. (Strauss would have become a pianist, said Bülow, "if he weren't something better," and Mahler's training at the Vienna Conservatory prepared him for a performing career if he had wanted it.)[4] Second, both figures' activity as conductors tells us much about their artistic values. With their choices of repertoire and their approaches to particular composers and works, they expressed their views on the Austro-German musical tradition and how that repertoire fit into European cultural life generally. (Particularly revealing is their treatment of Mozart and Wagner, the two deepest loves for both of them, through whose music they found their greatest success as performers and their greatest inspiration as composers.) Finally, conducting allowed them a place on the frontlines. Mahler and Strauss were both performers at heart; they lived for the miraculous moment of the musical present, and they would always be happiest retaining it for themselves, especially in their own works. If conducting was naturally also a business venture—answering a shared need for physical comfort as they pursued a life of creative exertion—it was even more the means of direct involvement in communicating their musical ideas. They needed to "make" music in every sense; creation and performance were in the end not to be disentangled.[5]

We can regard conducting, then, as another context in which they negotiated the relationship between individual and world. And here they helped each other, for each understood the other's experience better than anyone else. In his lifetime, Mahler had no stronger supporter on the podium than Strauss. Once Mahler had his own orchestra, he repaid the favor. But these choices were not primarily altruistic. Curiosity and imagination played stronger roles, as the greatest composers of their time eavesdropped on one another, each seeking insight into the creative process of his only peer.

In the nineteenth century, the privilege of conducting was a recognition of musicianship, and one reserved mostly for composers. The development of stick technique began when a young musician "was simply thrown in at the deep end and left to sink or swim," in the words of Herta Blaukopf;

Bruno Walter vividly described this thrill of suddenly receiving one's own "instrument."[6] Thus the fact that Mahler and Strauss became conductors at an early age, and became accomplished ones at that, reveals much about their knowledge of harmony, counterpoint, orchestration, score reading, and the art of musical hearing, and virtually nothing about their aptitude for waving a baton or dealing personally with musicians over whom they held authority. In fact Strauss did the first conducting of his life in a public performance with one of Europe's greatest orchestras, without a single rehearsal. In 1884 Hans von Bülow had commissioned the Suite in B-flat Major, op. 4, for performance by the Meiningen Court Orchestra on its fall tour. Shortly before the orchestra's November 18 concert in Munich's Odeonssaal, Bülow offered Strauss the chance to conduct his work, which the young man accomplished "in a daze [Dämmerzustand]" and without remembering anything except that "I made no blunders." Bülow's offer was not solicited by Strauss; he did it, as he told his erstwhile antagonist Franz Strauss, "because your son has talent."[7] The extraordinary depth of Bülow's respect would become clear only the following autumn, when Strauss made his second appearance as a conductor leading his own Second Symphony in his début (October 18, 1885) as Bülow's full-time (but unpaid) assistant in Meiningen (figure 3).

Mahler's talent did not win him so illustrious a beginning; to no avail he had applied, or begged, for the opportunity to work with Bülow, "even if I had to pay my tuition fees with my blood."[8] But if Mahler began with more modest positions, he ascended with incomparable speed. The broad outlines are impressive—from a summer engagement at a spa in Bad Hall in 1880 and a first contract as conductor of the eighteen-person orchestra in the Provincial Theater of Laibach in 1881, he climbed to director of the Vienna Court Opera in 1897—and the intermediate steps are equally striking, for example his engagement in 1888, after two years of working alongside Nikisch in Leipzig, as the twenty-eight-year-old director of the Royal Hungarian Opera in Budapest. Word of his abilities had spread far enough by this time that in accepting the position in Budapest he rejected an offer from the Metropolitan Opera in New York.

These achievements were not a function of social skills, political maneuvering, or popularity with his orchestras. They reflected a prodigious, overwhelming *Fachkenntnis* that even Mahler's antagonists never denied. In

Figure 3. Hans von Bülow in 1883. Courtesy of the Universitätsbibliothek Johann Christian Senckenberg, Frankfurt am Main.

Leipzig the critics who favored Nikisch gladly conceded both Mahler's musicianship and his results; their complaints focused rather on mannerisms—his tendency to indicate "every entry by moving his head, his hand, and his foot," or to "move about so much on the podium."[9] Nikisch himself, who seems literally not to have said a single word to Mahler during their time as colleagues, would later take the trouble to attend a performance of the Second Symphony in Berlin in March 1896, after which (according to Bauer-Lechner) he was "enormously and sincerely impressed by Mahler's work, and even promised to perform at least three movements of his Second during the coming winter."[10] This was probably the highest compliment Nikisch could pay to another musician, for it revealed his opinion of both Mahler's work in Leipzig and his accomplishments in an area where Nikisch fell short.

Mahler's final stamp of approval from a colleague came when at last he formed a genuine relationship with Bülow, after taking the job of first conductor at the City Theater in Hamburg, the city where the aging Bülow made his home and conducted a concert series. Rapid improvement in the opera house soon earned Mahler the extraordinary tribute of a laurel wreath inscribed, "To the Pygmalion of the Hamburg Opera. Hans von Bülow."[11] And this praise subsequently developed into the mentor-student relationship for which Mahler had so passionately longed, with the now thirty-one-year-old apprentice sitting near Bülow's podium during concerts so that the master could turn to him during interesting passages and point to the score.[12] Strauss enjoyed this same kind of interaction in Meiningen, attending Bülow's daily rehearsals and dreading the moment "when he suddenly turned from the podium with a question for the student diligently following in the score, who had to answer quickly in order not to earn a snarky put-down [spöttische Abfertigung] in front of the entire orchestra."[13] Early in this relationship Strauss would tell his father that Bülow, Franz's "fierce antagonist," was "the greatest executant musician [Musiker des Vortrags] in the world"; he retained this opinion in later years, giving credit for his own understanding of interpretation to "the model of all shining virtues of the performing [reproduzierenden] artist."[14] For Mahler he was "my spiritual home and my master," even more powerfully in death, when his funeral inspired the finale of the central work in Mahler's public career as a living composer, the Second Symphony.[15]

If the young conductors considered themselves Bülowites, what did they learn from him? First, lengthy rehearsal time and tireless attention to detail. "Long rehearsals, short programs," and "no artistic detail is ever insignificant" served as his creed of conducting (though "short programs" rings hollow from a pianist known for performing Beethoven's last five piano sonatas in a single recital). At Meiningen, Bülow held sectional rehearsals to go through parts bar by bar, ensuring the conductor's total control of phrasing, articulation, and bowing. He applied this approach most strictly with Beethoven, whose works he rehearsed exclusively for three months at the beginning of his Meiningen tenure.[16] The stated goal of this labor was not a subjective interpretation, but the realization of the composer's own intentions; as he told Strauss, "first learn to read the score of a Beethoven symphony *precisely*, and then you will have the interpretation" (emphasis in original).[17] Witnessing this approach to performance obviously influenced Mahler the composer with respect to the detail of his markings, and it found its way into his conducting through the adage (related by Anna von Mildenburg), "accuracy [Korrektheit] is the soul [Seele] of an artistic performance."[18] But something more lay in Bülow's readings than fidelity. During rehearsals at Meiningen, Strauss entered extensive annotations into scores of all nine Beethoven symphonies, which he kept until the end of his life.[19] Bülow's results in performance made an instant believer of Strauss, who wrote to his father that after hearing the *Eroica* he "cried like a child," for "the full light of Beethoven's sun shone on me for the first time in my life."[20]

Perhaps the most important lesson that they learned from Bülow is also the most difficult to pin down. The quality of performance that most struck listeners about Bülow, and later about both Strauss and Mahler, was his choice of tempi. Herta Blaukopf has argued persuasively that "what seems above all to have differentiated Mahler from his contemporaries was his tempi"; she notes particularly his tendency to emphasize the peculiarity of his choices when describing his conducting to people who had not heard it.[21] Strauss likewise was known for unorthodox choices, especially in works of Wagner, where dramatic content, the events onstage, and the singer's delivery would profoundly shape musical decisions.[22] Already in the first days of their friendship, Mahler and Strauss recognized themselves as kindred spirits in this specific sense, and Strauss shared that impression with Bülow. Shortly after meeting Mahler in 1887, Strauss wrote to Bülow with great enthusiasm about this "highly intelligent musician and conductor, one of the few modern conductors who knows about tempo modification."[23] For Bülow, tempo was especially crucial in the works of Beethoven and Wagner, and sure enough Strauss told Bülow that Mahler "in general had excellent views, particularly on Wagner's tempi (contrary to those of the now accredited Wagner conductors)." Precisely what he meant remains elusive; Klemperer, for example, was at pains to describe it, and could only say that Mahler's tempi were both extraordinary and "absolutely natural [...] it sounded quite different, but I could absolutely say 'yes' to it."[24] But the fundamental point is that Strauss believed he and Mahler were among a small minority who had mastered this elusive and essential feature of Bülow's approach.

That Bülow was more impressed with Strauss's talent than with Mahler's—perhaps even intimidated by it—is suggested by the fact that he programmed the early tone poems on his own concerts. In that choice Bülow ignored, for once, his instincts; his response to this music had not been much different from the comical scene in which he held his hands over his ears as he listened to Mahler play the "Todtenfeier" ("Funeral Rite," the title Mahler gave to the symphonic poem that became the first movement of the Second Symphony) at the piano. Bülow's advancing brain cancer may have played some role in this latter episode, along with his deepening conservatism—the same conservatism that ultimately left Strauss uncertain that Bülow could communicate his music accurately to an audience. Their new music, then, would be a source of increasing alienation, as it reflected a modernist musical orientation that baffled the mentor. Nonetheless, as interpreters Mahler and Strauss retained a powerful connection throughout their careers to Wagner and Mozart in the opera house and to Beethoven in the concert hall, which is to say to a musical tradition that in their opinion came to life most effectively by means of the techniques they learned from Bülow.

Modernist credibility, then, was perfectly consonant with an abiding fidelity to the intentions of the great composers. The classic example is Mahler's treatment of *Tristan und Isolde* on arriving in Vienna in 1897. He immediately restored all cuts, prompting newspaper reports warning an unsuspecting public that "the performance of *Tristan und Isolde* will henceforth begin at 6 p.m. and in all probability let out around midnight."[25] Mahler's reading of *Tristan* succeeded enormously, eventually achieving legendary status thanks in part to the singing of Anna von Mildenburg and, later, the sets of Alfred Roller. But the audience always gave credit primarily to Mahler, the visionary behind it all; even his detractors among the critics noted that at the beginning of the third act Mahler was (to his evident discomfort) traditionally showered with a "storm of applause lasting several minutes."[26] The cults of celebrity and of genius merged here into one of authenticity, with aesthetic and economic implications not unrelated to the success of such movements in our own time. And the fanatical Bülowian moral sense would seem to have played its role.

Mahler's fame as master of a historically authoritative musical truth reached its zenith with his Vienna productions of Mozart, especially the famous five-opera cycle from the 1905–06 season. Here, for once, Mahler found an arena in which praise resounded more or less unanimously. Applying the results of a meticulous historical curiosity, which led him for example to the restoration of secco recitative, Mahler reworked Mozart's three great *opere buffe*, along with *Die Zauberflöte* and *Die Entführung aus dem Serail*, from the ground up. "The legend tells of thirty rehearsals," wrote the critic for the *Wiener Abendpost* of final opera in the cycle, *Figaro*, "and the fruit of these rehearsals was a performance of indescribable tenderness and delicacy."[27] Another wrote flirtatiously (playing on the subtitle of the Second Symphony) that "it was a resurrection [Auferstehung] without equal, and I gladly confess that the immense wonder of this music was clearer to me yesterday than ever before."[28] By treating the works as novelties, Mahler gave them a level of care and fresh thinking that they had not received in decades. Yet his broader intention was to place his own definitive productions in the repertory as timeless documents of the works' true character, a tribute from the greatest Viennese conductor to the city's most illustrious composer of opera. In this quasi-historical enterprise, which may have been his finest achievement as a conductor, Mahler sought renewal rather than the merely new, and created productions "so noble, beautiful, and convincing, that one can rightfully believe in a powerful artistic Renaissance, the dawn of a new age of this magnificent artistic institution."[29]

Some ten years earlier, Strauss had collaborated with Ernst von Possart on a series of Mozart performances in the Munich Residenztheater (designed by François de Cuvilliés), offering what would grow into a regular summer festival of historically sensitive productions that served as a model for Mahler.[30] Strauss's connection to this approach went somewhat deeper than Mahler's, for he had learned the subtleties of classical performance from his earliest childhood, in daily music making with a first-rate *Hofoper* orchestral musician born before the death of Beethoven. (In fact, as late as 1897, when Mahler had a trial appearance with the Kaim Orchestra in Munich, critical opinion held that although he was "the right conductor for modern works [...] we are perhaps faced with a time when an impresario must engage two conductors, one classical and one modern.")[31] Strauss put his upbringing to work in an extraordinarily intensive rehearsal schedule; for the production of *Don Giovanni* that opened on May 29, 1896, he held twenty piano rehearsals, followed by seven further rehearsals with orchestra.[32] New productions of *Die Entführung* and *Così fan tutte* followed in 1897, and *Die Zauberflöte* in 1898. Recent commentators have tended to focus on Strauss's clever accompaniments of the secco recitative in these performances, overlooking the larger significance of this project, which took a substantial portion of Strauss's energy during his second term of employment in Munich. Indeed, he conducted Mozart more often than Wagner in the years 1894–98: ninety-eight performances of operas by the former to eighty-five by the latter.[33] Looking back on his conducting career Strauss would call the Mozart performances in that exquisite theater "among the truly wonderful memories of my life."[34]

The diligence with which Strauss rehearsed Mozart in Munich duplicated his earlier practice with Wagner, which in the first years of his conducting career had been a more pressing concern. Particularly in Weimar (1889–94), the first job in which he had both a degree of independence and some meaningful responsibility for productions of Wagner, Strauss had worked downright fanatically toward an authenticity calculated to impress Cosima and catapult him into the ranks of the principal Bayreuth conductors.[35] During the festivals he was a frequent guest at Wahnfried, where in private sessions Cosima walked him page-by-page through Wagner's scores and clarified the authoritative reading not just of the musical text but of all dramatic matters, from staging and costumes to individual gestures and movement on the stage. Back at Weimar, Strauss's requests for clarification during rehearsals could be comically precise: "Is it appropriate that at the words 'Fern von hier, in weiten, weiten Landen, dichtes Vergessen hat zwischen heute und gestern sich gesenkt,' Tannhäuser looks Elizabeth earnestly in the face, then turns away first at 'all mein Erinnern,' and that he makes no movement at all until 'Euch zu begrüßen,' where a small gesture of humility and worship [eine kleine demütige und anbetende Gebärde] might be appropriate?"[36] This request comes from Strauss's first season at the duchy (1889–90); as he grew more confident in his own judgment, and above all as he distanced himself from Cosima's Bayreuth (a process that was fully concluded by 1896, with the appointment of the marginally competent Siegfried as principal conductor of the *Ring*), Strauss paid less and less attention to input that did not come from within. He continued to believe rather strictly, however—and very much in line with Mahler—that effective conducting meant realizing the composer's intentions rather than imposing (as would happen so often in German productions in the twentieth century) a modern perspective on a "historical" artifact.

What then of Mahler's infamous *Retuschen*—changes of instrumentation, dynamics, articulation, and even pitch content? Such an approach would seem incompatible with an ideal of *Werktreue*, i.e., interpretation as a search for the composer's original vision. In a practical sense, altering a score was an everyday occurrence for an opera conductor, particularly one who had faced the challenges of putting on major works in small theaters such as Weimar or Kassel. As David Pickett has suggested, however, by the 1890s the practical motivations of Wagner's and Bülow's retouchings of Beethoven, for example, had been "supplemented by an obligation placed upon the interpreter to divine the intentions of the composer and, if necessary, to modify the text so as to be truthful to these original intentions."[37] Not only did one not rule out the other, one required the other. Bruno Walter affirmed that a spirit of faithfulness lay behind one of Mahler's most daring experiments—the use of an offstage orchestra for the B-flat march in the finale of Beethoven's Ninth Symphony. "He thought he had discovered by a glance into Beethoven's workshop his intention," wrote Walter, and this experience gave him the confidence to employ "means which Beethoven, hampered by the restrictions of his time, would not have dared to use."[38] This particular arrangement would be heard only once; the performance took place relatively early, on March 11, 1895, in Hamburg, and Walter himself called it an "audacious experiment." But the basic rationale for it remained a consistent feature of Mahler's artistic personality throughout his conducting career, including the New York period, when he shocked his Philharmonic players by reorchestrating passages of *Till Eulenspiegels lustige Streiche* and *Don Juan*, asking for a B-flat clarinet instead of the D clarinet for the hanging scene in *Till*, and adding bells to *Don Juan*, justifying this decision by saying that Strauss himself would have scored the work this way if he were writing in the present day.[39]

One searches in vain for such cases in Strauss's career; he would not have comprehended Mahler's desire to issue new versions of his works every five years, and he certainly would not have supercharged other composers' music with the latest technology. Practical considerations did occasionally move Strauss to an assertive brand of revision, most famously in his 1892 *Nuancierung* of *Tristan* to meet the limitations of the tiny Weimar orchestra (which at some rehearsals was staffed by a single cello). But there was for Strauss no connection between the self-evident imperative of keeping faith with the composer and the ever-evolving possibility of altering (intensifying, reinforcing, amplifying) a work's sound. The difference lies in the artists' conception of history. For Strauss, musical works became historical artifacts soon after their introduction to the public. A composition could retain its place in the canon, but it could not retain the quality of being "modern," because art moved on.[40] Strauss therefore would not have thought to update a ten-year-old Mahler symphony any more than he would a Mozart symphony—hence his efforts, unsystematic but nonetheless remarkable for their time, to perform Mozart's music in the manner in which it was first heard. Mahler did the same for Mozart, at least in Vienna, where he released half the string section from *Zauberflöte*, used a spinet or harpsichord for secco recitative, and eliminated unstylistic vocal freedoms. But he would not have transferred that practice to the music of Beethoven, or Wagner, or any nineteenth-century figure, because the music of his own century belonged to a living tradition of which he saw himself as the current leader. Where Strauss chose to leave works behind, or rather to allow them to document the historical moment from which they had emerged (as in the case of the "model productions" of his operas that he lovingly prepared with Clemens Krauss, only to see them go up in flames in the 1944 bombing of Munich), Mahler strove to make all music since Beethoven "contemporary," for the simple reason that the continued power of musical masterpieces had to be supported by all available means.

Mahler's supposed insecurity about the orchestration of his own music, as evidenced in his comments about Strauss's amazing facility, is thus exaggerated if not taken in context. Mahler did not lack confidence in his music; he lacked confidence that in every case he had said what he wanted to say in the clearest way possible.[41] The need to be understood rose in his case to the level of desperation, where on the other hand Strauss could satisfy himself by meeting a personal threshold of intelligibility beyond which listeners would have to sink or swim on their own. With less talented orchestras, Mahler took steps so extreme as to become legendary, as for example with his use of an entire rehearsal of Beethoven's Ninth in Prague to prepare the recitative passages for cellos and basses in the last movement.[42] Such attention was lavished on every detail, to the extent that time allowed, for Mahler considered himself a teacher of the orchestra. And everywhere he worked, he found the same errors: "As soon as they see a *crescendo* they immediately play *forte* and speed up the tempo, while a *diminuendo* makes them drop at once to *piano* and slow down. Subtle gradations like *mezzo-forte, forte, fortissimo* or *piano, pianissimo* and *pianississimo* you will seek in vain. Even more difficult to achieve are *sforzando, fortepiano* and *rubato*" (emphasis in original).[43] The only difference from orchestra to orchestra was the time required to eliminate those imperfections; after a guest performance with the splendid Kaim Orchestra in Munich, Mahler lamented, "I was not spared any of this, here any more than elsewhere."

To Strauss, "perfection" was an utterly alien notion, in performance as everywhere else. He generally took what he got, with a smile or at least without complaint, though he certainly appreciated his opportunities to work with great orchestras, above all the Vienna Philharmonic, the only orchestra to which he dedicated a composition.[44] "He did not rehearse very much, or for very long," Kurt Wilhelm candidly remarked, and his demeanor was calculated to put the players at ease.[45] When the young Herbert von Karajan finally had a chance to observe a Strauss rehearsal, before a 1926 performance of *Elektra* in Vienna, he witnessed a perplexing scene: "Strauss arrived, played the opening bars *fortissimo*, and broke off. 'Is there anybody here who doesn't already know the piece?' No. 'In that case, the rehearsal is over.'"[46] Perhaps because he did so much touring, he developed a remarkable efficiency that amazed the musicians even as it suggested detachment and boredom to audiences and critics. Relentlessly efficient in gesture—he cued predominantly with his eyes—he likewise crafted his interpretations by focusing on a few vital concerns, leaving peripheral details to work themselves out on their own. In Beethoven, for example, Strauss observed that "it takes an ictus, temperament and élan to bring out his greatness. The beauty of orchestral tone is less important than this particular fiery spirit."[47] Strauss's unchallenged musicianship, as well as his fame, allowed him to apply this philosophy without concern for the accusations of indifference to which it opened him. Idealistic fantasies troubled Strauss no more in this realm than in any other; he aimed for the compelling rather than the flawless.

Differences in their rehearsal methods notwithstanding, Mahler and Strauss shared a belief that conducting was a form of teaching, first of the musicians and then of the public. Just as he prepared his performances from the ground up, so did Mahler attempt to educate his audience on every aspect of their task as listeners. In Vienna this meant first of all darkening the hall, excluding latecomers, and eliminating the claque; audiences were to sit down, remain quiet, and pay attention, even and indeed especially during the now-uncut Wagner performances. Incredibly, the initial response to this high-handed discipline was overwhelmingly positive. The debut performance of *Lohengrin*, though prepared with a single rehearsal, was taken as a revelation, with "stormy acclaim" for Mahler's theatrical sense and particularly for his strange but dramatically penetrating tempi.[48] He went on to study all the basic repertoire from scratch, self-consciously reintroducing the best-known masterworks to an eager public. When taking over the Philharmonic in 1898 he began with a program of the *Eroica*, the *Coriolan* Overture, and Mozart's G-minor Symphony, K. 550, "pieces which our excellent orchestra have for years had so securely in their heads and fingertips that they could perform them passably in their sleep. This did not stop Mahler from studying them with the orchestra from scratch in three long and painstaking rehearsals."[49] Thus Eduard Hanslick, a critic with well-known educational impulses, concluded that "our Philharmonic could not wish for a better or more respected Director." And the public agreed; knowing full well what to expect after a full season of his operatic performances, they bought out the entire series as soon as Mahler's appointment was announced.[50]

Strauss's similar concern for the public's education as listeners was more explicitly a moral issue for him; for that reason he made his famous plea, not coincidentally in 1933, for a reorganization of the public schools to incorporate regular instruction in harmony, counterpoint, form, and score reading for all citizens.[51] But he put much less stock than Mahler in the finer details of performance. Complaining to Bruno Walter during World War I that *Elektra* was not to be found on the Munich *Spielplan*, and hearing Walter's response that a score requiring eight clarinets could not be performed in present circumstances, Strauss responded, "four will do!"[52] The opportunity to hear the music outweighed the nuances that Strauss had envisioned in his workshop. He felt the same way regarding alternate interpretations. After hearing Karajan's performance of *Salome* in Berlin in 1936, Strauss arranged a meeting to offer his comments. With typical self-deprecation, he concluded by observing that "you are much closer to it than I am, for whom it's so far in the past. It will be alright as it is."[53]

Mahler trusted no one in this way, except possibly Strauss. But Strauss's conception of the musical work, and of perceptions of the musical work, was fluid in a way that Mahler could never understand. The fact that Strauss lived much longer than Mahler had nothing to do with that insight; it was inborn, and Mahler had ample opportunity over the years to experience it and to be frustrated by it. It was the source of what Mahler perceived as flippancy, which in bitter moments he would link up with Strauss's apparent greed, conveniently forgetting which of the two was the first to use proceeds from conducting to build a beautiful mountain villa.[54]

CHAPTER 3

Husbands

STRAUSS AND MAHLER both reached creative maturity shortly after their respective marriages. *Till Eulenspiegels lustige Streiche* (1894), a Nietzsche-inspired manifesto of *Tonmalerei* (tone painting), was conceived in the first months of tender union with the ferocious Pauline de Ahna; the tone poem set his artistic course for the next half century as firmly as the general's daughter ruled his domestic life.[1] Mahler chose an equally strong woman—stronger than he bargained for, it would seem—at precisely the moment when his programmatic inclinations became clandestine. Neither composer would have wished to think that the linchpin of his oeuvre was supplied by a spouse. But each became himself only with the arrival of the most important woman in his life.

Marriage completed a process of coming to terms with the opposite sex, not only in romance but in all relationships. By his own testimony to Freud, Mahler spent his youth heartsick over the sufferings of an oppressed and weak-willed mother. In young adulthood he atoned for his father's sins by caring for sheltered sisters, especially the skillfully passive-aggressive Justine, and by tolerating the educated, musical, but, alas, plain and pathetic Natalie Bauer-Lechner.[2] His early adulthood was punctuated by stormy love affairs, most famously with the brilliant, needy Wagnerian soprano Anna von Mildenburg (who would marry Hermann Bahr in 1909).[3] With Alma he at last found a woman through whom he could explore his own predilections. That is not to say that Mahler the husband would give any sign of ending the studied avoidance of sexuality in his music, as Julian Johnson has pointed out.[4] But Alma's dual nature, a headstrong recklessness longing to be dominated (as she herself described it), offered Mahler the chance to live out his own divided personality as sensitive tyrant—and thus perhaps to return to his roots.[5]

Strauss too encountered his share of female victims, beginning likewise with his mother, a bundle of nerves whose pathological fragility was aggravated by a difficult and much older husband. Again we find a mousy sister, who as far as one can tell spent a full ninety-eight years sitting politely in the corner of life. In neither case did Strauss become the caretaker, however; unlike Mahler, he sought out older, psychologically mature women in his youthful affairs and ultimately in Pauline.[6] This choice served him well, for, in contrast to Alma, Pauline remained faithful, a source and example of personal strength.

Puzzling out the female character would have a powerful and only too obvious impact on the broad trajectory of each composer's career. Strauss's turn from male protagonists in the nineteenth century to female in the twentieth has often been remarked upon.[7] Less obvious is that it overlapped with his shift from orchestral to operatic composition; we see it prefigured in at least four of the tone poems—*Don Juan, Don Quixote, Ein Heldenleben,* and *Symphonia domestica*—where the spouse, idealized or not, powers the drama. The Eighth Symphony, with its treatment of Goethe's "eternal feminine" as metaphor of transcendent knowledge (elucidated in a letter of June 1909 to Alma), universalized the overtly autobiographical music relating to his wife that Mahler inserted into the Fifth and Sixth Symphonies.[8] After that process, no subsequent meditation on eternity, such as we find in the last works, can be divorced from the hopes he had placed in his relationship with his wife, or in whatever that relationship symbolized to him.

What we find, then, is that both composers used relationships with women as a laboratory for developing artistic viewpoints that played out philosophically, musically, and in the intersection between the two. That is not to say that the feminine provided the only approach, but it may have been the primary figurative means for contemplating topics that could not be expressed on their own terms. In Alma, Mahler bound his fate to a woman whom he could never quite fathom. In Pauline, Strauss surrendered himself to a force so powerful as to make all debate useless.

The late Stuart Feder opened his nuanced and influential study of Mahler's female companions "before Alma" by recalling the bourgeois chill with which the thirty-five-year-old composer imagined his future wife—"perfectly groomed and well-dressed," she would have to honor his creative need for solitude, "possibly several rooms away"—and his practical requirement of a "separate entrance."⁹ Detachment and control are common themes in Feder's dissection of the treatment received by Justine, Anna von Mildenburg, and Natalie Bauer-Lechner. Ever willing to accept solicitude, often in need of a sounding board, and dutifully concerned for the personal development of the women orbiting him, Mahler emerges in this account as part Pygmalion and part benevolent dictator. Emotional involvement from Mahler's side was never in question; affection, concern, and even love were expressed regularly, openly, and with a confident efficiency that one recognizes in all his endeavors.

What Feder's clinical approach does not capture with sufficient clarity is the Mahler who could lose his grip. The wretched wailings of Josephine Poisl's jilted lover, to Feder a "one-sided reflection of a young man's as yet unfocused passion and fertile imagination," bear an eerie similarity to the torrent that found its way some thirty years later into the sketches of the Tenth Symphony. Mahler in 1880:

Have mercy on me! Or I must despair of the light, of heaven.
[Erbarme dich meiner! (...) sonst muß ich an dem Lichte, an dem Himmel verzweifeln (...)]

I wander about like a corpse!
[(I)ch wandle umher wie eine Leiche!]

May the Lord have mercy on my poor soul! Oh, farewell, farewell!
[(G)nade der Herr meiner armen Seele! O, Leb' wol! Leb wol!]¹⁰

and in 1910:

> Have mercy!
> [Erbarmen!]
>
> Oh God! Oh God! Why have you forsaken me?
> [O Gott! O Gott! Warum hast du mich verlassen?]
>
> To live for you! To die for you!
> [Für dich leben! Für dich sterben!]
>
> Farewell, my lyre! Farewell! Farewell!
> [Leb' wohl, mein Saitenspiel! Leb wol! Leb wol! Leb wol!][11]

Verbal parallels reflect emotional ones here, lending gravity to both episodes notwithstanding the histrionics and despite the different personalities involved. And at the center of each breakdown is a revealing concern for the self, a desperate fear of personal annihilation through severance from the divine. Mahler dramatized this fear in a different way when writing to Poisl's mother shortly after the outcry quoted above. Having recovered his senses with the help of an Easter cake she had sent to him, he described with narrative detachment a lonely seven-hour walk through the Prater on Easter Sunday. The tale has all the makings of a romantic short story: having lost his way, the protagonist reaches the sandy banks of the Danube, where a nameless stranger sets him on the path home.[12]

No one observed Mahler more keenly than Mahler himself. And because he reflected often on how his behavior could be interpreted, he was adept at psychological manipulation. His handling of Anna von Mildenburg on their first meeting is a case in point. Henry-Louis de La Grange, and Feder following him, relate that during a private rehearsal of *Die Walküre*, Act II, Mahler responded to her tears by "terrorizing" and "insulting" her.[13] In fact Mildenburg's account, first published in the *Neue freie Presse*, tells a different story: "I laid my head on the piano and began to cry. My fear must have shown most comically on my face, for suddenly he began to laugh until his sides shook. Beside himself, hands buried in his pockets, he wandered through the room. But then he sat down quietly, wiped his glasses, and from his kind, earnest words I learned that I had done my job splendidly and had no reason to be afraid."[14] Of course

Mildenburg entered the rehearsal expecting the worst, having been led to expect it by seasoned members of the Hamburg company and knowing full well that Pollini had hired her without consulting Mahler. That she received something entirely different taught her that if he was a tyrant, he was a just one. And what it tells us, at the very least, is that both personas were calculated—behind uncontrollable rage and uncontrollable laughter stood a conductor coolly intent on getting what he needed from his performers.

There was also a kind of playfulness in Mahler's tendency to live at the extremes in his emotional relations with women. Companions sensed it, and if they found him exhausting, they nevertheless enjoyed the ride, as when Bauer-Lechner likened friendship with Mahler to "being on a boat constantly rocked and tossed to and fro on the waves."[15] From his perspective, however, the playfulness had a purpose. Flirtatious detachment and overblown emotionalism kept others off balance, "several rooms away," and protected his psychological "separate entrance."

This reality, in turn, leads inevitably to the conclusion that these people were something less than people to Mahler—or perhaps something more than people, personifications of an ideal that held more importance for him than the particular reality of the individual. As an artist whose creative work was his own first priority and, at his insistence, the first priority of his associates, Mahler interpreted all his experiences primarily as aesthetic phenomena, as Nietzsche might say.[16] That is, his tendency to look at life through the lens of German idealism—real vs. apparent, noumenal vs. phenomenal, eternal vs. transient—colored his personal relations such that any person and, indeed, any particular action or choice would be read as a work of art, for what universal truth he, she, or it might embody. A human being, even one close to him, was first of all a particularization, an appearance, a manifestation, and thus susceptible to being evaluated as a figurative projection of that underlying reality. If there is obviously a selfishness in such an attitude, it is a selfishness necessary for the production of great art, especially great art from the pen of a busy full-time conductor.

The outlines of this worldview can be gleaned from Mahler's letter to Alma on Goethe's "Ewig-Weibliche" [eternal feminine] written in June 1909, long after the completion of the Eighth Symphony (1907) but before the affair with Walter Gropius that destroyed his self-confidence regarding matters feminine.[17] In response to a query that sadly no longer survives (destroyed by Alma, along with the rest of her letters to Mahler), the composer presented the essence of his reading of *Faust*. Like any art work, said Mahler, Goethe's poem employed "rational aspects" beneath which the reader must delve, just as one might lift "a veil that obscures the object itself."[18] Given the epistemological conditions first described by Kant, reality can be expressed only by means of appearance—the "soul is in need of a body"—and indeed only by means that, due to their figurative nature, are "by definition *inadequate*."[19] The magnitude of Goethe's task required not just an allegory (Mahler uses Goethe's word, "Gleichniß") but a sort of ultimate allegory, adequate to the expression of the inexpressible. And the miraculous success of his poem lay in the choice of femininity as symbol of the "transcendental and unchanging" reality toward which humans strive.[20] As the culmination of a long series of allegories, the *Mater gloriosa* brings us as close as humanly possible to knowledge of the absolute. "*Eternal Femininity* has *carried* us *forward*. We have arrived, we are at rest, we are in possession of that which on earth we could only desire or strive for" (emphasis in original).[21]

In the opinion of Freud, it was no coincidence that Mahler's wife bore the middle name "Maria," which interestingly enough was also the name of his mother. (Freud actually guessed this fact, a stunning piece of psychoanalytic virtuosity that made a believer of Mahler.) At the beginning of Mahler's letter on *Faust* we find him already reflecting on the outer and the inner Alma; he observes that her interest in Goethe, which we might call a "rational aspect" of her everyday existence, "reveals much of your inner self."[22] No doubt Mahler looked at everyone and everything through some version of this same dualism. Yet femininity held for him a special "mythological" force, as "eternal bliss" did for Christians, and he stated explicitly that among symbols it stood as "the one most accessible to this era of world history."[23] Thus there lay a special urgency, philosophical by nature, in the connections that he drew between the central artistic subject matter available to him and the central woman in his life.

It cannot have escaped Mahler that if Woman might be seen as an allegory, and if Goethe's Maria was the culmination of a series, then his Alma Maria too stood as the last and most interesting embodiment of a type. Before 1901 he engaged with two sharply focused categories of women:

the maternal (Justine, who served the material functions of mother; Natalie, who as mature divorcée handled the emotional) and the romantic (principally Mildenburg, whose willingness to take direction and be molded brought to her some enormous professional benefits, though not her ultimate goal of marriage). These contrasting sides overlapped for the first and only time in Alma, who began as an eager, naive, but adventurous romantic partner and metamorphosed into a doting mother after Mahler found that she "no longer excited him." Whenever that shift may have occurred (after the birth of their first child?), only she embodied both dimensions of femininity for Mahler, and only she could claim to have been comprehensively a woman to him. As lover and caretaker she was doubly static, and thus Maria-like, "a *fixed point*, the *goal*." And, perhaps more important for his creative life, she could serve as "the antithesis of eternal longing, striving, motion towards that goal—in a word, Eternal Masculinity."

Embedded within these observations one finds a more nuanced explanation of why Mahler's works after 1901 tended to invoke not just femininity but Alma in particular. The typically Mahlerian moments of soft, still, floating utopian bliss are more than generically ideal in this period; they are figuratively feminine, and often specifically Alma-related. This quality, prefigured in the G-major quotation of "Die zwei blauen Augen" in the funeral march of the First Symphony (m. 83, reh. 10), found its classic expression in the Adagietto of the Fifth, a movement that Willem Mengelberg famously called a love letter to Alma, having heard the story from both Mahler and Alma.[24] It is no wonder that conductors lose track of time in this hymn to romantic bliss (consider Leonard Bernstein's eleven-plus minutes compared to the better-informed Bruno Walter's two recorded performances below eight minutes).[25] With a mode of expression drawn from the slightly earlier Rückert song "Ich bin von der Welt abhanden gekommen" ("I Am Lost to the World," 1901), but here deployed in an overtly amorous context, the music seems meant to erase time altogether, along with our sense of dissonance, in suspensions that resolve only after the desire for resolution has evaporated.[26] In the last movement, on the other hand, the principal motive brings a return to "Eternal Masculinity," with the straining forward motion common to the second and third movements now directed at a goal revealed in the magical stasis introduced by Alma.

The dreams lived by Mahler with his wife became raw material for a new art, one that matched the bravado with which the composer declared that his time would come after his death. It figures as prominently in the tragedy of the Sixth Symphony as in the triumph of the Fifth. At its core stood a secret programmaticism that Mahler concealed behind his rhetoric of "absolute music," much as Alma lay at the root of universals Mahler attempted to construct when using her as an artistic subject. The existence in the Sixth of an "Alma theme," in which he tried to "capture" her (as she proudly related in her memoir) was a strictly private detail.[27] In practice, which is to say before the public, that passage is meant to capture something quite different: a masculine experience of fleeting happiness in the midst of a terrible and hopeless battle. A family similarity with the Gaze motive from *Tristan und Isolde* emphasizes the quality of mediation; we are hearing not a woman but a hero's perception of her. (The same could be said of the Adagietto, in which Mahler employs the same rising stepwise motive.) To seize an absolute and retain it in an artwork, Mahler often enlisted a degree of autobiographical concreteness, which he then attempted to erase from the interpretive context of the work. Alma served as muse, as metaphor, and even as a kind of plaster mold.

Of course Mahler used himself, or a fantasy of his own tragic future, much more extensively to map out the plan of the Sixth. Alma/Woman provides only a few relatively short moments of relief in the midst of the battle—hence Mahler's breakdown after the dress rehearsal, which Strauss witnessed and laughed off with perplexed impatience. Hearing his own composed-out doom was obviously more than he could bear, yet one wonders in what specific sense the music was too real for him. Did he succeed too well, coming too close to the beyond, to a loss of contact with material world? Or was the music so compellingly personal that it prevented a transition to the universal/figurative, so that no deeper meaning could coalesce and the ideal vision fell flat? The latter seems more likely. For all his concern for the metaphysical, Mahler, it must be said, had his strongest emotional reactions when his own personal existence was at stake. Fear of death was his strongest motivator, to paraphrase Goethe; to conquer it he imagined, repeatedly, an ideal state symbolized by the feminine.[28]

The Eighth Symphony took a safer route to the noumenal, with preexisting texts that kept autobiographical connotations at a distance. The mystical feminine holds center stage as a firm and unmistakable goal, with a dominant protagonist, the *Mater gloriosa*, whose femininity was by definition symbolic and spiritual. With these elements keeping him focused, Mahler's chances of public success increased exponentially; as he readily admitted, his greatest failures had come when he himself had not been clear about his intentions. Moreover, the sentimentality of the Adagietto, beloved by the public and bemoaned by Strauss, returned here transmuted by orchestration into something otherworldly, ethereal, and far from physical; if the weightless arrival of the *Mater gloriosa* above harp and harmonium revels in its kitschiness (reh. 106), that first audience was not disappointed.

This process of detachment from materiality in the move from the Sixth to the Eighth mimics Goethe's own use of his Christian sources. Goethe immersed himself no less fearlessly than Mahler in a religious perspective that he would seem to have outgrown. Following Goethe, Mahler used what was to him effectively an adult fairy tale to seize a deeper knowledge of the inexpressible; he concluded that the more widely known his figurative mechanism, the more vivid the rendering of a realm that might not even exist. Thus his greatest artistic statement on woman served also as his strongest embrace of what Strauss would derisively call the "Christian, Jewish metaphysics."[29]

Combating that metaphysics would be one of the principal goals of Strauss's creative life. He would accomplish it through his own brand of autobiography, but rather than hiding his self-examination, he brought it crassly and some would say tastelessly into full view, especially when dealing with the subject of women. For Strauss the *Mater gloriosa* would not do. He never wanted Pauline to be anything but real, and when he used her as artistic material it was through hyper-illustrative programmaticism and/or detailed, mundane autobiography—artistic means that not only discouraged but even prevented the listener from extrapolating a deeper symbolic significance. In fact Strauss had already worked through the Mahlerian conception of woman as a static figurative embodiment of the noumenal during the period of his Schopenhauer critique, before his marriage. Wondering aloud whether the feminine might offer an alternative to Schopenhauer's "denial of the will," Strauss considered (in a diary entry of January 1893) the passive bliss of what he imagined to be the female sexual experience and asked, "is not the way to the redemption of the will to be sought here (in the condition of the receiving woman)!"[30] Judging by the events of *Symphonia domestica*, his understanding of feminine sexuality broadened significantly after marriage. In the meantime he had long since abandoned philosophical idealism of all types, in favor of a stimulating and marketable materialism that attempted to leave the entire debate behind. And his attitudes toward women underwent a concomitant change, whether as cause or effect.

Don Juan provides something of a musical analogue to the diary entry, with a G-major love object (mm. 232–301) making herself available as a goal, a static focus of seduction. As James Hepokoski has argued, that encounter changes the protagonist in some fundamental sense; he becomes a hero, complete with a *Heldenthema* as "breakthrough," and sets out on a vaguely Mahlerian journey that leads to the distinctly un-Mahlerian conclusion (the Sixth excepted) of quiet doom.[31] Inherent in this pessimism is a critical judgment about the efficacy of the redeeming feminine. If Strauss continued in 1893 to entertain the possibility in his notebooks, he had long since given it up in his music, in *Don Juan* but also in *Guntram*, which ends with the hero walking away from a beautiful and exceedingly frustrated woman, who then becomes a nun by default. As with his rejection of Schopenhauer, Strauss appears to have formulated his attitudes on redeeming femininity first in his music, before constructing an intellectual justification.[32]

The closest thing to a Faust work in Strauss's oeuvre is *Also sprach Zarathustra*, which contains nothing of the *Mater gloriosa*, and indeed none of Part II at all, but instead draws inspiration (as we see in the sketches) from Faust's encounter with the Earth Spirit. In what would be a crucial moment in Strauss's intellectual life, he cast the Earth Spirit's dark verdict—"you resemble the spirit whom you imagine, not me"—as the content of Zarathustra's breakdown, drawing a crucial connection between Goethe's and Nietzsche's suspicion of idealism.[33] This was the real moment of departure from Mahler, and from any shared conception of a symbolic metaphysical function for the feminine. Rejecting Mahler's metaphysics, he by extension rejected its related gender apparatus, in favor of a new and (as Schoenberg would say) "revolutionary" path.[34]

As if recapitulating this intellectual judgment, Strauss's two tone poems after *Zarathustra* offered a musical rendering of diametrically opposed philosophical alternatives. He conceived them as a pair but presented the "satyr play" first: *Don Quixote* (1898), a work of humorous sentimentality, contemplative but also mercilessly critical of his culture's discredited, persistent idealism. The brilliant illustration of the various episodes has always dominated commentary on this piece, yet the centerpiece is obviously the F-sharp vision of his chivalrous devotion to Dulcinea, a tour de force of ironic beauty (mm. 332–69). We are not meant to enjoy this music naively. It is a lie, told by a simple-minded romantic to himself after he is driven insane by too much reading. Strauss used much the same tone for the presentation of the rose in *Der Rosenkavalier* (1910), and if we listen carefully to the Marschallin, we know that here too the beautiful dream is in the process of evaporating. However powerful the feminine ideal, amorously and even religiously, it must eventually be dragged back to earth by everyday physical realities.

Yet for Strauss it is in precisely those realities that an authentic redemption can be found, as he tells us for the first time in *Ein Heldenleben* (1899). This heroism is inseparable from the mundane, although the former reaches the latter by a circuitous route. As in the partner-work, a woman stands at the center of the structure, surrounded by episodes and adventures experienced by the male. But this woman is far more active: coquettish, insistent, controlling, she renders the man static and closes in for the kill. We hear her as she is, not as the male sees her; we experience what she thinks and does, and we watch as he tries to cope with her mobility. Most important, she is a person of flesh and blood, no more but no less, and it is to this reality, to this mundane domestic bliss, that the hero retreats in his "Weltflucht." She is Pauline, as surely as Alma inhabits the Sixth Symphony, but Pauline brings all her flaws and prickliness, ensuring that our attention remains on the *diesseits*, grounded in an experiential reality.

Strauss pleased himself so fully with this vision that he could not help revisiting it, with the absurdly titled *Symphonia domestica*. The death of the symphony as a genre, and the rejection of its exalted aims, would find no clearer announcement. As Nietzsche had hoped, that death led not to nihilism but to joy, but a joy rather different in character than he had expected. Family, work, and nature would be the foundation of his happiness, Strauss declared to himself in the sketches:

> My wife, my child, and my music
> Nature and sun, they are my happiness.
> A bit of serenity [*Gleichmut*] and a lot of humor
> There the devil himself can't surpass me![35]

So it went for the last half century of his life. Only that which could be seen and felt, and which could be captured in virtuosic musical illustration, would be endowed with spiritual significance. The more bracingly physical, the better, or so one surmises; how else to explain the ability of a composer to stand before a hundred musicians and a thousand listeners and reveal the details of a vigorous, conventional sex life?[36] Pauline made for a strange muse.

Unfortunately the lack of familiarity nowadays with *Feuersnot* has erased for most listeners a crucial link between *Heldenleben* and *Symphonia domestica*. Konrad, a stand-in for Strauss, curses the town for its ill-treatment of the Sorcerer (Wagner), even as he cuts his own ties with the type of magic practiced by his forebear. This double break is the real reason for the loss of fire; Konrad's humiliation is only the proximate cause, a dramatic prop, like the potion in *Tristan*. The town returns to life through a robust simultaneous orgasm of just the sort enjoyed by the bourgeois composer and his wife in the tone poem. In their capacity as metaphorical constructions, Konrad and Diemut could not be thinner; for listeners ca. 1900 they obviously stood at the center of an autobiographical trilogy, an opera framed by tone poems. Mundane self-absorption in *Heldenleben* meets lights-on sexuality in *Feuersnot*, leading to a musical exhibitionism in *Symphonia domestica* that on its own seems absurd but in context stands as Strauss's most sincere confession of faith. Strauss wrote it to confirm in explicit terms that he had found his life, through Pauline.

How, then, does a composer work simultaneously on pieces featuring his wife and Salome? This juxtaposition is perhaps the strangest in a career filled with them. On one hand, *Symphonia domestica* closed out the orchestral portion of his output, while on the other, *Salome* opened the operatic (at least in terms of international success). Never more afraid than when he found himself without a creative project, Strauss had no difficulty winding up one work, or one career phase, while opening another. There is one important bit of common ground shared by those protagonists, however: self-determination. Salome makes her own decisions, and she follows her own inclinations wherever they may lead. Herodias wields none of the influence in Wilde's play that we find in the biblical source; her interests coincide with those of her daughter by chance. Thus while the bickering of mother and stepfather seem to keep alive Strauss's autobiographical streak—at least in the public details of his marriage, such as the stories told by Alma in her memoir—Salome's irrepressible drive captured what interested him most about women, on stage and in real life. She acts and others respond; she dictates the course of her action, "even unto death."

In all the records of a marriage that ended two days short of fifty-five years, there is no evidence that Strauss resisted any of his wife's inclinations, petty or grand. When they married, she wished to continue performing, and she continued performing. When she chose to stop, she stopped (figure 4). Strauss laid out no blueprint for her self-realization; he left her life to her, she devoted herself to him, and in the end her only regret was that it all went by so quickly. It is a mere fact, rather than a critical observation, that Mahler's willingness to marry Alma was contingent on her soul-crushing denial of her creative impulses.[37] Mahler made the demand from a distance, in writing, to prevent all doubt and preempt further questions. That is certainly a source of the bitterness with which Pauline is treated in Alma's memoir, in contrast to the admiration that Alma expressed for Strauss (notwithstanding the general view that Alma savaged both the composer and his wife). Alma could not take part in her husband's elevated conversations with Strauss because Pauline was there—a woman who possessed complete freedom in thought and action, and who chose to squander (in Alma's view) the opportunity. We do not know if it ever occurred to Alma to attempt a liaison with Strauss, although such an omission would perhaps be unexpected. He was a man of extraordinary artistic accomplishment (making him a plausible choice as a lover, according to the standard that she articulated to Mahler) and he

Figure 4. Pauline de Ahna as Elizabeth in *Tannhäuser*, Bayreuth, 1894. Courtesy of the Universitätsbibliothek Johann Christian Senckenberg, Frankfurt am Main.

lived where she lived, not in the clouds.[38] In any case, the Strauss family represented for Alma an overdetermined unattainable, feeding a desire that would have to find its satisfaction elsewhere.

Whereas an affair reduced Mahler's marriage to appearances (and brought on his final illness, if we accept the account of Feder), in Strauss's world the lone episode of this sort, a mistaken accusation brought by Pauline, was ridiculous enough to become material for a return to autobiography via middle-class sex farce. *Intermezzo* (1923) would seem to have pushed a well-worn formula a step too far, but none other than Arnold Schoenberg found it strikingly modern,[39] though obviously not for its musical technique. Schoenberg responded rather to the chasm separating this subject matter from that with which both Strauss and he had grown up. Here was a thoroughly fresh stimulus to musical creativity, and a content profoundly opposed to what the neoromantic idiom had been designed to express. Even as Schoenberg argued that his musical choices kept faith with a living tradition, he must have recognized that they likewise reinvigorated a certain romantic ideology of music, one that Strauss repeatedly, and here more impolitely than ever, heaved out the window.

However implausible the turbulent reality of Strauss's domestic life as an operatic happy ending, it gave him in this world something of the stability that Mahler and his romantic predecessors sought in the next. Strauss attached himself to a woman who would make her own decisions, a woman unlike any he had known in his youth, and by encouraging that independence he won for himself an everlasting stability. Mahler treated a similar woman in a different manner, and he paid a heavy price.

CHAPTER 4

Wagnerians

IT SPEAKS WELL of Mahler and Strauss that by their early twenties they had outgrown the Wagner-Brahms conflict, i.e., they had dismissed it as a framework for thinking about contemporary music. Close experience of aesthetic bigotry left them wanting something more than a choice between conservatism and "music of the future." Although Mahler's love of Wagner knew no bounds, he openly placed Brahms above Bruckner (on the grounds of his "extraordinarily compact" style); he called Bach, Brahms, and Wagner the only great German contrapuntists; and he rejected Liszt unequivocally for "paucity of content and shoddy workmanship."[1] The twenty-two-year-old Strauss felt himself sufficiently beyond the old controversy to draw on both Brahms and Wagner in the same compositions—parodically, in the *Burleske* (1886), and earnestly, in the ruminative chamber music context of the Violin Sonata (1887).[2] (The juxtaposition may have been prompted by Brahms himself, whom Strauss got to know in Meiningen in 1885 and who engaged with specific Wagnerian works more or less directly in his Third Symphony.)[3] Suggesting that Strauss or Mahler was at a given moment "for" or "against" Wagner thus gets us nowhere. As musicians and conductors they admired him; as composers they confronted a Freudian problem of unprecedented dimensions.

The fundamental challenge was to distance themselves from Wagner while maintaining faith. No one performing Wagner's music under Strauss or Mahler could miss the quasi-religious fidelity that held sway in the orchestra pit. The conductors were well known for restoring cuts (audiences be damned) and for taking all conceivable steps to learn Wagner's intentions, including consulting his dogmatic widow (at least while they found her a credible source).[4] Yet in their compositions they sought a new path, even undercutting Wagner's music explicitly when it served their purposes; here their militant preservation of his works' integrity on the stage allowed a certain license for guilt-free critique. Mahler the composer rejected the dramatic stage entirely (despite Strauss's encouragement), and in his symphonies he used Wagner's language to reconsider the viability of Wagner's aesthetic aims. Strauss on the other hand dared to write a tragedy as his first opera, yet the sophisticated Wagnerians among his inner circle saw it for what it was—a subtle parody—and that realization cost him some of his closest relationships. On the technical level, then, Mahler and Strauss could not have existed without Wagner, but their creative debts to him would be defined by critical appropriation: the deployment of Wagner's own art to express something self-consciously new.

The early experiences with Wagner's music indicate different levels of natural affinity. In this religion Mahler was a born disciple, Strauss a convert. At the time of his audition in Vienna in 1875, Mahler had already developed a Wagnerian compositional voice; indeed it was not his piano playing but his youthful compositions, "in direct descent from Wagner," that won the instant admiration of Julius Epstein.[5] Given the programming at the Iglau Municipal Theater—a steady diet of Mozart, Meyerbeer, and Italian bel canto—Mahler's knowledge of Wagner came predominantly if not entirely from scores, among them the Liszt arrangements that would have found their way to a teenage virtuoso known for playing Thalberg. In Strauss's music, conversely, there is no evidence of Wagner's influence before 1886, and the principal signs that the precocious adolescent knew of Wagner's existence come in mocking references in letters to Ludwig Thuille. (Note the Stabreim: "Nach langem und *s*ehnlichen, *s*aueren Warten/*h*ielt in *H*änden ich endlich die neidliche Post [Long I listed, in painful delay; Here I hold your mail at last in my fist]" [emphasis in original].)[6] Yet Strauss too was learning Wagner, if not yet applying the knowledge. Beyond the amusing tale of his secret candle-lit study sessions of *Tristan*, we find in the Thuille letters remarkably detailed descriptions of passages that Strauss heard in performances at the Munich Court Opera. "In general Wagner is very fond of sequences" is far from the only fair observation to be read in these pages, and his habit of filling the margins with notated musical recollections betrays a keen fascination.[7]

It is nevertheless a fact that Strauss required the intervention of a Wagnerian strongman, Alexander Ritter, to redirect his compositional style toward the New Germans. Having been pushed into territory that had tempted him, Strauss sorted out the differences between Wagner and the two non-German New Germans with characteristic swiftness. While the tone poems owe an obvious debt to Liszt, whose symphonic poems are a stronger precedent than any concert overture (even Beethoven's), Strauss took pains to point out where his tone poems would represent an advance, citing the "dramatic development" in the third movement of the *Faust* Symphony as the way forward, in contrast to the "mood pieces" (*Stimmungsbilder*) of the first two movements.[8] That interest in unfolding drama would lead in the direction of Wagner, principally by means of the leitmotivic apparatus, which Strauss substituted for Lisztian thematic transformation in the early tone poems, although he laid it over a double-function sonata plan clearly modeled on Liszt.[9]

This symphonic repurposing of Wagner's musico-dramatic technique holds far more interest than Strauss's decision to begin writing his own libretto for a Wagnerian tragedy, *Guntram*—a project that began in 1887, before any of the tone poems. The choices he made in the tone poems would result in a personal method of translating drama into music, a hybrid of tone painting and leitmotivic tapestry that would be as applicable in opera as in orchestral music. (Del Mar had good reason for calling the early operas "stage tone poems.") Thus while *Guntram* helped him sort out a personal response to the philosophical dead end of Wagner's art (see below), it played a surprisingly minor role in the evolution of a personal creative style based on Wagnerian principles of music and drama.

The young Strauss also confronted a bewildering variety in the available public and private Wagnerisms. By participating in the regular meetings of Ritter and his stable of young firebrands at Munich's Weinstube Leibenfrost, Strauss established fundamentalist credentials that ingratiated him with Cosima and strengthened his bargaining position with the establishment at the Munich Court Opera (figure 5).[10] But in maintaining cordial relations with Hermann Levi and Hans von Bülow he signaled a capacity for moderation and compromise, which, given his conservative lineage, seemed more believable to those in charge than his calculatedly conspicuous association with maniacal Bayreuth insiders. Thus as the private Strauss adapted Wagnerian tools to his tone poems and the six-year project of his first opera, he performed a similar juggling act in the social realm of musical politics. If he found the process confusing, however, he cannot have thought it unusual, for competition among the faithful was to be found everywhere, from the ongoing rivalries between Bayreuth and the major opera houses (Munich in particular), to the ever-shifting missions and memberships of the various Wagner societies, to the formation of relationships with older musicians who themselves had known Wagner personally and now could not get along with one another (Bülow, Levi, Hans Richter, Hans von Bronsart, Ritter, Franz Fischer, and so on). To be a Wagnerian in the 1880s was to be a chameleon.

On reaching Vienna as a student in 1876, Mahler quickly latched onto his own group of young Wagnerians, though they had no elderly leader and consumed vegetables rather than wine.[11] Mahler's enthusiasm developed a few years before Strauss's, and so he had opportunities for personal contact with Wagner himself. But whereas Hugo Wolf boldly waited in the hall of the composer's hotel in order to open his carriage door, Mahler lacked the nerve (or the bad taste) to bother the Master, even when a chance meeting in the Opera cloak room presented an opportunity to help Wagner into his overcoat.[12] In any case, for Mahler as for Strauss the attraction began with the music rather than the man; Mahler, Wolf, and Rudolf Krzyzanowski were known to spend hours playing and singing through Wagner's scores, on one occasion rendering the trio for Gunther, Brünnhilde, and Hagen in *Götterdämmerung*, Act II, with sufficient enthusiasm to get themselves evicted from the apartment they shared.[13]

Music making likewise held an important place in the meetings of the new Akademischer Wagner-Verein in Vienna, which Mahler joined in

Figure 5. "Enthusiasm at the climax": Strauss's ironic passion for Giacomo Meyerbeer's *Robert le diable*. Courtesy of the Richard-Strauss-Institut, Garmisch-Partenkirchen.

1877 and where he met Guido Adler.[14] In this setting, and particularly as Siegfried Lipiner began to assert his powerful intellect, the writings and ideas of Wagner became a new fascination for Mahler, and for the remainder of his life they would retain a force that he questioned far less willingly than did Strauss. When at a party in 1888 a fellow musician criticized one of Wagner's remarks on conducting, Mahler instantly retorted, "when Wagner has spoken, other people hold their tongues."[15] Shortly after Anna von Mildenburg took up her appointment at Hamburg she received Wagner's collected writings as a gift from Mahler, who admonished her that "an artist must own these works and continually read and absorb them."[16] And after his *Retuschen* of Beethoven's Ninth met opposition in Vienna, Mahler responded with a citation of "On the Performance of the Ninth Symphony of Beethoven," complete with reference to the edition and volume number. Especially where issues of musicianship were concerned, Mahler looked on Wagner's writings as a kind of scripture.

It is curious, then, to find that Mahler seems not to have attempted a systematic absorption of Wagner's philosophy, nor indeed of the principal intellectual sources of Wagner's mature worldview, above all Schopenhauer. Alma mentioned the philosopher only a single time in all her testimony, reporting, as did Bauer-Lechner, that "one of his favorite quotations was from Schopenhauer's *The World as Will and Representation*: 'How often have the inspirations of genius been brought to naught by the crack of a whip!'"[17] Naturally there was more to his reading than that; his use of the image of the "Ixion wheel" to describe the end of the Third Symphony confirms a basically Schopenhauerian mission in that work: a survey of the totality of existence culminates in the dissolution of the world of appearances, i.e., something like Schopenhauer's "denial of the will."[18] But there is no evidence that Mahler worked through Wagner's or Schopenhauer's philosophical texts with a critical eye, even to the extent of addressing, for example, the perennial question of how to reconcile Wagner's essay "Beethoven" (1870) with the dramatic theories of *Oper und Drama* (1851).[19] We have no comments from Mahler on Wagner's reading of Schopenhauer, and no indication that he recognized the Schopenhauerian elements of *Die Meistersinger*.[20] More important, Mahler seems not to have noticed the philosopher's ultimate conclusion regarding music, namely, that asceticism, not music, was the only legitimate path to a lasting denial.[21] If the

Third offers a vision of Schopenhauerian redemption, then, it simultaneously controverts Schopenhauer by deploying music to an end for which it had already been deemed insufficient by the philosopher himself.

At the same time, Mahler's idealism puts him firmly in a camp with these forebears, even if for him that outlook was more wistful sentimentality than genuine belief. In this light the critical stance toward Nietzsche in the broad outlines of the Third comes off as a kind of homage. The sequence of programmatic topics over the last three movements—Nietzsche's "Midnight Song," a Christian celebration, and a redemptive Adagio—indicates a straightforward repudiation of Nietzsche's Wagner critique, along lines that assume a seamless connection between Wagner and Schopenhauer. Such a move would have been entirely consistent with Mahler's abiding devotion to *Tristan*, a work that Nietzsche called Wagner's "opus metaphysicum" before turning against everything that he felt it embodied. Mahler did not spell out such a project; we know only that during the summer of 1895 he told Bauer-Lechner of having found "a glorious poem of Nietzsche's."[22] There would have been nothing out of character in Mahler's cherry-picking a creatively inspiring poem from a large work with an otherwise anti-Schopenhauerian disposition; selective appropriation seems likewise to have been his approach to Schopenhauer. (Walter found a sort of intellectual recklessness central to Mahler's nature: "systematic influence, the most important element of education, was foreign to his wholly ungoverned and impulsive character. Nothing in his life—as I quickly realized—was systematic.")[23] In any case, the superseding of Nietzsche by Christian and Schopenhauerian materials seems purposeful and prominent in this work. (The implications vis-à-vis Nietzsche are explored below in chapter 12.) Mahler's point was not so much to maintain faith with Schopenhauer's text as to look back fondly on the musical metaphysics that Wagner represented, a worldview captured best of all by the young, still-Wagnerian Nietzsche in that favorite text of Mahler's Vienna school friends: *The Birth of Tragedy*.

In describing his relationship to Strauss, Mahler famously dipped into Schopenhauer for an image that seems unrelated to anything deeper in the philosopher's thought: "Schopenhauer somewhere uses the image of two miners digging a tunnel from opposite sides and then meeting underground. That seems fittingly to characterize my relationship with

Strauss."[24] This style of quotation betrays the continuing influence of Lipiner, who according to Alma "always brought quotations to his aid in order to make anything clear; he never had anything of his own to say."[25] A closer look at this case suggests, however, that Mahler was not simply putting on airs. The comment came in a letter to Arthur Seidl, a learned music critic whose considerable philosophical training (he earned a PhD in philosophy from the University of Leipzig in 1887) and close personal friendships with Strauss and Mahler put him in a uniquely strong position to understand what issues were at stake. Moreover, the letter came in February 1897, in the midst of a growing confrontation between the two Nietzsche-related works, *Also sprach Zarathustra* and the Third Symphony. Given his acquaintance with Seidl, as well as his intimate knowledge of *Guntram* (which Strauss played to him from the manuscript in 1894) and *Till Eulenspiegel*, we can assume that Mahler now recognized Strauss's critical stance toward Wagner's Schopenhauerian metaphysical pretensions. Musically, the tunnels converged; the separation resulted from diametrically opposed receptions of the legacy of musical idealism. If Mahler knew Seidl's writings (for example his 1896 biographical essay on Strauss), he surely expected the critic to grasp this philosophical difference.[26]

Seidl actually commented in print, albeit briefly, on the metaphysical intricacies of *Guntram*.[27] These relate mainly to the ending, which dramatized Schopenhauer's rejection of music as a means of redemption—a step with momentous implications for the philosophical dimension of Wagner's music dramas. In brief, *Guntram* tells the story of a minstrel who, as a member of a mystic brotherhood, uses his art to promote spiritual transformation, then loses faith, breaks his lyre, and dedicates himself to a life of asceticism. The parallelism with Schopenhauer's "saintliness" as described in the fourth book of *Die Welt als Wille und Vorstellung* is no accident; in his private copy of Schopenhauer's text,[28] Strauss flagged the following sentence on the relationship between art and the human striving for denial of the will: "It [art] does not become for him an extinguisher of the will, as we shall see in the following book in the case of the saint who has attained resignation; it does not deliver him from life forever, but only for a few moments."[29]

This statement spelled for Strauss the end of a meaningful connection between music and Schopenhauer's philosophy, which is to say between music and metaphysics. He declared to Ritter that whereas Guntram would follow the philosopher's path, "*I am not giving up art, and I'm not Guntram either.*"[30] Shortly thereafter he announced his disengagement from Schopenhauer in correspondence with Cosima Wagner, Thuille, and the most gifted intellect among his friends, Friedrich Rösch. "I cannot help myself, the halo will never be my lot," he told Cosima.[31] Even more strikingly, he had the nerve to formulate his own critique of the fourth book of *Die Welt als Wille*, holding that Schopenhauer drew "conclusions that do not stand wholly in accord with the wonderfully objective attitude of the first books. Here I am thinking especially of the somewhat one-sided representation of the 'sufferings of the world' and the glorifying of the modification of the will in the life of the saints."[32] If metaphysical contemplation meant giving up music, Strauss had no interest in it. But he went so far as to question the possibility of such experience for any human, by any means: "our intellect, bound as it is to time and space, can go no further without becoming utopian."[33]

Ritter was under no illusions about what these developments meant for Strauss's understanding of Wagner—they amounted to a dissection, with the musical style detached from its philosophical grounding. "Nothing remains of Wagner's worldview in you," complained Ritter. "What alone has survived of Wagner in you? The mechanics of his art."[34] No truer statement about Strauss has ever been uttered, and no insight is more vital for the interpretation of his subsequent works. Even Strauss's experiments with Wagner's compositional style served the ultimate purpose of creating distance between the two composers. Seidl noted that *Guntram* stood alone among operas after Wagner for its overt juxtaposition of distinct Wagnerian styles: the aural world of *Tristan* alternates with those of *Meistersinger*, *Tannhäuser*, *Parsifal*, and so on, in ways that undermined the coherence necessary to sustain a metaphysical interpretation.[35] The work amounted to a "monstrous fantasy on Wagner's complete works" (*Münchener Bote*, November 19, 1895), motivated by a critical impulse that few listeners were equipped to understand.

The point became clearer in the subsequent tone poems, which explicitly targeted Wagner's high style. Transforming the *Tristan* chord into raspberries in the mouth of Till Eulenspiegel removed all doubt that a form of vandalism was in progress. The next work, *Also sprach Zarathustra*, brought back the transfiguring cadence of the "Liebestod" as an anemic vestige of itself (m. 965, reh. 56), decisively and impassively undermined by the repeating C's lurking beneath the philosophically loaded key of B major. At best musical elevation was now a beautiful memory, a quixotic dream rendered with exquisite empathy in the F#-major vision (discussed in chapter 3) at the heart of *Don Quixote*. All too often the aural beauty of such moments in Strauss obscures their essential irony, as in the glorious bombast of Jochanaan, whom Strauss called "a clown."[36] That critical impulse, one of the composer's strongest natural tendencies, had already revealed itself in *Don Juan*, when the chromatic intensification of the *Liebestod* becomes the vehicle for a none-too-subtle representation of male sexual climax.[37] But after *Guntram*, Strauss had a philosophical justification for his natural impulse; he grounded his critique in philosophy, and he implemented it in music. The message came through loud and clear in Bayreuth, where after his debut in 1894 Strauss would not conduct again until Cosima had died.

Though Mahler left no comment on Strauss's dismantling of Wagnerian musical metaphysics, he surely grasped at least the basic outlines. Indeed, this issue may partly explain the silence in their relationship from December 1895 through February 1897, which coincided with the production of *Zarathustra* and the Third Symphony. Certainly there is evidence that Mahler considered some familiarity with Schopenhauer the duty of every Wagnerian, though not with the same schoolboy fastidiousness as Strauss. Walter claimed that in the Hamburg period Mahler was "quite under the influence of Schopenhauer"[38]—sufficiently so that when Walter became his assistant, Mahler presented him with a complete edition of the philosopher's works.[39] The depth with which Mahler studied these texts remains questionable, however, as does the extent of the detailed knowledge of Wagner's writings he believed necessary for practical advocacy from the conductor's podium. Ida Dehmel reported him to have asked, "what is the use of all those volumes he [Wagner] wrote? You have to forget them before you can begin to love the genius of Wagner as it deserves to be loved."[40] At no time did Mahler turn Schopenhauer against Wagner, as

Strauss had done. The specifics apparently mattered less than the mere fact of once having read the material in the course of one's *Bildung*.

The idealism that lay at the heart of Mahler's love for Wagner was thus more an instinct or a natural inclination than a result of learning. Furthermore, it was at pains to justify itself in a modern world, as he recognized. The private discomfort of this position manifested itself as a hatred of materialism. Another of his gifts to Walter was Friedrich Albert Lange's *Geschichte des Materialismus und Kritik seiner Bedeutung in der Gegenwart* [*History of Materialism and Criticism of Its Significance at the Present Time*] (1866), an attack on "the oldest malady of human thought."[41] The neo-Kantian Lange wrote his work specifically to support opponents of materialism, and Mahler was not alone in finding it (according to Walter) "one of the most essential experiences of his life."[42] (The twenty-two-year-old Nietzsche, already deep into the Wagner infatuation from which he would later recoil, called this now little-known book the "most significant philosophical work to be published in the last one hundred years.")[43] Mahler had no tolerance for opposing viewpoints on this topic, particularly where Wagner was concerned. Richard Dehmel learned this lesson the hard way after remarking at a party attended by Mahler, Gustav Klimt, Alfred Roller, and Koloman Moser that "Wagner reminds me of a poppy, and I can't stand poppies."[44] The traumatized reaction, succinctly described by Alma—"silence fell, and the party broke up in gloom"—tells us that Wagnerian idealism remained an article of faith among this forward-thinking circle of intellectuals, as it was among the friends whom Mahler abandoned after Alma came along.

If Dehmel had known Mahler's reaction on his first hearing of *Parsifal*, at the Festspielhaus in 1883, he would have understood why the conversation halted so abruptly. Still grieving over the Master's recent death, Mahler described the experience to Löhr: "When I came out of the Festspielhaus, completely spellbound, I understood that the greatest and most painful revelation had just been made to me, and that I would carry it with me unspoiled all my life."[45] As a response to Wagner's most directly Schopenhauerian opera (the nineteenth century understood more readily than our own that *Parsifal*, not *Tristan*, was the standard in this respect), this effusion shows Mahler still holding to the principles of Nietzsche's *Birth of Tragedy*, a treatise that young Vienna Wagnerians treated as scripture and that of course was written ten years before *Parsifal*. Yet there is something even more antiquated about Mahler's focus on music as the source of "revelation." Mahler suggests, more or less directly, that the music offers an experience of idealism more authentic than one could find in any verbal text. Music, effectively composed and properly heard, superseded philosophy, in the manner described by E. T. A. Hoffmann and his fellow romantics. Where the youthful coming-to-terms with Wagner pushed Strauss toward a careful private study of philosophical texts, for Mahler it reaffirmed that while such study was indispensable on an educational level, it was not ultimately necessary in a spiritual sense.

Mahler's continuing defense of musical spirituality explains why in creative terms his interest in Wagner focused mainly on *Tristan* and *Parsifal*. The latter had an impact across his oeuvre: from the finale of the First (with the paraphrase of the Grail theme), to the angels' movement of the Third, to the slow movement of the Fourth, to the elevated atmosphere of the Eighth's *Faust* movement. As Mahler had predicted before work on any of his symphonies, *Parsifal* would be a model that he would never duplicate and always emulate. *Tristan* likewise shows up at important moments, especially after the arrival of Alma: the Gaze motive appears relatively undisguised in the Adagietto of the Fifth (an allusion that is worked out extensively in the finale); the "traurige Weise" of Act III forms the background of "Der Einsame im Herbst" (*Das Lied von der Erde*, movement two) and again in the Adagio of the Tenth.[46] Thus where Mahler's conducting activity encompassed the full range of Wagner's works—he made his Vienna debut with *Lohengrin*, for example (on May 11, 1897), and he moved quickly to rehabilitate the *Ring*—his compositional engagement lay primarily in the overtly metaphysical operas.[47] (The exceptions that prove the rule here are the *Ring*-like tetralogy-character of the first four symphonies, discussed most recently by Hartmut Hein, and the *Meistersinger* quotation in the manic finale of the Seventh.[48] The rarity of such moments confirms Mahler's antipathy for Pfitzner's Teutonic Wagnerism, which held that "the deepest and truest thing in Wagner was his Germanness"; according to Alma, Mahler responded that "the greater an artist was, the further he left nationality behind.")[49]

Strangely enough, the vivid quality of Mahler's Wagner allusions would hint at a critique, for he could not or would not sustain that mode of expression. Walter recognized before Adorno that Mahler's fondness for the archaic—for the traditional regarded from a sentimental perspective—contained an "unconscious reaction against Wagner."[50] The "apparent regression" of Mahler's musical material ("an idiom which is prevailingly pre-Wagnerian") and of his aesthetic orientation confirms by its sentimental character the inescapable reality of "transitoriness and impending death." There is no naiveté in this perspective. It is an appropriation of the bygone "as embodiment of that which is inexorably doomed to perish." (Adorno later elaborated on this point extensively without modifying its fundamental basis.) This persistent connection to pre-Wagnerian music conditioned Mahler's Wagner reception, which therefore must be viewed as a "strong" appropriation, i.e., as always somehow critical. In the aesthetic realm, as well, Mahler would remain attached not just to Wagner's neoromanticism but to the originary romanticism that culminated in Hoffmann's Beethoven reception—as though the two could exist side by side. Beethoven and Wagner were always Mahler's twin musical idols. "I usually spend my nights with them," he told Bauer-Lechner.[51] And at bottom he did not imagine a different relationship for himself with one than with the other. They both belonged to an irretrievable past, and they both made music about a beautiful but unreachable world.

Strauss's attack on Wagner would only become more assertive in the new century. With the encouragement of Ernst von Wolzogen, the comedically minded anti-Wagnerian brother of *Bayreuther Blätter* editor Hans von Wolzogen, Strauss turned to out-and-out parody in *Feuersnot* (1901).[52] The basis of redemption in this Bavarian *Erlösungsoper* (the libretto, in impenetrable Bavarian dialect, has yet to receive an English translation) builds from the ridiculous—a young wizard casts a fire-extinguishing curse after being publicly rejected by the mayor's daughter—to the overtly sexual—the curse is lifted after her submission to an equally public deflowering. Strauss delivered that earthy dramatic climax in the idiom of *Tristan*, and in so doing he burned the bridge to Bayreuth once and for all, no matter how compellingly he would later indulge in symbolism and musical sumptuousness in *Die Frau ohne Schatten* (1917), which in any case he considered a long overdue "last Romantic opera."[53]

Strauss would have his sentimental phase, however, some three and a half decades after Mahler's death, in the midst of a national self-destruction that made him reconsider the brash confidence of his youth. *Metamorphosen* (1945) is the closest thing in his oeuvre to irony-free Wagnerism, outstripping even *Tod und Verklärung*, a work seemingly based not on Strauss's own views but on Ritter's.[54] Unlike the earlier tone poem, *Metamorphosen* shows not a trace of hope; in his agony at the daily destruction of Germany's cultural artifacts (particularly Goethe's home in Weimar and the opera house in Munich) Strauss transformed the chromatic counterpoint of *Tristan* into a vehicle of pessimism. It took Strauss's son to bring back the old sanguineness. The so-called *Four Last Songs*, "commissioned" by the composer's son Franz, would be the consoling counterpart of *Metamorphosen*, mingling a staunchly un-Wagnerian lyricism with a *Ring* atmosphere (including quotations, such as the Magic Fire at the beginning of "September"). Here, finally, musical beauty wipes away questions of hope or its lack. In fact Strauss comes surprisingly close to the tone of the *Das Lied von der Erde*, particularly at Mahler's conclusion, where a beautiful past neutralizes concern for the future, leaving only a static, glowing present.

Mahler and Strauss lost faith in the Faustian striving that united Beethoven and Wagner, and in that respect they shared a modernist impulse. Neither of them pursued Wagner's spiritual or philosophical goals, however different their paths to that decision, and however unlike the private psychological repercussions. This divergence from Wagner must condition one's reading of the practical ways in which Mahler and Strauss remained Wagnerians. Walter said that his own youthful "Wagner-frenzy" was "purified and strengthened" by contact with Mahler, whose approach "was inspired by practical experience."[55] Strauss took similar lessons from Bülow and Levi, musically skilled pragmatists who by their old age had little interest in political, philosophical, or any other nonmusically concerned forms of Wagnerism. Wagner had provided a new model of musical practice, an alternative to the "formalism" of Haydn and Mozart; he taught that it "must evolve perpetually, like life," and that "for new content, one must create new forms."[56] These quotations show the composers appropriating a Wagnerian interpretation of Beethoven, as surely as Mahler would claim that Wagner was the only person who understood how to edit a Beethoven score.[57] Wagner thus indicated the way forward for the authentic German tradition, and in this strictly musical sense Mahler and Strauss proceeded as the most faithful of Wagnerians. This tendency was apparent to anyone with a basic awareness of the issues: the critics in New York, who praised Mahler's *Tristan* over Toscanini's for its protection of the voices from the orchestra, and the administration of the Court Opera in Munich, who recalled Strauss in 1894 because he offered them the best chance to preserve the credibility embodied by the ailing Hermann Levi.[58]

And yet, this authenticity acted simultaneously as an ossifying historicism, a kind of taxidermy, and therefore as a self-conscious step into the twentieth century and away from the living faith of Wagner's neoromanticism. It preserved the integrity of the musical guild mentality of *Die Meistersinger*, but it did so as a consolation, as a monument to something larger that was now lost. If they were to find a personal musical language that could express the modern human condition, Mahler and Strauss would have to search elsewhere.

CHAPTER 5

Businessmen

NOT THE LEAST NOTEWORTHY talent shared by Mahler and Strauss was the enormous skill with which they managed their professional careers. Mahler's difficulties as composer should not obscure the truly meteoric rise of his conducting career, which fully matched the rapid surge of Strauss's creative reputation. In both areas the triumphs brought to fruition a great deal of systematic effort. For Mahler to assume control of Europe's greatest opera house as a thirty-seven-year-old Bohemian Jew, and for Strauss to emerge as the leading creative force in Germany at a similarly tender age, both musicians had to devote considerable energies to the practical and even mundane requirements of conventional professional achievement. This kind of effort came easily to both of them; neither had any desire for a life of starvation in self-righteous obscurity, perhaps because they had vivid personal experience of overwrought neoromanticism—Hans Rott and Hugo Wolf in the case of Mahler, Alexander Ritter for Strauss. Yet it is easy to overlook the importance of this successful political dimension of their lives, or consciously to look the other way in order to avoid uncomfortable questions about the overlapping of artistic and commercial success.

There is something to be gained from an honest consideration of the strategies and tactics of career building. This context cannot be separated from the exalted creative products for which Mahler and Strauss are remembered today. Both musicians were brilliantly successful in the conventional sense; their methods of achieving success, however, were perfectly ordinary. Likewise their attitude toward financial matters was entirely standard and, from a bourgeois perspective, prudent. They hoped to make as much money as they could, for the freedom it would give them for their most important artistic activity—composition—and for the comforts it would provide to their families and support systems. Perhaps even more important than money was power, a commodity to be won in the administrative capacities that both men sought as early as possible, not only in the musical-administrative hierarchy—where for example Mahler worked toward the title of "director" at a remarkably young age— but also in professional organizations such as the Allgemeiner deutscher Musikverein (General German Music Association) and the Genossenschaft deutscher Tonsetzer (German Composers' Cooperative), which were always so important to Strauss. (This was of course also the principal attraction of the Nazi Reichsmusikkammer.)

Personal evidence is even more instructive in this area, and a surprisingly rich body of evidence exists given the thin treatment of the topic in the scholarly literature (if one discounts polemical writings). Mahler and Strauss were tough and effective negotiators, most especially in the early periods when reputation offered little assistance and survival depended on success. Both also showed a crafty awareness of political relations, the need to develop useful contacts, the value of capitulation and strategic obsequiousness, and the importance of storing up good will to be cashed in later. Once they assured their own positions in the musical world, they could be relied upon to assist those below them according to the unspoken customs that they themselves had learned and manipulated. Always, however, their first consideration in such situations was talent and ability, the crucial factor in a meritocratic political system that they would reform selectively but certainly not reject.

Franz Strauss was not just Strauss's first teacher of performance and composition. He also gave early lessons in entrepreneurship, hoping that, should his son pursue a career in music (which was not a foregone conclusion), he would not have to follow his father's arduous path. Franz made his way to the Munich Court Opera in 1847 via a post as court guitarist for Duke Max in Munich (beginning in 1837) and a long youthful record of pickup work playing violin, viola, clarinet, and every brass instrument. Richard would need neither that range of skills nor the willingness to say yes to whatever job came his way. (On one occasion the twelve-year-old Franz even sang the "Grâce" aria from Meyerbeer's *Robert le diable* at Regensburg when a soprano became ill.)[1] Rather, Franz ensured that when Richard's diligent preparation reached a professional level of accomplishment, it was heard by the right people. Hermann Levi was kept apprised of the young composer's progress, the aging Hofkapellmeister's interest carefully cultivated, so that with the completion of the First Symphony he not just willingly but enthusiastically arranged a performance by the Court Orchestra in the Musical Academy series at the Munich Odeon. That connection was then cemented eighteen months later with the dedication of the Concert Overture in C Minor (1883). The next year, with the completion of the Second Symphony, Franz took the remarkable and financially burdensome step of providing one thousand marks to cover the printing costs of the work's publication by Eugen Spitzweg, owner of the Munich publishing firm Joseph Aibl. Interest in this work had come from as far away as New York, where Theodore Thomas would give the symphony's world premiere with the Philharmonic on December 13, 1884, and Franz saw the need to be ready to accommodate requests for performance, which did, in fact, materialize quickly. (In 1885 the work was performed in Cologne, Meiningen, Munich, and Berlin.)[2]

Spitzweg would be a crucial figure in Strauss's rise to public prominence. The Berlin sojourn made by Strauss in the winter of 1883–84 produced many interviews with publishers but no contracts, so that the hometown option became the only option. In Spitzweg, Strauss found a publisher with "an artistic rather than a commercial temperament," according to Max Steinitzer, which allowed him to recognize talent that would pay well later if supported now.[3] The Piano Pieces, op. 3, had appeared in 1881 despite a colorfully negative assessment by Bülow: "*Do not care* for the piano pieces by Richard Strauss in the least... Lachner has the imagination of a Chopin by comparison." In 1884 Spitzweg paid

Strauss a fee for the minimally lucrative rights to the Horn Concerto, op. 11, saying of himself that "when publishers are hammering at your door, he will expect you to remember that he was not block-headed or broad-headed [a reference to Breitkopf und Härtel], nor was he goat-legged [cf. Bote und Bock]." When Bülow changed his opinion, on the evidence of the Wind Serenade, op. 7 (published by Aibl in 1883), the relationship was on firm ground.

Spitzweg would go on to publish some thirty of Strauss's works, gaining enormous financial rewards. The typical composer-publisher relationship in 1880s Germany prescribed a one-time fee for a new work, with royalties for future performances signed away entirely at the time of a composition's sale. For example, Strauss sold *Don Juan* for the paltry sum of eight hundred marks, and the continuing sting of that and other necessities figured powerfully in his lifelong activism on behalf of less-gifted composers. Friendship did not prevent Spitzweg from paying the lowest price possible for each piece, and from all appearances he followed Bülow's advice in July 1884 to "reveal nothing to him of his market value."[4] Yet Strauss responded to this challenge as forcefully as to any artistic one. When Spitzweg showed a reluctance to publish the admittedly difficult *Macbeth*, after having seen and recognized the potential of *Tod und Verklärung*, Strauss threatened to withhold the latter tone poem unless both were published or the composer were permitted to offer *Macbeth* to another publisher (Peters having expressed interest, according to Strauss). Spitzweg gave in, and Strauss learned how to mix business with friendship without compromising on either side.[5]

For all his preoccupation with artistic, intellectual, and spiritual ideals, Mahler was always deeply sensitive to the material world, both out of predisposition—his love for exercise and outdoor activity bordered on the compulsive—and the bald necessity of survival. When at the age of fifteen he left the relative safety and comfort of his home for a precarious existence in Vienna, he was barely able to keep a roof over his head and a coat on his back. At the end of each month he often survived on cheese rinds. Financial circumstances threatened his continued enrollment at the conservatory in the fall of 1876, when he claimed in a letter to the directing committee that "my father is unable to support me, and is even less able to pay my school fees." Only the intervention of Julius Epstein prevented his withdrawal.[6]

It is not surprising, then, that as a young man Mahler should have acquired, like Strauss, an aggressive and uncompromising personality as protector of his own financial interests. With the arrangement and completion of *Die drei Pintos*, which found considerable success in its early years and forecast a promising creative future, Mahler already showed the assertiveness and edge of an accomplished businessman. He knew, for example, not to give in too soon to a tempting offer. When in July 1887 he heard from the Leipzig publisher C. F. Kahnt, he wrote to his parents that "a publisher has already offered 20,000 marks for the piano-vocal and full scores but we do not want to hand them over just yet." His reason for holding out was one that would not dawn on Strauss until he had been victimized in his own early deals: "The most important revenue will be from the theatre royalties, which—if we're lucky—could easily be 4 or 5 times as much."[7] A month later he reported that his patience had borne fruit: Edmund C. Stanton, director of the Metropolitan Opera from 1885 to 1891, would attend the premiere in Leipzig on January 22.[8] "Well, he can bring a tidy sack of dollars with him," Mahler declared forthrightly, and indeed within a month he had paid off his substantial debts, sent one thousand marks home for immediate use, and invested the remainder as a nest egg for his parents, carefully calculating that within a year the principal ought to "grow until there is a sum of 30,000–40,000 marks [...] This capital ought to be *secure income* for you, then, so that you can give up your business and live however and wherever you like."[9]

Even as a young man, then, Mahler understood the value of a mark, and he took the trouble to learn what to do with money when he got it. His motivation was perfectly ordinary and perfectly reasonable: his family's material well-being and his artistic freedom depended on financial security. The same motives drove his early concern for administrative power, a quality particularly evident when Mahler came to Leipzig in August 1886 to serve as principal conductor alongside Nikisch, who held the same rank but enjoyed a stronger position because of seniority. After a year of getting acclimated, Mahler attempted with careful calculation to use his close relationship with the director, Max Staegemann, to gain the upper hand on Nikisch. He confided the details to his parents: "My relationship with my director is such a warm and friendly one that, because of this, of course, my position is a very dominant one. Even if Nikisch still gets to conduct the majority of the so-called 'significant operas' because of his seniority (which, by the way, will soon have an end too), it is still evident that my influence on things is stronger than his. If nothing intervenes, sooner or later I will have to be regarded as the *first*."[10] Competition for repertoire figured centrally in this struggle, particularly Wagner's works, and Mahler took satisfaction in already having acquired *Rienzi, Der fliegende Holländer, Lohengrin, Siegfried*, and *Die Meistersinger von Nürnberg*. That experience obviously would be necessary if he were to win a more prestigious position—and we should remember that Vienna was always the goal, even in these early days when it might have seemed unreachable. In that regard it is not surprising to find him admitting openly, at least among family, that vanquishing Nikisch would be of enormous public relations value. "In this case, this triumph over a Nikisch carries ten times more weight than one over a Slansky in Prague." Four years later it gave him satisfaction to find Nikisch taking the position in Budapest that Mahler relinquished to move to Hamburg.

In pursuing his own conducting career Strauss followed Mahler's lead by latching on to powerful figures, devising methods to set himself apart from competitors, and bouncing from job to job as he played institutions against one another. The mentorship with Bülow proved shorter than anticipated—a mere four months in the fall of 1885, after which the Meiningen orchestra was left to Strauss alone—but it transformed him in one season from an utter novice to a confirmed talent able to take over as third conductor in Munich. Hard experience during this first term of service in his hometown taught him that he would require further outside affirmation of his ability in order to climb the ladder to his ultimate goal, Hermann Levi's position as *Hofkapellmeister*. This reality as much as anything motivated his service to Bayreuth; he rightly saw that if he could secure a regular conducting position at the festivals he would be in the running for any opening in Germany. Beginning in 1889 he mounted an intense charm offensive in correspondence with Cosima and at soirées at Wahnfried, which, combined with his obvious gifts and his willingness to promote Bayreuth-influenced performance practice at Weimar (where he served in 1889–94), had the desired effect. Had Strauss not been ill in the spring of 1892, he would have made his debut at that year's festival; by 1894, when he conducted *Tannhäuser* twice (on July 22 and August 6), he had been recalled to Munich as Levi's heir apparent and was firmly established among the small group of musicians suited to the highest posts.[11] Strauss would not conduct again at Bayreuth for thirty-nine years.

Only once in their series of self-promotional intrigues did Mahler and Strauss step on each other's toes, and the special regard that they showed for each other in this difficult moment demonstrates the importance of the relationship to both of them, even at a relatively early stage. In January 1894, as Mahler negotiated with the Hamburg intendant Bernhard Pollini for a renewal of his contract, Strauss received an offer of twelve thousand marks for a conducting post at the same theater.[12] As Herta Blaukopf suggests, it is unlikely that Pollini intended to keep both conductors, and Strauss seems to have reached the same conclusion, for he wrote at once to inform Mahler that his boss had gone behind his back.[13] The famously shrewd Pollini may have counted on this move; Mahler's stalling tactics gave way quickly to a signature on the contract, and Strauss ended up in Munich, which everyone assumed had been his goal all along. But it is remarkable and even touching to find these professional competitors cooperating in an attempt, however clumsy, to thwart the machinations of a boss who stood to enrich one of them substantially. (Pollini's final offer to Strauss would be fifteen thousand marks, five times Strauss's salary at Weimar.) There is no evidence that in a similar situation either of them dealt so openly and generously with Weingartner, Mottl, Nikisch, Seidl, or any other leading conductor of the day.

In the field of composition they behaved even less as competitors, going to considerable lengths on multiple occasions to promote one another's works. Although after Mahler's death Strauss would privately question his friend's greatness as a composer, he remained proud until his old age that he had been responsible for the first public performances of several Mahler symphonies. In the margins of Willi Schuh's copy of Alma's *Gustav Mahler: Erinnerungen und Briefe* (Amsterdam: Allert de Lange, 1940), he sketched the following observations, disappointed that not only Alma but apparently Mahler himself had forgotten what he had done:

> The premiere of the Titan took place under my direction in 1894 in Weimar, likewise that of three movements of the Second Symphony (the last was not yet finished) in 1895 with the Berlin Philharmonic, and in 1902 the premiere of the Fourth under Mahler in *my* series of new music concerts in Berlin [emphasis in original]. Later in the Staatsoper I repeated the First Symphony and gave the first [Berlin] performance of Das Lied von der Erde. Likewise I included the first performances of the Third and the Sixth Symphonies on the program of the composer festivals [of the Allgemeiner deutscher Musikverein] in Basel and Elberfeld. All of this would have deserved mention.[14]

Alma's suppression of this long history of support has a complicated set of motivations. Some were individual slights, the most bitter of which involved the Third Symphony (see below). Much deeper, however, would have been lingering resentment of Strauss for a level of renown that even she freely admitted (calling him in the book's forward "the greatest master of contemporary music in the first decade of this century"), and that even in 1940 Mahler showed no sign of overtaking.[15]

Mahler reciprocated, where possible, over a similarly long period of time and even though Strauss's fame was assured by the early 1890s. (The debacle of *Guntram* only intensified the question of how soon Strauss would write an opera that matched the impact of his tone poems.) One of the few champions of *Guntram*, Mahler believed that while the opera as a whole was "childishly callow" and "pretentious," a few snippets were worth continued performance, especially the preludes to the first and second acts.[16] He would conduct the first-act prelude on behalf of Strauss on a Hamburg subscription concert in February 1895, then both preludes with the Vienna Philharmonic in February 1899 and again with the New York Philharmonic in March 1910.[17] (In New York he likewise gave many readings of the tone poems, especially *Till Eulenspiegel*.) Strauss's second opera, *Feuersnot*, received a particularly strong helping hand from Mahler, with a lovingly staged performance in Vienna in 1902 (an occasion memorialized by Alma in scathing terms, as she complained over Strauss's preoccupation with royalties). Mahler checked with Strauss on the staffing of the principal roles, asked for a score far longer in advance than usual (in order to get to know the work intimately), and offered private counsel when difficulties arose with the censors.[18] The first performance, on January 29, 1902, elicited from Strauss a lengthy and indeed emotional letter of thanks, which Mahler was unfortunately required to answer with the news that the "very eloquent attendance figures" would remove the work from the theater plan after four performances: "my good will, which you hopefully will not doubt, is not sufficient to ensure continued performances of an opera that the public will *not* attend" (emphasis in original).[19] Mahler's revival of the work in 1905 confirms his personal disappointment in that failure, yet despite a new cast and much strategizing the result was the same.[20]

On both sides of this relationship, the principal motivation for promotional assistance was belief in the quality, if not the genius, of the work. Mahler championed *Salome* in spite of political risk, not for political benefit; his efforts played no small role in his departure from Vienna, as he implied when telling Strauss that the "Cabinetsfrage" had been raised in his discussions with the censors.[21] The greatness of the music was indisputable; recall that he considered it "a *very powerful* work and without doubt one of the most significant of our time" (see the introduction).[22] It demanded his full support, however little he understood the "cocoon" from which the music emerged: "I don't understand the situation at all, and can only guess that the voice of the 'Earth-Spirit' has spoken from the core of genius, and that this voice seeks an abode that appeals not to human tastes."[23]

For Strauss, promoting Mahler's music presented the opposite problem. The consonance of this music's grandiose spirituality with its composer's private views, or hopes, was perfectly apparent to Strauss. Moreover, the music's carefully choreographed catastrophes and failures, its overt insecurity, embodied personal qualities that Strauss detested for the agony through which they put his friend, the person whose capacity for musical experience was among all contemporaries most like his own. Thus we find that, where Mahler promoted Strauss's music even though it told him nothing about his personality, Strauss promoted Mahler's music even though it did. For all the tendentiousness of Alma's memoir of Mahler, there is no reason to doubt her characterization of the premiere of the Third Symphony, the event that brought the basic philosophical incompatibility of these two composers most clearly into focus. Every detail rings true: Strauss's enthusiasm for the physically determined first movement, which brought him "right up to the podium, applauding emphatically as though to set his seal on its success"; the opposite trajectories of the work's ascent toward spiritual ecstasy and Strauss's waning appreciation, culminating in wild acclaim from the public as Strauss slunk from the hall; the brutal nonchalance with which Strauss expressed his disapproval, visiting Mahler's table in the café "in a lordly way . . . without noticing Mahler's extreme agitation or addressing a single word to him"; the crushing blow that this rejection dealt to the composer: "For some time he could not speak. His spirits sank and the public acclamation now seemed of no account."[24]

We must remember when considering this episode that the performance had been facilitated by Strauss, who had arranged it after having studied the score in advance. Whether or not Strauss's public reaction was calculated—and uncalculated public behavior was rare for Strauss—he was obviously responding not to the music but to the audience's reception of it. Jealousy falls short as an explanation here; no successful premiere of Mahler or any other composer could threaten Strauss's stature and reputation in 1903. Strauss meant to criticize the public celebration of a renewed musical spirituality, a spectacular and beautiful warming-over of the outdated Schopenhauerian dreams that Strauss had dedicated considerable creative efforts to vanquishing. Nothing in the entire affair, however, was unforeseen by Strauss. He had hoped for a success for his friend, which had come about, and he had hoped for an opportunity to show his disdain for Mahler's aesthetic goals, succeeding here as well. Yet if Strauss took pleasure in his double victory, it did not come without a measure of guilt, which he carried with him at least to the end of Mahler's life. Perhaps the most moving document of this entire friendship is Strauss's final letter to Mahler, written on May 11, 1911, when both knew well that this would be their last communication. As mentioned in the introduction, Strauss said farewell with a humane gesture of deference, announcing his plan to revive the Third; he would prepare it himself before handing the performance over to Mahler, "so that you will have no trouble, only joy." There is no doubt that Strauss intended to revive the memory of Crefeld; he said explicitly that "it will give me a great pleasure to hear your lovely work under your own direction once again."[25] And the performance did take place, with Strauss conducting the Staatskapelle Berlin on December 11, 1911. Thus a faithful friend demonstrated in the most meaningful way known to him that he would continue to promote Mahler's music after his death—that, as always, his respect for the music itself would guide his actions, whatever his feelings about the music's higher goals.

It was confidence in the integrity of each other's judgment, and conviction about the quality of each other's music, that allowed the single exchange in which the composers discussed the possible perception that they shared a mutual favoritism. In April 1900, in what was apparently his first letter to Mahler in three years, Strauss inquired whether Mahler would be interested in having the premiere of an as-yet-unwritten ballet on Paul Scheerbart's *Kometentanz* (Dance of the Comets).[26] After asking for a "straight yes or no"—because "receiving refusals from theater directors is for me routine"—he mentioned in passing that the Berlin public responded favorably to a performance of three of Mahler's orchestral lieder conducted by Strauss on April 9. At the end of the letter, recognizing the implication of a quid pro quo, Strauss facetiously blew the whistle on himself: "Naturally I have only performed your songs to secure your acceptance of my ballet. That's the way I am! Well known for it!"
Mahler's response contains an unmistakable blush. "You add cute marginalia!? The devil take it, what experiences you must have had, that you would risk *manus lavat* remarks even in jest! Believe me, I am delighted when I have the opportunity to show your works the diligent appreciation that they deserve."[27] But of course Mahler here put into words what both of them knew. It was only the power differential that existed between them—the fact that Mahler's works needed support while Strauss's would succeed on their own—that compelled Mahler to state the obvious. But just as obviously, Strauss recognized in advance that his request of Mahler could have carried with it an implicit threat: find a way to perform my work, or put at risk the relationship that has brought you more performances than any other. There is a touching sensitivity in the way that Strauss handled the matter, an uncharacteristic attention to the nuances not just of words but of feelings, and a concern to spare his friend unnecessary worry. Strauss was by no means an unfeeling person, but this level of care is unusual, and it tells us just how deeply he respected Mahler as

an artist. Only a creative genius on Strauss's level could have touched him in this way, and the only living musician of that stature, in Strauss's view, was Mahler.

Strauss's comments on himself also betray a certain cynicism that was borne out in subsequent biographical reception. It is by now a truism that critics have held Strauss accountable for a capitalist approach to music; they follow the lead of Adorno, who attacked the composer for using his position as "musical captain of industry" to gain access to the finer things in life. Photos confirm Strauss's taste for elegant clothing, carefully tailored and impeccably styled, whatever the occasion. He likewise stayed only in the very best hotels: the Vier Jahreszeiten in Munich, the Adlon in Berlin, and so on. At home, particularly in the splendid villa adjacent to the Belvedere on the Jacquingasse in Vienna, he surrounded himself with art (though some of it was of Bavarian folk origin) and reveled in the dictatorial protection of these luxuries by Pauline. Even during the catastrophic postwar period, the octogenarian found a way to maintain this lifestyle, at the cost of turning his manuscripts literally into capital.

It is more difficult to find in the Mahler literature an admission that he too enjoyed, in his mature life, essentially the same living standard as Strauss. And he "enjoyed" it in every sense; not only did he provide it for himself and his family, but he relished it. In her self-pitying commentary on the early years of her marriage to Mahler, Alma observed pointedly that "Mahler's suits were made to measure by first-class tailors, and his innumerable pairs of shoes were made by the finest English shoemakers."[28] When Ida Dehmel spent an evening with the composer, she noted in idealistic boilerplate that "Mahler both glows and illumines, points upwards and carries us with him far beyond the individual destiny." But in the same breath she confessed that "I detected a little envy of Strauss's success, in terms of money," and she concluded her reminiscence by describing the "feeling of complete satisfaction" she felt after spending an afternoon with Mahler in his "bright, comfortable, even luxurious flat," enjoying "good food and good wine."[29] Even as a young professional musician, Mahler found a way to acquire these comforts, though he provided them first to his family before giving them to himself. In early 1889 he sent salmon, lobster, pineapple and other delicacies to his parents on a regular basis.[30] One gift is accompanied by the note "the cognac is the finest in the world."[31] By 1890, after her parents' death, Justine had a private chambermaid.[32] Otto, the ill-fated and much-loved musical brother, was kept warm in winter by a coat tailor-made at Mahler's expense.[33]

It should surprise no one that Mahler, like Strauss, was a businessman, and a good one, with a good businessman's tastes and mode of life. What is surprising, rather, is that his acolytes would have felt the need to suppress a quality that Mahler considered normal and healthy. Certainly he knew how to protect his interests. Ludwig Karpath recalled that when Mahler took up his post in Vienna, he made a personal visit to every significant music critic in the city, following the long-standing custom of singers who knew where their bread was buttered. "For all his ideals and his deeply earnest creative effort, Mahler was by no means a saint; he operated always in the real world and understood very well how to distinguish between what aided him and what hurt him."[34] Ten years later, as relations with his superiors broke down, he knew well that as an appointee of the emperor he could be pensioned off (at fourteen thousand kronen per year) but not fired.[35] When in 1903 Strauss invited him to join the newly formed Genossenschaft deutscher Tonsetzer and sit on the board, Mahler wrote at once that, pending resolution of a legal conflict of interest, "I should be most glad to be a member of your society and, of course, to sit on the committee."[36] Unlike many twentieth-century composers, Mahler grasped that for art to succeed in the most meaningful sense—for it to reach listeners—certain demands of the market had to be met. He knew how to meet them, and he knew how to use the rewards to foster his own creative and performing activities. Adequate financial support made artistic expression possible. To suggest that Mahler thought otherwise, or lived otherwise, is to lose oneself in the covert romanticism of the Second Viennese School, a group that, in the full context of Viennese culture in the early years of the twentieth century, operated on the fringes. Mahler respected and supported their music, as did Strauss (to a greater extent than is recognized), but he did not want to live as they did, any more than did Strauss.

CHAPTER 6

Literati

◆ FROM THE VIBRANT DAYS of precocious childhood to the gloomy awareness of impending death, Mahler and Strauss immersed themselves in literature, with nearly the passion they felt for music. In fact, the parallel development is as close and striking here as in any area of the composers' lives. In his adolescence, Mahler developed literary impulses of sufficient intensity that for a time he considered giving up music for poetry.[1] Strauss distinguished himself in school by an extraordinary facility with ancient languages; the teenager's setting of a chorus from Sophocles's *Elektra* was less a musical novelty than a fond farewell to an enthusiasm of long standing.[2] In his mid-thirties, Mahler would tell Friedrich Löhr that books were his "only friends," and in his last days, the terminally ill composer carried on reading even when he no longer had the strength to hold a book upright, tearing the pages one by one from the binding.[3] Strauss likewise found a safe haven in books, particularly Goethe, as he faded from existence; on his deathbed he put visitors at ease by starting conversations about this greatest German literary figure.[4] The need for regular exposure to cultivated literary art was for both composers powerful and lifelong, as vital an ingredient in their artistic personalities as were their musical abilities and predilections.

The range of Mahler's and Strauss's reading can without exaggeration be called connoisseurship. Reviewing only the most extensively documented activity, one finds a thorough familiarity with ancient texts, in original languages, from Greek tragedy to Roman poetry and history; a fluent working knowledge of Shakespeare and his German reception; devoted and more or less continual rereading of Goethe, spanning most of his output and recognizing his stature as the ultimate model of *Bildung*; up-to-date knowledge of contemporary trends in drama and the novel (especially the Russians); and a wide experience of poetry, encompassing early nineteenth-century pseudo-folk poems, newly translated eastern masterworks, modernist experiments in socialism and sexuality, and bourgeois kitsch, culminating—in Mahler's case—in original poetry. Obviously Strauss and Mahler felt that to maintain their credibility as creative artists they had to be more than musicians, but the sheer volume of their reading cannot be explained as the mere fulfillment of an obligation. (How does a twenty-something Kapellmeister conducting several different operas per week find the time to become a Dostoyevsky disciple?) They both possessed an intense concern for literature, a trait that to some extent puts all scholars in the position of the forlorn Alma when Strauss said "come along, Mahler—let's go into your room for a bit."[5] Yet along with this common devotion to serious literary awareness, one suspects also a shared insecurity, judging by the patronizing attitude of Hugo von Hofmannsthal toward one and Siegfried Lipiner toward the other. Their credentials as literati matter less, however, than the fact of their having given all available energy to the attempt—which in any case they must have believed would yield a more credible result than the efforts of a poet to make sense of the technical mysteries of music.

For Austro-German artists in the nineteenth century, the beginning and end of the literary art was always Goethe. Strauss accepted this faith early and never gave it up. Goethe was the only poet he set in every decade of his life, from the 1870s to the 1940s. The complete (Propyläen) edition that Strauss acquired in old age is drenched in pencil annotations, almost none of which have to do with any known musical projects (figure 6).[6] According to his grandson, he read every work of Goethe at least twice, with the exception of the *Farbenlehre* (a forgivable lapse).[7] When traveling, he

Figure 6. A quiet moment in Strauss's study, 1945. Courtesy of the Richard-Strauss-Institut, Garmisch-Partenkirchen.

invariably took works of Goethe; on the 1892–93 trip to Greece and Egypt it was *Wilhelm Meisters Wanderjahre*, while during the tour to Rio de Janeiro in 1920 he brought the literary essays.[8] Creative difficulties often brought to mind analogous situations in Goethe, most famously during work on *Also sprach Zarathustra* (1896). At the shattering moment of Zarathustra's breakdown, Strauss added to his short score a quotation of the Earth Spirit from *Faust*, part 1: "Du gleichst dem Geist den du begreifst, nicht mir" ("you resemble the spirit whom you imagine, not me"). Hofmannsthal ascribed their successful collaboration in part to an unspoken connection, a "Goethean atmosphere" of "purification" that united *Der Rosenkavalier* (1910), *Ariadne auf Naxos* (1912; rev. 1916) and *Die Frau ohne Schatten* (1917).[9] Goethe lay behind *Metamorphosen* as well, in the work's undisclosed programmatic inspiration, the poem "Niemand wird sich selber kennen" ("No one can know himself").[10] Contemplating his own death and the apparent collapse of German culture, Strauss could find no more meaningful meditation on the nature of the self than what had been provided by Goethe (see the discussion in chapter 8). Later, in a less pessimistic frame of mind, he consoled himself with the thought that "when he died, Goethe was never so alive and renowned as he is today."[11] For Strauss, Goethe's brand of immortality was the only one that inspired hope.

Strauss's ongoing creative involvement with Goethe produced relatively few works drawing directly on the poet's writings: about a dozen lieder, the Brahmsian *Wandrers Sturmlied* (1884) for chorus and orchestra, *Metamorphosen* (1945), and the unfinished Singspiel *Lila* (1895). On biographical and philosophical levels, however, the depth of the connection is clear. Both artists lived long, relentlessly active lives, motivated by a love of work and a determination to develop their creative gifts through consistent activity; in Goethe's words—quoted by Strauss in the essay "On Melodic Inspiration"—"genius is hard work."[12] Both demonstrated in their creative activity a pronounced autobiographical tendency, while at the same time censoring outsiders' knowledge of their private views with a carefully constructed public persona. They also showed a fascination with landscape (especially Italy and the Alps), a touching devotion to an oddball wife, and a distant, conflicted, and intense relationship with a political figure of world-historical significance. And most important, both Goethe and Strauss began their careers with a publicly successful flirtation with romanticism, or, in Strauss's case, Wagnerian neoromanticism: *The Sorrows of Young Werther* for Goethe, and the early tone poems for Strauss. Each of these experiments conflicted with its creator's classically disposed nature, so that the romantic artifacts already contained the seeds of a critique; Werther's self-centered adolescent sentimentality, which ultimately turns on itself, finds an amplified echo in the overtly ironic use of Wagner's orchestra beginning with *Till Eulenspiegel*. If the elderly Goethe and Strauss were both regarded as aged reactionaries, they were by no means naive. Long experience left them confident in their distrust of theory, abstract thought, and metaphysics. From the perspective of the twenty-first century, their acceptance of fragmentation—indeed, their embrace of it, in works like the *Wanderjahre* or *Ariadne*—strikes one less as conservative than as modernist, in a neoclassical sense.

Mahler's passion for Goethe was fully apparent to all who knew him, even casual acquaintances such as the Vienna solicitor Richard Horn, who observed after a few days in Mahler's company that "Goethe and apples were about the only things he seemed to consume on a regular basis."[13] Although he set no texts by Goethe other than the final scene of *Faust* (in the second movement of the Eighth Symphony), he read widely, particularly enjoying the novels, the conversations with Eckermann, and the poetry.[14] In the summers he had the habit of reading Goethe aloud, but even in his busiest periods, according to Bauer-Lechner, he always found time for a bit of private study.[15] This habit would play a role in the formation of several important relationships. A discussion of *Wilhelm Meister* provided the first opportunity for Mahler and Natalie to get to know each other better, just as Alma's deep knowledge of the poet piqued Mahler's curiosity.[16] (When Alma was a mere eight years old, her father, with some ceremony, told her the story of *Faust*, then gave her a copy of the book with the words "this is the finest work of literature in the world.")[17] One finds quotations from Goethe's poetry in the early love letters to Alma, with flirtatious revisions that relied on an easy familiarity; apparently Alma found this habit charming, for it continued throughout their marriage, to the very last letter he wrote to her.[18] But Goethe could also be a weapon, for example when Mahler took up *Faust*, part 2, as justification for an indictment of her modernist reading material (principally Nietzsche, Maeterlinck, and Bierbaum).[19] Whatever use Mahler made of him, Goethe was an indispensable part of his daily life—so much so that leaving home without the necessary book could plunge the entire family into crisis.[20]

In the depth and breadth of his enthusiasm for Goethe, Mahler duplicated the attitude of Strauss. To some extent, however, his inclinations indicate a conservative streak that, like Mahler's continuing interest in Kant, Strauss would have found difficult to understand. Often Mahler expressed himself as Goethe's defender against present-day ignorance and misunderstanding. He considered Massenet's *Werther* "an affront to Goethe," for which the composer ought to be "condemned to hard labor."[21] On a rare trip to Frankurt am Main, Goethe's birthplace, Mahler complained about the lack of Goethe memorials.[22] The principal figures of literary modernism struck him as particularly oblivious to Goethe's importance, and thus he found himself astounded when Hermann Bahr's essay "Our Goethe," published in the *Neue freie Presse* in September 1910, for once echoed some of his own interpretive conclusions. "It [the general state of contemporary literature] reminds me of Pythia: a foolish woman sitting in clouds of vapor uttering nonsensical remarks which wise men interpret as pearls of wisdom."[23] Mahler particularly appreciated Bahr's theorizing of an "entirely worldly kind of immortality" for artists whose works and indeed whose "very existence" would continue to shape human life after an artist's death.

This reaction to Bahr exemplifies a broader trend in Mahler's approach to Goethe, one that had a more far-reaching significance than his reading of individual works. Mahler needed Goethe above all for the process of developing and honing his personal worldview. Interest in the philosophical implications of Goethe's thought was an important basis for Mahler's friendship with Lipiner, who in 1894 produced a dissertation at Vienna entitled "Homunculus: A Study of Faust and the Philosophy of Goethe."[24] Idiosyncratic philosophizing that took Goethe as a starting point would become a sort of daily devotional for Mahler; he was known to try out his ideas on houseguests during summer vacations, for example Erica Conrat, who relates that one evening Mahler came onto the porch unusually late (after 10:30 p.m.), recited poems from the *West-Östliche Divan* from memory, and then improvised a theory of the relativity of time. ("Then he spoke at some length, saying there was actually no difference between a rocket that shoots into the air then vanishes into the lake without a sound, and a sun that shines for a billion years.")[25] Most significantly, Mahler took from Goethe reinforcement of the dualism that lay at the heart of his idealist outlook. The famous letter to Alma on the final scene of *Faust* (June 1909; see chapter 3) reads as a compilation of binary pairs that define a neo-Kantian idealism: man/woman, striving/resting, body/spirit, appearance/reality, transitory/everlasting, Gretchen/*Mater gloriosa*. Stephen Hefling sees this "interplay of syzygial opposites" as evidence that Mahler's "views on immortality were deeply influenced by Goethe," if also reinforced in this vein by Kant's metaphysics, Nietzsche's Apollonian/Dionysian dichotomy, the eastern yin/yang pair (learned by Mahler via Schopenhauer), the teachings of Lipiner's mentor Gustav Theodor Fechner, and various other sources.[26] Walter characterized these antitheses as the root of Mahler's private religion—they were his "discoveries of all divinity," and his greatest source of consolation for his mortality.[27]

In the late nineteenth century Mahler was not unique in using whatever means were available to him, including Goethe, to reinforce a pronounced and conservative devotion to idealism. Indeed, as Carl Dahlhaus argued, the maintenance of that tradition seems to have been the mission of Austro-German composers in an otherwise enthusiastically positivist culture.[28] But it placed him severely at odds with Strauss, who had little use for *Faust*, part 2, but did marshal Goethe's support for his very different philosophical project. Already in *Wandrers Sturmlied*, Strauss confessed that he found setting Goethe difficult, because the music had to be "as deep and philosophical as possible."[29] But his critique of idealism came fully to the fore in 1895 with his unfinished setting of *Lila*, a little-known singspiel in which Goethe weighed the romantic metaphysical powers of music against its capacity for orienting humans rationally in the here and now.[30] The plot concerns a young noblewoman driven insane by a false report of her husband's death. Consumed by fear, she wanders the moonlit hills of what Goethe calls a "romantische Gegend," lamenting, "it will not release me, the Melody of Death."[31] The requisite happy ending is provided when the family doctor proposes to play along with her delusions, and thereby to bring about a gentle transformation from deranged psychosis to clear-eyed, rational stability.

Strauss saw in this subject an extraordinary opportunity to juxtapose Wagnerian neoromanticism with the lucid, preromantic world of Mozart and Haydn. "What attracts me to the work is that the polar opposition in music that exists today comes to a highly dramatic application and confrontation[:] 'music as expression' of the psyche [. . .] and music as sounding form, as pleasant, nerve-calming play of notes."[32] Strangely enough, he attempted to enlist Cosima Wagner as a collaborator on the project, and she accepted, perhaps believing that he meant to explore an alternative to Wagner rather than a critique. In fact his revival of classical materials— deployed "as though 'the works' [of Wagner] had never been written"— and his striking embrace of the conservative side of the Hausegger/ Hanslick debate had a philosophical agenda that was made explicit by the dramatic action: Lila can rejoin the community of the sane only when she is cured of her romantic delusions, and this remedy is embodied by music in the classical style—music that is just music, carrying no higher associations. What Lila needs most of all is to focus her mind on physical reality; the contrasting musical styles were to represent her problem and its solution. As her worried husband discovers just after his return, "her thoughts were always too little on the earth."[33]

Strauss gave up work on *Lila* in favor of a project even more critical of the Wagnerian musico-philosophical legacy: *Also sprach Zarathustra* (1896). As we have seen, this work provided Strauss with the occasion for his only direct musical engagement with *Faust*. But while Mahler was reading Goethe and Nietzsche at precisely this time (the summer of 1896, as we learn from Bauer-Lechner), the connections that he drew between them could not have been more different from Strauss's.[34] Mahler's Goethe brought the composer into contact with "not only the Earth Spirit, but the Universe itself, into whose infinite depths you sink, through whose eternal spaces you soar, so that earth and human destiny shrink behind you into an indiscernibly tiny point and then disappear."[35] Strauss's Goethe, on the other hand, seconded Zarathustra's "disgust at humanity"—his realization that the metaphysical longing of "afterworldsmen," "accusers of life," was a condition of all humanity.[36] It is doubtful that Strauss ever met an artist more deeply devoted to this idealistic target than Mahler, who called his Eighth Symphony and Goethean magnum opus "The True Symphony."[37] Mahler of course had no illusions about capturing such truth, but he subscribed to a hope that for Strauss was not only impossible but distasteful.

The search for an alternative to romanticism led Strauss toward overtly modernist literary figures, for example the *Jugendstil* poets whose writings he explored in lieder of the 1890s. During his second term as conductor in Munich, 1894–98, he found himself living in the geographical center of Austro-German literary modernism, and he did not remain on the sidelines. *Jugend*, the Munich periodical that would go on to become the most popular German-language art journal from the turn of the century to World War I, printed two Strauss lieder in the first full year of its existence. Among them was the notorious "Wenn," a setting of a poem by

Carl Busse, which flouted musical common practice by ending in a key a half-step higher than its beginning. At the moment of the forbidden modulation, Strauss advised "singers who intend to perform this work in public before the end of the nineteenth century to sing it transposed down by one semitone from this point onwards, so that the piece concludes in the key in which it began!"[38] But not all of Strauss's songs of this ilk were novelty pieces; in fact some of his best-known lieder are settings of *Jugendstil* poetry: "Morgen" (John Henry Mackay), "Befreit" (Richard Dehmel), "Traum durch die Dämmerung" (Otto Julius Bierbaum), and "Ruhe, meine Seele!" (Karl Henckell), among others.

Not the least attractive quality of these poets was that they were living; Strauss had personal friendships with the last three, though the relationships ended sourly. There does seem to be a contradiction, as Bryan Gilliam notes, between Strauss's interest in antiestablishment poetry and his position as comfort-loving court composer to a "philistine Emperor" in Berlin.[39] Yet Dehmel's advocacy of "free love" is not so far from the explicit sexuality of *Don Juan, Symphonia domestica*, and *Der Rosenkavalier*, and the common interest in Nietzsche had serious and obvious consequences for both composer and poet. For a time Strauss even showed sympathy for the socialist agenda of this group, setting Henckell's "Das Lied des Steinklopfers" ("The Song of the Stonebreaker"), among eight other Henckell poems, and thumbing through Mackay's novel *Die Anarchisten* (according to Arthur Seidl).[40] Soon after the turn of the century, however, Strauss's interests moved in other directions, as he found his way to Wilde and then Hofmannsthal.

For his part, Mahler mostly ignored the *Jugendstil* poets, and modernist poetry in general, although early in his relationship with Alma he occasionally called her by the nickname of "Lux," a pun on the Latin *lux* and German *Luchs* (lynx), which Dehmel used for a character in his cycle of love poems, "Zwei Menschen."[41] On one occasion Mahler politely turned down an invitation from Dehmel to set his poetry, saying of the latter's works, not without critical insinuation, that he "could imagine no higher task than to breathe new life into them by setting them to music."[42] Somewhat more candidly he warned Alma against the "tavern rhetoric of Bierbaum and Co.," advising her to follow his lead and ignore contemporary iconoclasm in favor of the classics. His most urgent warning he reserved for the seduction of a too-easy materialism: "surely this is no idea of yours, that the wonderful, profoundly unfathomable world we live in is nothing but a practical joke played on us by some numbskull, some stupid 'natural force,' which knows nothing either of itself or of us."[43] *Jugendstil*, with its focus on a pleasing, stimulating surface, and, perhaps more with its gutting of tradition, could offer nothing useful to a convinced idealist.

In fact for a time during his maturity Mahler would claim (to Anton Webern) that no poet held any interest for him as a composer but Friedrich Rückert, to whom he turned at the outset of what Hefling has called his "second maturity."[44] In Rückert he sought above all lyricism, which also happened to be what Strauss found most attractive about the *Jugendstil* repertory (or the portion of it that interested him).[45] In Mahler's case, however, the lyrical impulse answered a specific private need: it was a coping mechanism after the near-death experience of February 24, 1901, when the composer nearly bled to death from a severe hemorrhoidal condition. This ordeal, of which Mahler later said, "I thought my last hour had come," seems to have personalized in some new way the many family deaths he had experienced; until then his reactions to death, even the deaths of his parents, had been somewhat aloof, if one is to judge from his letters to Justine.[46] Rückert gave voice to the suffering of an individual, in a manner far removed from the flat character types of *Des Knaben Wunderhorn*, and he teased the tragedy from the mundane with an eloquence that taught Mahler something about his own life. (If Alma did not understand why Mahler would "tempt Providence" by composing the *Kindertotenlieder*, she ignored the reality that in Mahler's case fate had already acted.)[47] And the poet also provided an answer, one that resonates most strongly in "Ich bin der Welt abhanden gekommen" ("I Am Lost to the World," 1901), the centerpiece of all Mahler's Rückert lieder. With a new reliance on pentatonicism and an uncharacteristically strict application of motivic economy, Mahler created a musical analogue of spiritual acceptance, renunciation, and stasis, inventing a musico-spiritual language that would speak most powerfully in the late works. The close connection of this music to the Adagietto of the Fifth is just one of its operative associations; on the intellectual level it evokes just as strongly, through Rückert's orientalism, the eastern mystical strain that Mahler encountered in

Schopenhauer and Fechner and that he hoped eventually to trace to its source.[48] (This project would of course culminate in *Das Lied von der Erde*.)

If Rückert was capable on occasion of writing a bad poem, so much the better, in Mahler's view, for setting a perfect poem to music "was as if a sculptor chiseled a statue from marble and a painter came along and colored it."[49] (In this respect he must have understood the appeal someone like Dehmel held for Strauss.) He also knew perfectly well that Rückert's resurgent popularity ca. 1900, a function largely of sentimentalist appeal in a culture conflicted over its materialism, would likely bring him more performances than had been forthcoming for the *Wunderhorn* pieces. But such practical considerations are no more an indictment in the case of Mahler than they are for Strauss.

It is worth noting in this context, however, that Strauss's own limited musical settings of Rückert had in both of the principal cases considerable private significance. The first came with the *Deutsche Motette* (1913), the absurdly challenging choral work (twenty-three parts, a four-octave range, impossibly subtle dynamic nuances) that Michael Kennedy called "the choral equivalent of the *Alpensinfonie*.[50] Ulrich Konrad's study of the genesis of this work establishes that early conceptualization took place in the immediate aftermath of Mahler's death.[51] Konrad suggests that Strauss sought in Rückert's Persian *ghasel* a "lyrical pendant" to his own Nietzsche-inspired philosophy, which had flared up anew in a diary entry written in late May 1911, in the days just after his friend died: "I will name my Alpensinfonie the Antichrist, because it holds moral purification from one's own strength, freedom through work, and devotion to everlasting magnificent nature."[52] If we follow Konrad in considering the *Motette* as an "artistic-religious confession," we must also consider it a renewal of the struggle against Mahler's specific brand of idealism, now waged on Mahler's own turf.[53] Two decades later, however, he turned again to Rückert when brushed aside by the rising power of the Nazis, and this time the need for refuge and redemption had a distinctly Mahlerian tinge. Bryan Gilliam has placed particular emphasis on an unfinished choral setting, "Friede im Innern" ("Inner Peace"), a poem reflecting on the opposition of political and spiritual life, and on truths that cannot be spoken.[54] This would not be the only instance of Strauss feeling in old age an unexpected sympathy for a need that in youth he was prone to dismiss out of hand. Especially at difficult moments in his life, the inevitability of death elicited in the aging Strauss a tendency to contemplate that reality in something like the manner of Rückert.

At least once in his career Strauss turned to Friedrich Hölderlin at a similar moment, searching for an alternative, believable redemption, in poetry with Nietzschean resonances. That it was the young rather than the mature Nietzsche who rediscovered Hölderlin seems to have been known to Strauss; in the period of the *Drei Hymen* (1921), Strauss's main Hölderlin setting, the composer is also known to have enjoyed rereading *The Birth of Tragedy*.[55] Yet the operative poetic content—principally the depiction of natural images such as the sea, the desert, and the stars as embodiments of a transcendent love—served essentially the same purpose for the fifty-seven-year-old that the late Nietzsche had done for a younger Strauss: it invested nature, the here and now, with a higher significance without giving in to a metaphysical longing that Strauss, unlike Mahler, interpreted as weakness. In the 1920s and on to the end of his life, Strauss would remain dedicated to the pillars of his existence—family, work, and nature (see chapter 3)—as a reasonable substitute for religious or philosophical faith. The idiosyncratic spirituality of Hölderlin, deeply felt but neither romantic nor traditionally religious, offered a model. Thus there is an undeniable resonance between this group of orchestral songs and the *Four Last Songs*, not only in the lush valedictory tone but in the quotation of earlier works, which shows that, as always, Strauss was looking inward to his own creative products as the source of spiritual consolation.

One can imagine Hölderlin as a source of considerable disagreement between Mahler and Strauss, for although Mahler considered the poet "one of my favorites, both as a poet and as a human being," and indeed "one of the very greatest," what he took from him was very different from the faith in nature, art, and humanity that interested Strauss.[56] Mahler drew on Hölderlin in describing the program of the Third to Bauer-Lechner, explaining that "as life rises from stage to stage," from nature through humanity to the "angels," we hear "captive life struggling for release from the clutches of lifeless, rigid Nature."[57] This is an aggressively Schopenhauerian reading of Hölderlin (specifically of *Der Rhein*, one of the poet's major works), rooted as it is in the philosopher's hierarchical account of creation, a proto-evolutionary structure leading from dead nature to the living metaphysical will. Hölderlin's "Absolute Being," a primordial unity of subject and object, would seem too personal to allow this kind of easy adaptation, especially one that dissected creation into discrete levels. Yet Hölderlin's originality was responsible not only for his obscurity during his life but for his widespread and diverse appropriation later by such figures as Adorno, Heidegger, and the Nazis. At bottom, Mahler and Strauss found him equally inspiring, but in incompatible ways.

The same could not be said of Jean Paul, an oft-mentioned literary enthusiasm of Mahler who seems to have been utterly ignored by Strauss (like E. T. A. Hoffmann and, with a few exceptions, *Des Knaben Wunderhorn*). The documentary evidence of Mahler's affection for this writer is surprisingly thin, although Alma testified to a "passionate devotion to Jean Paul," and both she and Bauer-Lechner confirm the easy familiarity that allowed Mahler to produce a quotation at a suggestive moment.[58] The pilgrimage to Bayreuth in the summer of 1883 was also a pilgrimage to the city in which Jean Paul had died, and Mahler did not overlook the bonds linking his two idols, the romantic author and the neoromantic musician. Jean Paul also gave Mahler a model for one of his favorite narcissistic indulgences, the misunderstood artist, "wittier and more extravagantly gifted than anyone else; yet who reads or even knows of him today?"[59] But after being burned by the programmatic experiment of the First Symphony (in which the connection to Jean Paul seems superficial at best, and in any case a late add-on), Mahler kept this interest carefully separated from his creative work, even if its spirit remained in his predilection for formal experimentation.

Though Mahler and Strauss could differ widely on the meaning or value of particular literary figures, they nevertheless shared an important devotion to breadth of reading, along with a willingness to follow associations in whatever interesting directions they might lead. Just as Mahler could use Goethe in the Eighth Symphony to revisit the eschatological vision of Klopstock from the Second, so Strauss could find in Nietzsche a modern interpretation of a crucial scene in Goethe's *Faust*. Both were likewise thoroughly acquainted with Shakespeare, and Cervantes, and Virgil, and Homer, and were prone to use the familiarity with major texts to offer a pithy statement of their own personal perspective, whatever the current topic of conversation. The point was to deploy, in the great humanistic tradition, the wisdom of a great forebear in support of one's own opinions. Cervantes, for example, was for both of them an early enthusiasm, largely because his use of humor and irony to handle issues of gravity and even tragedy resonated with their own natural dispositions. He provided an example of the distance that both of them longed for—the boy Mahler, who forgot his pain during an illness when his parents placed a copy of *Don Quixote* on his bed, and the young man Strauss, who reconciled himself to his estrangement from the beloved mentor Alexander Ritter by remembering his friend affectionately, humorously, and critically as a modern-day Don.[60] Of course, for the mature composers this borrowing could involve considerable freedom, when such manipulation was necessary to make the argument. Unlike Cervantes's Don Quixote, Strauss's doesn't regain his senses, and Mahler's Faust finds his redemption in a musical grandiloquence that in the late period stands out like a sore thumb.

Ultimately the literary interests in Mahler's and Strauss's lives rose and fell according to the needs of real life. For example, when the ordinariness of modern life made tragedy seem impossible, Dostoyevsky showed them how to turn contemporary experience into poetry. Mahler expressed the greater attachment to the Russian, finding in him a darker version of Hoffmann, and asking with this favorite novelist of his early adulthood, "how can one be happy on this earth while a single being is unhappy?"[61] *The Brothers Karamazov* in particular had a powerful effect on him, especially during the Hamburg years, when according to Bruno Walter he wrestled with the brothers' Nietzschean question, "is God dead?"[62] Such broodings were not unusual in this era; it seems that a conversation about Dostoyevsky was the proximate cause of Otto Mahler's suicide. (The talented brother wrote in his suicide note that he had "handed back his ticket.")[63] Schuh reports that in the late 1880s Strauss's enthusiasm for Dostoyevsky outstripped his considerable interest in Schopenhauer, to the extent that he thought of giving *Guntram* the title "Schuld und Sühne," the German title of *Crime and Punishment*.[64] Neither composer maintained faith with this specific vision for long; Mahler's unquenchable appetite for tragedy retreated from the everyday world, while Strauss rarely indulged in a straightforwardly tragic mode, whether he set his works in Judea or Bavaria. But this encounter, like all the others, opened up possibilities that could be developed according to the independent artistic vision of a self-aware genius.

CHAPTER 7

Autobiographers

↩ FOR A READER SENSITIVE TO IRONY, few contrasts between Mahler and Strauss are more telling than their approaches to musical autobiography. On one hand, the supremely self-confident Strauss put himself comfortably and repeatedly on display over a period of seven decades, with an exhibitionism calculated to divert attention from personal convictions.[1] On the other, Mahler, the seething introvert who dreaded public speaking as much as he loved conducting, crouched behind nameless heroic protagonists who nonetheless voiced authorial confessions.[2] Somehow the very crudity of Strauss's self-promotion earned him the right to be taken seriously, and to negotiate a transition nearly impossible for Mahler during his lifetime: from talented composer to acknowledged creative genius. "And why should he not celebrate himself—admittedly the most talked-about composer of his time—as a hero?" asked Henry T. Finck in 1917, seconding James Huneker's acceptance of Strauss into a modernist pantheon that included Whitman, Rodin, d'Annunzio, Nietzsche, Tolstoy, Wagner, and Stuck.[3] Mahler had sworn off overt personal revelation when he explicitly rejected programmaticism in 1900, still stinging from the derisive reception of his early symphonies (among them the performance arranged by Strauss of the First Symphony at Weimar in

1894).[4] The rewards for this prudent adaptation were the moral high ground, satisfaction with his own sincerity, and nothing more. He longed to be discovered in his works, but he would not speak that desire out loud, contenting himself instead (as had Nietzsche) with fantasies of his posthumous vindication.[5]

Of the two composers, then, only Strauss made the leap to explicit autobiography. Mahler never gave a public indication that any of his pieces was about himself, however strongly he might have flirted with the idea.[6] Strauss wrote a symphony about himself (*Symphonia domestica*), an opera about himself (*Intermezzo*), and a tone poem about himself (*Ein Heldenleben*), the latter even staging the reception of his own music. Behind this divergence, however, we find an important commonality in the presence of multiple selves, a decenteredness that both of them recognized in themselves and in each other. Strauss's showman persona was to anyone who knew him, and indeed to anyone who has a feeling for Bavarian irony, a thin veneer; his first biographer, Arthur Seidl, called his personality a "disguise."[7] Good listeners have instinctively recognized this—even, I would hold, those like Adorno who indict him for an artifice that was both his charm and his point.[8] What we have not recognized, and what has only recently come to light through painstaking research of private diaries (which he kept carefully to himself, unlike his musical sketches), is that there was a personal level of intellectual reflection that figured importantly in his creative process—in decisions about musical style and structure—and that he shared with virtually no one.[9] A number of Strauss's most important compositions are models of his own philosophical reflections, a sort of musical autobiography for the sole consumption of the author himself, dedicated to the purpose of self-realization (*Bildung*). It is on this crucial but virtually unknown level that the only genuine autobiographical meaning is to be found in Strauss, although the superficial gestures do take on new connotations when read in this context.

By contrast, Mahler's "private" remarks in his working materials often seem designed to be discovered, as though they were written for an audience, even an audience of one. The outbursts in the score of the Tenth are hardly notes to self, but notes to Alma, and they have found their way to daylight.[10] In Mahler we are dealing not with a dichotomy of public and private personalities, as in the case of Strauss, but with a bipolar or (to follow Hefling) cyclothymic condition.[11] Mahler himself recognized this duality, calling it simply his natural "irritability" while admitting that it could take his music directly from "flowery Elysian fields" to "the nocturnal terrors of Tartarus."[12] In any case, the musical style of Mahler's manic side corresponds closely to Strauss's most puffed-up self-aggrandizement; compare, for example, the strangely off-putting boisterousness in the last movement of the Seventh Symphony and the similarly hollow climax of *Ein Heldenleben*. But here we are compelled to believe that Mahler means it, or wants to mean it. There is something Beethovenian about its excessive vigor (à la the disturbingly repetitive apparent triumph that ends Beethoven's Fifth Symphony) and likewise in the tragic core that it underlines by its difference. Tragedy is the center of gravity in Mahler's creative work, and all the tragedies are his own. Their not being advertised as confessional is what draws us in; genius makes them worth contemplating, while a staged lack of self-consciousness, the opportunity for the listener to participate in genius by discovering something unsuspected, provides the incentive for closer reading.

In the end, the composers' antithetical interests with respect to the audience—Strauss concealing himself through confession, Mahler confessing through concealment—do not preclude a common goal for the process of creation: both of them used music to practice philosophy, and both of them philosophized primarily about the chasm between the subject and objectivity.[13] It was for this reason as much as any that Mahler could call the two of them "old friends" by 1897.[14] Like the rest of the Austro-German world in the nineteenth century, they had no answer for Kant, no way across the gap between what could be experienced, and what could not be experienced but must exist. But with the decline of romanticism they could not address these questions merely by composing music. They had to use music to explore the self, and to finds its limits.

If the story is to be believed, the five-year-old Mahler's dreaming-up of a "Polka with Introductory Funeral March" illuminates a divided personality structure that no life experiences or creative evolution were likely to overcome. The fact of the two sides' coexistence, whether as juxtaposition or complementarity, would grow into a central facet of both his character and his musical oeuvre. Alma and Natalie Bauer-Lechner left ample evidence of his instant changes of mood, both accounts filled with understanding and even admiration, and Natalie's largely without self-pity.[15] The First Symphony corroborates a psychological binarism as effectively as any personal testimony. In particular the third movement stages the basic divide of his interiority: a crass, harsh, mundane here-and-now contrasts with a floating utopia too good to be true. Paul Bekker, well positioned to judge Mahler's personality and its relation to his works, heard a fragmented state of mind, with a "painfully happy dream mood" (the G-major section at m. 83) that "is only properly achieved through the opposition to the weighty oppression of the D-minor movement."[16] To highlight the distressed subjectivity, Mahler contrasted what Bekker called the work's "deep, inwardly experiential aspect" with musical representatives of externality, beginning with the determinedly nonmusical *Naturlaute* (nature sounds) of the first movement's introduction.[17] The dual confrontations—within the hero, and between the hero and an antagonistic externality—set the terms of conflict for Mahler's entire creative output. A basic theme of division, reflected in contrasts between tragic and trivial, real and dreamlike, present and past, triumphant and defeated, joyful and jilted, musical and merely aural, and so on, is overdetermined in its reflection of both Mahler's own personality and his relationship with the world.

The First presents itself as a collage of autobiographical fragments meditating on a reality from which it hopes to escape. Its musical sources, the *Wayfarer* songs, document (by his own testimony) his unrequited love for their dedicatee, Johanna Richter. But they do not attempt to persuade her; rather they dramatize his position as "a wandering journeyman, who, having suffered a misfortune, heads out into the world and roams."[18] This loss, ordinary enough for a young man, would come to stand for something much deeper, as Freud would discover when they discussed Mahler's taste for musical banality.[19] The composer's various attempts at programmatic labeling of the First suppressed a content that was too personal to make plain: the lonely suffering of a child whose only protector (his mother) lived under daily attack. A "band of very bad musicians"—musicians of a sort that Mahler would spend his life abusing, with methods no less painful for being psychological rather than physical—pointed in the third movement to his separation from his mother, by evoking Mahler's aural memory of moments when mother and child could not protect one another.

When Mahler confessed to Löhr that he found the *Wayfarer* songs "inadequate,"[20] he announced a need to reopen the wounds in the broader context of a symphony, where the "outcry of a deeply wounded heart" (at the beginning of the fourth movement) could be made audible, indeed so powerfully audible as no longer to be musical.[21] The noise of subjectivity contrasts with the noise with which the symphony opens: mere sounds, meant to be played and heard as such (however rarely that ideal is achieved), which indicate a passive state of blissful nonexistence made explicit in the innocent trio under the linden tree. Of course this work ultimately chooses "breakthrough" over death, but that is a sign of its immaturity; the presence of death as a choice tells us that the seeds of the late Mahler were there from the beginning.

Strauss's path to musical autobiography began, like Mahler's, with his first attempt at the musical genre that would define his output—in this case, opera. Had it been successful, *Guntram* (1893) would likely have preempted six tone poems and made Strauss at once into an opera composer, as surely as Mahler was a composer of symphonies. Its failure (which puzzled Mahler, who liked the work) can be ascribed first of all to a mistake that he never repeated: the piece dealt explicitly with a private philosophical dilemma.[22] As I have suggested above (see chapter 4), in *Guntram* the protagonist is Strauss's opposite, an alter ego, built to live out the metaphysical conception of music that the composer was attempting to reject. For both the composer and the character, adulthood began at the moment when they concluded that music had no power to effect spiritual goals.

This process of self-reflection moved Strauss a long way toward creative maturity, but as artistic subject matter it was the kiss of death (confirming his prediction).[23] By the light of the first three tone poems, this opera must be considered an experiment, for none of those orchestral works takes a serious autobiographical stance. This is most forcefully true of *Tod und Verklärung*, which, popular opinion notwithstanding, reflects nothing of Strauss's own experience; often mistaken for a record of the composer's serious bout with pleurisy (which took place in 1892, three years after the work's completion), it traces rather the frustrated life—and fantasizes the apotheosis—of Alexander Ritter, the beloved mentor alienated by the philosophical conclusions of *Guntram*.[24] (For the sake of chronological clarity it should be noted here that although Strauss began working on *Guntram* in 1887, before any of the tone poems, the opera's autobiographical philosophizing was a product of a late revision made in the winter of 1892–93.)[25] *Guntram* thus came about as a lurch into an autobiography of sorts (biography of an anti-self), a crude first attempt following three substantial works that gazed outward rather than inward (aside from the sexual energy of *Don Juan*, of which Strauss obviously had some personal experience).[26] It did not help matters that anyone who knew Strauss could recognize *Guntram* as a declaration of principles, and that at least one friend (Arthur Seidl) published the fact.[27]

Only with *Till Eulenspiegels lustige Streiche* did Strauss begin to find a Mahlerian level of artistic productivity in the contemplation of his self, in the sense that he could project elements of his personality into the work and hold them there for his own consideration without making the music into a dry intellectual exercise.[28] Building on the critique laid out in *Guntram*, *Till* used spectacularly exciting music, energized by bald-faced tone painting, to give voice to a postmetaphysical conception of music with which Strauss would keep faith, though ever less joyfully, for the remainder of his career.[29] The hero's subjectivity is entirely more stable and whole in this tone poem than in Mahler's First, in that we see the same side of him, the prankster, in a rondo structure that simply changes the backdrops. Strauss, for whom self-doubt was not born but acquired, would take some time before identifying himself as a fragmented subject. Like Mahler, however, he was able here to use music as a laboratory, to place his ideas in the mouth of a protagonist in order to evaluate their worth and believability. As in *Guntram*, these ideas were critical rather than constructive—his music would go its own merry way, like Till, ruffling feathers and reveling in nihilism—but here this orientation produced a public success. Perhaps by watching Mahler, Strauss had learned that it was easier to tear down an ideal than to represent one.[30]

It should not surprise us that with the opening movement of the Second Symphony, Mahler's autobiographical ruminations converged at death.[31]

As a pair, the first two symphonies contained, in Mahler's words, "the inner aspect of my whole life [...] everything that I have experienced and endured."[32] But the animating concern of the "Todtenfeier" was Mahler's terror at imagining himself "dead, laid out in state, beneath wreaths and flowers."[33] From this work forward, his mortality would condition everything he created; however different the topics, moods, and styles of his creative products, and whatever other concerns the works might have addressed, they all served in some way to help him come to terms with death. The early example of the "Todtenfeier" shows us just how easily this fear came to him; we are confronted by "a mighty being still caught in the toils of this world; grappling with life and with the fate to which he must succumb."[34] Devising a compelling continuation, on the other hand, took six years.

One close confidante of Mahler, Bruno Walter, would claim that in the Second "the composer turns away from personal experience," an assertion that flatly contradicts Mahler's own statements.[35] It may hold at least a grain of truth about the outer movements, however, which ultimately tell us little about Mahler beyond the intensity of his fear and the immensity of the means that would be required to control it. He speaks of himself far more directly in the inner movements, especially in the scherzo, where various levels of alienation (as Jew, Bohemian, introvert, manic-depressive, abused child), coalesce in a lonely figure peering through a window at a happy crowd dancing to music that he cannot hear.[36] All these various sufferings were sublimated by Mahler into the ultimate suffering of spiritual alienation, the separation of the subject from an ultimate reality that he knew must exist but could not touch or even fathom. In a situation of such hopelessness—and we should admit in all honesty that it is this feeling, and not that of the closing movement, that controlled Mahler's existence before and after the Second—one suspects that the "outcry of despair" at the end of the scherzo, like the scream from the finale of the First, is tinged with a certain envy of the fish to whom St. Anthony preaches.[37] Mahler's loneliness was rooted in a dual exclusion, from the crowd of humanity on the other side of the window, and from the metaphysical permanence that he spent so much effort imagining.

What better symbol of Mahler's subjectivity, then, than the "little red rose" of the fourth movement ("Urlicht"), standing alone in the meadow?

The power and depth of this enormously complicated emblem duplicates the sophistication of the Wunderhorn poems, and also the complexity of Mahler's character. Longing to experience again the "state of a chrysalis," he nevertheless chose the most advanced musical means possible, both orchestrationally, with timbral contrasts and clarity anticipating the late works, and tonally, replacing a diatonic deceptive cadence (m. 24) with a *Tristan*-esque tritone appoggiatura over a cadence to the flat submediant (m. 60). The paradox of his fleeting existence in an anchorless universe, of the survival of the child in the suffering adult, of the inexplicable feelings of love and beauty in a world offering no escape from tragedy, found expression in the mystery of Wagnerian transfiguration. In a practical sense the symphony ends here—for this movement, like the third and unlike the finale, captured something permanent. If the solution provided in the finale had been adequate, the results for his creativity would have been disastrous; "if my existence were simply to run on as peacefully as a meadow brook, I don't think that I would ever again be able to write anything worthwhile."[38] But no solution would ever prove adequate for Mahler; in this respect above all he was a modernist, recognized as such even by so old-fashioned a character as Brahms, who after studying the score of the Second remarked, "I don't quite understand why Richard Strauss is proclaimed as the revolutionary of music; to me, Mahler is the king of these revolutionaries."[39] Not surprisingly the Third and Fourth, which as philosophical documents are best regarded as a complex, wrestled with the same problem as the finale of the Second. Mahler hunted for the metaphysical systematically in the Third (or "scientifically," for he appropriated Nietzsche's term, the "gay science," for an anti-Nietzschean project that he called "*my* gay science" [emphasis mine]), before trying to sneak into heaven disguised as a child in the Fourth.[40] And still the question remained: what could one say with certainty about existence after death?

It is not a coincidence that Mahler's autobiographical ruminations went underground at about the same time that Strauss produced the first of his three overtly, indeed flamboyantly, autobiographical works. Mahler's Fifth Symphony, begun in the summer of 1901, followed shortly after *Ein Heldenleben* (1899), a work that Mahler had studied carefully by October

1900.[41] We have seen that both composers spent the 1890s writing orchestral music that confronted personal philosophical dilemmas, which in Strauss's case were strictly private but no less absorbing personally. At the end of the decade, both Mahler and Strauss reached a moment of transition. Strauss's first public presentation of himself as artistic subject coincided with a private loss of faith in the notion of the "self," whereas Mahler renounced musical programmaticism even as he redoubled his efforts to reconcile truth and subjectivity through music.

With the bitonal ending of his fifth tone poem, *Also sprach Zarathustra*, Strauss announced his Nietzschean conclusion that no absolute—philosophical, religious, artistic, or otherwise—had a meaningful relation to human existence.[42] In his private worldview the implications for the self were as significant as those for external, absolute reality; both sides of the subject-object equation had been unmoored. *Ein Heldenleben* thus presents us with a cardboard cutout of Strauss, a one-dimensional character whose willing correspondence to popular caricatures not only hides the real Strauss but questions the very existence of a real Strauss. As he must have realized, a parodic confession is a step that cannot be undone; an artist who calls his own seriousness into question has raised a permanent doubt. Here that step represents a defining moment of honesty. The subtle brilliance of this otherwise disturbingly overblown work lies in the protagonist's inability to decide what his own music might mean. The dense collection of swirling quotations, justifiably the most remarked section of the tone poem, leaves the protagonist almost as confused as the listener.[43] The fragments draw connections among related works—the iconoclasm of *Don Juan* and *Also sprach Zarathustra*, the idealism of *Guntram* and *Don Quixote*—but they offer no vision of a productive way forward from these compositions, which is to say of a meaning that could generate further artistic achievement. They are an end point, a memory, and thus they float freely, inviting the listener to make of them what they will. In the meantime, the composer retreats, abandoning the struggle against the critics but also, and more importantly, the struggle to control the meaning of his music and the outlines of his own character. Explicit, pictorial, high-definition autobiography undermines the notion of artistic self-expression by casting doubt on the artist's control of his subject matter.

This too was a kind of confession, but an entirely modern one in that it abandoned the essential romantic artistic vision, the special power of the creator to see truth that eluded regular people. Strauss's next orchestral work returned to this same project, with greater focus and an equally strong emphasis on superficial autobiography. The program of *Symphonia domestica* (1903) brings Strauss even more decisively down to earth than *Ein Heldenleben*, giving up all pretense of heroism and marginalizing Papa's creative activities as exalted daydreaming. (His "Schaffen and Schauen" ["creating and contemplating," m. 599, reh. 55] are marked by their dreaminess as a departure from the work's authentic dramatic space and its tone of realism.) As discussed in chapter 3, the sketches show a personal grounding not at all parodic in nature: "my wife, my child, and my music, nature and sun, these are my happiness."[44] But resonance with the program of the *Eine Alpensinfonie*, in which Strauss linked the same complex of family, work, and nature to a Nietzschean anti-metaphysical agenda, confirms that despite its outward silliness *Symphonia domestica* was still engaging with philosophical concerns on a private level.[45] Reading the work thus depends on the realization that the public program represented the practical implementation of private reflections. Blatant and crass self-absorption publicized the obsolescence of autobiographical self-expression and meditation, without revealing the thought process that had brought Strauss to that conclusion. The interdependency between artistic surface and private meditation in these late tone poems must take some responsibility for the works' aesthetic failures, particularly a decline in dramatic efficiency and power compared to *Till Eulenspiegel*, *Also sprach Zarathustra*, and *Don Quixote*. But for Strauss these earlier tone poems seem to have been essentially negative, i.e., critical, designed to satisfy himself as to what he should not be attempting artistically, and only preliminarily intended to propose what he might do instead. He found the critical dimension more inspiring musically, in other words, at least in this period.

When Mahler reached his own crossroads ca. 1900, an equally complicated set of contradictions would need to be worked out. As I describe in the next chapter, Mahler would at this time reject verbal programs unequivocally.[46] But Mahler's new opposition to programs restricted itself to what the audience should be told in words; it implied nothing as to what role a program might play in the compositional process, or what might be communicated through the music. In many cases his expectations of what the audience would perceive were quite specific. Bauer-Lechner reports of the "Blumenstück" from the Third Symphony, for example, that Mahler felt he had successfully captured the view of a flowery meadow from his villa in Steinbach: "'Anybody who doesn't actually know the place,' said Mahler, 'will practically be able to visualize it from the music.'"[47] His frustrations stemmed not from listeners' interest in extramusical meaning in his music, but from listeners' inability to draw that meaning directly from the music (without a verbal text). Thus after having tried and failed in the first four symphonies to assist the process by offering various programmatic hints, Mahler decided to let the communication of extramusical ideas succeed or fail on the music's own ability to speak clearly.

The Fifth Symphony, the work with which the defender of absolute music ostensibly nailed his colors to the mast, actually invites just this kind of straightforward programmatic interpretation, along autobiographical lines. Preceded by four symphonies in which the composer himself surfaced now and again as "hero," and followed by a work that imagined his own tragic future,[48] it includes (according to Mengelberg) the most profoundly autobiographical document imaginable, a love letter that began the crucial human relationship of his life.[49] Moreover, the symphony's five-movement plan and formal anomalies (progressive tonality [ending in a different key from that in which it began], a funeral march as opening movement, a massive scherzo as central hub, a finale built on parodic treatment of a chorale) suggest that, like Berlioz's *Symphonie fantastique* (which critics so often accused Mahler of imitating, in various works), this symphony tells the story of a life.[50]

One is strongly tempted, then, to interpret the symphony's peculiarities in the context of his personal experience. ("There is an easy temptation to give this symphony a programmatic interpretation," Paul Bekker would write, arguing for a more "general and purely human reading" but conceding that Mahler's claims of autobiographical content in the First and Second Symphonies "apply in their fundamental meaning to the Fifth and those that followed it just as they did to the older works.")[51]

The funeral march initiates the story, with death, the atmosphere of Mahler's own childhood. The second movement traces a long struggle, beginning with orthodoxy (the straightforward sonata-form exposition), leading to an attempted breakthrough (to D major, m. 464) that falls short (sinking back to A minor at m. 557, in which key the movement ends) while preparing the way for a later successful attempt (the work's conclusion in D major). This musical equivalent of a lengthy and endlessly difficult apprenticeship then gives way to the scherzo, "an expression of enormous strength": Mahler as mature musician, "at the summit of his life," taking his place as a leader of European music without downplaying any of his "daring" features in the slightest.[52] Finally, the first, belated experience of real love (Adagietto) gives rise to the awkward spectacle of a euphoric, jubilant Mahler, indulging in a manic celebration so oddly overstated that Alma herself would tell him directly it did not suit his personality.[53] Whether provoked by his near-death experience of early 1901, or his unexpected metamorphosis into husband and father, or the feeling that his music's difficult reception demanded a change of direction, Mahler seems to have required here an artistic summing-up of his life's course, in preparation for some unknown future.[54]

Without the addition of the "tragic" Sixth (as Mahler himself labeled it) and its completion of the cyclothymic complex, Mahler's Fifth would not have made sense.[55] The victory of boisterous optimism (despite inner conflicts, especially in the second movement) was for Mahler all too clearly unsustainable, and the work becomes an antecedent phrase, answered in the Sixth by a return to heartbreak as the composer's psychological default setting. One might hear this homecoming as an early sign of the resignation that would define the late works; acknowledgment of defeat fulfills the main prerequisite for this final stage. Mahler's breakdown in the green room at Essen indicates that he understood the implications at the time, but Strauss missed them entirely, as evidenced by his insensitivity on that occasion (see the introduction).[56] The pain of this incident for Mahler stemmed partly from his colleague's apparent disregard of the symphony's homages to Strauss: the Straussian attempt to "express" his wife "in a theme" (cf. *Heldenleben*),[57] and the allusion to the son's theme in *Domestica* at the scene of children's "arrhythmic playing" in the scherzo (mm. 273–80, oboe, D major, in the Sixth; cf. mm. 218 [eight measures before reh. 19] in *Domestica*).[58] It did not help that precisely these moments were identified as defects even by Mahler's supporters; of the "Alma" theme, Bekker would write, "there are indisputable weaknesses," albeit in the melody's aesthetic qualities rather than "the meaning of the sound."[59] If Constantin Floros is correct to hear in the Sixth hints of the striving protagonist in *Tod und Verklärung*, it would seem that one goal Mahler sought to attain—with mixed success—was a compelling emulation of Strauss, picking up on tendencies of the latter's outwardly autobiographical music.[60]

Why then would Strauss turn up his nose at the Sixth, with behavior that, given his sensitivity to musical allusion, was at least cold and perhaps deliberately humiliating? In all likelihood Strauss found himself at that moment as angry as Mahler, and for the same reason: having been misunderstood. The gaudy self-portraiture of *Heldenleben* and *Domestica* was no more a sincere expression of Strauss's self than the feigned confusion about his friend's emotional state. Not only did Mahler overlook that irony, he appropriated the music for a work that maintained romantic claims of confessional authenticity, which is to say, the very target of Strauss's faux-autobiographical critique. With both composers now well into their forties, Strauss could see that they were speeding in opposite directions—Mahler intensifying his efforts to stabilize a "constructed musical subjectivity" (in Peter Franklin's phrase), Strauss facing ever more serious questions about the plausibility of a coherent subjectivity, musical or otherwise.[61] That is not to say that Mahler's music from this period is any less fragmented than Strauss's; rather, whereas Strauss began to see fragmentation as a condition of human thought, Mahler renewed the tradition of using art "to control and unify the protean character changes that define its discourse."[62]

Of course, with Strauss we have the advantage of looking back on this period through his late reflections, in which he explicitly identified a mercurial subjectivity as the key to understanding his oeuvre. Even as he claimed that "the confession of *Intermezzo*, of *Capriccio*, is exactly what differentiates my dramatic works from the typical operas, masses, variations,"

Strauss emphasized the variety of his subjective guises and the centrality of "the deliberate tone of mockery, of irony" that had built through the tone poems to a definitive expression in *Feuersnot*.[63] In *Metamorphosen* Strauss would extend this line of thought to an explicit proclamation of decentered subjectivity, drawing on Goethe's "Niemand wird sich selber kennen" ("No One Can Know Himself") as a decisive confirmation of psychological fluidity.[64] The compositional choices of Strauss's "Indian Summer" take on a purposeful tone in this context; indeed they come into focus as an autobiographical-historical project, reviewing his early period (the concertos and sonatinas), the phase of programmatic orchestral composition (*Metamorphosen* and the Duett-Concertino), and the Wagnerian dramatic vocal music (the *Four Last Songs*). The overriding truth acknowledged by this review is the inadequacy of particular artifacts, alone and grouped, to capture the whole significance of an individual who nonetheless contributed immensely to the store of German cultural expression.

Strauss was not a pessimist but a realist, of a sort that Mahler could not possibly understand. Mahler's inability to abandon the hope of an afterlife, his compulsion to continue struggling against doubts that in the end could never be vanquished, is inseparable from a confidence that the only barrier to adequate self-expression lay in the precision of his musical technique. This is the real source of his obsessive revisions: unlike Strauss, he never questioned what he meant to communicate, only the means that he used. When we hear him repeating himself in his late style, then, we should not mistake these moments for detached reflection. He is simply trying again. Stephen Hefling's careful study of *Das Lied von der Erde* traces these connections with extraordinary sensitivity; instructively, he begins the account with a cogent distillation of Mahler's entire symphonic output through the Eighth Symphony.[65] Thus Bauer-Lechner's most important revelation concerning Mahler's autobiographical streak— "to understand these works properly would be to see my life transparently revealed in them"—applies as readily to the late works as to the early ones.[66] As we follow Hefling's reading, the composer's familiar goal emerges; the staging has changed, as resignation and acceptance provide a different emotional coloring, but the paradox of continuing hope never fades. This is essentially the conclusion that Strauss reached in his distraught private outpouring after learning of Mahler's death (see chapter 6): "the Jew Mahler could still find elevation in Christianity," Strauss claimed, for the same reason that "the hero Richard Wagner descended to it [Christianity] as an old man, under the influence of Schopenhauer"—an enduring, indestructible idealism.[67] Mahler's inability to give up what Strauss could never tolerate leads us closer to an understanding of their divergence.

CHAPTER 8

Programmmusiker

IN THE VIEW OF CARL DAHLHAUS, European musical modernism began in 1889, with Strauss's *Don Juan* and Mahler's First Symphony.[1] Looking beyond the works' fundamental differences—in genre, structure, mood, sonority, heroism—Dahlhaus perceived a common vision of contemporary music, built on overt, challenging programmaticism. Gone was the dreamy ellipticism of Liszt. Music would now evoke the physical, the ethnic, the sexual, the violent, all in gruesome detail using an ultraprecise pictorial technique derived from Wagner and Berlioz. Unwelcome guests invaded the concert hall, making their presence felt regardless of how much or little verbal guidance the composers provided their audience (which varied widely in the case of Mahler's symphony).

Listeners reacted unpredictably. On Strauss's side, the first tone poem succeeded far better than expected: somehow its "enormous performance difficulties," "audacity of conception," and "altogether unusual demands [...] on the listener's power of comprehension" added up to what even Bülow would call "a quite unprecedented success."[2] Most important, audiences rarely felt confused; music and program reinforced one another while each offered something exciting, provocative, and new. When *Tod und Verklärung* confirmed the success with its premiere at Eisenach on

June 21, 1890, Strauss found himself an internationally famous and frequently performed composer, the leader of the *Programmmusiker* while still in his twenties.

Mahler embraced programmaticism no less enthusiastically at the outset of his career, only to see his first two symphonies meet with incomprehension, ridicule, and apathy. The premiere of the First in Budapest (November 20, 1889) set the tone, eliciting vocal protests from the audience and critical complaints of "bizarrenesses," "meaningless tone-figures," a "stunning hodgepodge of painful cacophony," and so on, all of which placed him (said one commentator) among Richter, Bülow, Mottl, Levi, and Wüllner as conductors who could not compose.[3] A long decade of similar experiences would eventually see him boil over, announcing to a gathering of friends (in Munich after an October 20, 1900, performance of the Second) that he was abandoning program music; to seal the decision, "Mahler took up his glass and emptied it with a cry of 'death to programs!'"[4]

A cursory overview thus leaves one with the impression of a successful program musician who rode the wave as far as it would take him, and a failed one who after long effort rebooted his career (beginning with the ostensibly "absolute" Fifth Symphony). The truth, however, was not so simple. First, as Constantin Floros has argued, Mahler by no means barred extramusical content from his post-Wunderhorn symphonies.[5] Though the works do not have publicized programmatic content, they often show clear extramusical inspiration on a private level—an "inner program," as Mahler described it to Max Kalbeck.[6] This dimension betrays itself repeatedly in Mahler's sketches and correspondence, in recollections of intimate associates, and in his compositional style. Indeed, the Munich episode, related with theatrical intensity by Ludwig Schiedermair, Mahler's first biographer, actually served to introduce a new strategy for revitalizing programmaticism, by pushing it underground and divorcing it from a label that had acquired problematic associations. The details of this new tack were provided by Bruno Walter, who, writing in Mahler's name, offered Schiedermair a sort of manifesto in which the term "program music" became a straw man that Mahler vanquished in order to protect the credibility of orchestral music as a vehicle of idealism (see below). This was, in other words, a carefully prepared rear guard action, offered to a young writer who seemed well positioned to spread the word.

Strauss too had a nuanced private conception of program music, which came into focus as a response to the reception of his first mature works. Early in 1890, shortly after finishing *Tod und Verklärung*, the young composer was compelled to theorize a distinction between two different types of programmaticism, in order to defend himself against a well-meaning but firm critique of *Don Juan* by Cosima Wagner. To complement the kind of pictorialism for which he was becoming famous—the virtuosic illustrative technique labeled "Tonmalerei" (tone painting) by his contemporaries—Strauss argued for the deeper significance of "poetic" inspiration, as established by Liszt (program music as the "telling of inner processes") and by Wagner in his 1857 essay on Liszt's symphonic poems.[7] No doubt Cosima appreciated the deft use of the ultimate authority. She did not quite accept, however, that the two forms could coexist without the physical overwhelming the spiritual. The impasse, in which Strauss faced a choice between fidelity and independence, would push him forcefully toward a critical stance vis-à-vis Wagnerian musical metaphysics.

The material below explores these two episodes in some detail, arguing that the apparent disagreement between Mahler and Strauss on programmaticism was far from a matter of simple pro or con. It involved, rather, two parallel internal struggles over what purposes extramusical content should serve in a musical work: in its creation and in its reception. Just as the composers began with similar positions, they ended at essentially the same place, though the roads to it diverged widely.

One of the best-kept secrets about Mahler—thanks to his admirers, and to some extent the composer himself—is his enthusiasm for tone painting. Early on he developed a fondness for the musical imitation of natural phenomena, which remained strong throughout his life. John Williamson has commented on the various natural inhabitants of the *Lieder und Gesänge* of 1880–83: "lark, bees, and crickets."[8] Nearly three decades later, an anonymous New York musician told of encountering a beetle one day while on a walk with Mahler, then discovering the next winter a musical version droning in Mahler's latest music. "There is our beetle of last summer's walk," Mahler remarked.[9] Among Strauss's works he was especially partial to *Till Eulenspiegel* and *Don Quixote*; he conducted the former with the New York Philharmonic ten times, using it to close out the last of his 1909–10 "historical concerts" (on March 30, 1910), while the latter he "applauded wildly" at a Munich performance in June 1910.[10] Similar tendencies would surface in his music even at the most profound, spiritual moments, for example the opening of the Ninth Symphony, when he composed out his own heartbeat in oblique reference to *Tod und Verklärung*.[11] There is not so great a distance from this representation of physical subjectivity and the sound effects that open the First Symphony, where the direction "like a sound of nature" ("wie ein Naturlaut") is meant to be taken seriously: this music is not to be heard merely as music.

Such examples are easy enough to understand even without explanatory programs, as Mahler learned the hard way. That in spite of it all he maintained a lifelong interest in these conceits—whether he considered them Handelian, "characteristic," New German, Straussian, or something else entirely—indicates that even on the illustrative level he remained a program musician at heart. What seems even more interesting about the First, however, is that it shows us a composer interested in every conceivable kind of programmaticism, who applies so many layers of extramusical content that the programmatic nature of the piece becomes massively overdetermined. A sizable portion of the musical material for this symphony was drawn from previously existing texted sources, principally the autobiographical song cycle *Songs of a Wayfarer*, but also Liszt's *Dante Symphony*, Wagner's *Parsifal*, the student song "Bruder Martin," and several other early songs of his own. These works were more than musical "building blocks" (in Bauer-Lechner's phrase); the various allusions create a fragmentary narrative of a hero's life, with episodes spanning the full range of emotional experience from happiness and naive wonder to violent struggle and triumph.[12]

To survey the types of programmaticism in the First is to make a catalogue of the approaches available to a young modernist ca. 1890. The opening measures' hovering between sound and music calls to mind the appearance of the birds in the second movement of the *Pastoral* Symphony, which Beethoven famously described as "more expression of feeling than painting." The naive Mahler offers no such qualification; expression and painting are equally welcome. The subsequent incorporation of music drawn from texted works naturally invites extramusical inference, particularly when that music is parodied (as in the third movement's minor-mode version of "Bruder Martin," with its accompanying programmatic reference to the huntsman's funeral and the woodcuts of Jacques Callot). The *Wayfarer* songs carry the above-mentioned autobiographical connotations of a painful amorous misadventure, recalled in the consoling haze of "Die zwei blauen Augen meiner Schatz" ("The Two Blue Eyes of My Sweetheart"). With its *per aspera ad astra* trajectory the symphony strongly implies a dialogue with Beethoven's Fifth, while it calls on Berlioz in its tracking of the hero through various scenes, with each new appearance marked by a musical sign (the falling perfect fourth as a kind of idée fixe). Finally, the title *Titan*, though apparently added late and somewhat halfheartedly (according to Bruno Walter), made possible the kind of interpretation that Wagner found so important in Liszt's symphonic poems: here the composer, by indicating the title and nothing more, could use the uniquely powerful language of music to explore the story's inner content. With boundless youthful enthusiasm, then, Mahler here presented a piece of program music that left no manner of extramusical reference unused. And that attempt, daring though it was, likely bore as much responsibility for the work's difficult reception as any confusion about the relationship between the music and this or that specific referent.

In spite of the work's contrapuntal programmaticism, Mahler provided no verbal explanation at the 1889 premiere in Budapest, even for the unconventional (or conventionally unconventional) number of movements (five, with the soon-to-be discarded "Blumine"—a number seemingly inspired by the *Pastoral* Symphony and the *Symphonie fantastique*) and the two-part structure. He did not keep the program a secret, at least from his friends; hints in a review by August Beer indicate that he discussed the extramusical issues openly in informal settings. But his practice was a quasi-schizophrenic one that Max Kalbeck, in a 1905 review of the Fifth Symphony, identified as the problem that doomed his early symphonies: "Mahler-the-poet outlined a poetic text; Mahler-the-musician tore up the program after using it."[13] Mahler himself, on the other hand, would blame the lack of a written program for the work's failure (though he also implicated the orchestration of the first version); subsequent performances saw not just a revision of the musical score but an overabundance of programmatic indications, first at Hamburg in October 1893 and then again at Weimar in June 1894. Surely one consideration here was the success of *Don Juan* and *Tod und Verklärung*, with their poetic texts that seemed effective at advertising the musical content. (As mentioned above, Strauss would host the Weimar meeting of the Allgemeiner deutscher Musikverein where the First had its 1894 performance.) In this new multimedia guise, the symphony included freely invented programmatic titles for each movement, along with references to the woodcuts of Callot for the third movement, Dante for the fourth movement, and Jean Paul's *Titan* for the whole. Even Mahler's champions found this range of extramusical information overwhelming; after the Weimar performance, which was energetically hissed, Ernst Otto Nodnagel called the program "a succession of disconnected words, from which I could extract no meaning" (though by 1902 he would be a firm supporter of Mahler), and Richard Specht would later write that it was "so extravagant, hazy, and disconnected from the music, that it seemed to come not from the composer but from one of the worst examples of the stereotypical 'enthusiastic commentator.'"[14]

By the turn of the century, with his compositional efforts still facing skepticism and apathy from a resistant public, Mahler admitted the need to find a new way. The reception of the Second, and of partial performances of the Third, taught him that in this arena he could not ride Strauss's coattails; he would have to set himself apart in the minds of listeners—"to distance himself consciously," in the words of Floros, "from the illustrative program music of his friend and rival Richard Strauss"— in order to rehabilitate his existing works and prepare a smoother path for the new ones.[15] This is the context of the declaration recorded by Schiedermair, made after the Munich performance of the Second in 1900:

> [Schiedermair recalls Mahler's words:] "Away with programs, they arouse false impressions. Leave the public to their own thoughts about the work they are to hear, do not force them to read while they are listening and fill their minds with pre-conceived ideas! If a composer himself has forced on his listeners the feelings which overwhelmed him, then he has achieved his object. The language of music has then approached that of the word, but has communicated immeasurably more than the word is able to express." And Mahler took up his glass and emptied it with a cry of, "Death to programs!"[16]

This melodramatic scene, which apparently left the company motionless and discreetly glancing at one another, would be followed in December 1901 by a more substantial, dispassionate explanation in a manifesto of sorts written out by Walter. Its proximate cause was a request of Schiedermair, who intended to produce a set of analyses of Mahler's works. The composer himself not having the time or the inclination to construct a detailed argument, he directed Walter to do so, then approved the lengthy text and forwarded it to Schiedermair with the request that it be published in full, without emendation.[17]

In this significant and underappreciated document, Walter presented an ostensible critique of program music, laying the groundwork for Mahler's future compositions and reinterpreting the first four symphonies as "absolute music" (Walter's words). Opening his essay with the unambiguous pronouncement "Mahler utterly loathes all programs," Walter proposed the unity of musical form and content, echoing Hanslick's metaphor of the wine as its own bottle: "music can be both kernel and husk."[18] The specific point at issue was Schiedermair's request for information on the program of the Fourth, which brought the remarkable assertion, "no program will bring one to an understanding of this work or any other Mahler symphony." Given that all of the previous symphonies actually had printed programs, Walter recognized the need to elaborate, and he did so with comments on the locus classicus of unhelpful programs, the third movement of the First Symphony. In this work, Walter explained, many extramusical ideas might be used to hint at the content of the music, but all of them fall short, because only music can express that content fully and with emotional specificity. If Mahler himself gave in to the temptation to put the musical meaning into words, the composer nevertheless recognized throughout that "this movement was not composed to depict any of these images"; it was composed to express something deeper, something that was accessible only to music.[19] Ultimately the program was not genuinely a part of the work, a fact that would remain beyond dispute irrespective of the nature of the program, the number of separate and potentially incompatible programs, and even the composer's own responsibility for introducing those programs in the first place.

Moving from this specific composition to a general theory of programmaticism, Walter took a powerfully philosophical tack, confirming, it would seem, that even in a new century the basic tenets of neoromantic musical idealism would hold sway. Mahler's highly advanced musical technique, in combination with his "incomparably ripe and complicated emotional life," allowed him to express things that could not be expressed in any other way, "since they come from a sphere beyond space and time, beyond the form of individual appearances."[20] Walter repeatedly appealed to the notion of "absolute music," drawing on ideas familiar from the third book of Schopenhauer's *Die Welt als Wille und Vorstellung*; for example, we hear of music that "*her kingdom is one step closer to the gods than that of the other arts*" (emphasis in original)—music, that is, expresses the essential being, the noumenal "reality" behind the phenomenal world of appearances, in a way that no other art can. And for that reason, no program could ever bring us closer to the meaning of Mahler's works than the music itself.[21]

The critical dimension of this letter had an important musico-political task to accomplish with respect to Mahler's reception as composer: to distance him as far as possible from a realm where he would have to compete head-to-head with Strauss, and where he had thus far proven himself incapable of finding the right tone. Thus Walter reduced "program music" to its vulgar definition, i.e., the overt attempt to imitate musically the information contained in a verbal program attached to the score. Against this lower music he counterposed Mahler's brand of music—"absolute" music. "One who has grasped the being of music in this way—as the simile of the deepest being of things, and therefore incapable of reproducing the individual appearances of these things—can never write music to a program."[22] Strauss and Mahler found themselves in a hierarchy, with Mahler on top.

Of course, Mahler knew full well that the theory of programmaticism articulated by Wagner in the 1857 essay on Liszt's symphonic poems had used precisely this argument to distinguish between Berlioz and Liszt, with Berlioz as a composer devoted to capturing the particular in music, and Liszt as one who used music to convey the deep meaning that lay beneath the programmatic content—a meaning that could only be communicated by music. In essence, then, Walter and Mahler meant to appropriate Wagner's theory of deeper, spiritual programmaticism and return it to absolute music, a type of music that Mahler now proposed to lead and indeed to defend. Hanslick himself would have been impressed by this maneuver; indeed, it is not unthinkable that during Mahler's early years in Vienna he had absorbed the essentials of Hanslick's own idealism and now found a useful personal application for them.

Today it is more difficult for us than it was for Schiedermair to accept the claim that Mahler was never a program musician in the first place. Even if, as Walter claims, the fundamentally absolute quality of Mahler's music put him "in the position to name a long series of images whose nature is related to that of his work"—in other words, to suggest multiple, apparently conflicting extramusical connections to a piece like the third movement of the First—the fact is that Mahler did attach specific indicators of programmatic content to some of his music.[23] Moreover, there is substantial evidence that for virtually all of his untexted music, extramusical content played a role during the compositional process. Mahler did not deny that fact in private, and so we must conclude that the Walter letter has greater significance as a public document—which was its intended purpose—than as a definitive expression of Mahler's own views.

Strauss too left us with a sort of mission statement, but one that had a strictly private purpose: to address doubts expressed by Cosima Wagner after he played *Don Juan* for her at the piano in February 1890. (Cosima visited Weimar on February 16–20 to hear Strauss's performance of *Lohengrin* on the nineteenth; already she was grooming him for a conducting position at Bayreuth.) This exchange is remarkable not only for the uncharacteristically assertive tone taken by Strauss, who was otherwise understandably obsequious in his dealings with Cosima, but for the clear distinction made by both correspondents between tone painting and the deeper kind of programmaticism that Wagner admired in Liszt. Cosima began the discussion on February 25 with a letter in which she praised his highly developed compositional technique but admonished him, gently but firmly, "to listen closely to your heart, and here and there ask your intelligence, which possesses a ready wit, to be quiet."[24] In particular she was taken aback by the graphic moments of the piece, not so much for their sensual character (they hardly surpassed the sexual intensity of the last five minutes of *Tristan*), but because they focused so sharply on particular events in an unfolding narrative. These moments of "intelligence" had such power, she believed, that they would inevitably distract the listener from the work's "feeling" (*Gefühl*), the bearer of authentic, spiritually meaningful programmaticism.

To his credit, Strauss declined to back down: "With respect to the outweighing of feeling by the intelligence, I believe (generally speaking) that in the case of a broad and generously disposed artistic nature, the unconscious and the instincts, which together form the fundamental basis of every true and productive creative urge, whether in the creative or the interpretive artist, will always be more powerful than the intellect, no matter how highly developed the latter may be."[25] No amount of tone painting, in other words, could ever harm the deeper programmatic significance of a piece, if that level was well founded; a good composer could give his pictorial imagination free rein, without fear of compromise. As one might imagine, Cosima responded to this self-serving claim with some consternation, asserting forcefully that the "free play of the rational mind" (*der spielende Verstand*, as opposed to the spirit) imposes "unease" (*Unruhe*) on the listener, interfering with the perception of the work's spiritual content and preventing the composer from bringing to light the emotional core of the programmatic subject.[26] Strauss had violated the Wagnerian principle of "simplicity" (*Einfachheit* is her word, as implausible as such a claim might seem) by introducing a "play of the intelligence against feeling."[27] An intensive musical focus on physical particulars could not help but damage the artwork's ultimate effect, for "our art leads us back to eternal motives."[28]

With that last phrase Cosima played her trump card: "eternal motive" is the very term used by Wagner to distinguish the content of Liszt's symphonic poems from the musico-narrative experiments of Berlioz. As if to confirm that she knew the source she was citing, Cosima added obliquely, "I would have said the same thing to Berlioz about any of his works if I had had the opportunity."[29] This assertion of authority seemed to make an impression; Strauss claimed to have understood her, and he suggested furthermore that at their next meeting he would present compositional evidence to put her mind at ease.[30] But that evidence turned out to be the new tone poem *Tod und Verklärung*, a work replete with heartbeats, labored breathing, ticking clocks, spasmodic convulsions, and other vivid products of Strauss's "intelligence"—if also a spiritual apotheosis that he rightly expected would please her. We have no record of her reaction, but she must have seen the writing on the wall. He chose a subject that invited both kinds of programmaticism, and he followed both paths. He even disavowed personal control for the choice, referring Cosima to Schopenhauer's essay on free will and observing that a program "forces itself on one with inevitable necessity." She had lost, then, even if Strauss concluded the exchange with politic self-effacement: "if anything I have said seems, perhaps justifiably, dumb, please take it with goodness and indulgence."[31]

There is nothing in Strauss's music after this debate that suggests a change of heart with respect to tone painting. If anything, the tendency becomes more pronounced, so that in the last two tone poems (now ironically called "symphonies") it overpowers the music just as Cosima had predicted—and by no means unwittingly on Strauss's part. In the *Symphonia domestica*, the jarringly oxymoronic title forecasts something overtly nonsymphonic, a vast collection of painterly moments including a toddler's bath, an alarm clock, games between parent and child, a stroll, an argument, and likely many more that Strauss never bothered to explain. (We know as much as we do about *Till Eulenspiegel* and *Don Quixote* only because tenacious friends pestered Strauss for details.) In a tour de force of programmatic illustration, even music itself is "imitated," when the composer plays (or hears in his head) Mendelssohn's "Venetian Gondellied." And the first nonpictorial music that we hear, the G-minor rapture for oboe beginning at m. 5, is meant as Papa's creative reverie and thus appears as a kind of quotation.

As Strauss obviously recognized, all of this serves to connect the music directly and explicitly to the physical realm, and thus to detach it from the metaphysical level to which Cosima had been clinging. Strauss's "scene d'amour" betrays its ancestry in the "Liebestod" by its quasi-pornographic climax, but the music's ugliness, taken together with the uncomfortable fact that we know who is having sex and what they look like, creates an effect rather gruesome and certainly not in the slightest degree spiritual. The noisy fugue serves much the same function; counterpoint no longer represents absolute objectivity, a retreat from the phenomenal to the pure, but instead its complex intertwinings mimic the overlapping screams of a rambunctious argument.

This same kind of reduction to the physical applies also in *Eine Alpensinfonie*, a work begun earlier than *Symphonia domestica* (in 1899, the latter having been composed in 1903) and directly inspired by Nietzsche. That Strauss considered naming it "The Antichrist,"[32] and that he did so as a direct response to Mahler's death, speaks eloquently to his grasp of the interrelationships among Wagnerian musical style, Mahler's musical idealism, and the relentless critique of this tradition in Nietzsche's late works. In this most comprehensively pictorial work in Strauss's oeuvre, tone painting finally serves overtly as philosophical critique, which the composer implements by short-circuiting nineteenth-century listeners' instinctive tendency to listen deeper than the illustrative surface. The target was one musical ideology with two labels: the idealistic brand of programmaticism identified by Wagner in Liszt's symphonic poems (and promulgated by Ritter, who believed Strauss would extend that tradition), and the "absolute music" of Mahler and Walter, which had similar noumenal aspirations but promoted them by cutting all ties with program music. *Eine Alpensinfonie* thereby culminated a critical process operating in all the post-*Guntram* tone poems, from *Till Eulenspiegel* and *Also sprach Zarathustra*, to *Don Quixote* and *Ein Heldenleben*, and ending with *Symphonia domestica* and a work inspired by the mountain that greeted Strauss each morning through his workroom window. After the third pair he seems to have been satisfied, for he didn't return to programmatic composition for orchestra until 1945, when the destruction of Germany found expression in *Metamorphosen*.

Mahler was hardly alone in maintaining faith with musical idealism. Dahlhaus observed that a neo-Schopenhauerian perspective was thoroughly mainstream ca. 1900.[33] To defend one's idealism by means of a reactionary attitude toward program music was likewise not unusual, though neither was it necessary; as early as 1929 a philosophically informed critic such as Felix M. Gatz considered it self-evident that idealism represented the common goal for musicians on both sides of the "absolute music"/"program music" debate.[34] Mahler's choice seems as much political, then, as aesthetic; he took the path that he believed would attract listeners and advertise the integrity of his artistic mission. (Some critics did see through this move, incidentally, referring to the new Mahler as a "bashful [*verschämt*] program musician.")[35] It cannot have been easy for him, for the programmatic layer of musical meaning would always be essential to his creativity—both the emotional stimulus of psychological challenges, and the immediate musical inspiration of the physical world. (Consider his need, for example, to compose near a lake because "the lake talked to him.")[36] In private he kept the faith with his programmatic creative practice, as we have seen with the beetle; in overlooking the contradiction between his public and private views he staked out a position not unlike what Strauss had articulated to Cosima concerning "intelligence." But what Mahler did not do, and would never have considered doing, was to turn one kind of music against the other in order to divorce the art from an outdated metaphysics. In this crucial respect Mahler was a musician of the nineteenth century, Strauss of the twentieth.

Strauss did at least manage to teach Mahler (by example) how to use extramusical content to shape the reception, which is to say the consumption, of his music.[37] The greatest popular success that Mahler ever experienced, the premiere of the Eighth Symphony in Munich on September 12, 1910, took Goethe's poem not just as dramatic material and creative inspiration but as a sort of defense mechanism, a guide to interpretation that was to hold good for Mahler's entire oeuvre. Composing *Faust* Part II gave Mahler a unique compositional freedom, for it provided him not just a license but indeed an imperative to draw on any kind of music imaginable, the better to create the impression of all-encompassing totality sought by Goethe. Yet at the same time, the crucial and assertive feature of the famous last scene, the scrupulously figurative dimension of Goethe's relationship with his Christian subject matter (recall that Goethe was emphatically not a Christian), controls the interpretation of the whole. Goethe tells us that nothing in his poem, and thus nothing in the world, is meant to be taken literally; all is metaphor, symbol, appearance, and thus inadequate to express an ultimate reality that nonetheless exists and can only be approached in this imperfect manner. Mahler took great pains to explain this point to Alma as clearly as possible in the letter of June 1909 (see chapter 3), because it had become for him a philosophy both of life and of creation, and one grounded securely in the greatest intellectual authority of the German tradition.[38]

Mahler reveals himself in this letter as remarkably up-to-date concerning the crisis of truth and subjectivity ca. 1900. Clearly he recognized that something more was at stake than the subject's access to truth; the existence of an enduring truth was itself being questioned, leading to the oxymoronic notion of a "subjective truth": "truth is a subjective concept, and it varies for each of us and in every new epoch."[39] Mahler did not intend to accept that state of affairs, however, but to define all human endeavor, including a human notion of truth, as allegory, and thereby to draw from Goethe a renewed hope for some supra-allegorical reality that would be accessible only after death. "All transitory things," says Mahler's paraphrase of Goethe, "by the very nature of the unworldliness, are *inadequate—but when* freed from their outer shell of human frailty, they are *accomplished*, and there is no further need for circumlocution, comparison—or *allegory*" (emphasis in original). The need for allegory explained Goethe's use of Christian symbolism, "this beautiful, sufficiently mythological concept—and the one most accessible to this era of world history"—a curious choice for a poet who counted Christianity among the four things he most detested (along with tobacco smoke, bed bugs, and garlic).[40] Christianity here was only a means, but one that could communicate a deeper and otherwise imperceptible truth.

Whenever Mahler suppressed the programmatic elements of his compositional process—elements that, while private, are easily uncovered in every symphony from the Fifth to the Tenth—he did so because he calculated that audiences would not recognize their allegorical function in this Goethean sense. The programmatic markers would have been taken as the content, rather than a symbol of the content, just as had occurred in the reception of the First. Peeling away this layer of symbolism in advance carried an element of risk, for the listeners would have to provide their own analogues for the music's emotional/spiritual content, or they would have to learn to comprehend his peculiar musical language—a challenge that for most had so far proven impossible. ("People have not managed to penetrate my musical language," he told Bauer-Lechner, in a passage not included in her published memoir but unearthed by Floros. "They have no idea what I am saying or what I mean, and it seems to them senseless and incomprehensible.")[41] But publicizing a program carried the much greater risk that audiences might abandon the search for a deeper level of meaning altogether. And that would have undermined Mahler's entire musical project, which was devoted with extraordinary passion to the ordinary notion—ordinary for the time, that is—that music offered humans their only glimpse of truth in this life.

During Mahler's lifetime, Strauss dedicated his orchestral music to undermining that very notion, with the help of precisely those superficializing tendencies of programmaticism that Mahler (and Cosima) feared. Strauss too believed that any truth available to humans was subjective, but unlike Mahler he dropped the issue there and contented himself with the beauty to be found on earth, complemented by a wry nihilism rather less optimistic than Nietzsche would have liked. The pessimistic streak became more pronounced as Strauss got older, and it found a culmination of sorts in *Metamorphosen*, his last programmatic work for orchestra. The Goethe poem on which it is based, "No One Can Know Himself," offers a brilliantly prescient and pithy formulation of decentered subjectivity. The limits of knowledge, Goethe tells us, prevent knowledge not just of the outside but of the inside.[42] Thus where Mahler found in Goethe a way out of subjectivity—by means of a figurative signifier of an unreachable signified—Strauss took from him an intensified sense of alienation, with unmoored subjectivity as the only reality.

Ironically, that particularly bitter moment of hopelessness led Strauss back to the kind of program music that he had abandoned. Unique among his programmatic works, *Metamorphosen* entirely foregoes tone-painting in order to seek a deeper reality, an "eternal motive" that resists nonmusical definition. As Mahler had done in his late works, Strauss became unusually serious, focusing on the loss of what had been and the uncertainty of what was to come. But he parted ways with Mahler on the question of hope. If one finds consolation in this music, it is a merely human consolation, and one that doesn't hide from the prospect of inevitable annihilation. *Metamorphosen*, then, constitutes Strauss's most aggressive attack on spiritual program music, for rather than undermining it with tone painting, Strauss returned to it only to compel it to endorse its own destruction. The eternal motive expressed by this music was eternal nonexistence, eternal meaninglessness—a claim, in other words, that music's promise to Wagner and other idealists had been a lie.

CHAPTER 9

Imports

WHAT ATTRACTED MAHLER AND STRAUSS to the United States? Money, one supposes, and in fact they admitted as much. Strauss openly described the States as a cash register, in a December 1907 conversation with Mahler that was witnessed by Karl Moll. After Mahler wondered aloud whether he should bother going to New York—"where none of the preconditions for understanding what I am trying to do are to be found"— Strauss responded blithely, "but Mahler, you are and remain a child. Over there you get up on the podium and do this—(he waved an imaginary baton)—and then you go to the cashier and—(a gesture of counting money)."[1] Mahler, despite his ethical pretensions, concluded that an established conductor who refused to tap the mind-boggling wealth of the American nouveaux riches was only cheating himself. Writing to Alma from Berlin in June 1907 with news of the final negotiations with Heinrich Conried, director of the Metropolitan Opera, he signed off with the following:

<pre>
   kiss   kiss
         6 months a year @ 125,000 crowns
              1/2 million crowns
       or annual guest contracts of 6–8 weeks
</pre>

       50,000 crowns fee
     total of 200,000 crowns in four years
kiss   kiss[2]

  Perhaps, then, a more pertinent question than "Why did they go to America?" might be "Why did they wait so long?" Strauss's first tour, in 1904, came thirteen years after a lucrative invitation in January 1891 to become the conductor of the New York Symphony Orchestra.[3] Mahler held out a full two decades between the Met's initial approach in 1887 and his acceptance in 1907.[4] Clearly they put it off as long as they could, but eventually common sense, and curiosity, prevailed. The composer who dedicated a work to the twentieth century (literally: *Also sprach Zarathustra* is "dem 20. Jahrhundert gewidmet") would have to visit the country of the twentieth century, just as Mahler would insist on seeing the "charming boy" before it grew into a "frightful Philistine" like its parent, Europe.[5]

  A closer look suggests a network of motivations for these visits, with material factors overlapping with artistic ones. In middle age, Strauss and Mahler saw more easily than before that money could be a means to higher ends. Especially in America, where enormous investment in artistic institutions was producing world-class results—at the Met, for example, which by the early 1900s had attracted the greatest collection of singers in the world—the potential relationship between financial power and elevated creative achievement was readily apparent. Money meant artistic freedom, of a sort craved by both figures. Here we must remember that in 1907 Mahler decided in the spring, not the summer, that it was time to move, which tells us that it was more the consequence of a daily grind than of the tragedies of June that are commonly held to have driven him from Vienna.[6] At the end of another long season at the Court Opera, in the midst of a hostile press campaign, and increasingly weary of opposition from members of his orchestra, he saw deliverance in a contract that would double his salary (36,000 kronen in Vienna, the equivalent of 75,000 at the Met) while reducing his season from ten months to three.[7] For the first time in his career he could devote himself primarily to composition, dreaming that soon he, like Strauss, would be a composer who conducted rather than a conductor who composed.

  Of course, Strauss had achieved that status while managing an equally heavy workload. He would hold full-time conducting positions until 1918, even as he maintained a busy guest-conducting schedule that brought him extra income on a scale approaching that of Mahler's New York salary. (The fees for these events are recorded, concert by concert, in the daily calendar that Strauss kept from 1894 until the end of his life.)[8] But his plan all along had been to retire from the podium once he had a sufficient nest egg. It was his highest goal, one that found expression in the valedictory warmth of "The Hero's Flight from the World and Consummation," the final section of *Ein Heldenleben*. Thus travel to America ultimately served the purpose of *Weltflucht*, as it did for Mahler, who in the summer of 1908 retreated with his hard-earned money to idyllic Toblach and produced *Das Lied von der Erde*, a work nearer to his heart than any other (and one he never heard).

As longtime Wagnerians, Mahler and Strauss knew that artistic productivity was not only compatible with, but could be a function of, the creature comforts in which Americans specialized. The star treatment that came with a US sojourn—a level of celebrity more intense than anything either man had experienced before—encouraged Mahler to emulate Strauss in this area. He discovered happily that in New York he would be "on the same level as Caruso," and he learned to treat himself like Caruso—relaxing more, taking naps, and pampering himself (relatively) in a manner he had so often noticed in Strauss.[9] The latter had preached this lifestyle consistently to Mahler, advocating a bourgeois version of Wagner's predilection for satin and tapestries. Now the advice was taken, particularly in light of the diagnosis in July 1907 of a defective heart valve; Mahler specified the physical conditions necessary for his creative work, stipulating in his Met contract free accommodations at a first-class hotel (the Majestic in 1907–08, the Savoy at Fifth Avenue and Central Park South in the other three seasons), where he would be kept in a style befitting the trophy that he was: in a "ready-made home," as Alma called it (figure 7). He relaxed in the opera house as well, turning a blind eye to cuts that he had resisted strenuously in Vienna.[10] And when Conried left his position and Mahler found himself eyed as his successor, he categorically refused to become once again a director, even if this choice would reduce his influence at the Met and thus open an opportunity for Toscanini. After two decades, conducting would now cease to be a matter of life and death, and it would take a back seat to composition.

Figure 7. Mahler on the streets of New York, 1910. Courtesy of The Kaplan Foundation, New York.

As a presumed onetime visitor, Strauss, whose tour lasted from February 24 through April 28, 1904, enjoyed even greater luxury.[11] In city after city he was wined and dined, at receptions, banquets, and high society men's clubs (the Strollers Club, the Lotus Club), always welcoming the adulation with bemused gratitude. Other American experiences, however, interested him more. At one posh dinner, Walter Damrosch concluded his *laudatio* with the wish that Strauss would compose a "Symphonia Americana," complete with music to capture "the effect of great twenty-four-story skyscrapers."[12] Not surprisingly, precisely this notion was already percolating in the composer's imagination; walking the streets of Manhattan, Strauss gazed in rapt awe at the achievements in architecture and engineering, which even at that early date far exceeded anything in Europe. "To my eye the giant twenty-story buildings are splendid and beautiful," he wrote to his parents in a mood of aesthetic wonder. "In their proportions they are wonderfully wrought."[13]

Technology proved to be an area where the guests and their hosts could learn from one another. In the city's towering architecture, Strauss and Mahler saw a reflection of their own compositions—marvels of musical engineering that Americans for all their ingenuity could neither conceive nor construct nor manage. Critics struggled for the words to describe the technical miracles in Strauss's tone poems. "The marvel of their technical construction is never-ending," wrote Richard Aldrich in the *New York Times*; a counterpart in Boston raved, "his grasp of the orchestra and its possibilities seems almost super-human."[14] One form of technological miracle met another, as "modern Germans" taught their new friends the logistics of achieving in art what had been formed in the skyline.[15] With their money Americans would buy a lesson in the technical know-how necessary for this kind of artistic achievement.

Up-to-date practical knowledge was no less important in the performance hall, where Americans hoped to learn from the Europeans' management style. Neither conductor disappointed. Mahler had a cross word for no one (at least in the early going), but he made his high expectations clear enough. "I am the most amiable man in the world, but I expect my people to do their duty and to do it quickly," he explained to his Met players.[16] Preparing the March 21, 1904, premiere of his *Symphonia domestica* with the Wetzler Orchestra at Carnegie Hall, the ever-efficient Strauss took two rehearsals to accomplish what Hermann Hans Wetzler had not brought about in thirteen. And in business dealings too they showed a tendency to quiet ruthlessness. Even while negotiating with Conried, Mahler communicated separately with Oscar Hammerstein, Conried's archenemy, putting all sides on notice that he would control his destiny.[17] Strauss, after conducting two performances of the Philadelphia Orchestra in Boston, raised his fee for an engagement leading the city's own orchestra, knowing that Boston society could not allow Philadelphia to have the upper hand in this unrepeatable opportunity.[18]

As they explored interrelationships among wealth, technology, and art, all in the context of a visit to a foreign land, Mahler and Strauss found a unique opportunity for self-reflection. They could read about themselves in newspapers (with the help of bilingual friends), watch the reactions of unexpectedly cultured audiences, and learn from the buzz they created in a country eager to define itself through its reception of important European artists. This opportunity came just as the first biographical treatments of Mahler and Strauss were beginning to circulate; Gustav Brecher's *Richard Strauss: Eine monographische Skizze* appeared in 1900, Erich Urban's *Richard Strauss* in 1901, Ludwig Schiedermair's *Gustav Mahler: Eine biographisch-kritische Würdigung* in 1901, and Richard Specht's *Gustav Mahler* in 1905. Both composers had some inkling, then, that they were to be historical figures, and this realization had an impact on men who, in their early forties, had long careers behind them and a hope, if not an expectation, of many more years in which to shape a creative legacy.[19] Who were they, really, and how would they be perceived by posterity? America provided them with a chance to look at themselves from a new vantage point.

Self-obsession may have been the strongest bond between these two composers. For both of them, the question of the self's relationship to the world—the confrontation of subject and object—served as the ultimate motive for creative activity. It formed the setting of a parallel evolution, through phases of youthful impetuosity, mature confidence/bravado, and late resignation. Mahler and Strauss used music not only to express themselves but to define themselves, to invent themselves. And for both of them the American visit came at a crucial moment in this unfolding narcissism.

Each composer had spent the 1890s creating orchestral works that dramatized confrontations between subjectivity and objectivity. The battles of Till, Zarathustra, Don Quixote, and the hero of Strauss's "heroic life" were not far removed from the saga of the protagonist who lived, died, and found redemption in Mahler's first two symphonies, nor from the encounters between creation and individual ("what the flowers in the meadow tell me," "what the animals in the forest tell me," etc.) presented in the Third. All of these works trace the progress of an individual—implicitly the composer himself—trying to find his place in the world.

When the time came to present themselves to America as composers, Strauss and Mahler chose works that foregrounded these issues. Strauss made the centerpiece of his trip the unveiling of the *Symphonia domestica* (1903), his first tone poem in five years and the only one to receive its first performance outside of Germany. A sequel of sorts to *Ein Heldenleben*, this conflicted work includes moments that match the most beautiful and compelling in Strauss's oeuvre, but its lasting impression is extensive, detailed, almost photographic programmaticism leading to an absurdly boisterous climax that makes the ending of Beethoven's Fifth seem psychologically understated. The symphony is anything but "domestic," in other words, and it offers little help to the listener in deciding whether these are the monomaniacal ravings of an unchecked ego or a serious claim (made through irony) about the fading aesthetic justification for symphonic grandiloquence. Of all Strauss's autobiographical statements to that point, this one seems at once the most accurate and the most strange.

Mahler had similar works available when he decided, in his second season (1908–09), finally to present one of his own works.[20] His Fifth and Seventh Symphonies cry out for programmatic explanations—notwithstanding his claim to have given up program music—and they end with famously manic, over-the-top celebrations that made even those who loved him uncomfortable.[21] Sandwiched between these is the heart-rending Sixth, a crushing tragedy so personal that he could barely stand to conduct it. (As mentioned in the introduction, his breakdown in the green room after the dress rehearsal was interrupted by Strauss, who asked obliviously, "what's the matter with him?")[22] But after briefly considering a debut with the Seventh, Mahler turned away from his recent works and their cyclothymic zigzagging, returning instead to the Second, a symphony identified by Stephen Hefling as perhaps his most intricately autobiographical.[23]

The reception of these two performances—the premiere of *Symphonia domestica* on March 21, 1904, and Mahler's performance of the Second with the Philharmonic Society on December 8, 1908—highlights an important distinction in how the composers were regarded even before their arrival. Strauss came to America having established himself, as far as this audience was concerned, as "the man of the hour in the musical world" (*New York Times*, February 28, 1904). In Boston, home of the nation's best orchestra, a critic could write that "Richard Strauss is universally acknowledged to be the greatest of living composers" (*Boston Globe*, March 6, 1904). Chicago billed him as "Dr. Richard Strauss, the Greatest Living Composer" (*Chicago Tribune*, April 3, 1904), and Philadelphia, Cleveland, and Pittsburgh followed suit. "This is not a matter of conjecture, but a fact," readers were told as far west as Portland, Oregon (*Sunday Oregonian*, March 13, 1904) (figure 8).

When it came time for critics to pass judgment on *Domestica*, then, they trod lightly, notwithstanding flirtatious provocations from the composer. In the lead-up to the premiere, which took place in the culminating fourth concert of Wetzler's Richard Strauss Festival, Strauss played coy with reporters who wanted programmatic details. "Be kind enough to accept a work of mine for once without any other explanation than its title. The music must speak for itself, and I regret exceedingly that I do not find it in my power to add thereto any preliminary glossary of my own."[24] Of course the music made him a liar, with alarm clocks, a baby's bath, several minutes of energetic connubial activity, and a violent argument. But what was the response? In a word, deference. "Whatever opinion may be held of Dr. Strauss's musical ideals, of his methods, and of the results of them as embodied in his music, it is unquestionable that he is the foremost figure in the world of music to-day," wrote the usually imperious Richard Aldrich.[25] Critical reservations were voiced here and there—"the whole thing seems incredibly out of proportion"; "Dr. Strauss's desire to have this work heard as music and to speak for itself under its title is an inexplicable one"[26]—but in the end, critics found ways around their own judgments in order to jibe with the predictable adulation of the public: "I find that with greater familiarity the programme part recedes more and more, and I listen to the works now almost entirely as music pure and simple."[27] With the collected elite of New York regarding him expectantly—"princes of finance, dictators of society, queens of opera, autocrats of the baton, lords and ladies of the piano and violin, and all the rest"[28]—Strauss made

> **STRAUSS, THE MOST FAMOUS OF LIVING COMPOSERS.**
>
> *Dr. Richard Strauss and his wife Mme. Strauss (de Ahna)*
>
> With the appearance of Dr Richard Strauss at Symphony hall this evening and Tuesday afternoon, the famous Philadelphia orchestra will make its Boston debut by presenting for the first and only times in this city the acknowledged master of modern music, who will conduct this splendid organization in his own works.
>
> The place that Richard Strauss will occupy in the records of the future is yet to be determined. There is, however, no gainsaying the fact that he stands today the towering genius of his immediate age. He is accepted and welcomed as such by his own countrymen. He has been so acknowledged by all of Europe, including staid and stolid London.
>
> Immortalized in poetry by the late Henley in his last and perhaps his greatest poem, and therein ranked with Tolstoi and Rodin, he now comes to this newer part of the world to enlarge his conquest and broaden the foundation upon which he rests his fame.
>
> By common consent he is the arch revolutionist in the world of music. Whether or not his leadership will result in a new republic of musical thought and expression remains to be seen. One thing is certain—his attack on the very essentials of what we have heretofore accepted as a standard has won the sympathy if not the support of the critical and intellectual world.
>
> The only way to form any idea of his rightful claim to greatness is to hear his works as interpreted by himself, and now this opportunity is ours. For the first time in our history we are privileged to view the workings of a master mind in the morning strength of its development.
>
> Second only to the appearance of Dr Strauss will be that of his gifted and charming wife, Frau Strauss de Ahna, who will sing at both of these concerts her husband's songs, accompanied by him. Thus is the opportunity given of viewing the man from two standpoints, and in each instance of having the most authoritative vantage point possible. It is said that those who have not heard Richard Strauss' songs sung by her have not heard them at all.

Figure 8. *Boston Globe*, March 7, 1904.

himself inscrutable, and he got away with it. After that night, as before, he was welcomed as "the one great musical spirit which has made for something new since Wagner laid down his pen."

Mahler had a different experience. Certainly he came to New York as a musician of international reputation, but his compositions were barely known, the Fourth Symphony having received a single performance in 1904, the Fifth in 1905 and 1906. And even as a conductor he was considered at best a second coming of Anton Seidl. "The spectre of the defunct conductor was waved at Mahler from every journalistic side," wrote Marc Blumenberg in the *Musical Courier* of January 8, 1908, "until he must have begun to wonder whether he had come among a nation of children or of fools."[29] William Henderson of the *New York Sun* showed what Mahler could expect, describing him pointedly as an "interpreter" and cautioning that "we do not grow excited over the arrival of new interpreters from Europe, for the sufficient reason that we have already heard many of the best Europe has ever known, and we are fully informed that the present generation is distinctly inferior to that which enlightened us."[30]

The Second would not receive a free pass, then, though Mahler had some reason for confidence, having used it for debuts in Vienna, Munich, and Paris. Moreover, the work's parallels with *Domestica* surely did not escape him; massive forces, grandiloquence, detailed autobiography, programmatic content that the composer refused to divulge—all of this had been a recipe for his friend's success just four years earlier. And for good measure, the Second's choral finale, a none too subtle reference to Beethoven's Ninth, would highlight the essential common ground between Beethoven's and Mahler's artistic projects: contemplation of the individual's place in the world, the striving toward unity between the singular and the collective. Not for the first time, however, Mahler's tendency toward the all-inclusive would hurt him. Aldrich complained of "trivialities and crass contrasts," which undermined "the deep seriousness of the composer's work." Henry Krehbiel noted the audience's positive response—"far more than mere politeness"—but concluded that the work lacked originality; it was more a cleverly assembled pastiche than an authentic emotional confession. Finck too missed the "big thoughts" indicative of a compelling authorial presence, while Henderson heard "passages where the reaching out after infinite detail of expression issued herculean effort and nothing more." And Gilman, the only critic to issue a wholly negative review, juxtaposed the obvious programmaticism with Mahler's reputation as an "unrepentant denigrator of programme-music," then pronounced his judgment: "the thought is without wings."[31]

By and large the response to these two works would be typical of the composers' American reception. For each figure, however, there was one exception. Well before Strauss's arrival, *Tod und Verklärung* had gained a reputation among US audiences as the most profound, serious, and heartfelt among his works.[32] Knowing a winner when he saw one, Strauss included this early tone poem in thirteen of his twenty-two orchestral concerts, in every case as the final piece on the program. (The next most frequently performed were *Till Eulenspiegel* [ten] and *Don Juan* [seven].) One of these concerts was Strauss's lone performance with the New York Philharmonic (March 25, 1904), at which the work's "mystery, the feeling of suspense and of impending fate; the realization of human struggle and aspiration" so captured the audience that the entire twenty-five-minute composition was repeated.[33] Boston listeners responded just as ecstatically, particularly to the work's climactic C-major coda: "Just when he and the orchestra appeared to have given their ultimate degree of power and thrill, there was found to be yet something more in reserve, until the audience was excited to such enthusiastic and voluminous plaudits as perhaps no purely orchestral performance has ever or at any rate rarely before aroused here. Everybody felt the life and freedom of the whole thing."[34] It was not easy to earn that kind of reaction to a performance by the Philadelphia Orchestra in Boston, a city fiercely proud of its own ensemble's reputation as the best in the country. With *Tod und Verklärung*, the impossible was possible. Strauss did not often consent to lower the mask of irony and humor, but in the one case when he did (or at least affected to), he satisfied a powerful craving of his American audience.

Mahler would for once experience something like a sympathetic response after the first American performance of his *Kindertotenlieder*, given on January 26, 1910, with the New York Philharmonic, an orchestra that had been effectively rebuilt for him to take over in the 1909–10 season. More than any work in his oeuvre, this song cycle presents a single, uniform, coherent emotional character, projecting an artistic voice that listeners found easier to process than Mahler's usual mode. Here even Krehbiel, the powerful, pontificating *New York Tribune* critic who gradually became the composer's most vocal antagonist, found something positive to say. "We have not heard any music by Mr. Mahler which has so individual a note," he declared, nor any "so calculated to stir up the imagination and the emotions."[35] What struck Krehbiel particularly was the songs' "poignant sincerity," a confessional aspect that according to

Edward Ziegler of the *Herald* left the audience in a state of stunned reverence: "absolutely no attempt at applause was made until the series ended[;] the audience called the singer and the composer out again and again." The elevated tone resonated even with critics who rejected the set, such as Max Smith, who noted "the composer's honest and energetic efforts to express the most profound feelings" but found "not a scintilla of inspiration."[36]

The reactions to these two cases of high seriousness are most notable for what they lack: complaints about aesthetic disorder and fragmentation, which were staples of the critical discussion of both composers in positive as well as negative reviews. Strauss seems almost to have invited this objection, for he allowed the first concert of the tour (February 27, 1904, at Carnegie Hall) to begin with *Also sprach Zarathustra*, his most difficult and diffuse tone poem, and he left it to be conducted not by himself but by Wetzler. In this way he faced down his opposition at the first opportunity; when the next day predictable laments of unevenness arrived—"the power and beauty of much of this music are felt as well as its ugliness"—they had already been trumped by an ovation lasting several minutes from a "large and uncommonly distinguished audience."[37] The rapture that followed the premiere of the *Symphonia domestica*— enthusiasm that motivated the addition of two infamous concerts in Wanamaker's department store at Broadway and Ninth Street—did not preclude grumbles about its "unbelievable noise" and "confusion."[38] Often the technical accomplishment was contrasted with a perceived artistic disorder or outright incoherence; a critic who heard *Also sprach Zarathustra* and *Ein Heldenleben* found that "the marvel of their technical construction is never-ending," but held nonetheless that Strauss had failed in his "larger purpose," so that "the philosophy of the philosophical piece, the psychology of the psychological one do not make their success as such."[39] After a Chicago performance of *Zarathustra* a critic remarked that Strauss's very grasp of Nietzsche was a liability, leading him to produce a work "devoid of melody and beauty," and a New York critic found *Don Quixote* "crassly materialistic prose."[40] Strauss himself would admit of the latter work that "if each part does not come through, it's just chaos"—which in fact is precisely what developed at the second Carnegie Hall concert, when a performance of the tone poem with Pablo Casals had to be restarted.[41] (The incident was reported by Ferruccio Busoni to his wife.)[42]

Nonetheless, Strauss could afford to ignore such reservations, even when he shared them. For Mahler they became an indictment that he could not shake. Damrosch, for example, observed plaintively that "[Mahler] was never able to write in the style of Mahler"; the conductor's vast knowledge overwhelmed the composer, who slipped all too easily into unintentional pastiche, juxtaposing all manner of derivative material in ways both abrasive and incomprehensible.[43] With a performance of his star-crossed First Symphony, offered in New York on December 16, 1909, he used the work's darkness-to-light dramatic contour to position himself once again as a modern-day Beethoven. The critics simply thought it was strange, especially because Mahler declined once more to distribute a program for an obviously programmatic work, and thus left himself misunderstood.[44] The episodic qualities of these ostensible symphonies, programmatically motivated or not, were irreconcilable with traditional (classico-romantic) musical structure and meaning—which is to say that they were incoherent. Reginald De Koven complained in these terms about the Fourth (heard with the New York Philharmonic on January 17, 1911), a work as different from the early symphonies as one can find in Mahler's oeuvre. Although "the composer writes fluently with even Haydnesque simplicity at times," and in spite of "Mr. Mahler's expressed disclaimer that he never wrote program music," his desire to keep up with Strauss moved him "to shake out the whole bag of tricks of the modern musical juggler [...] with bewildering and quite unintelligible effect."[45] For Krehbiel, Mahler's fondness for folksong, "one of the most amiable traits of his musical nature," was here corrupted by "so much modern sophistication in harmony, modulation, and orchestration," that "a general effect of fragmentariness and disjointedness is conveyed instead."[46] Aldrich likewise noticed the juxtaposition of modernist "daring" with the "naive" and "archaic," which he interpreted as irony, if not comedy: "it is hard to take this symphony seriously [...] it is what the painters would call 'amusing.'"[47]

It emerges here that American critics with very different attitudes could listen to very different works and hear stylistic elements that we would identify as central to Mahler's art: the ironic, the trivial, the irrecoverable naive, the transitory sublime, and the piecing-together of all these in a manner highlighting rather than hiding the "fractures" in which Adorno would locate Mahler's ethical authority.[48] What they did not hear was a "why." They did not perceive a reason for these choices, and indeed they did not recognize in Mahler's music the authority or confidence that in their narrow view distinguished artistic "choices" from the necessities imposed by lack of ability. Or, to put it in romantic terms, they did not hear a distinctive self striving for expression through coherent artistic means. They heard a mishmash of irreconcilable selves—and that, although they did not realize it, was precisely the point of the music.

An informed reading of Mahler's utterances in the popular press might have been sufficient to overcome this problem. In the *New York Times*, for example, he gave a remarkably direct statement of his creative project, for those capable of grasping his meaning: "The longing to express myself musically comes over me only in the realm of obscure feelings, at the threshold of the world beyond, the world in which the categories of time and space rule no more."[49] Without a background in German philosophy the New York critics could not see the implications of pursuing that kind of metaphysical project sixty years removed from Schopenhauer's *Die Welt als Wille und Vorstellung* (1844). Mahler knew that he could never cross that threshold. For the romantics, a fragmented subjectivity (such as Schumann's) could still look to the musical metaphysics of an E. T. A. Hoffmann as a dream of a higher unity. For a composer looking back sentimentally on romanticism from a postmetaphysical age, fragmentation meant the musical embodiment of a vain hope, a discredited Absolute—the building up of musical triumphs that cannot help but undermine themselves. In this respect the formal disjunctures of Mahler and those of Strauss share a crucial philosophical honesty, though neither of them managed to get the message through to audiences in the United States. If American listeners seemed to give Strauss a fairer hearing than they did Mahler, it was because they misinterpreted the symptoms of critique differently in the two cases.

Such considerations begin to explain Mahler's extraordinary devotion as conductor of the New York Philharmonic to *Till Eulenspiegel*, Strauss's "manifesto" of postmetaphysical subjectivity.[50] In November 1909, facing a debut with his new orchestra that would be even more closely scrutinized than his first performances at the Met, Mahler opted to close the program not with something of his own but with Strauss's fable of individual rebellion against the collective. He would go on to perform it nine more times that season, more than any other composition; for the final program, the last of the "historical concerts" surveying the Western canon, he would place it once again at the end of the evening. But what attracted Mahler to this tone poem above all others? Strauss managed here, with a likeable iconoclasm that no one could emulate, to spell out the dilemmas that Mahler's listeners would have to understand if they were to make sense of his own very different solutions. The nature of the modern subject was mercurial, ironic, and critical—certain of nothing but the insufficiency of any authority, whether religious or scientific, to define an intellectual or moral absolute. The guises in which Till appears thus embody a kind of musical nihilism, in that they each refer back to the spirit of iconoclasm generated by the takedown of Wagner's *Tristan* chord (m. 47). This rejection of centeredness would receive a more grim embodiment one year later with the clash of B and C at the end of *Also sprach Zarathustra*. In the context of this and the other later, grander, weightier Strauss tone poems, *Till* had a unique incisiveness, which lifted it from a surefire crowd-pleaser to a musico-philosophical statement that after only fourteen years justified (in Mahler's view) the label "historical."

The tone poem succeeded under Mahler's baton as under Strauss's, but it did nothing for Mahler's own works. The First was a "failure," he wrote to Schoenberg with not a hint of surprise.[51] In the end even that first attempt was too big a leap into the future for these American audiences. They resisted the pull, as they resisted the more forward-looking features of Mahler's conducting. Even the favorably disposed Aldrich could not help noting with raised eyebrows that Mahler "does not hesitate to revise Beethoven's scoring," a tendency that Aldrich identified explicitly as "modern."[52] (Many German critics took the same view; Robert Hirschfeld, for example, wrote of the revised Ninth Symphony, "with it Mahler has asserted himself as a modernist.") Mahler of course granted the point, and reinforced it with the Philharmonic's "historical concerts," in which original instrumentation was respected (right down to Mahler's performance of continuo parts on a "spinet" specially prepared for him by the Steinway company).[53] But with concerts not marked as "historical," Mahler did not hesitate to revise his own compositions or other composers'—even Strauss's—because "in every performance the work must be born anew."[54] No means must be spared, he believed, because to play music was to attempt the impossible, to bridge the gap between the free-floating individual and a realm of truth that did not exist. It was an act of hope, on a plane of private philosophical contemplation and private philosophical action that Americans could not begin to fathom.

Strauss saw this danger all too well. In his own performances of other composers' music in America, he maintained a discreet reserve, which was appreciated. His concert with the Philharmonic included a reading of Mozart's *Jupiter*, in which "there was no injection of the unquiet modern spirit into its serene and lovely utterance," according to the critic for the *Times*. He continued: "there were subtle touches that gave animation, spirit, vivacity, to it, and there was an understanding of the music as a vital expression of emotion, in the eighteenth century idiom […] all this was delicately and suggestively realized in the spirit of Mozart."[55] That is not to say the interpretation was flat, or impersonal; a different critic for the same newspaper wrote that "Dr. Strauss touched some unfamiliar and peculiarly responsive chords through his performance of one of the most familiar works of Mozart."[56] Understanding full well the American suspicion of the "virtuoso conductor," who "is tempted to magnify his office and justify his existence by giving 'new' or 'original' or highly 'characteristic' readings," Strauss applied a dose of his typical modesty, and it took him a long way.[57]

CHAPTER 10

Allusionists

ANY BROAD CONSIDERATION of musical style in Mahler and Strauss immediately confronts a paradox. The mature music of each composer is instantly recognizable; no experienced listener would mistake one for the other, even in the remarkable moments when the artists pay unspoken homage to one another. (One example: after the music of a child's games in *Symphonia domestica* turned up in the Sixth Symphony, Strauss returned the favor by echoing the Sixth's cowbells in *Eine Alpensinfonie*.)[1] Yet in like manner no connoisseur listens for long without hearing unmistakable traces of other people's music. This feature holds true across the composers' work, from student experiments through late masterpieces. If these derivative moments have slowly faded from consciousness with the shrinking number of listeners deeply familiar with the repertoire, they nonetheless drew enormous attention, both negative and positive, during the twenty-five or so years when Mahler and Strauss were both active creatively. For the composers and for their audience it represented a defining feature of the music, for better or worse, and most especially with respect to these works' character as harbingers of twentieth-century musical style.

The variety of allusive modes tempts one to formulate a typology of borrowing: out-and-out quotation has a different effect than subtle allusion, accidental reminiscence, technically determined stylistic echo, and so on.[2] Often, however, disentangling the categories proves impossible or hopelessly speculative, not only because the composers would not tell us what they were doing but because they themselves did not know. The instinctive dimension is already clear from the fact that one type is rarely activated to the exclusion of all others. We can see easily enough, for example, that imitation formed the core of the learning process, whether in the formal training that Strauss received from Friedrich Wilhelm Meyer or the informal autodidactic regimen practiced by Mahler in Iglau.[3] But for artists at this level, maturity arrived unexpectedly early and in flashes, so that imitation became manipulation before anyone realized what was happening, in a manner that in hindsight one might dare to call "original." Allusion was itself a tried-and-true device of musical romanticism, and one that in the Schumann-Brahms relationship showed how a style whose day had passed, at least as a living aesthetic, could bridge the gap to a modern present while also reaching back to an even more remote past (classicism).[4] Given the battles raging over style during Mahler's and Strauss's youths—with journals and composers' societies that sharply defined the lines of the conflict—a young composer was required to put influence on display out of political necessity. All of these factors encouraged creative borrowing, then, before we even begin to consider the effect of the rising modernist aesthetic of appropriation that would be so fundamental to European composition in the first decades of the new century.

It makes less sense to look for a stable meaning in these instances, then, than to consider what competing or collaborating possibilities might exist. Strauss obviously enjoyed composing out his own response to music, whether it was the eighteenth-century cosmopolitan repertoire from which he fashioned the collage of *Capriccio*, or his own youthful works, already judged classics (with tongue in cheek) in *Ein Heldenleben*.[5] Mahler's examples may seem less overt, but if we bear in mind the musical knowledge and stylistic sensitivity of his well-educated audience, his citational freedom seems just as determinedly provocative. "Music about music," to use a phrase that critics applied to the works of both composers, might almost be called the music they most longed to create.[6]

The first career goal set for the young Strauss by those in charge of his artistic development was to become a skilled musical parrot. Yet imitation was not just the principal tool of musical pedagogy; it was the principal tool of all pedagogy, in a time when the humanistic tradition of emulating literary and intellectual authority figures reigned supreme in the gymnasium. Thus when Meyer demanded chamber music and then smaller orchestral movements in the style of Mozart and Haydn, he required the equivalent of what Strauss's schoolmasters asked regarding the classical poets through whose works the youngster learned Latin and Greek. These assignments suited the student's talents and personality almost too well, for despite the brilliant accuracy of his imitations, we do not see, as in the case of Mendelssohn, a striking early move toward originality. (The seventeen-year-old Strauss produced nothing like the miraculous overture to *A Midsummer Night's Dream*, despite musical training and opportunities similar to Mendelssohn's, if less posh.)

Curiously, one finds that as Strauss approached maturity he intensified the citational quality of his music. The borrowings become more obvious, not less, and the sources are frequently the best-known works in the canon. As a result, the listener's contemplation of intertextuality becomes a compulsory element of the interpretive process. The op. 10 lieder are a case in point. This set announced the arrival of a composer whose gift for song composition would place him alongside Schubert and Schumann; it has been among Strauss's most performed works for over a century. In perhaps the most beautiful number, however, "Die Nacht," Strauss offered music so overtly indebted to Schumann's "Mondnacht" (from the Eichendorff cycle, op. 39) that ignorance of the source removes the song's principal level of meaning. The delicate, shimmering chimes of the accompaniment, over which the lyrical vocal melody floats past, are themselves a commentary on Schumann's uncanny synthesis of emotional expression and pictorialism. Strauss brings us back to that moment as if to gaze at it from the outside, and thus perhaps to highlight its potential, to recall it as a cherished model of technical and expressive possibility.

Calling attention to preexisting music would soon become a hallmark of Strauss's mature artistic personality, in direct contradiction of an imperative to originality that remained widely in effect even with the approach of a new century. (It would be the most powerful inner compulsion in Schoenberg's personality, for example.) The more obvious these references, the better, even in the pieces with which the young man tried to make his reputation, such as the Piano Sonata, op. 5, the first movement of which openly and excessively rehearses the motive from Beethoven's Fifth Symphony.[7] Reflecting on this and similar instances (many of them discussed by R. Larry Todd in his seminal essay on the early music), Franz Strauss may well have thought that his demand of faithfulness to the classics had backfired, although in these early years the potential of this technique to function as a critique of the source would not have been clear to him and perhaps not to his son. The crucial step for Strauss, and one that he took fairly quickly (i.e., in the mid-1880s), was the recognition that citations could be played off one another, made to comment on the sources' individual expressive capacity and on the personality of the creator who had placed them in juxtaposition.

From this standpoint, the crucial observation to be made about Strauss's musical personality in the 1880s is not his apparent shift from becoming a second Brahms (following the formula Haydn/Mozart+Schumann/Mendelssohn=Brahms) to becoming a fourth New German (or "Richard the Third," as Bülow christened him, there being no room for a "Richard the Second"). The essence of Strauss at this stage is rather a consistent aesthetic of appropriation and juxtaposition, a witting critical method wide enough to encompass *Aus Italien* (1886), the *Burleske* (1886), and the Violin Sonata (1887). We need not be perplexed that the first programmatic orchestral music predated a major chamber work—or indeed that the Violin Sonata came after the ostensible "conversion"—if we note that in all three works an aggressive but playful pastiche takes center stage. Brahms confronts Wagner in the *Burleske*, Liszt meets Brahms in the Sonata, and in *Aus Italien*, dedicated to Bülow (friend and enemy of both Brahms and Wagner), all three modern masters are brought into contact with their classical and romantic forebears. This game, played with increasing finesse and even, on occasion, elegance, would remain a staple of

Strauss's creative technique as he traveled from genre to genre over the next six decades.

Mahler wrote far less music than Strauss in his childhood and teenage years, and little survives—even from his three-year tenure at the Vienna Conservatory, where he distinguished himself in the eyes of everyone, whether they liked him or not. The dearth of student compositions reflects first of all the lack of encouragement to compose; while the father provided a piano so that Mahler could develop his obvious talent, he did not demand creative products (as did Franz Strauss). But if the urge to compose came late, the need to know the full range of existing music, and to perform this music, was as strong in Mahler as in any great musician. (In fact Mahler holds the extraordinary distinction of having been beaten by a parent for practicing too much.)[8] His skill as a pianist, which in his mid-teen years gained him a reputation as a rising virtuoso and later would be the proximate cause of his departure for Vienna, reflected no desire whatsoever for the kind of spotlight directed at a professional soloist. It was a byproduct of his private interest in music, as Julius Epstein, the conservatory teacher who accepted him into his class, instantly recognized. What really got Epstein's attention was the Wagnerian tone of Mahler's adolescent compositions (if they were "compositions" at all and not improvisations written down after the fact). Only here, in the compellingly authentic appropriation of Wagner's powerful voice, did Mahler strike Epstein as potentially a genius.

From the beginning, then, Mahler's fortunes as a composer were bound up with issues of citation—what seemed to be overt attempts to make a meaningful artistic statement with previously existing material. Rarely would this tendency win him admirers again. During his lifetime it would elicit the repeated accusation that he composed "gigantic pots-pourris," a complaint that would persist even in the 1960s as Leonard Bernstein struggled to convince a skeptical Vienna Philharmonic.[9] Among supporters, it would mostly be ignored; even Henry-Louis de La Grange would conclude his extended systematic study of the types of borrowing (including an appendix of some sixty-one examples) with the oddly dismissive remark that "they really do not matter all that much."[10] Most strangely, Mahler was known to complain of reminiscences in others' music (for example Zemlinsky's), and even confessed annoyance with himself for unintentional borrowings from Beethoven and Brahms in the Fourth Symphony.[11]

None of this endangers the dual conclusions, however, that listeners in Mahler's time were right to hear a pastiche quality in his music (given the average educated person's considerable familiarity with the repertoire from which he borrowed), and that Mahler both recognized this tendency and let it run free, because he thought it served some artistic end. Two factors condition a reading of his motivations: first, his often-remarked willingness to draw from all types of music, exalted or trivial, cultivated or folk; and second, his rarely discussed treatment of all these types as equally capable of expression, both in terms of emotional power and of type of affective content. The early symphonies make it perfectly clear that in the juxtapositions of high and low, or significant and trivial, or learned and vernacular, the deepest feelings, whether tragic or hopeful, may be attached to either side of the equation. His remarks to Freud on the connection of the tragic and the trivial in his music only confirmed what was always obvious; what mattered was not what he cited but what it could be made to do. (In musical technique, Wagner and Brahms would likewise value treatment over material, as a response to the problem of how to make every moment of music significant.)[12] Moreover, the vast range of uses to which Mahler put his preexisting music—La Grange identifies no fewer than ten, ranging from conscious quotation, homage, and allusion to unconscious reminiscence—itself indicates that he consciously shut down whatever editorial faculty he possessed that would have purged such things. He did not want to purge them, and he did not want to control them, at least not in a simplistic, intention-based sense inappropriate in a work of art. He wanted them to speak, in whatever manner his unfettered creative instincts might bring about.

The importance of this element of Mahler's creative personality can be seen in the fact that it was untouched by accusations of a lack of "internal coherence" in his music. When this charge was directed at his expressly programmatic compositions, Mahler gave up program music. When it was aimed at his citational extravagance, he continued as before. That is why one can find more or less the same intertextual approaches operating in the major groupings of his works: the *Wunderhorn* symphonies, the ostensibly absolute symphonies of the middle period, and the late works. In the third movement of the First Symphony, the most striking example of borrowing is not the programmatically motivated "Brother Martin" funeral march, or the otherworldly "Two Blue Eyes," but the grotesquely jovial gypsy band that intrudes "with parody" into a musical genre that holds no place for bad music or bad musicians.[13] Where the other two examples rely for their effect on the listener's knowledge of a specific source, this manipulative device had a more general efficacy because it used not a piece but a style, one that any concertgoer could both recognize, and recognize as inappropriate. The "parody" serves only to intensify the strangeness of its emergence in this context.

This passage enraged the work's first listeners, because it disallows internal coherence and subjectively centered originality, focusing our attention on the creator's reception of external sources rather than on some revelatory inner vision. We hear not the artist but the confrontation between artist and world. Just this kind of disruption returns in the fifth movement of the Fifth Symphony, another work that is thought to have initiated a discrete period in Mahler's output. The reliance on Bruckner is strong in this symphony, even for Mahler, but it is simultaneously undermined by our hearing not only Bruckner but, even more powerfully, the Baroque sources from which Bruckner drew his inspiration. As in the First, however, these are parodied, not with ill will (and there was no ill will in the First) but with the closest thing to Nietzschean "high spirits" that is to be found in Mahler. Now it is the *treatment* of the source, not the source itself, that seems inappropriate; the greater emphasis on the parodic dimension prevents the listener from engaging with the music as a mere neo-Baroque composition (analogous to the stylized historicist architecture to be found in cities like Vienna and Munich). It is an aggressively distortive reception, a parody, as in the First. Again the source is a style, not a particular work, and thus the citational quality can be missed by no one. And again the treatment diverts our attention from the composer to the composer's relationship with something external; we leave aside reflection on originality to focus on creation as reception.

In the non-western tone of *Das Lied von der Erde*, especially the overtly eastern gestures of "Von der Jugend," parody is in a strict sense impossible; as recognizable as the stylistic allusion may be (in its vaguely "oriental" quality), no one, including Mahler, had sufficient knowledge of authentic Asian music to know the difference between a faithful appropriation and a manipulative one. There is no doubt that manipulation, albeit unconscious, is going on here, however; we simply do not know what has changed. And thus we are left again perceiving Mahler as a composer who operates through encounters with the outside. His music stages the process by which the composer finds meaning in music that is not his own, and thus it creates its own meaning. A pentatonic string of eight notes played by the oboe and flute is sufficient to draw the distinction between the composer and a distinct external source (mm. 3–6). Whatever affective differences may obtain among the contentedly generic eastern stasis of this movement, the manic historicism of the Fifth, and the coarse rural processing of the First, these instances represent a consistent citational technique that worked because almost no advance preparation was required (certainly not the knowledge of particular musical works). Its main result, whatever other effects it may have had, was to make the reading of art itself the subject of art. And that practice can be found across Mahler's oeuvre, perhaps because he always knew that his art would pose unique challenges to interpretation.

Although composed musical works begin as monologues, they become conversations when the composer introduces (consciously or otherwise) "external" music, whether it be a particular work or merely a distinguishable musical style. This expressive disunity, the aural splintering of authorial perspectives, binds the music of Mahler with that of Strauss more strongly than any purely stylistic common ground—harmonic language, orchestrational virtuosity, formal magnitude, polyphonic density, and so on. Within their works, different kinds of music confront one another, not necessarily in a struggle for supremacy, but with a disruptive heterogeneity that proposes an alternative truth to the metaphysical essence revered by romantic musical thinkers from Wackenroder, Hoffmann, and Mendelssohn to Schopenhauer, Wagner, the young Nietzsche, Schoenberg, and indeed Hanslick.[14] Their works conceive and embody a modernist truth, overt perspectivism, a critique that does away with the old category but substitutes something more interesting, refreshingly honest, and "earthly" (as Nietzsche might say).

The disruption produced by intertextuality is equivalent to the physicalizing (de-metaphysicalizing) effect of tone painting, which begins to explain the similarly violent reaction against both among Mahler's and Strauss's critics. Tone painting challenges the integrity of a musical utterance, by introducing sounds the ultimate source of which is obviously different from the centered creative subject presumed to be controlling the artwork. The technique produces, as its critics often insist, not music in any pure sense, but musically inflected noise. And as such it interrupts the seamless aesthetic experience required by a listener who hopes to be transported to what Dahlhaus called an "alternate reality" (*Gegenwelt*). Probably the most important contribution of Adorno to our understanding of Mahler is his clarification of the composer's own role in his works' failures—the music problematizes the redemption that it seeks, but in the process of failure generates a fleeting image of what redemption might look like.[15] Tone painting and intertextuality are close collaborators in this process; in fact they are two sides of the same coin, for in drawing our attention to the composer's handling of an external source, they both break the spell of autonomy.

One may hear the cofunctioning of these elements in the Sixth Symphony, Mahler's composed-out fantasy of his own downfall. The composer's fondness for march rhythms here reaches what Jean Matter called an "obsession," which, beyond the specific associations of the military or some more general kind of struggle, again puts Mahler in the position of making music about a specific type of music.[16] Scholars often identify this tendency in Mahler (recently, for example, Anette Unger) without, however, noting the impetus for requiring the art to reflect on itself: the music and the musician ask whether they are capable of being what they are believed to be, knowing in advance that they are not.[17] The downfall of the composer in the Sixth is likewise the downfall of his art; we know this from precisely the self-consciousness of the recurring march topic, a clamorous insistence that testifies to its own inadequacy. This stylistic link to the world outside the work is complemented by some bracingly specific intertextual allusions, for example to Saint-Saëns's *Danse macabre* (with the xylophone) and to Strauss's *Symphonia domestica*. (As mentioned above, the trio of the scherzo movement, a delicate but lively 3/8 theme in D major for the oboe, represents the "arrhythmic playing" of two children with a near echo of the music used by Strauss for his "childlike play, parental happiness.")[18] Constantin Floros pointed out parallels with *Tod und Verklärung* (the hammer) and called the Sixth the "counterpart to Strauss's *Ein Heldenleben*."[19] The most powerful attempt to reach outside the work, however, comes with the shocking intrusion of the cowbells, an idea that he did not get from Strauss but that shows Mahler responding positively to the trend in Strauss's later orchestral works toward musical imitation of sounds in the real world. Musically rendering the sounds that he hears in his everyday environment, Mahler blurs the distinction between music and sound, and between himself as composer and the aural world. The finale intensifies the process by resorting to bells, a hammer, a whip, and a wood rattle; the line between work and world is no longer capable of keeping anything out, just as it no longer separates the artist from the world he addresses.

In *Eine Alpensinfonie*, which served not only as musical "Antichrist" but as elegy for Mahler, the most direct homage to Strauss's dead friend involves the Sixth Symphony. As Tim Ashley and Norman Del Mar have observed, Strauss's incorporation of cowbells, Mahlerian birdcalls, and a static magical, bucolic atmosphere act as a plaintive memorial in the midst of a work methodically devoted to personal fulfillment through anti-Mahlerian ideals.[20] When Strauss rededicated himself to the *Alpensinfonie* after Mahler's death (see chapter 6), he confirmed that he saw the Mahler of the Sixth as the authentic Mahler, a pathetic figure who embraced his own doom. Four years later Strauss would ponder the physical and the metaphysical, without mentioning Mahler but obviously with him in mind: "[I] am a German [*Germane*], to whom the *sight* of a magnificent mountain vista, the blue sky above it, in the radiant, warming sun, represents the summit of the attainable and the desirable. I rejoice in it, it keeps me healthy and gives me joy for *work*. An unproductive race such as that of the Jews could concoct this Christian, Jewish metaphysics, would put speculation in the place of production [...] When will the German race finally have expelled the frightful bacterium: Christianity, i.e., Neo-Judaism, from its blood?" (emphasis in original).[21] If Strauss's life had a central meaning for him at that time, it was that through a deeply reflective artistic project he had confronted the musico-intellectual tradition of metaphysical romanticism and rejected it. Thus the *Alpensinfonie* was at once a regretful reminiscence of Mahler, a Nietzschean critique of Mahler's central weakness, and a celebration of the personal strength—intellectual, artistic, spiritual—that had allowed Strauss to triumph where his friend had been destroyed.

The locus and character of that celebration are carefully laid out in the *Alpensinfonie*, through a network of allusions set off by the carefully painted arrival on the summit. Strauss clinches the self-reflective point not just by citing himself, as he did in other autobiographical works (*Heldenleben*, *Symphonia domestica*, and, later, *Intermezzo*), but by citing music in which he had cited someone else. A reference to the "Nature" theme from *Also sprach Zarathustra* (m. 597, two before reh. 80), leading to a chorale alluding to the "Brotherhood" theme from *Guntram*—which itself was modeled on the "Grail" leitmotif in *Parsifal*—culminates in the so-called "Bruch-Stelle" (m. 607)—a simultaneous quotation of the Adagio from Max Bruch's Violin Concerto and Strauss's own song "Anbetung," op. 36, no. 4—with its overwhelming *Steigerung* toward a C-major climax as powerful as any that Strauss ever wrote.[22] Thus we have engagement with Nietzsche, engagement with Wagner, and engagement with the music of a conductor's routine, and all three are juxtaposed in an openly pictorial context that restricts our ability to separate music from the mere aural experience of the protagonist. Because the protagonist is himself the composer, we are not permitted to lose ourselves in his vision; we must do as he does, and we must reflect on his own perception of the experience as we wait to see whether the apotheosis is lasting.

Of course it is not, and we return eventually to the bookend of "Night," which interestingly is both an allusion to the main theme of Strauss's Second Symphony and an effective aural depiction of darkness. The need to go back down the mountain is required by more than the mundane reality of the program; Strauss absorbed no Nietzschean lesson more strongly than the fact of always remaining, to some extent, the person one has always been. (Hofmannsthal had by 1915 powerfully reinforced that bit of wisdom in his interactions with his collaborator.) The mountain would have to be climbed every day, in an everlasting cycle between the B-flat minor of "Night" and the C major of the summit. At the work's outer edges, as at the center, the combination of a vivid piece of tone painting with an overt self-referential allusion provided a double-strength critique of autonomy, and thus of the ideology from which Strauss was once again distancing himself, now more forthrightly than ever before. It also recalled Mahler's own fondness for the very same techniques, even as it made the point—a tragic one, in Strauss's view—that Mahler had shied away from the critical potential of these tools, declining to harness their destructive power. In the end, Strauss would have said, that choice had kept Mahler from full self-realization as a thinking musician.

For Strauss and for Mahler there were of course many types of intertextual activity, ranging from deliberate cases that raise complex aesthetic questions, to pure accidents. Even these latter instances, which seem barely worth noting, reveal something important about the topic as a whole. If Mahler tended to grouse when he discovered an unconscious allusion, Strauss often chuckled, even in front of a crowd; he actually used the term "Bruch-Stelle" in rehearsals of the *Alpensinfonie*. Dual careers as conductor and composer made such slips of the pen inevitable, one supposes. Yet for composers who intended to give intertextuality a central role in the creative process, and who recognized (or were beginning to sense) the impossibility of controlling a work's meaning at any stage of its life, carelessness was itself a creative tool, perhaps not wholly distinguishable from inspiration. A composer who borrowed unconsciously would also create meanings that he did not anticipate. Or, to put it in terms of productive uncertainty, a composer who set free his instinctive borrowing also set free his music's creative power.

The fluidity of meaning is a central but rarely discussed element in the "distance" that scholars so often remark in Mahler and Strauss. Henry-Louis de La Grange rightly notes of Mahler that "what makes him already a twentieth-century composer is his manner of distancing himself from his material."[23] Leon Botstein likewise says of Strauss that neither tragedy nor comedy were accessible to him after *Elektra* "without a dimension of distance, self-criticism, and doubt."[24] Implicit in these readings, however, is a separation not just from the material but from the stable conception of self that obtained in Europe for centuries before collapsing in the decades around 1900. Mahler and Strauss retreated from the self at about the same time, and in roughly the same ways. Just as their works leave conflicts unresolved, refusing to impose solutions that would imply a centered creative presence, they allow, and indeed stage, incursions from external presences. And in the composers' recognition of the collapse of the self, and in their abandoning of artistic "self-expression"—the purpose of which had been for most of the nineteenth century to offer a focused, special, individual insight into the world—they left the formation of meaning to the vagaries of interaction between work and audience.

Mahler, for example, had his own "Bruch-Stelle"—an inexcusably obvious allusion to a widely known and loved work—with what we might call the "Brahmsstelle" at the beginning of the Third Symphony (mm. 62–65 in Brahms's First Symphony, fourth movement; mm. 1–4 in the Mahler). Imagining that he did not consciously hear this connection is even more difficult than imagining that he would have let it stand had he recognized it. For reasons that he did not articulate, he chose to engage with Brahms openly, in the main theme of a major work, having been taken to task for such things before (and perhaps also remembering that Brahms had been accused, with precisely this theme but in a later section than the one used by Mahler, of borrowing from Beethoven). The cheekiness of this move seems uncharacteristic of Mahler, but by this time his naiveté had long since been vanquished by experience; he would have known that listeners would take note, and that they would argue over its meaning. The solutions that they proposed could cause no greater difficulties for his music than it had already experienced. The fact of the conversation, however, led people toward the kind of contemplation, sophisticated and open-ended, that Mahler believed was required for an appreciation of his conflict-laden and solution-resisting music.

As discussed in chapter 7, Strauss's "Indian Summer"—a period when he considered his creative life to have officially ended—yielded a series of works that reminisce about the main phases of his compositional activity. Concertos and sonatinas hark back to his youthful love for "absolute" genres; *Metamorphosen* revisits the tone poems, albeit with a striking pessimism far removed from the daring of the 1880s and '90s; and the *Four Last Songs* take up Wagner, using the older composer's harmonic and orchestrational manner to support a lyricism that is fully Straussian. Taken as a group, these works bring Strauss's career to a close in a beautifully open-ended way, tying them together in a set of recollections that simultaneously raise new questions. Whichever Strauss we consider—the promising follower of Brahms, the brash scandal-mongering tone poet, the gifted Wagnerian-turned-traitor who wrenched the Master's technique from its spiritual underpinnings—we find a composer who created by reacting to others' music. These encounters raise questions but cannot provide answers, at least in any final sense. The swirling allusive mélange of *Capriccio* is no more stable than that of *Die schweigsame Frau*, or *Ariadne auf Naxos*, or *Feuersnot*, or the *Burleske*. It sets up opportunities for meaning to be generated in the encounter between listener and music, by placing the composer's own reactive experiences at the center of the artwork. The process is not meant to be controlled by the artist, and he has not foreseen the outcome; that is why so many of Strauss's works end with an understated gesture. The music stops without bringing to an end the process that it initiates.

Mahler's endings attempt the opposite, or seem to, but as Adorno suggested, the struggles that precede those conclusions rule out the apparent closure in advance. The authorial presence in Mahler's music is no less fragmented than in Strauss's; that explains why the composers find it so easy to adopt one another's mode, at least temporarily. (Think of the C-minor gravity shared by *Tod und Verklärung* and the Second Symphony, or the boisterousness of *Symphonia domestica* and the Seventh Symphony.) Neither composer maintained false claims of aesthetic independence, and both turned that reality to their advantage through a new kind of creative honesty.

CHAPTER 11

Ironists

EVEN CASUAL FANS of Mahler and Strauss know that on occasion the music's surface contradicts its meaning. Ochs's amorous waltzes inspire anything but passion; they know how silly they sound, if he does not. Swooning contortions in the Ninth Symphony's "riotously sardonic" Rondo-Burleske stage "an iconoclastic parody of fugal style."[1] The bombast in the *Symphonia domestica* ridicules itself and every similar grand climax. And Bruckner was never less Brucknerian than in his boisterous cameo at the end of the Fifth Symphony. The examples proliferate as one becomes attuned to them; indeed, it is difficult to find a substantial work by either composer in which a precise and expressive musical style is not made to communicate its opposite.

The profusion of these moments has proven overwhelming to critics, especially in Mahler's case. Julian Johnson has surveyed the increasingly nuanced typology, leading from Robert Samuels's "useful distinction between parody (as distortion) and irony (as opposition)," to Alain Leduc's three categories of irony ("parodistic," "critical," and "tragic"), to Stephen E. Hefling's six ("parody, ingenue irony, tragic dramatic irony, ironic ambivalence, bitter incongruity, ironic nostalgia"). Ultimately Johnson concludes, sensibly, that each work might require its own type: "the closer one gets to individual songs and movements, the more discrete categories give way to the particularity of tone in each instance."[2]

Especially in a comparative context, it seems advisable to take a step back. More than any of their Austro-German predecessors, Mahler and Strauss raised questions about their music's seriousness, or more broadly, about the difference between literal and figurative meaning in their works. Mahler pointed explicitly to Aristotelian irony in an 1896 letter to Max Marschalk on the First Symphony's third movement—the definitively Mahlerian moment of the early works—calling it "ironic in the sense of Aristotle's *eironeia*."[3] What did he mean? Drawing on his classical education, Mahler here cited what philosopher Melissa Lane calls "Aristotle's attempt to circumscribe and stabilize the meaning of *eironeia* to suit a technical purpose of rhetoric."[4] Aristotle forcefully appropriated a mercurial Socratic concept, limiting it to the opposition of literal and figurative meaning. Mahler likewise sought to enlist the power of the open lie. Paul Bekker, for one, would read the movement in precisely this way; the work is meant to convey "the feeling that accompanies a shattering emotional event," yet "this event is not given in an agitated, passionate language, but in an apparently unfeeling and unmoving representation," which "heightens the oppressive nature of the impression."[5] Naturally Mahler was influenced as well by romantic precedents, directly and, as Jeremy Barham points out, through mediating influences such as Gustav Fechner's "romantic-ironic penchant for mixing serious and humorous conceptual processes."[6] But in the end his fundamental goal was straightforward: to establish that any expressive gesture could mean its opposite.

Here the mischief began, because a method for increasing precision had the effect of multiplying possible meanings. Strauss and his works would follow a similar path. The young Strauss did not set out to become an ironist; he spent his teenage years gaining a technical mastery of the full spectrum of nineteenth-century styles (and indeed of eighteenth-century ones, especially Mozart). But the resulting facility for musical imitation—imitation being the method by which he learned musical composition—taught him that musical expression could be wielded from an emotional distance. Music could deceive, in other words, and Strauss's knack for musical role-playing gave him a wealth of options for practicing that kind of manipulation. In their emotional specificity these tools were powerful and up-to-date; as Strauss would later explain, the defining quality of late nineteenth-century music was its unprecedented expressive precision. Never before had the musical audience been so finely attuned to such a wide range of stylistic-affective associations, expressive signs that, for a composer with real skill, could be deployed with powerful expectations of reliability. Through Wagner, in particular, music had realized its destiny of a "progression from the reproduction of hazy or general associations to the expression of a more and more precise, individual and intimate circle of ideas."[7] This also meant that expression became more than ever before a function of the technical, at least as long as audiences responded appropriately (and the continuing power of the postromantic style in Classic Hollywood scores of the 1930s and '40s shows just how resilient was this expressive mechanism). Turning these capacities to manipulative purposes was, to a composer of Strauss's facility and sense of humor, a perfectly obvious step.

The classic example of musical irony in Strauss's early maturity is the sumptuous A-flat hymn he provided for "Von den Hinterweltlern" ("Of the Backworldsmen")[8] in *Also sprach Zarathustra* (mm. 35ff.). If the marginalia in his private copy of Nietzsche's text are an accurate indication, this section of the book occupied him more than any save "Der Genesende" ("The Convalescent"), which provided the programmatic stimulus for the breakdown and recovery at the center of the tone poem. Strauss marked four separate passages in "Von den Hinterweltlern," as follows (the second and third are adjacent lines but flagged separately):

> Then the world seemed to me the dream and fiction of a God; colored vapor before the eyes of a discontented God.
> [Traum schien mir da die Welt und Dichtung eines Gottes; farbiger Rauch vor den Augen eines göttlich Unzufriednen.]
>
> Thus I too once cast my deluded fancy beyond mankind, like all afterworldsmen. Beyond mankind in reality?
> [Also warf ich einst meinen Wahn jenseits des Menschen, gleich allen Hinterweltlern. Jenseits des Menschen in Wahrheit?]

> Ah, brothers, this God which I created was human work and human madness, like all gods!
> He was human, and only a poor piece of man and Ego: this phantom came to me from my own fire and ashes, that is the truth. It did not come to me from the "beyond!"
> [Ach, ihr Brüder, dieser Gott, den ich schuf, war Menschen-Werk und -Wahnsinn, gleich allen Göttern!
> Mensch war er, und nur ein armes Stück Mensch und Ich: aus der eigenen Asche und Gluth kam es mir, dieses Gespenst, und wahrlich! Nicht kam es mir von Jenseits!]
>
> Listen rather, my brothers, to the voice of the healthy body: this is a purer voice and a more honest one.
> [Hört mir lieber, meine Brüder, auf die Stimme des gesunden Leibes: eine redlichere und reinere Stimme ist diess.][9]

Having begun his tone poem with the famous C-major vision of Nature, Strauss now moved directly to nature's polar opposite: metaphysical hope. No listener would have doubted Strauss's sympathetic attitude toward Nietzsche here, and so even the most basic familiarity with the philosophical context tells us that Strauss intends to produce a musical lie, a "dream and fiction" that would have to be rejected in favor of the "voice of the healthy body." The composer supplies a beautiful dream indeed ("with devotion" ["mit Andacht"], mm. 35ff.), with the soft spirituality of A-flat, his preferred mystical key, complemented by a lush string texture, piously maudlin thirds, and a lengthy dominant pedal supporting an ecstatic cadence (m. 66) that seems quite appropriately too good to be true. The accumulated vapors gradually dissipate in a short but patient epilogue, and we return to reality and a distinct sense of unease.

The critical dimension of this music must have seemed perfectly obvious to Strauss: he had painted a seductively beautiful image of the metaphysical fantasies that more than any other single factor drove Nietzsche's creative and intellectual enterprise. But in his expectation that listeners would grasp this implication easily and willingly, Strauss made one of the great misjudgments of his career. Surely some among his peers recognized this music as a parody of religion's hollow promise, a beautiful depiction of a realm that did not exist, an overwhelming warmth that signified the cold reality of delusion. Yet as far as one can tell, no critic in Strauss's time spoke unequivocally to the ironic character of this passage.[10] The musical rapture, a function of enormous technical command, presented itself too believably, it would seem, so that listeners were thrown off the work's main philosophical argument. Without recognizing the contrast between natural, earthly, antimetaphysical C major and an A-flat-major hallucination, the listener cannot hope to follow the considerably more involved treatment of humanity's struggle to overcome idealism. And so Strauss's most personally meaningful tone poem was doomed to obscurity and confusion, and he moved in directions that required less of his audience.

Mahler's first symphonic experiment with overt irony met the same uncomprehending response, for opposite reasons. No one who attended the early performances of the First Symphony failed to see the third movement as the most unusual and distinctive part of the work, and thus on some level as the most important. Likewise, listeners instantly recognized the bizarre distortion of "Bruder Martin" as some kind of irony, with tragic implications but otherwise inscrutable. Max Graf, the Vienna critic who went from ardent supporter of Mahler to cruel opponent and back again, wrote in an enthusiastic 1900 review that the work's main obstacle was generational. Established audience members for whom Mahler was a young composer (even at forty) had no patience with satire, which brought feeling and intellect into an unnatural relationship. "They demand not a parody of feeling—which is always the result of a struggle between mind and heart—but the pure play of mind (wit) or the pure play of the heart (humor)."[11] For these older listeners the head was the location of ironic distance, and in the serious context of a tragedy it had no place, for it endangered the emotional connection necessary for tragic feeling. The younger generation arrived in the concert hall already suspicious of emotional sincerity, however; Mahler's work spoke to them alone, because "only they can enjoy its parody and distortion of sacred emotion."[12] (Hanslick confirmed that at this performance, at least, the younger members of the audience cheered while the older remained befuddled.)[13] "Enjoy" means something like "accurately interpret" here, in a modernist dramatic context that assumed the inefficacy of any sincere utterance, tragic or otherwise. Tragedy had become the new comedy, we might say, appropriating distortion and even a kind of buffoonery in order to reinvigorate dead feelings.

The G-major idyll in this movement (m. 83) is the exception that proves the rule. Graf correctly observed that here "the true and perfect feeling surfaces for a moment," an oasis surrounded on all sides by "caricature."[14] This music is unquestionably heartfelt in a way that one could never claim of Strauss's "Hinterweltlern." Where Strauss adopts a tone of candor and profundity to declare his own skepticism, and thus to clear the air, Mahler indulges the first of his many death fantasies. If this one, like the others, was not quite believable even to the composer, it nonetheless seems to mean what it says, or to wish it could believe in what it proposes. One might say, with Pierre Boulez, that it occupies "the borderline between sentimentality and irony, nostalgia and criticism which is sometimes impossible to define."[15] The ironic distance almost disappears, along with the reflection compelled by a distortive musical technique. Theodor Helm heard this moment as an interruption of a "drive toward the openly parodistic," which had begun with the distorted folk song and continued with the "conspicuously Hungarian" melody marked explicitly as "Parodie."[16] Robert Hirschfeld likewise felt that the few moments of clear "seriousness," including also the Brucknerian D-flat melody in the Finale, stood out as noteworthy exceptions in what he described sarcastically as a "satire of the symphony" and a "parody of the symphonic spirit."[17] That description could well have been applied to Strauss's A-flat smoke and mirrors, but as the cruel but honest Hirschfeld suggested, there was nothing the slightest bit dishonest in Mahler's linden tree music. However the average listener may have consumed these two applications of high seriousness, the composers themselves well knew the difference between critical irony and the pleasant indulgence of a futile yearning.

Graf would go on to complain that Mahler intermingled head and heart—that the struggle produced impurity, a "parody of feeling" rather than real feeling. In this respect he recalled Cosima's perceptive and vitally important reaction to *Don Juan*.[18] She too found intelligence incompatible with feeling and thus hostile to music's unique purpose and power. The kind of intellect at issue here is not the reflection on musical processes: form, counterpoint, development, and so on. These could operate in the background of one's perception and contribute more or less passively to the act of expression. It was critical reflection on expression itself that bothered Cosima and Graf. In their separate ways, which focused on distortion on one hand and tone painting on the other, Mahler and Strauss called attention to emotional expression and raised questions about its authenticity. This step had far-reaching implications, as Cosima and Graf realized perhaps before Mahler and Strauss. Once the music no longer took for granted an authentic emotional connection between composer and listener, the basic condition of the romantic expressive enterprise was lost. Irony was an all-or-nothing proposition, in other words: once released, those doubts could not be controlled.

Having taken a step that could not be undone, both composers attempted to conceive a new sort of expression, in which reflection on staged emoting could be the source of a second level of emotional involvement. For Strauss this process unfolded in two tone poems and an opera: the explicitly paired *Don Quixote* and *Ein Heldenleben*, and the comprehensively satirical "non-opera" (*Nichtoper*, Strauss's term) *Feuersnot*.[19] The tone-painterly intellect against which Cosima inveighed was given free rein in the first tone poem, aside from one moment highlighting the other dimension: the carefully distanced, exquisitely beautiful vision of the high chivalry inspired by Dulcinea (mm. 332–69, in F-sharp major; see chapter 3). For this one moment, Ritter's "Ausdruck," inspired by Hausegger, is placed onstage under lights for our enjoyment and clinical reflection. As in *Zarathustra*, there is an obvious distancing here, because this is someone else's vision. Through the personal connection to Ritter, however—an unspoken and subtle nuance—the resigned meditation on the Don's fate maintains a certain sentimental power. This music might just as easily have been written about Mahler, if it had been composed a decade later. The poignancy unfolds without a curled eyebrow, yet it never compromises its critical dimension.

If *Don Quixote* represents an idealistic perspective that was shared by Ritter and Mahler (at least in a general sense), *Ein Heldenleben* turns the lens on the composer's own choices, with a bracingly honest assessment of his superficiality. For a piece of over half an hour in length, the formal plan of this work is stupefyingly simple, both in musical respects—with a crude, common, but overgrown sonata plan—and programmatically, with a limited number of excruciatingly clear episodes. In no other work would Strauss so assertively shun ambiguity. But even as the tone poem mercilessly undercuts the idea of heroism, with a protagonist and enemies who fight an everyday battle in the here and now (the composer against his critics), its satirical technique treats its targets with deadly seriousness rather than humor. This choice reflects their nature. Strauss wrote that in this work he struggled against "inner enemies" as well as outer ones: "doubt, disgust," Nietzschean catchphrases for his discomfort at rejecting idealism in a culture addicted to musical metaphysics.[20] Depicting this conflict artistically required a double dose of dramatic irony; in the penultimate section we watch the composer as he watches himself, and we witness the dawning realization that his evolution toward Nietzschean anti-romanticism would bring him only alienation and artistic solitude. Hence his *Weltflucht*, to a personal realm where he became the only standard for his creations.

When at the end of his life Strauss offered a reading of his artistic personality—in a fragment no less revealing for its brevity (see chapter 7)—he pointed specifically to the irony emerging in the sequence of works from *Guntram* to *Feuersnot*.[21] Opera had always been the most important genre to him, but it was through a "non-opera" that his defining tendency first came self-consciously to the fore. "In *Feuersnot* the deliberate tone of mockery, of irony [. . .] represents individual novelty." As Strauss pulled back from the debate over metaphysics and began constructing a way forward, he realized that the critique of metaphysical objectivity had implications for subjectivity as well. In the absence of a stable objective framework—which he had disallowed on a categorical basis by his critique of metaphysics—Strauss's works focused on a new reading of the subjective. Critics would miss this point entirely, as the eighty-five-year-old lamented: "Why do they not see what is new in my works, how the individual [behind the works] becomes visible in them as only in Beethoven?" But the critics missed it because Strauss now confronted them with the paradox of a subject without a stable identity—a flamboyantly contingent individuality that cut itself loose from any objective mooring. If, as he claimed, "confession" was "exactly what differentiates my dramatic works from the typical operas, masses, variations" of his contemporaries, it was the confession of a subject who presented himself only through ironic means, who wore many masks because he had nothing to offer but masks. And perhaps most importantly, and most confusingly, Strauss took this step lightly and optimistically, without any sign of hesitation or apprehension.

The stylistic heterogeneity of *Feuersnot*, which Morten Kristiansen has interpreted as a manifestation of fin de siècle *Stilkunst* (style art), raised the postmetaphysical fragmentation of subjectivity to the level of an artistic principle. Embracing "the dominant element of cultural life during this period, namely its pluralism and fragmentation," Strauss composed an opera in which the full spectrum of Munich's musical life—from Wagner to Bavarian folk songs, historical styles to operetta, waltzes to personal stylistic predilections—was at once parodied and celebrated.[22] Through a freewheeling circus of juxtapositions, the composer obliterates the listener's sense of a stylistic center of gravity, confirming by means of style his conclusion that music did not exist to communicate some deeper reality outside itself. The only feature of the work more bewildering than its mixtures of competing styles—which are catalogued meticulously by Kristiansen, particularly with respect to Wagnerian allusions—is the pervading sense that none of these is the composer's own "authentic" manner of expression.[23] In stylistic terms, Kristiansen is right to find in *Feuersnot* a powerful statement of the incipient postmodernism theorized by Leon Botstein with respect to Strauss's works of the 1920s, '30s, and '40s.[24] This pastiche does not indicate a new "objective aesthetic," however, but rather a disengagement from both objectivity and subjectivity as they were traditionally construed. As in his first opera Strauss concluded that music had no connection to objectivity, which is to say "reality" in the philosophical sense, he recognized with his second opera that the end of objectivity meant the detachment of subjectivity from any stable grounding. Contingency and decenteredness would now be unavoidable intellectual realities. And in artistic terms, that meant that the only philosophically honest approach to style was irony. One can find in *Feuersnot* a version of virtually every musical style available in Munich at the turn of the century. But one cannot find any one of those styles deployed without circumspection, without a sign of ironic distance either parodic or sentimental.

And that goes above all for anything that passes for a uniquely Straussian style.

Strauss, it would seem, was no less obsessed with the self than Mahler, even as he abandoned all pretense of confessional authenticity. "Neither I nor, I think, anyone else," wrote the Dresden music director Fritz Busch, "has managed to solve the riddle of the Straussian nature, which, though bearing the most astounding talents, is neither permeated nor possessed by them as are other artists, but merely wears them like a suit that one can take off."[25] Mahler, on the other hand, carried on constructing potentially genuine selves. The Sixth Symphony is a case in point, not just for its explicitly autobiographical vision but for the way it holds the self-portrait aloof from irony, as though distance, skepticism, doubt had no place when the topic was this personal. There is a stark contrast with the Fifth Symphony, which moves from tragedy to burlesque via a heartfelt confession (the Adagietto) that becomes the material for a manic but good-natured pseudo-Baroque romp. Alma's reaction to the Fifth must have hurt Mahler deeply, for not only did it echo a flippant and dismissive reaction to the Fourth ("I think Haydn has done that better"), but it suggested that Mahler had betrayed or at least forgotten some essential element of himself. In particular the closing chorale, which she called "hymnal and boring," compelled her "to make clear to him the radical difference between his nature and Bruckner's." Flirtation with Brucknerian Catholic orthodoxy, even when disguised with playful excess, highlighted "a rift in his being which often went so deep as to bring him into serious conflict with himself."[26] The irony that Alma read in this movement was thus of an unwitting sort—Mahler's music betrayed him, the buoyant surface communicating a darker interior that, at least in Alma's view, had for the moment escaped the composer's notice.

These comments obviously affected him as he planned his next symphony, a work that attempts a more truthful self-assessment by exchanging optimism for tragedy. In the Sixth, Mahler treated himself as heroic archetype; both the classically influenced outlines and the monochromatically tragic tone direct the listener from the specific to the general, ensuring that no one would mistake this for a crude self-portrait à la *Ein Heldenleben*. Despite the autobiographical content, then, Mahler stands with us outside the action, adopting a posture of dramatic irony; together we witness the hero's downfall, dreading the fulfillment of a destiny that we foresee and the protagonist does not. For the composer personally, sustaining that ironic separation proved impossible. He seems to have held a genuine "fear of the symphony's prophetic power," to the extent that he removed the third hammer blow in the finale for no other reason than superstition.[27] It was this terror that boiled over in the green room at Essen, in perhaps the most painful misunderstanding that Mahler and Strauss ever shared (see the introduction).[28] This personal significance explains the sentimentality of the Andante theme, which Bekker called "almost ironizingly popular" in a touching attempt to rescue the composer from himself.[29]

That Strauss would have misunderstood what was happening, and why it was happening, is of course not credible. The music's redemptive aspirations, conveyed by means of conspicuous *Parsifal* references, spoke eloquently to a Wagner conductor who by 1906 understood Mahler's worldview from long experience. He did not need to hear that the F-major theme in the first movement related to Alma; he would have known it instantly, by its contour, orchestration, rhythmic impetuosity, and context (within a musical self-portrait), and indeed he likely chuckled at the contrast it represented with his rendering of Pauline in *Heldenleben*. Likewise, Strauss did not need to be told of the connection to Beethoven's op. 132, made clear not just by the profile of that same theme but by the exceptional use of the key of A minor for a symphony. Strauss behaved as he did after the rehearsal not because he misunderstood the work and Mahler's reaction to it, but because he understood them all too well. By a calculated display of thoughtless impatience, and a crude reference to the death of the mayor and the resultant need for appropriate music, Strauss meant to restore some perspective to a friend who had been brainwashed by his own symphony. The mourning of tragic heroes through music was hopelessly outdated, Strauss seemed to say, not to mention the staging of such ceremonies with oneself in the title role.

The transitions in each composer's creative output around 1900—Strauss moving decisively from tone poem to opera, Mahler from program music to "absolute" music (his word)—involved a role reversal in the handling of irony. The daring experiments in musical parody that characterize Mahler's Wunderhorn symphonies passed to Strauss, who in *Feuersnot* and especially in *Salome* proved that he could sell the grotesque and the distorted to an audience without being dismissed as strange or incoherent. The infamous moments of *Salome*, above all the dance and its aftermath, appropriate a technique from the scherzi of the Second and the Fourth, in which unpleasantness and even a sort of nausea repel the listener from the music and thus demand a distanced reflection. (Bekker used the word "demonic" for this quality in Mahler, conflating parody, irony, and sarcasm in a larger category "often malicious, often bitter, seldom and only in quickly fleeting moments unintentional.")[30] But in Strauss's hands these tools reached listeners with an immediacy that Mahler could not duplicate and could not understand, any more than he could fathom why Strauss's experiments in orchestration always worked the first time. By the same token, Mahler after 1900 veered away from satire toward an expressive tone like that of Strauss's first three tone poems, which could be consumed unproblematically by ears calibrated to Beethoven, Berlioz, and Brahms. Even the Seventh Symphony, with its rowdy celebrations and outlandish lack of discipline, represents a historical allusion to Beethoven's over-the-top celebratory mode. There is no indication in a public or private utterance that Mahler chose this path from a failure of nerve. He desperately wanted to be heard and appreciated, and by this time he knew well that undisguised irony would not be his ticket to success.

The relationship with Hofmannsthal would encourage Strauss's natural tendency to use musical style to reflect on the nature of the art. Indeed, this practice would become ever more explicit, culminating in the figure of the Composer in *Ariadne auf Naxos*, a character whom, in the second and final version of the opera, Strauss pondered in great detail precisely because at a gut level he abhorred him. In one of the most difficult episodes of the friendship between composer and librettist, Strauss insisted that in the revision the composer would be a pants role, an indispensable physical sign of Strauss's distance from an artist who could exclaim that "music is a holy art."[31] Only once in his life did Strauss flirt with such a notion, when he described melodic inspiration as "the unconscious mouthpiece of the World-Spirit," the "highest gift of the divinity," and the "absolute revelation of the ultimate mysteries."[32] For Strauss these were exceptional effusions, instantly diverted (in this same essay) from the metaphysical to the physical. A life of experience suggested to him, he said, that "human blood contains chemical elements which, when flowing through certain nerves or when coming into contact with certain parts of the brain, cause this highest stimulation of spiritual and mental activity which produced the masterpieces of art." Even the loftiest expressions of the spirit had their cause, according to the aged and increasingly sentimental Strauss, in the physical realities of the human body. "Brain, nerves, blood—which is the strongest factor?" he asked rhetorically.[33]

Such thoughts did not occur to the Composer in *Ariadne* (1912; rev. 1916), an incurable and archetypical romantic. Within a decisively un-Wagnerian libretto and dramatic context, this character speaks the old language of idealism, in his words but more importantly in his music. But now the Wagnerian harmonic and orchestrational technique finds itself a specimen within an experiment in historicism, a self-consciously modern work that roams the western canon plucking distinctive styles from their contexts for use in a parodic pastiche. Mozart, Schubert, Bellini, Donizetti, the French rococo, the commedia dell'arte, and so on—the historical formation of the western canon is no less a central dramatic theme than the creation of the Composer's opera and its comedic counterpart. But if, as Bryan Gilliam suggests, *Ariadne* "forges a new relationship between composer, performer, and audience," it does so not to create parody for its own sake, but to make the new relationship apparent to everyone involved. With the ironic dimension of his music now overdetermined by the juxtaposition of parodies, Strauss demanded more assertively than ever before that his audience reflect on music's power and their own expectations of the art. The stylistic counterpoint, itself the major force in our perception of each element as a parody, disallows the immediacy that defined romantic music and that the Composer continues to celebrate. Thus in *Ariadne* it is no longer Strauss's distance from his music that defines his modernism, but the enforced distance between music—any kind of music—and its listeners.

When the elderly Strauss returned to this mode in *Capriccio* (1941), creating once again (with the help of another Viennese librettist, Clemens Krauss) a musical pastiche that doubled as aesthetic rumination, he brought the same modesty and lighthearted wisdom that made *Ariadne* a uniquely refreshing example of musical modernism. The relationship of this work to *Die Liebe der Danae* is not unlike the connection between *Ariadne* and *Die Frau ohne Schatten*, a project with roots that predate its predecessor. *Danae* gives the lie to Strauss's claim of *Die Frau* as the "last Romantic opera"; neither of them is unproblematically Wagnerian, but both suspend their disbelief long enough to indulge in what once was. There is thus in this late work a return to the subtle irony of *Also sprach Zarathustra*, with a dead style presented so powerfully that one could almost believe in it. But now the critical dimension is softened by something like Schiller's sentimentality, a regretful glance at something beautiful and irrecoverable. The entire late period shows evidence of this mood, with its review of Strauss's youthful modes. Having described this tactic in terms of autobiography (chapter 7) and intertextuality (chapter 10), I would call attention here to its ironic dimension. Each of the late works betrays—wittingly, it would seem—some sign of alienation from the model. In *Metamorphosen*, the tone poet left aside his trademark impish tone painting. The classically inspired works he called "wrist exercises"; unlike the music of the 1880s, they held no pretense of continuing a living tradition. And the *Last Songs*, despite an orchestrational and harmonic luxuriance redolent of the Bayreuth master, seem in their rapturous lyricism to float effortlessly away from Wagner rather than engaging critically with him. In reviewing his past selves, then, Strauss could not resist employing irony to separate himself from each one, even though it ruled out the discovery of a final, stable, personal identity.

Where the late Strauss turned his ironic impulses on himself, composing out the fragmentation of his subjectivity as a history project and separating his current self from all the former possibilities, Mahler took one thread from his past as the basis for a final attempt as consolation. The quiet resignation of Rückert's poem "Ich bin der Welt abhanden gekommen" ("I Am Lost to the World"), reflecting Eastern and Schopenhauerian influences, had pushed Mahler to the creation of a musical style of eternal stasis, a hybrid of pentatonicism and common-practice harmony that with its capacity "to diffuse goal-directed Western tonal processes" provided a musical representation of his mature worldview.[34] *Das Lied von der Erde* was unquestionably a search for self, and one that considered past attempts not as equally viable responses to an unanswerable question, but as failures. "If I am to find the way back to myself again, I must surrender to the horrors of loneliness," he wrote to Bruno Walter, perhaps the closest thing he had to a kindred spirit among musicians (including Alma and Natalie).[35] The difficulty here lay not in the fear of death, or so he claimed. It resided rather in the alienation from other people, implicit in the unbridgeable gap between the subjective and the objective—the principal obsession of Mahler's entire artistic career. Mahler did not feel cut off from himself; indeed, one feels that he would have regarded such a predicament as a relief. Rather he felt an inability to communicate, which, for an artist with a deep confidence in his ability to wield the most powerfully communicative art known to humanity, left him in a hopeless position. It was this hopelessness that made him into, as Bekker would say, the "summoner of dark forces and shadows" in the middle movements of the Ninth, where he indulged in "harsh parodies of life, obtained by caustic mockery."[36] In that sad state, irony could identify the problem, it could serve a critical purpose, but it could offer no way forward. For that reason, if not for others, the endings of *Das Lied* and the Ninth Symphony strike us as personal and positive but not optimistic. Optimism concerns the future, and for these works there is only present.

CHAPTER 12

Metaphysicians

ONE OF THE DEEPEST shared experiences of Strauss and Mahler, and one of the least discussed, is the private negotiation of release from an inherited religious tradition. Neither composer came from a secular household, so they both knew the challenges of rejecting one's ancestors in this most profound and radical way. The racial implications of Mahler's religion—"unfortunately, it is the race that matters," Mahler observed of Viennese anti-Semites—complicated the process of separation for him, but it involved few bonds of a spiritual or philosophical nature.[1] Indeed, by his mid-teens, in the first full flush of intellectual maturity, Mahler, like Strauss, decisively scrapped what he saw as quaint and simple-minded customs that had nothing genuine to offer a young genius in search of a nuanced worldview.

Practical rejection nonetheless opened new spiritual possibilities—modes of communion with what had been lost—once the young artists formed the habit of figurative thinking. The exciting trendsetter Nietzsche would teach them to regard all life—including philosophy and religion—as an "aesthetic phenomenon," just as Goethe, with his awe-inspiring spiritual depth and unimpeachable credibility, had done by example. No reasonable and educated Austro-German at the end of the nineteenth century would read the second part of *Faust* as an embrace of Christianity; rather, it applied the comparativist's approach close to home, treating familiar religious trappings as symbols of something more real and meaningful but impossible to grasp literally. It used Christianity, in other words, much as Freud would use his ancient materials—to consider modern issues via symbolic artifacts still meaningful but practically defunct. This method carried with it the satisfaction of mirroring the "progress" that was so evident technologically in one's daily life. But its basic motivation lay in its utility as a technique for an artist-intellectual to think about the unthinkable. That is why two composers who were essentially atheists—Strauss admitting it, Mahler not daring to—returned so often and so powerfully in their music to religious themes they seemed to have outgrown.

Metaphysical thought in an age of positivism could avoid dishonesty only by maintaining distance, through either an overtly critical attitude or a staged fantasy-atmosphere. If Strauss leaned one way and Mahler the other, those choices should not obscure the underlying fact of a lacuna at the center, where each composer's own views might lie. In long series of creative religious interactions, spanning the full length of their careers, these two composers asked unanswerable questions about God. Sometimes this predilection brought discomfort, even fear, which too found its modes of expression. If we cannot point to a moment where their personal views harmonized—even in the very late music, or the works that grew from personal crisis or self-doubt—we can nonetheless identify a common set of problems and a consistent mode of limiting the discussion, grounded in firm convictions about the limits of human endeavor.

Strangely enough, Strauss's liberal perspective on religion, and his critical reception of Christianity in general and Catholicism in particular, were not reactions against what he was taught at home but freely faithful applications of the principles he had learned. The *alt-katholisch* faith practiced by Strauss's parents originated in the 1850s but did not officially exist until 1871, when a convention held in Munich and led by the church historian and priest Johann Joseph Ignaz von Döllinger broke decisively with Rome over the conclusions of the First Vatican Council (1869–70). The proximate cause of the schism lay in the Council's doctrine of papal infallibility with respect to faith and morals, though the new "Old Catholic Church" took liberal positions across the board, introducing the vernacular into the liturgy and in 1874 removing the requirement of celibacy for priests. Döllinger's excommunication gave the movement a measure of credibility as a sort of second Reformation, and in Austria and Bavaria the church associated itself with nationalist currents, with the support of Bismarck, who pursued policies increasingly hostile to the Catholic Church.[2]

In her well-known "Jugenderinnerungen," Strauss's sister Johanna von Rauchenberger-Strauss made no mention of the family's religious practice, but in a brief interview with Robert Breuer she noted, with more subtlety than the interviewer could detect, that having been raised in an *alt-katholisch* household "Strauss became a freethinker early in his life."[3] For someone who in his youth watched his Catholic parents abandon the Roman Church and risk their own excommunication, it was a short step to religious independence—certainly much shorter than we have imagined. Likewise, there are several layers of meaning to another religious anecdote provided by Johanna, in which Strauss responded to a friend's request for a mass with the comment, "this is rather impossible for me." Certainly it was impossible for a precocious atheist, but it was likewise impossible for a son of parents who did not want their child's artistic energies squandered on controversies of dogma and ceremony. Franz and Josephine Strauss thus created, perhaps unwittingly and perhaps not, a tolerant atmosphere in which over the span of one generation religious observance could transform itself from an individual's most profound inner reality to a cultural veneer concealing spiritual independence.

From all appearances, Pauline saw eye to eye with her husband on these matters. Their wedding ceremony took place in the parish office in Grassau, but their life did not include regular or even sporadic attendance of a church, aside from the christenings of their son and grandsons, the family marriages, and Strauss's funeral. There seems to have been nothing unusual or ostentatiously iconoclastic in this lifestyle, for comments on it by friends and associates of the family are virtually nonexistent. Thus while in Strauss's music we find religious belief singled out in ways that provoke, or were meant to provoke, confrontations, in regular life neither he nor his wife interacted with others on this topic, and by and large they were left in peace.

The religious atmosphere in Mahler's childhood home likewise admitted the possibility of independent thought and liberal attitudes, in the context of a firmly Jewish orientation. From birth he experienced the special difficulties faced by Jews in central Europe, along with the characteristic adaptability necessary for survival in difficult conditions. Bernhard Mahler, an illegitimate child by virtue of a law that allowed only the firstborn son of a Jewish family to marry legally, could transplant his family to Iglau from Kalischt only after restrictions were lifted on the movement of Jews, and he did not enjoy full civil and political rights until the Compromise of 1867.[4] Yet these difficulties did not prevent him from raising his family in the orthodox tradition, a choice made possible by the easy relations among Jews and Christians in Iglau. As an adult, Mahler would of course never observe the religious practice of his youth, nor would he seek in any way to align himself with a Jewish community. But he did learn the Old Testament with extraordinary depth, and he did not forget what he had absorbed. As a nine-year-old in his first year at the gymnasium, he earned a grade of "excellent" in only one course: religion; throughout his school career his grades would generally be fair, but in this subject his performance was never less than outstanding. Later, when he underwent instruction for his 1897 conversion, he would enjoy putting difficult questions to his catechist, with a "sudden surging up of Old Testament pride," as Alma put it.[5] Mahler was proud of the wisdom of the Jewish people, as we learn regularly in anecdotes such as his remark to Bauer-Lechner that the invention of Jacob as a symbolic figure would have been sufficient to ensure the Jews' status as a "formidable people," and his praise of the Jewish treatment of freed slaves who longed to return to bondage.[6]

At the heart of Mahler's Judaism, however, lay a desire to unite it with Christianity, in a synthesis that retained nothing of ceremony and dogma but melded symbols in a spiritually meaningful agglomeration. The cooperative and tolerant atmosphere of his hometown set the stage for this development: as a child Mahler performed regularly with the choir at

Iglau's Sankt Jakob church, in this way coming to know Beethoven's *Christus am Ölberge*, Haydn's *Die sieben Worte*, Rossini's *Stabat mater*, and Mozart's *Requiem*. If Mahler would later become, as Alma called him, "ein christgläubiger Jude"—a Christian-oriented Jew intent on racial as well as religious unification (consider, for example, his choice of wife)—this tendency would seem to have been lifelong, permitted if not fostered by his parents. The boy who shouted "Be quiet! Be quiet! It's horrible!" on first hearing the singing of hymns in the synagogue, and who took his place alongside young Catholics for the performance of beautiful music of a foreign faith, would ultimately take an independent musical path toward knowledge of "the world's inmost being," the term that Bauer-Lechner used for Mahler's musical conceptualization of God in the Third Symphony.[7]

Prior to the mid-1880s Strauss showed no evidence whatsoever of an interest in religious music. Chamber works, piano music, and Lieder abound, augmented by orchestral music as he reached his late teens, but sacred genres did not exist for him. It is all the more striking, then, that the most important composition he produced before the age of thirty—the work on which he pinned his hopes of "arriving" as a mature force in German music—was a *Parsifal* remake, *Guntram* (1893). Written under the influence, and indeed the supervision, of the devoutly Roman Catholic Wagnerian Alexander Ritter, this opera revived the central themes of Wagner's last music drama, the work in which, according to Nietzsche, Wagner "collapsed before the Christian cross." A religious community, an act of transgression, a deeply felt need for atonement, a strong woman who transforms herself from sex object to idealized Mary figure, and a carefully choreographed redemption: all the ingredients were present for an epigonic revival of the Christian ceremony with which Wagner had unexpectedly made his farewell (see chapter 4 for a discussion of the plot). Given that Strauss worked on *Guntram* from 1887, before any of the tone poems, through 1893, we must regard this expansive religious meditation as the central creative product of his early career.

And yet, if on this superficial level it seems to have been the exception that proved the rule, in its details it was no exception at all. The redemption proffered here does not reinforce the dogma of the group, but destroys it. Instead of passively waiting for redemption, as does Amfortas, Guntram seeks it actively himself, in the process rejecting the authority of his ancient brotherhood and declaring, as though a medieval forerunner of Luther, that to find "the Savior's Grace" one must reject authority, tradition, and dogma and withdraw to an ascetic life "in eternal, solitary contemplation of the divine."[8] It is telling that while Ritter and almost everyone else reacted with shock at this unexpected denouement, his father took it in stride. The rejection of an obsolete authority in order to follow one's own conception of true Christianity was personal experience for Franz Strauss, despite the fact that he broke with the Roman church as part of a group. This example, and the Schopenhauerian claim of asceticism as the sole path to redemption, were for Strauss manifestations of a spirit shared with Luther, a religious attitude that made independence and idiosyncratic personal insight a sine qua non of spiritual conviction.

With this one vitally important religious work of his youth, then, Strauss applied the example of his parents and took a single decisive step toward spiritual independence. The importance of this maneuver for his personal development is seen not just in the diligent study and systematic reflection that went into its production, but in the extraordinary fact that this first musical interaction with religion was not in the slightest degree ironic. In this sense, too, *Guntram* is extraordinary if not unique in Strauss's music. As though this deadly serious contemplation had left him in need of fresh air, the next major works, *Till Eulenspiegels lustige Streiche* and *Also sprach Zarathustra*, would more than make up for the opera's dull literalism. The spiritual sincerity embodied by both Guntram and his Brotherhood is the subject of the full-blown parody of spiritual grandiloquence in "Von den Hinterweltlern" ("Of the Backworldsmen," *Zarathustra*, mm. 35ff.; discussed in chapter 11). That irony has a straightforward antimetaphysical purpose: to state in eloquent musical terms what Strauss said in words to Ritter: "I am not Guntram."

Till, on the other hand, does give the impression of an alter ego, in his mischievousness but also in his intermittent but palpable anxiety. Disguising his protagonist as a pastor "dripping with unction and morals" ("trieft er von Salbung und Moral"), Strauss unleashed a critical barrage (mm. 179ff.) that he must have believed would allow a softer touch in subsequent efforts such as the "Hinterweltlern" passage.[9] Humor and contempt are inseparable, especially in the satirically sweet thirds and bouncing square rhythms, which anticipate, in a livelier tempo, the style at the related moment in *Zarathustra*.[10] Yet Till's insecurity, the "secret horror that seizes him in spite of his mockery of religion," likewise reflected Strauss's own feelings more or less directly, as we learn from correspondence and from the musico-programmatic workings of *Zarathustra*. For Strauss the discrediting of Christianity was less problematic than the rejection of Schopenhauer, which caused him considerable personal unease in the early months of 1893 (that is, immediately after the completion of the third act of *Guntram*) and burst forth in letters to Ludwig Thuille, Friedrich Rösch, and Cosima Wagner that I have described elsewhere.[11] At bottom, though, they were different manifestations of the same issue: the debate over a higher metaphysical plane of existence, which Strauss wished to jettison but instead found, as did Zarathustra, to be a source of ever-renewing misgivings. Whatever else that crucial tone poem may be, then—and it is certainly a history of human struggles with religion, as Strauss said—it is also a coming to terms with the fact of his own continuing instability and doubt, a condition that Nietzsche (the later, anti-Wagnerian Nietzsche, who made his appearance with *Human, All Too Human*) tells us is the very definition of humanity.

Mahler suffered the same insecurities, of course, but he wanted nothing to do with Nietzsche's recommendation to accept them, celebrate them, and love them. His faith would always remain with the Nietzsche of *The Birth of Tragedy* and the *Untimely Meditations*, and with the fundamental conclusion of Siegfried Lipiner that, in the words of Stephen E. Hefling, "religion, art, and metaphysics are both inextricably intertwined and necessary to human existence."[12] Thus when he came to write his own Nietzschean work in the mid-1890s, he followed Strauss in producing a history, but one devoid of the irony he had deployed with such virtuosity in the First and Second Symphonies. The operative movements of the Third, which is to say the end-state toward which the rest of the work drives itself, are the fourth and the sixth, the "profoundly serious" movements, according to Mahler. In the sixth, "What Love Tells Me," we hear what Constantin Floros calls "the first typical Mahler Adagio": a serene vision of reconciliation and acceptance. In a remarkable anticipation of the late style's essence (consider the endings of *Das Lied von der Erde* or the Ninth), Mahler wrote a finale in which, as he told Bauer-Lechner, "everything is resolved into quiet 'being,'" the "Ixion wheel" finally brought to rest.[13] Despite the expressly Schopenhauerian intent, Mahler associated this denouement with his highly personal reading of Nietzsche, writing to Fritz Löhr of a "deeply painful spiritual involvement, which, however, is gradually resolved into blissful confidence: 'the joyful science.'"[14] Recently Carl Niekerk has argued forcefully for the fidelity of this ending to the late Nietzsche, interpreting Mahler's musical image of love as "an affirmative attitude toward life on earth," and thus *übermenschlich* in its embrace of the here and now.[15] Floros, on the other hand, has highlighted Mahler's own claims that the love he intended to communicate here is "godly love"—God and love being one and the same—in direct contrast to "earthly love."[16]

In one crucial respect, the dream of a final relaxation of the struggle for transcendence flies in the face of what the mature Nietzsche tried to accomplish with his "joyful science," as Mahler certainly would have known. The very essence of eternity in Nietzsche's worldview is a recurrence of the same doubts that Mahler sought here to bring to rest. Nietzschean joy, *amor fati*, resides in a clear-eyed disavowal of the redemption conceptualized in the sixth's movements Brucknerian tones.[17] Here Niekerk's reading begins to show strain, and likewise Peter Franklin's relating of the finale to the *Übermensch*.[18] Eternal recurrence for Zarathustra and for Nietzsche meant the endless renewal of doubt, which is to say a "redemption" that celebrated the impossibility of redemption—a difficult hearing to manage in Mahler's sixth movement unless we hear it ironically, following Donal Henahan and wincing at the "sentimental slush."[19] Mahler's misreading (or strong reading) of Nietzsche is no less assertive in the fourth movement, where the philosopher-psychologist's seductive poetic gifts—the warmth of mood, the chiming of the word "eternity," the urgent cries of warning to humankind—deflected the composer's attention from the main point: the joyful, eternal acceptance of the very struggles that Mahler hoped to transcend. By insisting on that transcendence—or if not transcendence, at least a staged resolution—Mahler created a monument to the willful rejection of Nietzsche, at precisely the historical moment when the philosopher, and in particular his late persona with its anti-metaphysical, anti-Wagnerian, anti-Schopenhauerian tendencies, found broad public appreciation.

It is tempting, then, to see in this work a premeditated misreading, not only because Mahler surely must have recognized that Nietzsche could not be made into Schopenhauer, but because the placement of the angels' song in the fifth movement aims at the heart of Nietzsche's real argument. The poem tells the story of Peter's redemption and absolution by Jesus, celebrating "heavenly joy that has no end" by means of the "sweet" singing of the angels. Just as Mahler can have had no doubts about the anti-Christian disposition of Nietzsche, he can hardly have expected that a *musica coelestis* echoing *Parsifal* and embodying heavenly joy would submit to a Nietzschean reading, no matter how strongly it leaned toward fantasy. Here Niekerk attempts valiantly to connect the use of a children's choir to Nietzsche's inversion of the Gospel of Matthew in the fourth book of *Zarathustra*: "Unless you become as little children, you shall not enter *that* kingdom of Heaven" (i.e., Nietzsche's alternative to heaven).[20] But such nuances can easily fade when one hears lines such as "The heavenly joy was granted to Peter/through Jesus, and to all mankind for eternal bliss," which explains the long (and reasonable, one must say) critical tradition questioning Mahler's Nietzschean intent. What the movement does, in terms directly and overtly at odds with Nietzsche, is to present a beautiful, simple memory of what redemption once was; it performs, that is, an outdated version of the *Erlösung* offered in the fourth and sixth movements. For those not attuned to the anti-Nietzschean subtleties of those two movements, the fifth movement's Christianity draws attention briefly but powerfully to the distance from the philosopher—to the issues, in other words, that led Mahler in conversation with Bauer-Lechner to change "the joyful science" to "*My* Joyful Science" (my emphasis).[21]

Mahler's deep familiarity with Goethe, and his respect for him as a model of intellectual and spiritual development, would have allowed the composer to appropriate Christianity as a critical tool, and even in the Eighth to treat it as a living myth. As discussed above, Goethe had been openly hostile to Christian dogma, most colorfully in his *Venetian Epigrams*.[22] Yet this judgment did not prevent him from deploying Christianity figuratively, just as one might any other mythology, as discussed above in connection with *Faust*, Part II and the Eighth (see chapters 3 and 8).

Elsewhere, to be sure, Alma makes a compelling case that Mahler felt a deeper connection to this religion than the merely figurative. Certainly the 1897 baptism was undertaken for the practical reason of removing the final obstacle to his Vienna appointment (a scenario that Alma blamed on Cosima Wagner). The fact of his having taken that step under duress tells us nothing, however, about his attitudes toward Christian teaching or ritual. Alma confirms that Catholic ceremony attracted him in a way Jewish practice never did. "He could never pass a church without going in; he loved the smell of incense and Gregorian chants."[23] The "mysticism" appealed to him above all, no doubt for both its promise of an eternal redemption—Mahler's lifelong obsession—and its offering of that state to anyone who chose it. Mahler was not afforded a choice in his Jewishness; whatever his attitudes toward the Jewish religion, racially and culturally he would remain what he was born. In temperament and personal disposition, however, he was according to Alma a Christian through and through, and most especially in his musico-spiritual utterances. "His religious songs, the Second, the Eighth, and all the chorales in the symphonies are rooted in his own personality—and not brought in from the outside!"[24]

The central feature of the examples cited by Alma is their inclusiveness: they invite participation, and indeed they stage a kind of universal acceptance. That quality is the decisive idiosyncrasy of Mahler's private Christianity, the feature that allowed him to be on some level "a believer in Christianity."[25] Mahler saw that if Christianity was open to anyone, its redemptive power must in the end include everyone, for the exclusion of individuals on the basis of the by-then discredited notion of free will made no sense in the modern world. This is the central message of the Second Symphony, a work that does away with the concept of judgment, a foundation of the Jewish religion and an inescapable reality in the daily life of Jews in an anti-Semitic culture. Witnessing this dream of forgiveness up close, Alma suffered pangs of guilt, for while Mahler would never find a practical recognition of his Christian inclinations and indeed would incur persecution for them, she herself "was a Christian Pagan and got off scot-free." Yet the meaningful dimension of Mahler's life was the interior, and in that realm, Christianity provided him with a powerful metaphor of the ultimate spiritual stability he craved.

Strauss distinguished himself from Mahler, and virtually every other composer he knew, by his deep antipathy for both Christianity and Judaism. As in the case of Goethe, those feelings did not stand in the way of artistic engagement. But in no sense can we say that Strauss drew on religious sources to use them as figurative equivalents for similar but higher or more real spiritual experience. For Strauss they were the means of a historical study of human psychology: a reflection on the contemporary human psyche as viewed through the prism of its sources. In *Salome*, we struggle to decide who comes off worse: the Jews or the Christian hero Jochanaan. Both are parodied mercilessly, and with a notable lack of the good-natured humor that lends Herod his buffoonish qualities. Religious authority is taken seriously in this opera, and it is held responsible for the havoc it wreaks on the mind of an adolescent girl. Salome's obsessions, her sickness, her "nervousness" (in that most characteristic of modernist jargon terms), travel back in time to confront their roots. The ancient conspiracy of the "Christian, Jewish metaphysics," which Strauss held responsible for Mahler's downfall (emotional, spiritual, psychological, philosophical, artistic), comes face to face with the consequences of a millennia-long hatred of life.[26] The wages of sin are death: death for the humanity-denying ascetic, for his dogmatic alter egos—the Jews, who pursue his goals by the opposite means—and for the creature who embodies natural impulses gone haywire at the end of an age of guilt and self-hatred.

After this forceful critical statement, any further direct engagement with Judeo-Christian history was bound to bore him, and so it is remarkable to find that in 1912, just a year after Mahler's death, he took up the tale from Genesis of Joseph and Potiphar's wife.[27] Michael Kennedy plausibly suggests that if the libretto for the first act of *Die Frau ohne Schatten* had been finished a year earlier, this unfortunate ballet would never have been composed. Thanks to Nijinsky it exists, however, and it does offer us a useful window into the mature Strauss's religious views, particularly in that it confirms just how deeply and comprehensively settled he was in his spiritual attitudes after years of doubt and struggle. Where *Salome* had elicited a powerful sharpening of his tools of attack, in the process giving rise to Europe's most influential work of proto-Expressionism, *Josephs Legende* did absolutely nothing to stimulate his intellect or spiritual feeling. "The chaste Joseph himself isn't at all up my street, and if a thing bores me I find it difficult to set to music. This God-seeker Joseph—he's going to be a hell of an effort! Maybe there's a pious tune for good-boy Joseph lying about in some atavistic recess of my appendix."[28] Atavism has a dual meaning here: it stands for the ancient religious fantasy that for a person of Strauss's education had already ended in the eighteenth century (Strauss being well familiar with French thinkers of the Enlightenment), but also for the tired personal dilemmas that he had long since put to rest and had no interest in revisiting.

Hofmannsthal showed his naiveté and his incomplete knowledge of Strauss's development with the comment that the composer should look for "some bridge between this boy Joseph and the recollection of your own adolescence."[29] Suggesting that Strauss should concentrate on Joseph's dance, and on Potiphar's wife as "something lofty, radiant, hardly attainable above you, waiting to be taken by force"—as a sexual object, in other words, or so Strauss would have read such a suggestion—Hofmannsthal attempted with surprising openness to revive the clash of religion and sexuality that had energized the composer of *Salome*. But that side of his personality, the "Vulcan who labors under a heap of slag" (in Mahler's words), had burned itself out. Even the *Alpensinfonie*, the work with which Strauss made his most direct statement of his spiritual views, and which in spite of a sixteen-year genesis he insisted on completing, was only finished during another lull in operatic activity. An Eighth Symphony, or any appropriation of Judeo-Christian religious myth—figurative, modernist, ironic, or otherwise—was not to be expected from an artist whose creative adulthood began when he put aside that tradition for good.

The closest Strauss ever came to a sympathetic attitude toward Christianity was in his alter ego Barak in *Die Frau ohne Schatten*, the cheerful workhorse whose modesty and apparent superficiality hide a profound if unconscious wisdom. Bryan Gilliam makes an explicit comparison of Barak to the New Testament's "blessed one," noting that the dyer "provides for all, is referred to by all as 'father,' and through suffering attains transcendence."[30] This comparison might well have been a conscious one for

Strauss, for even as the character remains untouched by Christian dogma, he serves as a prophet of the personal religion of family, work, and nature articulated in the sketches for *Symphonia domestica* (see chapter 3). Strauss's preoccupation with "Erlösung" ended when he determined that the things of this earth—his family, his artistic mission, and that part of the universe that was perceptible to him—would be his salvation, or such salvation as he would seek. It was a predictable stroke of Nietzscheanism that he would find a Christlike figure to preach that philosophy, and that Hofmannsthal, who spent a lengthy automobile tour with Strauss discussing the plot (indeed, it was the longest period they ever spent together), would see Barak as a Straussian character just as the dyer's wife was a recollection of Pauline. In some ways Hofmannsthal's most subtle and sophisticated work, this opera was likewise the deepest personal expression of Strauss's own worldview, an unmatched dramatic harmony of librettist and composer and, not surprisingly, in Strauss's view the best opera they produced.

Mahler was no less spiritually invested in his children than Strauss, and the few anecdotes provided by Anna Mahler, the younger daughter who like her mother survived to a ripe old age, suggest that he took great joy from the everyday proceedings of life with a child. His creative inspiration manifested itself here too, in discipline (for example when he asked a recalcitrant Anna to step out of the room and fetch her other personality), tolerance (he not only tolerated being watched as he worked but took pleasure in the child's concern for the scratched-away notes), and finding time to know them in the midst of an uncommonly busy schedule. Yet the mere earthly existence of his family, their actions and relationships considered purely on their own terms, could never have been for him the core of a worldview. Mahler lived to imagine, through art and whatever other means he could find, a transcendental plane that ultimately would wash away any memory of life on earth. He sought, in other words, what Lipiner called "true and serious pantheism," reached only "when we have ceased to know and to feel ourselves as individual beings."[31] Notwithstanding the many happy moments he enjoyed, his children and wife interested him most insofar as they brought him glimpses of that higher realm (figure 9). Alma reports that when Maria lay on the dining room table in

Figure 9. Maria Anna ("Putzi") and Anna Justine Mahler ("Gucki") with their parents, Maiernigg, 1905. Courtesy of the Kaplan Foundation, New York.

Maiernigg dying of scarlet fever, Mahler had to be kept out of earshot, so as not to have any reminder of the earthly struggle in which his child would spend her final hours. Reading between the lines, one senses Alma's disappointment in a kind of cowardice. But for Mahler, Maria was undergoing the terrifying birth into a new state that he envied in spite of his instinctive dread. Paradoxically, he felt closer to her by cutting off his relationship to her doomed physical presence. To console himself in his agony he rushed toward a reunion in the unseen sphere that for his whole life had been his natural home. And at the end of his own life he arranged a posthumous symbol of that reunion, with the reburial of her body beside his own at the cemetery in Grinzing, under a single stone with no inscription but the words "Gustav Mahler."

If Mahler had sought his redemption in this world rather than the next, as Strauss recommended and practiced, he would not have been Mahler, any more than if he had taken Strauss's advice to write operas and restrict his conducting. While they could agree on the impoverished state of traditional religions in the new century, they could not find the slightest agreement on how to proceed. And in that divergence we see what may have been the fundamental difference between them.

Epilogue

INDIVIDUALS

◆ BY WAY OF EPILOGUE, I propose in this last chapter to survey again the human qualities of my protagonists, drawing a few conclusions about how this improbable relationship could have formed in the first place. It must be said that on merely personal terms a friendship was not foreordained. Strauss was a model of equilibrium, self-sufficiency, and emotional detachment; with few exceptions, he was unfazed by any difficulty, including what he perceived to be the absolute indifference of Nature to his existence. Mahler thrived on self-deprivation, unfulfilled needs, and idiosyncratic religiosity, deploying his artistic gifts in a series of spectacular, doomed attempts to control a pitiless universe. Naturally this association of modern titans had its share of unpleasantness, and those moments too deserve to be scrutinized. Two bonds, however, ensured that these differences would be overcome: the challenge of living with a level of musical talent that only the two of them could understand, and the need to come to terms, emotionally, spiritually, and artistically, with the mystery of mortal life. The former made them brothers, of sorts—antagonists, opposites in many ways, but connected by an authentic bond—while the latter motivated the constant, unrelenting creativity that defined their lives and ensured their abiding interest in one another.

The profundity of Mahler's and Strauss's natural musical ability deserves broader awareness. One can only imagine that a quasi-magical power of that sort must be ever-present in the consciousness, as fact and as responsibility. Willi Schuh writes with amusement of the musical get-togethers at the home of Strauss's uncle Georg Pschorr, where the family delighted in young Richard's accomplishments. There is something more than cute, however, about a preteen who loathed technical practice but could toss off virtuoso showpieces to amuse his elders.[1] Bülow was not kidding when he remarked, after the twenty-two-year-old Strauss performed Mozart's C-minor Piano Concerto with the Meiningen orchestra in his one and only appearance as piano soloist, that Strauss could have made a career as a pianist.[2] As Bülow recognized, only a matchless aural and musico-intellectual gift could allow someone to fake it as a virtuoso ("he's going to make a success of the Mozart concerto as of everything else the first time he tries," he told the Berlin agent Hermann Wolff) and indeed to intimidate professionals with decades of experience.[3] But what struck the elder man most of all was Strauss's modesty and his inexhaustible desire to learn. At no moment in the Strauss-Bülow relationship did Strauss overestimate his own talent. In June 1885 he traveled to Frankfurt to attend Bülow's master classes at the Raff Conservatory, where he soaked up as much wisdom as he could while building his credibility with Princess Marie of Meiningen, the musically inclined daughter of his prospective employer, Duke Georg II.[4] In Meiningen he attended all of Bülow's orchestral rehearsals with score in hand, quietly observing the rehearsal process and responding to pop quizzes when prompted. This attitude of modesty was fully in keeping with a childhood that saw him intellectually active at every moment, his genius for music supplemented by a genius for work. And in fact Strauss would make precisely this point in his late essay "On Melodic Inspiration," saying that "industry and joy in one's work are innate and not only the results of training."[5]

Mahler too enjoyed a purely musical gift that allowed him to play virtuoso showpieces without undertaking the athletic training and finger memorization typical of professional performers. Performing Liszt in public at the age of twelve without the benefit of a systematic approach to technique—an approach invented for the Lisztian repertoire—is already a shocking anomaly.[6] Transposing the Schubert *Wanderer* Fantasy on the fly in performance after having started in the wrong key is an accomplishment of a different order.[7] Mahler's natural self-consciousness does not seem ever to have limited him in musical performance, however; one suspects that in this episode he simply lost himself, repeating a behavior that occurred daily in his family's living room. As with Strauss, aptitude reinforced desire, and a child who wet his pants rather than step away from a military band concert became a youth who "would not leave the piano, even to eat."[8] He played anything for which he could find scores—symphonies, opera arrangements, salon pieces—with a love for the art so deep that it left no room for critical judgment. (Even as a mature conductor Mahler could find something to interest him in any work that circumstance required him to conduct. "The work he happened to be rehearsing was accorded his complete devotion," according to Herta Blaukopf.)[9] He did not know how to give less than everything to an activity that he could have done well without giving anything, and to those lazier and less able he showed no mercy, even in his teens, when he instructed a stubborn pupil to write "I must play C sharp, and not C" a hundred times.[10]

The fanatical drive that we find in such scenes, an overwhelming zeal that indicates a psychological illness or at least a character flaw, is not a trait that we normally associate with Strauss. Balance stood as an ultimate value for the sensible Bavarian; we cannot imagine him saying with the young, already self-abusing Mahler, "my most ardent desire was to read day and night without stopping."[11] A taste for suffering always held a prominent place in Mahler's personality. When he nearly starved while living with the Grünfelds, he did not complain and only came home when his father visited and found him shoeless, freezing, and emaciated.[12] Such experiences held a strange appeal, reflected in the "awful," "quite dreadful" food that was served at his own family's table in his adult years, according to his younger daughter Anna.[13] A bourgeois ascetic, Mahler ate "only for health," feeding an appetite for deprivation that was its own form of excess and somehow a precondition of creative activity. As a conductor and a composer, Mahler might best be defined by an apparent need to drive himself to exhaustion.

For Strauss, a glut of anything, including music, had unhealthy results. The daily skat game became in his mature years an indispensable ritual; five hours on the conducting podium could not yield to sleep without the intervening card game. Too much of one activity produced stagnation, curable only by a different activity. Even in composition—in fact, especially there—limits had to be enforced; when working at night, if the music would not come, he would abandon the effort without guilt or struggle, "and when I wake up in the morning, lo and behold! I have found the continuation."[14] The secret of Strauss's successful marriage lay to a considerable degree in Pauline's recognition of this necessity. She felt his innate need for routine and managed it with the precision of a general's daughter. Perhaps because she herself had been a successful professional artist, she did not underestimate the value of a clear schedule: discipline, consistency, rest, precise expectations. If Strauss's music tended to work without revision, as Mahler noted, that quality had something to do with his resolution during the creative process that once the work was finished he would not return to it.

Thus a dual talent for music and for work led in one case to extreme balance and in the other to a radical avoidance of balance; one can already detect natural inclinations toward or against romanticism. The physical demands that Mahler placed on himself reflect a kind of self-obsession, in which all material realities were bent to the requirements of his artistic and spiritual self. The attitude is oddly reminiscent of Wagner, but where Wagner demanded tapestries and silk pajamas, overcoming the physical by sating it, Mahler drove his body into submission. In both cases the point was to create the necessary conditions for the supraphysical activity of artistic creation. Specifically, to bring his abilities to fruition, Mahler required that the external world, including the physical realities of his own body, should submit to his control. Thus his deepest need from nature was that it should take account of his existence, and his greatest fear was that it would not. During Mahler's youthful affair with Josephine Poisl, his letters called on nature as witness to both happiness and despair. In the early days of courtship, a summer rain provided an evocative backdrop to his "stories of the horn-player Siegfried, who woke Brünnhilde from her magic sleep." After his jilting, the Prater welcomed him (as described in chapter 3) and almost refused to let him go.[15] In the end, however, nature seemed not to care, as in Müller and Schubert's *Winterreise*. When nature did take an interest in him, it was with frightening assertiveness, as when he told Bauer-Lechner in the summer of 1900 that the forest "dominates me and steals into my world of sound [. . .] one does not compose, one *is* composed!" (emphasis in original).[16] Such realities threatened his subjectivity, so that he attempted to manage nature by composing it into his music. "Indeed, there is no end to the infinite oceans of the world. And in every work of art, which should be a reflection of nature, there must be a trace of this infinity."[17] The purpose of such an appropriation, however, as for example in the Third Symphony's course through nature back toward a human-inflected love, was to theorize a place for the individual in an indifferent world.

Strauss, for his part, could not have been more indifferent to nature's indifference toward him. In his encounters with nature he took no notice of himself, or of what effect he might have had on the world. He had a feeling for something like infinity, but a cold, unknowing, physical infinity, one that would stimulate his creative mind not by seeming to empathize with his human concerns but by presenting a mountain range with a musically suggestive profile. In both of Strauss's nature pieces, *Aus Italien* and *Eine Alpensinfonie*, the outside world is not a character but a fact, and the subjective protagonist reacts to nature without forming a relationship with it. Strauss approached his "Symphonic Fantasy" with the conscious determination to use nature as a sounding board—to meditate, with its help, on the various options available to him as symphonic composer. Writing a series of landscapes allowed him to produce a multimovement work with traditional forms that simultaneously entertained different kinds of programmaticism—painterly, and "expressive" à la Hausegger— that were then competing for his attention. This was a clinical exercise, a compositional étude, not a cry for help from the individual to the collective. The point becomes explicit in the finale, a romp based on a tune about a fascinating new piece of technology—"Funiculi, funicula," celebrating a funicular built on Mount Vesuvius in 1880. This piece of mechanical equipment was just as legitimately a part of the landscape to Strauss as any mountain or lake, because its lifelessness, or soullessness, replicated the beautiful everlasting indifference embodied by the rest of the world.

A need to reiterate this early belief stood behind the lengthy but inexorable drive to complete the *Alpensinfonie*, whose seventeen-year genesis was sixteen years longer than Strauss required for any other orchestral work. The eerie B-flat-minor framing device, built on a quotation of his Second Symphony, reminds us at the end that, from nature's perspective, nothing has happened. All the intervening action—the ascent, the triumphant arrival at the summit, the "vision"—involves a character who exists only as a witness. He gives nothing to nature, he has no effect on it, and he has no expectation that his presence will elicit any interest on the part of the world. The Nietzschean qualities of the work, focused on the physical as a foil to an outdated metaphysics (hence the provisional title "The Antichrist"),[18] include also a recommendation as old as *The Birth of Tragedy*: the treatment of life "as an aesthetic phenomenon." Nature had meaning for Strauss only insofar as he himself could draw meaning from it. It would not reach out to him; he had to make sense of it on his own terms. He understood that this responsibility lay with him, and he accepted it without complaint, without regret, and indeed without any emotional response that we can discern.

Strauss's attitude toward nature presents one instance of a trait with broad significance across his personality: his utter, unfailing self-sufficiency. When his parents had provided the technical training required of a professional musician, and when Bülow had given him a forum for demonstrating his abilities in public, Strauss could apply in practice what was always his deepest personal inclination: to get what he wanted by doing it himself. Emotionally, psychologically, artistically, practically, Strauss needed very little from other people, the major exception being his relationships with opera librettists, the frustrations of which are striking and at times pathetic. At heart Strauss was a lone wolf, an independent mind who, given a stable family life and a secure routine, could go on fulfilling his artistic mission indefinitely. With respect to self esteem he approached something like perfection; he did not overestimate his talents, but neither did he underestimate them, even in the most difficult moments of his career, and he never questioned his ability to excel in the art for which he seemed to have been born. Moreover, he was fully conscious of this dimension of his personality, and he gave himself credit for it. For Strauss the belief in himself, and the concomitant dedication to self-improvement, was an ethical disposition reflected in his characterization of the personal meaning of *Eine Alpensinfonie*: "moral purification through one's own strength."[19]

The impatience that Strauss felt with Mahler's religious tendencies was matched by bemused indulgence of the petty jealousies and insecurities that burst forth every so often from Mahler's side of the relationship. The early years of the composers' correspondence are peppered with Mahler's complaints about perceived snubs by Strauss. In 1893 he remarked pointedly to Strauss, who at that time was primarily a conductor, that no living conductor was interested in his compositions.[20] In 1894, after negative reviews of the performance of the First Symphony organized by Strauss, he suggested to Arnold Berliner that Strauss himself might have been behind the critics' reaction.[21] In 1895 Mahler went silent after Strauss had to decline an invitation to attend the first full performance of the Second Symphony.[22] Over time, the list grew: Strauss allegedly mistreated him at a social gathering; Strauss neglected to ask him about his latest compositions; Strauss stole the credit for introducing the E-flat clarinet into the orchestra.[23] And, most distressingly to Mahler, Strauss included criticism in his generally favorable remarks on Mahler's compositions, for example concerning the finale of the First, the Adagietto of the Fifth (a critique echoed by Adorno), and the Sixth in general, which he called "overinstrumented."[24]

Such incidents never swayed Strauss from his practical support of Mahler's musical creations. Even three decades after his friend's death, when he found that Alma had distorted his unblemished record in this area, he expressed no regret for what he had done, only disappointment. But insofar as he reflected critically on Mahler's life, as opposed to promoting Mahler's activities, Strauss saw irremediable weaknesses— weaknesses of character and of morality, which had a destructive effect however indispensable they may have been to the nature of the creative output. And the flaws that Strauss noted were relatively muted examples compared to the private complaints that Mahler for his part shared with Alma and Bauer-Lechner, to the effect that Strauss could "see only the pedestal" on which Mahler stood, or that his own praise of Strauss to Arthur Seidl had been "not completely sincere."[25] A genuine interest in Mahler's personality, beyond an affection or shared professional interest, taught Strauss that within this complex persona lay insecurities that were the real pillars of his character, and to which both ethics and aesthetics accommodated themselves.

Mahler would have said much the same thing of Strauss, laying blame, however, not at a religiosity motivated by private insecurity but at a personal detachment bordering on the pathological. It is doubtful that Mahler drew satisfaction from the fact that Strauss never lashed out at him with anything like jealous anger. Apathy, not security, would have been Mahler's explanation; the charge of "coolness" was the most frequent and the most passionate that he directed at Strauss. He recoiled from what he called "something *cold* about Strauss that has nothing to do with his talent but with his *character*" (emphasis in original).[26] He longed for "a little more warmth," for relief from the "offhanded, self-important attitude." He feared that it might be contagious: "Strauss has such a sobering influence; in his world one scarcely recognizes oneself."[27] Ultimately Mahler admitted a certain bitterness toward Providence, and complained that the interior and exterior contradicted one another: "beneath a pile of rubble smolders a living volcano, a subterranean fire—not just a display of fireworks."[28]

Mahler complained most vocally when he sensed that Strauss was as detached from his own music as he was from anyone else's. He did not understand why Strauss refused to draw the kind of spiritual meaning from music that Mahler saw as the art's greatest strength. Nevertheless, Mahler was most deeply hurt by those cases where Strauss's aloofness took the form of good taste in handling a disagreement that could never be mediated. To take the most famous example, it was clearly the intensification of spiritual content in the Third Symphony that moved Strauss to walk out of the premiere (June 9, 1902, at Krefeld) and later that evening to visit Mahler's table without mentioning the work. Alma said that after this treatment Mahler's "spirits sank and the public acclamation now seemed of no account."[29] But for Strauss the alternative to silence was contempt. Walter Panofsky claimed that Mahler reminded Strauss of Jochanaan, in his straddling of Judaism and Christianity but more deeply in what Strauss considered the simple foolishness of outdated metaphysical yearning.[30] (Recall that Strauss described the character of John the Baptist in his opera *Salome* as "a clown" preaching in the desert and feeding on locusts.)[31]

By 1902 Strauss had spent the better part of twenty years trying to destroy the worldview that the Third meant to resuscitate. No one was in a better position to recognize this attack than Mahler; indeed, the simultaneous composition of two philosophically opposed Nietzsche works in 1896 must have been something of a private competition to the two composers. From then on, a fundamental alienation must have seemed inevitable; if Alma judged correctly that in Mahler's opinion "[no one] had said anything of value about the nature of music" aside from Wagner and Schopenhauer, then Strauss can hardly have suppressed a demeanor that on some level was "cold."[32] But in this judgment Mahler was reacting against not just a dry personality or a crude obsession with royalties, but against a philosophical argument, coming from the most technically gifted composer of the day. For an educated, reflective musician such as Mahler, who was loath to give up Schopenhauer, Strauss represented an enemy whose worldview moved Mahler to Schopenhauerian laments: "it's enough to make you retreat into an impenetrable forest and cut yourself off from the outside world."[33]

Retreat would become for Strauss, as for Mahler, a dream pursued in both art and life. As discussed above, *Guntram* ends with the protagonist abandoning "the curse of sinful humanity" in favor of a solitary ascetic existence in the forest. Likewise, in the most personal of the tone poems, *Ein Heldenleben*, composed just four years after *Guntram*'s horrific failure in Munich, the hero's journey culminates in a "flight from the world" that dreams of a future with a minimum of human contact (but now with at least the "companion" for company). These cases of course fantasize an intensification of Strauss's practical career planning, but it is worth noting that he limited his attempts to make the fantasy a reality. In the notations of his guest conducting engagements in his private calendar, which meticulously record when and where the performance took place as well as how much he was paid, one sees an interest in something more than the cumulative total of his earnings, which of course he could have learned from his banker at any time. The process, the activity, the ongoing connection to the world of music was something that Strauss could not give up, and the fact that he earned money for this activity told him in a tangible way that his abilities were valued by other people, who, as Goethe would say, determine whether or not the process of artistic communication had been consummated. If the day-to-day aggravations of practicing the art could now and then tempt him to quit, the reality of his art's connection with human interaction would never allow it. The films of the late Strauss conducting with obvious pleasure and quiet emotion corroborate the evidence provided by his continued activity in the concert hall and recording studio: only physical decline could take him from the podium.

Mahler found the same to be the case for himself; one senses that no matter how long he had lived, his death would have come, like Strauss's, not long after his last appearance on the podium. The final years in New York, which in a relatively short time would have brought him the means to retire, likewise facilitated longer summer breaks than he had enjoyed in Vienna. But Henry-Louis de La Grange has argued that the New York engagements in fact laid the groundwork not for retirement but for further and expanded activity, building on an already heavy schedule (typically at least three performances per week).[34] The three weeks immediately preceding his breakdown in February 1911 saw him conducting the Philharmonic in eleven concerts with eight different programs. He considered this level of activity a light workload, augmenting it where circumstances and his health allowed. Thus as much as Mahler may have dreamt of retirement, he was no more keen than Strauss to see that hope fulfilled.

The close association between withdrawal and death in Mahler's work suggests a basic insight that holds good for both composers, at least generally. The art cannot be dissociated from the process of accepting death. The peace toward which many of Mahler's compositions strive, from the Third and Fourth to *Das Lied von der Erde* and the Ninth, forms by dissolving the boundary between love and immortality. The "Abschied" of Mahler's final orchestral song must have been offered to Alma, as Peter Franklin claims, but the nature of the farewell is to create an intense experience of love, a religious vision of sorts, through which the composer's sense of self could melt into something eternal. Mahler used love to rehearse for death. In the Fourth, he imagined the face of his dead mother, transposed into the visage of a saint, to provide himself with an antidote to the horror of the previous movement and a transition to his own apotheosis in the closing heavenly song. The similar moment in the Eighth, with the *Mater gloriosa* descending in a quasi-operatic tableau, presented (in spite of the histrionic stylization) the sincere exegesis of Mahler's worldview described in chapter 3.[35] It was an attempt to express what could not be expressed, an oblique glimpse of eternity through an overloaded maternal symbol: Mary, his mother Maria, and Alma Maria, who filled a role recognized and explained in short order by Freud. Thus death and love and family coalesced into a vision of a future after death, a retreat from life toward something that could be imagined only imperfectly but that allowed a life on earth that would not be dominated by dread of what lay after.

We can infer from Strauss's voracious reading of Goethe at the end of his life—to the near-exclusion of all else, apparently—that he, like Mahler, believed with the poet in the fear of death as the strongest force in human life. Strauss dealt with this fear through his domestic spirituality, putting this worldview into practice at the villa in Garmisch (completed in 1908). This retreat in a spectacularly beautiful setting became the center of Strauss's existence during the last half of his life, in a way that Mahler could identify with but did not live to enjoy for long. Yet even in Strauss's sixties, seventies, and eighties, forays into the real world remained a necessity, right through 1947, when he travelled by airplane for the first time and was regaled in London as a twentieth-century Haydn. The urge documented by these trips has a parallel in late works' review of his creative life, in which he considered at a remove the implications and wisdom of decisions made in earlier days. He came away convinced that he had lived up to the responsibilities of his gift; "I have done my job—there is nothing left to do," he told his daughter-in-law just before his death.[36] The creative immersion in his own art was also a surrender to death, however, for he believed openly that the only part of him to live on would be his works. The aged Strauss composed music about his own music because that was the closest he could come to experiencing a believable vision of immortality.

In a roundabout way, then, this artist who seemed for eight decades utterly detached from a stable self, surrounded himself psychologically in the end with nothing but the products of his own mind. We do not know what he said to Pauline in his final weeks, but from the reports of Alice Strauss and Rudolf Hartmann it seems that Strauss lived this period absorbed in musical memories, emerging periodically to report on the experience but otherwise on his own. Touchingly, he lived out something like the apotheosis of his hero in *Tod und Verklärung*, as he explicitly reported to Alice. "It was exactly like that," he told her, meaning not just that the approach of death felt like the sound of the C-major coda, but that in the ultimate loneliness of dying he found himself surrounded by an ideal vision of his own work, a long-sought image of himself as a fact in the world. Forced to confront himself by the imminent reality of his nonexistence, Strauss found some consolation in reflecting that his works had become a fixed part of the world he left behind.

Mahler was not so lucky at the end. Though similarly disengaged from his family and the outside world in the terrible aloofness of death, the composer seems not to have reflected substantially on his own creations. Instead he read *The Problem of Life* by Eduard von Hartmann, imagined future productions (including *The Barber of Baghdad*, strangely enough), and, in the very last moments, said again and again, "Mozart!"[37] In this crisis, his own compositions were not enough for him. Indeed, his creative work may even have caused him some regret for the time it cost him with other people, or such would seem to be implied by the remark, "My life has all been paper!" which he made more than once to Alma. In the agonizing death struggle, physically so different from Strauss's, he could draw little comfort from the countless times he had imagined this moment in his music. Even his request for a funeral marker with his name alone—because "any who come to look for me will know who I was, and the rest do not need to know"—shows a striking pessimism whether his creative work might offer him a kind of continued existence.

Only one photograph exists of Mahler and Strauss together (figure 10).[38] Taken from about twenty feet—close enough to reveal details, distant enough to be frustrating—it shows them standing at the entrance of the Graz opera house in May 1906. Alex Ross and others suggest a date of May 16, when *Salome* had its Austrian premiere.[39] Strauss apparently needed more to fill up a day, for he arranged a chauffeured outing for himself, Gustav, and Alma to the waterfalls in Golling an der Salzach, fully 140 miles west of Graz.[40] Alma described the event at length, in the sympathetic, energized tone familiar when Strauss was not accompanied by

Figure 10. The only known photograph of Strauss and Mahler together. Graz, May 1906. Courtesy of the Gustav Mahler—Alfred Rosé Collection, University of Western Ontario, London, Ontario.

his wife. The Strauss she remembers is cool as a cucumber: unfazed when the car skids off a wet road, lingering endlessly over simple food in a local inn, seemingly immune to stage fright. She wonders briefly whether it is all a façade, but of course this is the Strauss we have come to know. Mahler, likewise, plays true to form. Overstressed by the calm, he fidgets and pleads, and by midafternoon has had enough: "If you won't go, then I will—and conduct in your place."[41]

Alas, the photo's eastward early afternoon shadows suggest that we are looking at a different day.[42] The mood, however, seems the same. Mahler furrows his brow, gazing exasperatedly into the distance. Strauss, smiling and active, with limbs heading in different directions, entertains the onlookers as a doorman waits and Mahler stands poised to enter. As always, carefree patience contrasts with restive urgency. A stout woman wearing a hat with a massive bow—could it be Alma?—looks away, duplicating Mahler's aloofness while the others stare rapt at the lanky bundle of energy. Strauss acts, immersed in the present; Mahler contemplates, waiting his turn.

In a private lapse of modesty that has since become famous, Mahler remarked to Alma in 1902, "my time will come when his is over."[43] He was half right; his time did come, if later than it should have. It came, however, not because Strauss's ended, but because it continued. These distinct musical oeuvres strengthened each other, just as the profound, unavoidable differences between their creators somehow improved both of them. Then as now, the two sides depended on each other. And by the same token, we can understand each better because we know the other. Their irreconcilability is not a problem. It is what gives life to the subject, and to the art.

Notes

INTRODUCTION: FRIENDS

1. Herta Blaukopf, "Rivalität und Freundschaft: Die persönlichen Beziehungen zwischen Gustav Mahler und Richard Strauss," in *Gustav Mahler, Richard Strauss: Briefwechsel 1888–1911*, ed. Herta Blaukopf (Munich: R. Piper, 1980), 129–220; translated as "Rivalry and Friendship: An Essay on the Mahler-Strauss Relationship," in *Gustav Mahler, Richard Strauss: Correspondence 1888–1911*, ed. Herta Blaukopf, trans. Edmund Jephcott (Chicago: University of Chicago Press, 1984), 103–58. The translation is abbreviated in this volume as *Rivalry*.

2. The first modern scholarly treatment in English was Stephen E. Hefling's "Miners Digging from Opposite Sides: Mahler, Strauss, and the Problem of Program Music," in *Richard Strauss: New Perspectives on the Composer and His Work*, ed. Bryan Gilliam (Durham, NC: Duke University Press, 1992), 40–53. Peter Franklin deals almost exclusively with Mahler in "Strauss and His Contemporaries: Critical Perspectives," in *The Richard Strauss Companion*, ed. Mark-Daniel Schmid (Westport, CT: Praeger, 2003), 31–61. A creative and even-handed account opens Alex Ross's *The Rest Is Noise: Listening to the Twentieth Century* (New York: Farrar, Straus and Giroux, 2007), 3–32. Among recent biographers of either composer, few even treat the relationship as a discrete topic. Jens Malte Fischer's 2003 biography at least offers a six-page overview in a book of 766 pages

(in translation), along with numerous other brief references; see Jens Malte Fischer, *Gustav Mahler*, trans. Stewart Spencer (New Haven: Yale University Press, 2011), 474–79.

3. Admittedly, Adorno is a complex case, thanks to his evolution from admirer to antagonist of Strauss. Long before his withering 1964 attack on Strauss as "composer-captain of industry," the philosopher-musicologist had written in 1924 with something like admiration, acknowledging in this music a capacity to be critical—to address, as did the music of Mahler, the plight of the modern individual. For the twenty-one-year-old Adorno, Strauss "escaped the fate of [. . .] lyrical form-anarchy," even as he proved himself "charmed against the temptation of empty forms, which give the appearance of objectivity and yet possess, at best, the objectivity of the machine." See Theodor W. Adorno, "Richard Strauss at Sixty," trans. Susan Gillespie, in *Richard Strauss and His World*, ed. Bryan Gilliam (Princeton, NJ: Princeton University Press, 1992), 406–15, quotation from 409; idem, "Richard Strauss. Born June 11, 1864," trans. Samuel Weber and Shierry Weber, *Perspectives of New Music* 4 (1965): 14–32, and 5 (1966): 113–29. On Schoenberg's transition from Straussian to Mahlerian and its motivations in Strauss's criticisms of the younger composer's turn to atonality, see Andreas Jacob, "Ein sachlicher Heiliger? Schönbergs Mahler," in *Gustav Mahler und die musikalische Moderne*, ed. Arnold Jacobshagen (Stuttgart: Franz Steiner, 2011), 145–56, esp. 146–48.

4. Carl Dahlhaus, "Gustav Mahler und Richard Strauss. Die Geschichte einer problematischen Freundschaft in Briefen," *Frankfurter Allgemeine Zeitung*, November 8, 1980.

5. Throughout their relationship Mahler and Strauss addressed each other with the formal *Sie* rather than the familiar *Du*. One ought not to overinterpret this choice, however, as both figures reserved the *Du* form to intimate relationships, such as family and acquaintances from childhood. Thus Mahler was *geduzt* with Siegfried Lipiner and Friedrich Löhr but not with Bruno Walter, Alfred Roller, or Willem Mengelberg; Strauss with Ludwig Thuille and Arthur Seidl but not with Hugo von Hofmannsthal, Alexander Ritter, Hans von Bülow, or Clemens Krauss. Certainly a meaningful connection as colleagues, artists, and human beings was not irreconcilable with the formal mode of address.

6. *Rivalry*, 108.

7. Gilbert Kaplan, exec. prod, *Mahler Plays Mahler: The Welte-Mignon Piano Rolls* (New York: Kaplan Foundation, GLRS 101, 1993, CD).

8. Bernhard Pollini (1838–97), born Baruch Pohl, managed the Italian Opera in St. Petersburg and Moscow before serving in Hamburg from 1876 until his

death. Under his leadership the Stadttheater gained a strong reputation as a modern opera house, particularly for performances of Wagner.

9. Henry-Louis de La Grange holds that "Strauss's role in this affair is far from clear," but while the details of the latter's communications with Pollini are not known, there is no doubt that Strauss informed Mahler of his negotiations before they reached a conclusion (in a letter now lost but received by Mahler on February 3, 1894), and that Mahler wanted to confront Pollini but "should not wish to do so without your [Strauss's] consent." *La Grange I*, 290. Mahler to Strauss, February 3, 1894 (two separate letters written on the same day). *Mahler/Strauss*, 28–29.

10. It is easy to imagine why Strauss preferred the peculiar thrill of this lurch from C to D over the normalized version at mm. 631–36, one measure before reh. 53. Strauss's letter is lost, but the reply from Mahler is clear enough: "that you wish to find the conclusion and, as it were, a summary of the whole piece at the point you refer to merely shows me that I have not expressed myself at all *clearly* [. . .] Just one thing today: at the place in question the conclusion is merely apparent (in the full sense of a 'false conclusion'), and a change and breaking-down that reaches to the essence is needed before a true 'victory' can be won after such a struggle." Mahler to Strauss, July 19, 1894. *Mahler/Strauss*, 37. The term "breakthrough," much used by Adorno and subsequent commentators on Mahler, was coined by Paul Bekker, whose *Gustav Mahlers Sinfonien* (Berlin: Schuster & Loeffler, 1921) has appeared recently in translation. See Kelly Dean Hansen, "*Gustav Mahler's Symphonies (Gustav Mahlers Sinfonien)* by Paul Bekker (1921): A Translation with Commentary" (PhD diss., University of Colorado, 2012); for discussion of breakthrough in the First Symphony, see 114, 153.

11. Otto Lessmann concluded his review of this performance (which took place on June 3, 1894) with the observation that a portion of the audience had "tried to thwart the applause by loud hissing." "Die XXX. Tonkünstler-Versammlung der Allgemeinen Deutschen Musikvereins—Weimar 31. Mai-6. Juni," *Allgemeine Musik-Zeitung* 25 (1894): 348.

12. The philosophical substance of *Guntram* consists in its dramatization of Schopenhauer's conclusions about art vis-à-vis the Will, namely that lasting "denial of the Will" (*Willensverneinung*) cannot be achieved through art, but only through "saintliness" (*Heiligkeit*). The implications for Schopenhauerian musical metaphysics, the default orientation of Austro-German composers in the late nineteenth century, were profound. See Charles Youmans, *Richard Strauss's Orchestral Music and the German Intellectual Tradition* (Bloomington: Indiana University Press, 2005), 68–82.

13. Ibid., 88–113.

14. James Hepokoski, "Framing Till Eulenspiegel," *19th-Century Music* 30 (2006): 4–42.

15. See chapter 12 for a discussion of Nietzschean issues in the last three movements of the Third.

16. Peter Franklin, "A Stranger's Story: Programmes, Politics, and Mahler's Third Symphony," in *The Mahler Companion*, ed. Donald Mitchell and Andrew Nicholson (Oxford: Oxford University Press, 1999), 181–82.

17. Mahler's terms are "seinesgleichen warm zu halten," "platten Korybanten," and "Industrieritter." Mahler to Max Marschalk, December 4, 1896. *Mahler Letters*, 200.

18. Franklin, "A Stranger's Story," 174.

19. Mahler to Strauss, August 12, 1897. *Mahler/Strauss*, 46.

20. Strauss to Mahler, February 22, 1897. Ibid., 45.

21. Hofmannsthal expressed his opposition freely to Strauss, first citing concern that Strauss would put his own interests above those of the institution, then adding the broader complaint regarding the composer's "neglect of all the higher standards of intellectual existence." Hofmannsthal to Strauss, August 1, 1918. Franz Strauss and Alice Strauss, eds., *The Correspondence between Richard Strauss and Hugo von Hofmannsthal*, trans. Hanns Hammelmann and Ewald Osers (Cambridge: Cambridge University Press, 1980), 308–309.

22. Fritz Busch, *Aus dem Leben eines Musikers* (Zurich: Rascher, 1949), 169. Here Busch attributes the quotation to both Strauss and Max Reger, claiming that the two expressed the same view of Mahler's compositions, "in the same Bavarian dialect" ("Sö, Busch, der Mahler, dös is überhaupt gar ka Komponist. Dös is bloss a ganz grosser Dirigent").

23. Strauss to Mahler, February 4, 1902. *Mahler/Strauss*, 66.

24. Strauss to Mahler, July 11, 1901. Ibid., 56.

25. Adorno stated specifically that without the scherzo "Strauss's *Rosenkavalier* would hardly be thinkable." Theodor W. Adorno, *Mahler: A Musical Physiognomy*, trans. Edmund Jephcott (Chicago: University of Chicago Press, 1992), 102–103.

26. Alma Mahler, *Gustav Mahler: Memories and Letters*, ed. Donald Mitchell, trans. Basil Creighton (London: Cardinal, 1990), 24. In confronting the "Alma problem"—the notorious tendentiousness and indeed flat-out falsifications in her memoirs and "editing" of Mahler's correspondence—one must nonetheless guard against throwing out the baby with the bathwater. Much important work has been done in recent years to separate fact from fiction, most importantly by

Henry-Louis de La Grange, Günther Weiss, and Knud Martner in the German edition of the correspondence, and by Antony Beaumont in his expanded translation (jointly abbreviated here as *Gustav/Alma*, with citations referring to the translation unless otherwise noted). Moreover, even uncorroborated anecdotes have the potential to shed useful light when the question at hand has less to do with factual matters than with the emotional puzzles of human interaction. I have done my utmost not to spread lies, while accepting that, for better or worse, Alma was Mahler's most intimate relationship.

27. *Memories and Letters*, 88–89.

28. Mahler to Alma Mahler, May 22, 1906. *Gustav/Alma*, 233.

29. Ibid.

30. Mahler to Alma Mahler, January 10, 1907. Ibid., 255.

31. In Strasbourg, Mahler had expressed concern when he found out that Strauss had not yet composed the dance; he could not understand how one could compose an opera on Salome without having the dance in mind. Those doubts apparently subsided when he finally heard the complete opera. *Memories and Letters*, 89.

32. Ross, *The Rest Is Noise*, 8.

33. On January 14, 1907, Strauss reported to Mahler that he believed Adolph Fürstner would agree to Strauss's request to provide Mahler with a copy of the score for private study. Mahler would write on February 6, 1907, "Many thanks for *Salome*. It simply will not leave my desk." *Mahler/Strauss*, 96–97. On *Das Lied von der Erde*, Niekerk argues that Mahler's song cycle "is conceived as a direct dialogue both with Strauss's opera and its libretto and with the Orientalist imagery that both evoke," while also emphasizing important differences, especially Mahler's avoidance of *Salome*'s "exuberant sexuality." Carl Niekerk, *Reading Mahler: German Culture and Jewish Identity in Fin-de-Siècle Vienna* (Rochester: Camden House, 2010), 197–208; quotations from 197 and 203.

34. *Memories and Letters*, xliii.

35. Strauss's self-description, related in Walter Thomas Anderman, *Bis der Vorhang fiel: Berichtet nach Aufzeichnungen aus den Jahren 1940 bis 1945* (Dortmund: K. Schwalvenberg, 1947), 241.

36. *La Grange IV*, 976. We will see below (in the Epilogue) that the "hostile reaction" that Mahler perceived in Strauss (so described by Mahler to Julius Korngold) had much to do with the work's content. See Julius Korngold, *Die Korngolds in Wien: Der Musikkritiker und das Wunderkind: Aufzeichnungen* (Zurich: Edition Musik & Theater, 1991), 141.

37. "Blaues Tagebuch," Richard-Strauss-Archiv (RSA) quoted in *Rivalry*, 151.

38. *Mahler/Strauss*, 100.

39. "Gustav Mahler nach schwerer Krankheit am 19. Mai verschieden./Der Tod dieses hochstrebenden, idealen, energischen Künstlers ein schwerer Verlust./Die ergreifenden Memoiren Wagners mit Rührung gelesen./Lectüre *[D]eutsche Geschichte im Zeitalter der Reformation* [italics mine] Leop. Ranke: durch sie wird mir hell bestätigt, daß alle dort die Cultur fördernden Elemente seit Jahrhunderten nicht mehr lebenskräftig, wie alle großen politischen u. religiösen Bewegungen nur eine Zeitlang wirklich befruchtend wirken können./Der Jude Mahler konnte im Christentum noch Erhebung gewinnen./Der Held Rich. Wagner ist als Greis, durch den Einfluß Schopenhauers wieder zu ihm herabgestiegen./Mir ist es absolut deutlich, daß die deutsche Nation nur durch die Befreiung vom Christentum neue Tatkraft gewinnen kann [. . .]/Ich will meine Alpensinfonie: den Antichrist nennen, als da ist: sittliche Reinigung aus eigener Kraft, Befreiung durch die Arbeit, Anbetung der ewigen herrlichen Natur." Entry in Strauss's personal calendar, May 1911, RSA. A facsimile of this page has been published in Stephan Kohler, "Richard Strauss. Eine Alpensinfonie op. 64," *Neue Zeitschrift für Musik* 143/11 (November 1982): 42–46. See also *Rivalry*, 152–53, and Walter Werbeck, *Die Tondichtungen von Richard Strauss* (Tutzing: Hans Schneider, 1996), 198.

1. CHILDREN

1. Strauss's sister and only sibling, Johanna von Rauchenberger-Strauss, left a forthright and at times poignantly detailed account of Strauss family life in her "Jugenderinnerungen," in *Richard Strauss Jahrbuch 1959/60*, ed. Willi Schuh (Bonn: Boosey & Hawkes, 1960), 7–30.

Natalie Bauer-Lechner reported a few of Mahler's own observations on his childhood—perhaps more than we know, as her "Mahleriana," now owned by Henry-Louis de La Grange, has yet to be published in its entirety. The most recent version of this source is Herbert Killian and Knud Martner, eds., *Gustav Mahler in den Erinnerungen von Natalie Bauer-Lechner* (Hamburg: K. D. Wagner, 1984); for an English translation see *Bauer-Lechner*. A publication of Bauer-Lechner's complete recollections—or as complete a version as can be gathered—is reportedly in the offing; see Morten Solvik and Stephen E. Hefling, "Natalie Bauer-Lechner on Mahler and Women: A Newly Discovered Document," *Musical Quarterly* 97 (2014): 19, n. 2.

Mahler's boyhood friend Theodor Fischer shared numerous revealing anecdotes in his widely excerpted "Aus Gustav Mahlers Jugendzeit," *Deutsche Heimat: Sudetendeutsche Monatsschrift für Kunst, Literatur, Heimat und Volkskunde* 7 (1931): 264–68. The biographies of Willi Schuh and La Grange—both of which owe their status as definitive works to the fact that they are less biographies than enormous repositories of primary sources—are peppered with family members' stories of the composers' childhoods.

2. *La Grange I*, 18.

3. Richard Strauss (the composer's grandson), personal conversation with the author, June 24, 1994.

4. Theodor Adorno, for example, called Strauss a "son of rich parents," though he surely knew that the maternal grandparents' wealth had relatively little impact on their daughter's family. Adorno, "Richard Strauss. Born June 11, 1864," 15. Peter Franklin has observed that the "popular mythic version of Mahler's life-story" originated with the composer himself. Peter Franklin, *The Life of Mahler* (Cambridge: Cambridge University Press, 1997), 14. Indeed, to Bauer-Lechner the composer called the living conditions of his first home (in Kalischt) "wretched," without noting the considerable improvements during the family's time in Iglau. *Bauer-Lechner*, 69.

5. Graues Heft IV, 5, Richard-Strauss-Archiv (RSA).

6. Robert Breuer, "My Brother, Richard Strauss," *Saturday Review* (New York), December 27, 1958, 32.

7. Rauchenberger-Strauss, "Jugenderinnerungen," 15, 24.

8. Ibid., 10.

9. *La Grange I*, 26.

10. Strauss's mother, Josephine Strauss (née Pschorr), on numerous occasions required extended treatment in sanatoria, for psychological breakdowns brought on, it seems, by Franz Strauss's volatile temper. Details on these episodes, and on the father's role in them, can be found in *Chronicle*, 83–84; see also Bryan Gilliam, *The Life of Richard Strauss* (Cambridge: Cambridge University Press, 1999), 27–28.

11. Donald Mitchell, *Gustav Mahler*, vol. 1, *The Early Years*, rev. and ed. Paul Banks and David Matthews (Berkeley: University of California Press, 1980), 24.

12. A useful treatment of this philosophy, and especially the roots of its modern form in Herder and Goethe, is W. H. Bruford, *The German Tradition of Self-Cultivation: Bildung from Humboldt to Thomas Mann* (Cambridge: Cambridge University Press, 1975).

13. Kurt Wilhelm, *Richard Strauss: An Intimate Portrait*, trans. Mary Whittall (New York: Rizzoli, 1989), 197.

14. Stefan Zweig, *The World of Yesterday* [1942], trans. Anthea Bell (London: Pushkin Press, 2009), 52–53.

15. Mahler to Max Marschalk, December 1896. *Mahler Letters*, 200.

16. Indeed, William McGrath argues in the first paragraph of his well-known monograph that cultural, political, and social issues raised in high school provided the impetus for a mutual attraction among this diverse group of thinkers, whose "shared intellectual development has been largely overlooked." William J. McGrath, *Dionysian Art and Populist Politics in Austria* (New Haven: Yale University Press, 1974), 1. Among Strauss's peers, two especially strong forces were Arthur Seidl (1863–1928), a dramaturg and critic of considerable repute who served in 1898–99 as an editor of the first edition of Nietzsche's correspondence, and Friedrich Rösch (1862–1925), a boy-genius who became a professional conductor but gave it up to practice law, with important results for Strauss's battle for composer's rights. A biographical sketch of Seidl can be found in Ludwig Frankenstein, *Arthur Seidl: Ein Lebensabriß* (Regensburg: Gustav Bosse, 1913), 7–14.

17. Richard Specht, *Gustav Mahler* (Berlin: Gose & Tetzlaff, 1905), 17.

18. Mahler to Josef Steiner, June 18, 1879. *Mahler Letters*, 55.

19. On Strauss's idiosyncratic taste in poetry, see Susan Youens, "Actually, I like my songs best": Strauss's Lieder," in *The Cambridge Companion to Richard Strauss*, ed. Charles Youmans (Cambridge: Cambridge University Press, 2010), 151–77, esp. 151–55.

20. *La Grange I*, 23.

21. Ibid., 25–26.

22. Schuh writes that "at a children's concert on 19 March 1876 Richard performed Weber's *Invitation to the Dance*." *Chronicle*, 25.

23. *La Grange I*, 42.

24. Ibid., 18.

25. The complete correspondence between Strauss and Thuille, which began in October 1877, when Strauss was thirteen and Thuille sixteen, has been published as Franz Trenner, ed., *Richard Strauss, Ludwig Thuille: Ein Briefwechsel* (Tutzing: Hans Schneider, 1980). A good selection of letters in English translation appears in Susan Gillespie, trans., "Selections from the Strauss-Thuille Correspondence: A Glimpse of Strauss During His Formative Years," in *Richard Strauss and His World*, ed. Bryan Gilliam (Princeton, NJ: Princeton University Press, 1992), 193–236.

26. See above, note 16.

27. Rudolf Krzyzanowsky (1859–1911), was perhaps Mahler's first friendly rival as a composer. In 1876 Mahler persuaded his friend to accompany him to Iglau, where they took part in a concert benefiting a local school; the first movement of Krzyzanowsky's Piano Quartet was followed on the program by a com-

plete performance of Mahler's own Piano Quartet, the latter work having won first prize that year at the conservatory. *Mährischer Grenzbote*, September 17, 1876, quoted in *Life, Work and World*, 25. Later the two would work simultaneously as conductors in Hamburg under the manipulative Bernhard Pollini, who encouraged Mahler to leave in 1896 by giving Krzyzanowski the duty of conducting *Tristan und Isolde* and *Die Meistersinger von Nürnberg*. The *Götterdämmerung* anecdote is in *La Grange I*, 43–44.

28. Rott (1858–84), whose Symphony in E (1878–80) occasionally finds its way to modern concert programs, has yet to receive a substantial biographical treatment but was the subject of a recent essay collection: Frank Litterschied, Helmuth Kreysing, and Maja Loehr, eds., *Hans Rott: der Begründer der neuen Symphonie* (Munich: Text+Kritik, 1999).

29. *La Grange I*, 49.

30. Undated letter in the archive of the Gesellschaft der Musikfreunde, quoted in *Life, Work and World*, 26.

31. Jens Malte Fischer, "Mahler. Leben und Welt," in *Mahler Handbuch*, ed. Bernd Sponheuer and Wolfram Steinbeck (Stuttgart: Metzler, 2010), 18–19.

32. "Sowol die *Mitwirkenden*, als auch das ganze *Publikum* waren aufs Tiefste ergriffen von dem mächtigen Bau und den wahrhaft erhabenen Gedanken, und ich erlebte zum Schluß der Aufführung, was ich für größten Triumph eines Werkes halten: das Publikum blieb lautlos sitzen, ohne sich zu bewegen, und erst nachdem der Dirigent und die mitwirkenden Künstler ihre Plätze verlassen, brach der Beifallssturm los." Mahler to Bruckner, April 16, 1892, Österreichische Nationalbibliothek. Alas, such sentiments only rarely translated into performances with Mahler at the podium.

33. "His antitraditional impulse thumbs its nose at its own class but never really means it." Adorno, "Richard Strauss. Born June 11, 1864," 24.

34. On Strauss's relationship with Ritter (1833–96), his Lisztian/Wagnerian mentor, see Charles Youmans, "Ten Letters from Alexander Ritter to Richard Strauss, 1887–1894," *Richard Strauss-Blätter* 35 [new series] (1996): 22; see also idem, *Richard Strauss's Orchestral Music*, 16–19 and 59–68. Strauss would later credit Ritter with curing him of his prejudices against Wagner and Liszt, introducing him to Wagner's writings and the philosophy of Schopenhauer, clarifying the terms of the Hausegger/Hanslick debate, and demonstrating that the sonata form had become an "empty shell." "New ideas must search for new forms [. . .] became from that day the guiding principle for my own symphonic work." See "Recollections of My Youth and Years of Apprenticeship," in *Recollections*, 138–39. Undoubtedly there is a degree of overstatement in this assessment, arising

from regret over their 1893 estrangement. The first and only biography of Ritter is Siegmund von Hausegger, *Alexander Ritter: Ein Bild seines Charakters und Schaffens* (Berlin: Marquardt & Co., [1907]).

35. A detailed overview of these compositions, most of which remain unpublished, can be found in Scott Warfield, "The Genesis of Richard Strauss's Macbeth" (PhD diss., University of North Carolina at Chapel Hill, 1995), 36–82.

36. A careful account of this relationship remains to be written. A recent attempt, but one that (like its predecessors) takes into account only a small portion of the correspondence, is Alan Walker, *Hans von Bülow: A Life and Times* (Oxford: Oxford University Press, 2010), 319–22, 383–84, 456–58. The complete correspondence is available in Gabriele Strauss, ed., *Lieber Collega! Richard Strauss im Briefwechsel mit zeitgenössischen Komponisten und Dirigenten* (Berlin: Henschel, 1996), 14–101.

Mahler of course developed a close relationship with Bülow during the former's tenure in Hamburg (1891–97), though by that time the younger figure was far more colleague than protégé. An attempt by Mahler in 1883 to secure a position as Bülow's assistant was bluntly rebuffed; in fact Bülow took the petty bureaucratic step of forwarding the letter to Mahler's current employer at Kassel. *La Grange I*, 113.

37. This difference would be felt even in the negotiations over repertoire and conductors at Bülow's funeral. Fed up with distasteful political wrangling, Strauss flatly refused to participate, to the horror of Mahler, who wrote frantically, "be *sure* to attend Bülow's funeral service" (emphasis in original). For details on this episode see *Mahler/Strauss*, 30–33.

38. Typically Strauss called on such language to spice up critical commentary on a musician's abilities, as for example in an 1891 comment on a performance of Peter Cornelius's *Der Cid* conducted by Hermann Levi: "Once again our Jewish provost beat time, so the performance was quite mediocre." Strauss to Cosima Wagner, June 20, 1891. Franz Trenner, ed., *Cosima Wagner, Richard Strauss: Ein Briefwechsel*, with the assistance of Gabriele Strauss (Tutzing, Hans Schneider, 1978), 95. Mahler for his part was not averse to pejorative remarks about Jews outside his bourgeois sphere; see the collection in Julian Johnson, *Mahler's Voices: Expression and Irony in the Songs and Symphonies* (Oxford: Oxford University Press, 2009), 256.

39. Schnitzler was quoted by Richard Batka in a review of a performance of Mahler's Seventh Symphony, *Prager Tagblatt*, September 20, 1907. See Karen Painter, ed., *Mahler and His World* (Princeton: Princeton University Press, 2002), 322; see also the discussion in Niekerk, *Reading Mahler*, 194–95.

40. Breuer, "My Brother, Richard Strauss," 33. On the origins of *alt-katholisch* theology, see chapter 12.

41. Most famously, perhaps, in the 1857 essay "Über Franz Liszt's symphonische Dichtungen: Brief an M. W." in *Gesammelte Schriften und Dichtungen von Richard Wagner*, vol. 5 (Leipzig: C. F. W. Siegel, [1907]), 182–98, where he draws the distinction between the excessively narrative programmaticism of Berlioz and Liszt's dramatically concentrated approach.

42. Describing the last movement of the Fourth, and specifically its character as summation of the "higher world" of the first three movements, Mahler commented, "the child—who, though in a chrysalis-state, nevertheless already belongs to this higher world—explains what it all means." *Bauer-Lechner*, 178.

43. Constantin Floros has discussed the song's position as both foundation and "the top of the symphony's pyramidal structure." Constantin Floros, *Gustav Mahler: The Symphonies*, trans. Vernon Wicker and Jutta Wicker (Portland, OR: Amadeus Press, 1993), 131.

44. A useful table of thematic connections between the song and the remaining three movements can be found in James Zychowicz, *Mahler's Fourth Symphony* (Oxford: Oxford University Press, 2000), 17.

45. *Bauer-Lechner*, 152–53.

46. Because the sketches of the first 599 measures of the work are missing, we do not have for this moment the taut verbal programmatic descriptions that often can be unearthed for the themes in Strauss's tone poems. An early plan, however, lists themes for "Papa" and "Mama," then for "Bubi, a mixture, but greater resemblance to Papa." Werbeck, *Die Tondichtungen*, 173–76.

47. In fact the varied components of the father's theme group seem intended by their very heterogeneity to undercut the notion of a stable, authentic subjectivity. See Charles Youmans, "The Twentieth-Century Symphonies of Richard Strauss," *Musical Quarterly* 84 (2000): 248–50.

48. When Mahler balked at allowing Strauss to perform the Fourth in Berlin before the Third had been heard there, Strauss called him a "pig-headed fellow," half in jest. Strauss to Mahler, July 11, 1901. *Mahler/Strauss*, 56. Bauer-Lechner was present for the rehearsals of the December 16, 1901, performance of the Fourth (conducted by Mahler) with Strauss's Berliner Tonkünstler-Orchester. She reported that Mahler "felt closer to the work at each successive rehearsal, [and] was finally quite swept off his feet by it, especially by the third movement." *Bauer-Lechner*, 184. Strauss engaged in a tug-of-war with Richard Sternfeld over the work in October 1901, before its Munich premiere (November 25, 1901). Strauss to Richard Sternfeld, October 10, 1901. Franz

Grasberger, ed., *Der Strom der Töne trug mich fort: Die Welt um Richard Strauss in Briefen* (Tutzing: Hans Schneider, 1967), 139.

49. Donald Mitchell, *Gustav Mahler: Songs and Symphonies of Life and Death* (Berkeley: University of California Press, 1985), 78.

50. Seeing the score of this symphony for the first time at the home of Hermann Levi, Strauss was especially struck by the third movement, "which we immediately played four-handed from the score." This anecdote, from one of Strauss's "gray notebooks" now held at the RSA, is quoted in *Mahler/Strauss*, 19.

2. CONDUCTORS

1. Raymond Holden's *Richard Strauss: A Musical Life* (New Haven: Yale University Press, 2011) focuses primarily on Strauss's career as a conductor. Holden gives a thorough account of what, when, and where Strauss performed, without going deeply into the specifics of his interpretive style (which is preserved in a healthy number of recordings) or attempting to relate his approaches to composition and interpretation.

2. "Remembering Mahler," in Kaplan, *Mahler Plays Mahler*.

3. Wilhelm, *Richard Strauss: An Intimate Portrait*, 206.

4. *Recollections*, 123.

5. While in New York, Mahler would tell Bruno Walter that "my only pleasures are the rehearsals of a work that is new to me." Mahler to Walter, December 19[?], 1909. *Mahler Letters*, 346.

6. Herta Blaukopf, "Mahler as Conductor in the Opera House and Concert Hall," in *The Cambridge Companion to Mahler*, ed. Jeremy Barham (Cambridge: Cambridge University Press, 2007), 165.

7. Richard Strauss, "Reminiscences of Hans von Bülow," in *Recollections*, 119.

8. Mahler to Hans von Bülow, spring/summer 1884, quoted in *Life, Work and World*, 57.

9. *La Grange I*, 151.

10. *Bauer-Lechner*, 51.

11. *Rivalry*, 110.

12. Bülow was known to bow in Mahler's direction, and even to offer (facetiously, but with generosity and uncharacteristic humility) to turn over the baton. On the respect and friendship between Bülow and Mahler during the Hamburg period, see Walker, *Hans von Bülow*, 427–28.

13. Strauss, "Reminiscences of Hans von Bülow," 121.

14. *Chronicle*, 92; Strauss, "Reminiscences of Hans von Bülow," 118.

15. Morten Solvik, "Mahler and Germany," in *The Mahler Companion*, ed. Donald Mitchell and Andrew Nicholson (Oxford: Oxford University Press, 1999), 127.

16. *La Grange I*, 112.

17. Strauss, "Reminiscences of Hans von Bülow," 121.

18. Anna Bahr-Mildenburg, "Meine erste Proben mit Gustav Mahler," *Neue freie Presse*, May 26, 1912.

19. These survive at the Richard-Strauss-Archiv.

20. Strauss to Franz Strauss, January 31, 1886. Willi Schuh, ed., *Richard Strauss: Briefe an die Eltern* (Zurich: Atlantis, 1954), 84–85.

21. Blaukopf, "Mahler as Conductor," 173.

22. Strauss gave a brief explanation of his rationale in his earliest published essay, a discussion of the 1891 production of *Tannhäuser* at Bayreuth. See "Brief eines deutschen Kapellmeisters über das Bayreuther Orchester. (Tannhäuser-Nachklänge)," *Bayreuther Blätter* 15 (1892): 126–32; published as "On the Production of 'Tannhäuser' in Bayreuth" in *Recollections*, 57–66.

23. Strauss to Hans von Bülow, October 29, 1887. Gabriele Strauss, *Lieber Collega!*, 66.

24. Blaukopf, "Mahler as Conductor," 174.

25. *Illustrirtes Wiener Extrablatt*, October 14, 1897.

26. *Fremden-Blatt*, February 22, 1903.

27. "Die Legende erzählt von dreißig Proben. Die Frucht dieser Proben war eine Aufführung von unbeschreiblicher Zartheit und Delikatesse." *Wiener Abendpost*, March 31, 1906.

28. "Es war eine Auferstehung ohnegleichen und ich bekenne gerne, daß mir das große Wunder dieser Musik gestern klarer aufging, denn je." *Illustrirtes Wiener Extrablatt*, March 31, 1906.

29. "Hier äußerte sich wirklich das Walten eines neuen, nicht bloß neuerungssüchtigen Geistes so edel, schön und überzeugend, daß man gern an eine mächtige künstlerische Renaissance, an den Anbruch eines neuen Blütenzeitalters des beliebten herrlichen Kunstinstituts glauben mochte." *Fremden-Blatt*, March 31, 1906.

30. The "Cuvilliés-Theater," built in 1751–55 by François de Cuvilliés the Elder for Elector Maximilian Joseph III, was destroyed on March 18, 1944, but not before its painted wood carvings and other decorations had been removed to a safe location. These were installed in the Neues Residenz-Theater, completed on the original site in 1951. Franz Strauss, for his part, believed the acoustics in this hall were bad.

31. David Pickett, "Arrangements and *Retuschen*: Mahler and *Werktreue*," in *The Cambridge Companion to Mahler*, ed. Jeremy Barham (Cambridge: Cambridge University Press, 2007), 179.

32. *Chronicle*, 388.

33. Raymond Holden, "Kapellmeister Strauss," in *The Cambridge Companion to Richard Strauss*, ed. Charles Youmans (Cambridge: Cambridge University Press, 2010), 261.

34. Michael Kennedy, *Richard Strauss: Man, Musician, Enigma* (Cambridge: Cambridge University Press, 1999), 105.

35. Strauss had responsibility for *Tannhäuser*, *Lohengrin*, and *Tristan und Isolde*, but Eduard Lassen, the Weimar Hofkapellmeister and thus Strauss's immediate superior, retained control of *Der fliegende Holländer*, *Die Meistersinger von Nürnberg*, and the *Ring*. *Chronicle*, 175.

36. Strauss to Cosima, March 3, 1890. Trenner, *Cosima Wagner, Richard Strauss*, 30.

37. Pickett, "Arrangements and *Retuschen*," 182.

38. Ibid., 188.

39. The reminiscences come from Alois Reiser and Benjamin Kohon, who played in the New York Philharmonic under Mahler. The former recalled that in *Till Eulenspiegel*, Mahler asked for a B-flat clarinet to play the high passage for D clarinet in the hanging scene. See "Remembering Mahler," in Kaplan, *Mahler Plays Mahler*.

40. Strauss elaborated his theory of the avant-garde in a 1907 essay, claiming that "modern" works were those that built meaningfully on artistic precedents and were accepted by the public. The teleological implications of this view would be belied by his compositional practice—especially its critical and intertextual dimensions—but such contradictions did not trouble him. See "Is There an Avant-Garde in Music?" in *Recollections*, 12–17.

41. Examples of the playing-out of this tendency are explored in Klaus Aringer, Orchesterbesetzungen und Instrumentation," in *Gustav Mahler: Interpretationen seiner Werke*, ed. Peter Revers and Olver Korte, vol. 1 (Laaber: Laaber, 2011), 431–34.

42. Josef Stranksy, "Begegnungen mit Gustav Mahler," *Signale für die musikalische Welt*, July 19, 1911, quoted in *Life, Work and World*, 141.

43. Ibid., 123.

44. The *Wiener Philharmoniker Fanfare* (1924).

45. Wilhelm, *Richard Strauss*, 202.

46. Ibid., 206.

47. Ibid., 201–202.

48. *Neue freie Presse*. May 11, 1897; *Neues Wiener Tagblatt*, May 12, 1897; *Wiener Abendpost*, May 5, 1897.

49. *Neue freie Presse*, November 7, 1898, quoted in *Life, Work and World*, 137.

50. Ibid.

51. Richard Strauss, "Timely Remarks on Music Education," in *Recollections*, 85–88.

52. Wilhelm, *Richard Strauss*, 205.

53. Ibid., 206.

54. For Mahler's instructions to the architect of the villa on the Wörthersee, see *Life, Work and World*, 142.

3. HUSBANDS

1. Walter Werbeck dates the earliest *Till* sketches from the first months following Strauss's marriage on September 10, 1894. Werbeck, *Die Tondichtungen*, 127.

2. Recent evidence, in the form of a sixty-page letter from Bauer-Lechner to Hans Riehl, indicates that this tolerance extended to two brief sexual encounters, in 1892 and 1901; otherwise Mahler imposed on their relationship what she called an "entirely senseless celibacy." See Solvik and Hefling, "Natalie Bauer-Lechner on Mahler and Women," 33–36, 39–42 (quotation from 40). This letter also includes a revealing assessment of Mahler's relationship with Justi: "In order to understand Mahler's life, it is necessary to know that, from the death of his parents up until his marriage, this favorite sister of his constituted the most important source of happiness and also of misfortune in his existence [...] Indeed, had she not been his sister, she would certainly have been one of his greatest passions." Ibid., 35–40, quotations from 36 and 38.

3. At a low point in their courtship (February 7, 1896), a spurned Mahler wrote, "I am in *a hell*, from which there is *no redemption*" (emphasis in original). Franz Willnauer, ed., *Gustav Mahler, "Mein lieber Trotzkopf, meine süße Mohnblume": Briefe an Anna von Mildenburg* (Vienna: Paul Zsolnay, 2006), 78. An exhaustive account of the Mildenburg relationship is given in *La Grange I*, 333–81. Bauer-Lechner's letter to Riehl also provides useful information, along with the implausible claim (as Solvik and Hefling note), ostensibly from Mildenburg herself, that the relationship "left her an untouched maiden." See Solvik and Hefling, "Bauer-Lechner on Mahler and Women," 41–44 and 63 (note 63). An insightful discussion of conflicts between the family-figure women in Mahler's life and his lovers can be found in Stuart Feder, *Gustav Mahler: A Life in Crisis* (New Haven: Yale University Press, 2004), 75–91.

4. Commenting on the aesthetic distance between Mahler's music and Viennese modernist trends as manifested in the Secession, Johnson writes, "nothing marks this difference more acutely than the absence of an erotic dimension in Mahler's work." Johnson, *Mahler's Voices*, 229.

5. In the extravagantly uncensored account of their courtship in Alma's diary, the reaction to Mahler's demand that she renounce composition is especially instructive from a psychological standpoint. Where on December 20, 1901, she wrote, "give up my music—abandon what has until now been my life? My *first* reaction was—to pass him up," by the next day she had embraced subordination: "I must admit that scarcely any music now interests me except his [...] Yes—he's right. I must live *entirely* for him, to make him happy." Of course she knew that more than music was at stake; on December 22 she asked again: "*must one of us be subordinate?*" And on January 16, 1902, two weeks after the consummation: "He wants me different, completely different. And that's what I want as well. As long as I'm with him, I can manage—but when I'm on my own, my other, vain self rises to the surface and wants to be let free." Alma Mahler-Werfel, *Diaries 1898–1902*, selected and trans. Antony Beaumont (Ithaca, NY: Cornell University Press, 1999), 462–63, 468. The need for an oppressor against whom to struggle seems to have been one of her principal attractions to the relationship. Or, as Feder observed, "paradoxically, the outrage she solicited in those confidantes with whom she shared the letter, seemed only to increase her resolve." Feder, *Gustav Mahler*, 106.

6. Strauss's deepest early love affair, in 1883–84, involved the divorcée Dora Wihan-Weis, four years his senior. See *Chronicle*, 161–68. His letters to the actress Cäcilie Wenzel, from 1886–87, appear in J. Rigbie Turner, "Richard Strauss to Cäcilie Wenzel: Twelve Unpublished Letters," *19th-Century Music* 9 (1986): 163–75.

7. For example in Gilliam, *The Life of Richard Strauss*, 6.

8. Antony Beaumont dates that letter provisionally to June 22. *Gustav/Alma*, 326.

9. Stuart Feder, "Before Alma: Gustav Mahler and 'Das Ewig-Weibliche,'" in *Mahler Studies*, ed. Stephen E. Hefling (Cambridge: Cambridge University Press, 1997), 78.

10. Mahler to Josephine Poisl, March 18, 1880. Bayerische Staatsbibliothek, Ana 600, B, I, 2b.

11. *La Grange IV*, 1489–90.

12. Mahler to the (unnamed) mother of Josephine Poisl, March 29, 1880. Bayerische Staatsbibliothek, Ana 600, B, I, 2b.

13. *La Grange I*, 333: "Then he began to insult her." Feder, "Before Alma," 91: "he terrorized the young singer, bringing her to tears."

14. "Ich legte den Kopf aufs Pianino und fing zu weinen an. Mein Schreck mußte sich aufs komischeste in meinem Gesicht ausgedrückt haben, denn er begann nun unvermittelt so zu lachen, daß es ihn nur so schüttelte. Die beiden Hände in den Hosentaschen vergraben, lief er wie ratlos durchs Zimmer. Dann aber setzte er sich ruhig hin, putzte seine Augengläser, und aus seinen ernsten guten Worten erfuhr ich nun, daß ich meine Sache famos gemacht und bis jetzt noch keinen Grund hätte, bekümmert zu sein." Bahr-Mildenburg, "Meine ersten Proben mit Gustav Mahler."

15. *Bauer-Lechner*, 65.

16. Near the end of section 5 of *The Birth of Tragedy*, Mahler's favorite book by the philosopher, Nietzsche announced that "only as an *aesthetic phenomenon* are existence and the world *justified*" (emphasis in original).

17. Mahler to Alma Mahler, June 22, 1909, in *Gustav/Alma*, 326–28 (German edition, 388–90). The precise date of the letter is uncertain.

18. "Das *Rationale* daran (d.h. das vom Verstand Aufzulösende) ist fast immer das nicht Wesentliche: und eigentlich ein Schleier, der die Gestalt verhüllt" (emphasis in original).

19. "Eine Seele einen Leib braucht." "Alles ist nun ein *Gleichniß*, für Etwas, dessen Gestaltung nur ein *unzulänglicher* Ausdruck für das sein kann, was hier gefordert ist" (emphasis in original).

20. "Es läßt sich eben *Vergängliches* wol beschreiben; aber wir fühlen, ahnen, aber nie *erreichen* werden (also was hier ein *Ereigniß* werden kann) eben das hinter allen Erscheinungen Dauernde, Unvergängliche ist *unbeschreiblich*" (emphasis in original).

21. "*Das Ewig Weibliche* hat uns *hinangezogen*—Wir sind da—Wir ruhen—Wir besitzen, was wir auf Erden nur ersehnen, erstreben könnten" (emphasis in original).

22. "läßt in Dein Inneres blicken."

23. "Der Christ nennt dieß die 'ewige Seligkeit' und ich mußte mich dieser schönen und zureichenden mythologischen Vorstellungen als Mittel für meine Darstellung bedienen [two lines illegible]—das adäquatesten, die dieser Epoche der Menschheit zugänglich ist."

24. A splendid facsimile of the page of Mengelberg's personal score on which he detailed this anecdote is presented in Gilbert E. Kaplan, ed., *Gustav Mahler, Adagietto: Facsimile, Documentation, Recording* (New York: The Kaplan Foundation, 1992), 20. Kaplan considers the validity of the claim on 21–29, concluding

that the story is valid and has important implications for performance (see below).

25. Mengelberg recorded the movement in 7:04. Kaplan suggests plausibly that the differences in tempi originate in a misconception of the work's character as funereal rather than amorous. See ibid., 16–19.

26. On the relationship between the song and the symphonic movement, see Stephen E. Hefling, "The Rückert Lieder," in *The Mahler Companion*, ed. Donald Mitchell and Andrew Nicholson (Oxford: Oxford University Press, 1999), 358–60. Hefling notes that "while the Rückert lied is a study in serenity, the symphonic Adagietto, although intimate in character and scoring, is suffused with yearning that reaches passionate culmination just prior to the movement's conclusion" (358). Kaplan makes a similar case ("'Ich bin der Welt abhanden gekommen' ends in a mood of hushed withdrawal, and the Adagietto with passionate commitment") in *Gustav Mahler, Adagietto*, 26; on chronology, see 35–37.

27. See the discussion in Floros, *Gustav Mahler: The Symphonies*, 163; also Seth Monahan, "'I have tried to capture you . . .': Rethinking the 'Alma' Theme from Mahler's Sixth Symphony," *Journal of the American Musicological Society* 64 (2011): 119–78.

28. Like Goethe's Harper, "all his passions seemed to have resolved themselves into the single fear of death." Goethe, *Wilhelm Meisters Lehrjahre*, book 8, chapter 9.

29. November 22, 1915, "Brown Diary," RSA. See the discussion in chapters 10 and 12. The full text of the passage appears in chapter 10, note 21.

30. "Wäre nicht hier (im Zustande des empfangenden Weibes) der Weg zur Erlösung des Willens zu suchen! Nicht in der Verneinung des Willens, sondern in dem 'Bewußtsein' der Bejahung?" Excerpts from the diary appear in *Chronicle*, 309–13 (German edition, 316–20). The original is held at the RSA.

31. James Hepokoski, "Fiery-Pulsed Libertine or Domestic Hero: Strauss's *Don Juan* Reinvestigated," in *Richard Strauss: New Perspectives on the Composer and His Work*, ed. Bryan Gilliam (Durham, NC: Duke University Press, 1992), 157–58.

32. On the chronology of Strauss's critique of Schopenhauer, see Youmans, *Richard Strauss's Orchestral Music*, 59–82.

33. "Du gleichst dem Geist den du begreifst, nicht mir!" Idem, "The Private Intellectual Context of Richard Strauss's *Also sprach Zarathustra*," *19th-Century Music* 22 (1998): 117.

34. Schoenberg famously claimed that "*the only revolutionary* in our time was Strauss" (emphasis in original). Arnold Schoenberg, *Style and Idea: Selected Writings of Arnold Schoenberg*, trans. Leo Black (Berkeley: University of California Press, 1984), 137.

35. "Mein Weib, mein Kind und meine Musik/Natur und Sonne, die sind mein Glück./Ein wenig Gleichmut und viel Humor/Drin thut mir's der Teufel selbst nicht vor!" Werbeck, *Die Tondichtungen*, 173.

36. Notwithstanding its unmistakably direct content, and Strauss's reluctance to provide any details about the program, the *Symphonia domestica* had a largely enthusiastic and markedly unscandalized reception at its New York premiere at Carnegie Hall on March 21, 1904. See chapter 9.

37. His letter stating this demand—"from now on you have only *one* profession: *to make me happy*"—is dated December 19, 1901. See *Gustav/Alma*, 78–84.

38. "I remarked to him once during a walk:

'All I love in a man is his achievement. The greater his achievement the more I have to love him.'
'That's a real danger. You mean if anyone came along who could do more than I—.
'I'd have to love him,' I said.
'Well, I won't worry for the time being. I don't know anybody who can do more than I can.'" *Memories and Letters*, 71.

39. Bryan Gilliam notes that Schoenberg, in a letter to Webern, "seems almost embarrassed to admit that he is favorably inclined toward the new opera." Bryan Gilliam, "Strauss's *Intermezzo*: Innovation and Tradition," in *Richard Strauss: New Perspectives on the Composer and His Work*, ed. Bryan Gilliam (Durham, NC: Duke University Press, 1992), 279.

4. WAGNERIANS

1. *Bauer-Lechner*, 37 (Brahms), 37–38 (Liszt). The remark on counterpoint is quoted from Anton Webern's reminiscences of Mahler; see *Life, Work and World*, 185.

2. R. Larry Todd, "Strauss before Liszt and Wagner: Some Observations," in *Richard Strauss: New Perspectives on the Composer and His Work*, ed. Bryan Gilliam (Durham, N.C.: Duke University Press, 1992), 7–14; Norman Del Mar, *Richard Strauss: A Critical Commentary on His Life and Works*, vol. 1 (London: Barrie & Rockliff, 1962), 46–51.

3. See the treatments in David Brodbeck, "Brahms, the Third Symphony, and the New German School," in *Brahms and His World*, ed. Walter Frisch

(Princeton: Princeton University Press, 1990), 65–80, and A. Peter Brown, "Brahms's Third Symphony and the New German School," *Journal of Musicology* 2 (1983): 434–52.

4. In Strauss's case this consultation is documented, in Trenner, *Cosima Wagner, Richard Strauss.*

5. *Neues Wiener Journal*, August 6, 1905, quoted in *Life, Work and World*, 22.

6. Strauss to Ludwig Thuille, October 28, 1878. Gillespie, "Selections from the Strauss-Thuille Correspondence," 212.

7. Richard Strauss, "Reminiscences of My Father," in *Recollections*, 132. Strauss to Thuille, April 4, 1878. Gillespie, "Selections from the Strauss-Thuille Correspondence," 208.

8. Strauss to Ludwig Thuille, November 19, 1890. Trenner, *Richard Strauss, Ludwig Thuille*, 115.

9. See the discussion in Youmans, *Richard Strauss's Orchestral Music*, 150–69.

10. For an account of the wine-lubricated sessions in which Ritter indoctrinated Strauss, Ludwig Thuille, Arthur Seidl, Friedrich Rösch, and other young musical intellectuals in Munich in the late 1880s and early 1890s, see *Chronicle*, 128–31.

11. Guido Adler's account of the Vienna Academic Wagner Society can be found in *Life, Work and World*, 28–29; compare the reminiscences of Friedrich Eckstein in the same source, 35–36.

12. *La Grange I*, 43.

13. Ibid., 43–44.

14. Ibid., 43.

15. The story was reported in 1903 by Max Steinitzer, later to be an early biographer of Strauss. Sikkus [Steinitzer], "Porträtskizzen und Momentbilder: Gustav Mahler," *Rheinische Musik- und Theaterzeitung*, July 31, 1903, quoted in *Life, Work and World*, 70.

16. Bahr-Mildenburg, "Meine erste Proben mit Gustav Mahler."

17. *Memories and Letters*, 47. Bauer-Lechner, 194.

18. Bauer-Lechner, 67, 203–04.

19. Wagner's immersion in Schopenhauer during the mid-1850s led him eventually (in "Beethoven") to allot music a world-redeeming primacy not found in the earlier treatise; in the pithy formulation of Dieter Borchmeyer, "the metaphysical aspect is absent from *Oper und Drama*." See Dieter Borchmeyer, *Richard Wagner: Theory and Theater*, trans. Stewart Spencer (Oxford: Clarendon Press, 1991), 102.

20. The latter work's Schopenhauerian themes are discussed in Kevin Karnes, "Wagner, Klimt, and the Metaphysics of Creativity in fin-de-siècle Vienna," *Journal of the American Musicological Society* 62 (2009): 247–97.

21. On aesthetic experience: "it does not deliver him from life forever, but only for a few moments." Arthur Schopenhauer, *The World as Will and Representation*, vol. 1, trans. E. F. J. Payne (New York: Dover, 1969), 267.

22. Bauer-Lechner, 40.

23. Bruno Walter, *Gustav Mahler*, trans. Lotte Walter Lindt (New York: Knopf, 1958), 13.

24. Mahler to Arthur Seidl, February 17, 1897. *Mahler Letters*, 212.

25. *Memories and Letters*, 25–26.

26. Arthur Seidl, "Richard Strauss: Eine Charakter-Skizze" [1896], in *Straussiana: Aufsätze zur Richard Strauß-Frage aus drei Jahrzehnten* (Regensburg: Gustav Bosse, 1913), 11–66.

27. Ibid., 34–37.

28. The edition of Schopenhauer given to Strauss by his parents for Christmas in 1889—*Arthur Schopenhauer's sämmtliche Werke*, 5 vols. (Leipzig: F. A. Brockhaus, 1888)—survives today at the RSA.

29. "Daher wird sie ihm nicht, wie wir es im folgenden Buche bei dem zur Resignation gelangten Heiligen sehn werden, Quietiv des Willens, erlöst ihn nicht auf immer, sondern nur auf Augenblicke vom Leben." Arthur Schopenhauer, *Die Welt als Wille und Vorstellung*, vol. 1 (Stuttgart: Philipp Reclam jun., 1987), 384. The translation comes from Schopenhauer, *The World as Will and Representation*, 267.

30. *Chronicle*, 285.

31. "Ich kann mir nun einmal nicht helfen, der Heiligenschein wird mir doch nie beschieden sein." Strauss to Cosima Wagner, March 1, 1893. *Cosima Wagner, Richard Strauss*, 148.

32. Schopenhauer "Schlüsse zieht, die nicht ganz mit der wundervollen objektiven Haltung der ersten Bücher im Einklang stehen. Ich meine hier speziell die etwas einseitige Darstellung der 'Leiden der Welt' und die Glorifizierung der Modifikation des Willens im Leben der Heiligen." Ibid.

33. "Das bis jetzt einzig erkennbare *Ziel des Willens* ist: daß er sich im Menschen seines Wollens *bewußt* geworden ist, daß er *erkennt*, ob er (Kraft der Prädestination im einzelnen Individuum) bejahen oder verneinen *will*— weiter kann, glaube ich, unsere allerdings an Zeit und Raum gebundene Erkenntnis nicht gehen, ohne utopistisch zu werden" (emphasis in original). Ibid.

34. "Von Wagners Weltanschauung steckt also gar nichts mehr in Ihnen. Was ist Ihnen von Wagner einzig noch geblieben? Die Mechanik seiner Kunst." Ritter to Strauss, January 17, 1893. Youmans, "Ten Letters from Alexander Ritter to Richard Strauss, 16.

35. Seidl, "Richard Strauss: Eine Charakter-Skizze," 34.

36. Strauss to Stefan Zweig, May 5, 1935. Max Knight, trans., *A Confidential Matter: The Letters of Richard Strauss and Stefan Zweig, 1931–1935* (Berkeley: University of California Press, 1977), 90.

37. James Hepokoski, "Fiery-Pulsed Libertine or Domestic Hero?" 155.

38. *Bauer-Lechner*, 203.

39. *La Grange I*, 312–13.

40. *Memories and Letters*, 92.

41. *La Grange I*, 312–13. On Mahler's reading of Lange, see Constantin Floros, "Mahlers intellektuelle Neugier," in *Mahler im Kontext/Contextualizing Mahler*, ed. Erich Wolfgang Partsch and Morten Solvik (Vienna: Böhlau, 2011), 11.

42. *La Grange I*, 313.

43. Friedrich Nietzsche to Hermann Mushacke, November 1866. Friedrich Nietzsche, *Werke und Briefe: Historisch-kritische Gesamtausgabe*, R. I, vol. 2, *Briefe der Leipziger und ersten Basler Zeit, 1868–1869*, 184.

44. *Memories and Letters*, 79.

45. *La Grange I*, 106.

46. Floros, *Gustav Mahler: The Symphonies*, 253, 302; see also David Matthews, "Wagner, Lipiner, and the 'Purgatorio,'" in *The Mahler Companion*, ed. Donald Mitchell and Andrew Nicholson (Oxford: Oxford University Press, 1999), 510–14. Stephen McClatchie has described the Wagnerian roots of Mahler's fondness for motives that "overflow the boundary of a single work." Stephen McClatchie, "Mahler's Wagner," in *Mahler im Kontext/Contextualizing Mahler*, ed. Erich Wolfgang Partsch and Morten Solvik (Vienna: Böhlau, 2011), 415.

47. McClatchie describes Mahler's overhauling of the *Ring* in Vienna; see Ibid., 416–29.

48. Hartmut Hein, "Vierte Symphonie," in *Gustav Mahler: Interpretationen seiner Werke*, ed. Peter Revers and Oliver Korte, vol. 1 (Laaber: Laaber, 2011), 357–58.

49. *Memories and Letters*, 79–81.

50. Walter, *Gustav Mahler*, 189.

51. *Bauer-Lechner*, 66.

52. The most thorough treatment of this work as a strong reading of Wagner is Morten Kristiansen, "Richard Strauss's *Feuersnot* in Its Aesthetic and Cultural

Context: A Modernist Critique of Musical Idealism" (PhD diss., Yale University, 2000).

53. Strauss to Hugo von Hofmannsthal, July 28, 1916. Strauss and Strauss, *The Correspondence between Richard Strauss and Hugo von Hofmannsthal*, 259.

54. See the discussion of *Metamorphosen* in Gilliam, *The Life of Richard Strauss*, 173–74.

55. Walter, *Gustav Mahler*, 12.

56. *Bauer-Lechner*, 147. Strauss to Hans von Bülow, August 24, 1888. Gabriele Strauss, *Lieber Collega!*, 82.

57. *Bauer-Lechner*, 140.

58. On Toscanini's "overpowering" orchestra in *Tristan*, see for example the review in the *New York Times* of November 28, 1909, where we read that with Toscanini "it was sometimes difficult to tell by the ear alone whether or not there was a singer singing behind the orchestra," whereas in Mahler's hands the orchestra "can build up climaxes and an express the sum of all he attributes to it, and yet hide the tone and enunciation of no singer's voice."

5. BUSINESSMEN

1. *Chronicle*, 7–8.
2. Warfield, "The Genesis of Richard Strauss's *Macbeth*," 70–71.
3. The quotations in this paragraph come from *Chronicle*, 49 and 78.
4. Warfield, "The Genesis of Richard Strauss's *Macbeth*," 152.
5. Ibid., 169–80, 210–15.
6. *La Grange I*, 33–34.
7. Mahler to his parents, late November 1887. Stephen McClatchie, ed., *The Mahler Family Letters* (Oxford: Oxford University Press, 2006), 44.
8. Mahler to his parents, late December 1887. Ibid., 45.
9. Mahler to his parents, January 29, 1888. Ibid., 47.
10. Mahler to his parents, early June, 1887. Ibid., 40–41.
11. Franz Trenner, *Richard Strauss: Chronik zu Leben und Werk*, ed. Florian Trenner (Vienna: Verlag Dr. Richard Strauss, 2003), 117–18.
12. *Chronicle*, 343.
13. *Rivalry*, 115.
14. Strauss dated these marginalia December 28, 1946. A copy of the source is held at the RSA; the original is presumably in the possession of Schuh's family.
15. *Memories and Letters*, xli.
16. *Chronicle*, 365.

17. Knud Martner, *Gustav Mahler im Konzertsaal: Eine Dokumentation seiner Konzerttätigket 1870–1911* (Copenhagen: 1985), 41, 59, 131.

18. Mahler to Strauss, June 1901, June/July 1901, July 6, 1901, ca. August 20, 1901. *Mahler/Strauss* 52, 53, 56, 60.

19. Strauss to Mahler, February 4, 1902. Mahler to Strauss, February 18, February 21, and February 28, 1902. *Mahler/Strauss*, 66–69.

20. Julius Korngold called the opera a "burlesque composed with the means of Wagner's music dramas, which suffers mainly for not being very amusing," and complained of Strauss's "artful and colorful, but inwardly cold music." *Neue freie Presse*, June 6, 1905. The anonymous critic for the *Illustriertes Extrablatt* described it as "a footnote to *Die Meistersinger*." *Illustriertes Extrablatt*, June 6, 1905.

21. Mahler to Strauss, mid-March 1906. *Mahler/Strauss*, 92.

22. Emphasis in original. *Memories and Letters*, 88. Mahler to Alma, January 10, 1907. *Gustav/Alma*, 255.

23. Mahler to Alma, January 13, 1907. Ibid., 258.

24. *Memories and Letters*, 41.

25. Strauss to Mahler, May 11, 1911. *Mahler/Strauss*, 100.

26. Strauss to Mahler, April 22, 1900. Ibid., 46–47.

27. Mahler to Strauss, late April 1900. Ibid., 48.

28. *Gustav/Alma*, 205.

29. *Memories and Letters*, 90, 93.

30. Mahler to Justine Mahler, late February/March 1889. *Mahler Family Letters*, 64.

31. Mahler to his mother, April 1889. Ibid., 68.

32. Mahler to Justine Mahler, June 10, 1890. Ibid., 75.

33. Mahler to his parents, December 1888. Ibid., 61.

34. "Mahler war, bei all seinen Idealen und seinem hochernsten Schaffen und Wirken, durchaus kein Heiliger, er stand immer auf realem Boden und wußte sehr genau zu unterscheiden, was ihm frommte und was ihm schadete." Ludwig Karpath, *Begegnung mit dem Genius*, 2nd ed. (Vienna: Fiba, 1934), 55–56.

35. Ibid., 60, 185.

36. Mahler to Strauss, late January/early February 1903. *Mahler/Strauss*, 72.

6. LITERATI

1. Specht, *Gustav Mahler*, 17.
2. *Chronicle*, 54.

3. Mahler to Löhr, spring 1894. *Mahler Letters*, 153. *Memories and Letters*, 197. Mahler's literary impulses have been usefully surveyed in Herta Blaukopf, "*Bücher fresse ich immer mehr und mehr. Gustav Mahler als Leser*," in *Mahler Gespräche. Rezeptionsfragen—literarischer Horizont—musikalische Darstellung*, ed. Friedbert Aspetsberger and Erich Wolfgang Partsch (Innsbruck: Studien Verlag, 2002), 96–116, and Margarete Wagner, "Mahlers Verhältnis zur zeitgenössischen Literatur," in *Mahler im Kontext/Contextualizing Mahler*, ed. Erich Wolfgang Partsch and Morten Solvik (Vienna: Böhlau, 2011), 291–335.

4. Rudolf Hartmann, "The Last Visit with Richard Strauss," trans. Susan Gillespie, in *Richard Strauss and His World*, ed. Bryan Gilliam (Princeton: Princeton University Press, 1992), 298.

5. *Memories and Letters*, 50.

6. The edition still resides in the Strauss villa in Garmisch, which remains a private residence but also houses the RSA.

7. Personal communication, Richard Strauss (the composer's grandson), June 24, 1994.

8. Strauss to Hugo von Hofmannsthal, October 5, 1920. Strauss and Strauss, *The Correspondence between Richard Strauss and Hugo von Hofmannsthal*, 340.

9. Hofmannsthal to Strauss, March 8, 1912. Ibid., 121.

10. Timothy L. Jackson, "The Metamorphosis of the *Metamorphosen*: New Analytical and Source-Critical Discoveries," in *Richard Strauss: New Perspectives on the Composer and His Work*, ed. Bryan Gilliam (Durham, NC: Duke University Press, 1992), 93–142.

11. Gilliam, *The Life of Richard Strauss*, 183.

12. Richard Strauss, "On Melodic Inspiration," in *Recollections*, 116.

13. *Memories and Letters*, 103; translation from *Gustav/Alma*, 244.

14. *La Grange I*, 101–102.

15. Ibid., 276, 524.

16. *Bauer-Lechner*, 24.

17. Alma Mahler, *Mein Leben* (Frankfurt am Main: Fischer, 1960), 16.

18. Mahler to Alma Mahler, December 14, 1901, December 24, 1901, January 29, 1904, October 14, 1904, January 17, 1907, September 5, 1910. *Gustav/Alma*, 65, 89, 144, 179, 264, 390. The quotation from "Rastlose Liebe" in the letter of September 5, 1910, would become the title of Alma's collection of Mahler's letters: *Ein Glück ohne Ruh'*.

19. Mahler to Alma Mahler, December 19, 1901. Ibid., 80–81.

20. Mahler to Alma Mahler, September 6, 1909. Ibid., 341.

21. Henry-Louis de La Grange, "Mahler and France," in *The Mahler Companion*, ed. Donald Mitchell and Andrew Nicholson (Oxford: Oxford University Press, 1999), 141.

22. Mahler to Alma Mahler, December 2, 1903. *Gustav/Alma*, 141.

23. Mahler to Alma Mahler, September 3, 1910. Ibid., 383.

24. Ibid., 328.

25. Ibid., 175–76.

26. Stephen E. Hefling, "*Das Lied von der Erde*," in *The Mahler Companion*, ed. Donald Mitchell and Andrew Nicholson (Oxford: Oxford University Press, 1999), 441–42. Constantin Floros likewise observes that Mahler's "belief that the spiritual is primary and the material is secondary likewise traces back to Goethe." Floros, "Mahlers intellektuelle Neugier," 12.

27. *La Grange I*, 101.

28. Carl Dahlhaus, "Neo-romanticism," in *Between Romanticism and Modernism: Four Studies in the Music of the Late Nineteenth Century*, trans. Mary Whittall (Berkeley: University of California Press, 1980), 1–18.

29. Strauss to Humperdinck, March 27, 1885. Gabriele Strauss, *Lieber Collega*, 203.

30. Johann Wolfgang von Goethe, *Lila (Ein Festspiel mit Gesang und Tanz)*, in *Sämtliche Werke nach Epochen seines Schaffens, Münchner Ausgabe*, ed. Karl Richter et al, vol. 2.1, *Erstes Weimarer Jarzehnt, 1775–1786, I*, ed. Hartmut Reinhardt (Munich: Carl Hanser, 1987), 131–60.

31. Ibid., 142.

32. "Was mich an der Arbeit reizt, ist, daß die zweierlei Art Musik, die heute existiert, darin zu höchst drastischer Anwendung und Gegenüberstellung kommt; verstehen Sie mich genau? 'Musik als Ausdruck' der menschlichen Psyche [. . .] und Musik als tönende Form, als angenehmes, nervenberuhigendes Tonspiel." Strauss to Cosima, September 30, 1895. Trenner, *Cosima Wagner, Richard Strauss*, 215–16.

33. Goethe, *Lila*, 138.

34. Bauer-Lechner, 73.

35. Ibid., 62.

36. Youmans, "The Private Intellectual Context of Richard Strauss's *Also sprach Zarathustra*," 112.

37. Richard Specht, *Gustav Mahler's VIII. Symphonie. Thematische Analyse* (Vienna: Universal, 1912), 6.

38. *Chronicle*, 448.

39. Gilliam, *The Life of Richard Strauss*, 75.

40. Seidl, "Richard Strauss: Eine Charakterskizze," 32–34.
41. Mahler to Alma Mahler, January 3, 1902. *Gustav/Alma*, 95–96.
42. The letter from Mahler to Dehmel is not dated. *Life, Work and World*, 135.
43. Mahler to Alma Mahler, December 19, 1901. *Gustav/Alma*, 81.
44. Hefling, "The Rückert Lieder," 338.
45. Christine Getz, "The Lieder of Richard Strauss," in *The Strauss Companion*, ed. Mark-Daniel Schmid (Westport, CT: Praeger, 2003), 338–40.
46. *La Grange II*, 335. Less than a month after their mother's death, which came only eight months after their father's, Mahler would tell a grieving Justine, "you must not surrender yourself to this mood, because you are young and the sun will shine again for you." Mahler to Justine, mid-October 1889. McClatchie, *The Mahler Family Letters*, 71.
47. *Memories and Letters*, 70.
48. Hefling, "The Rückert Lieder," 358–59 for the Adagietto. On Mahler's thoughts about common ground between Rückert and Fechner, see M. Wagner, "Mahlers Verhältnis zur zeitgenössischen Literatur," 297.
49. *Memories and Letters*, 93.
50. Kennedy, *Richard Strauss*, 184.
51. Ulrich Konrad, "Die *Deutsche Motette* op. 62 von Richard Strauss. Entstehung, Form, Gehalt," in Bernd Edelmann, Birgit Lodes, and Reinhold Schlötterer, eds., *Richard Strauss und die Moderne* (Berlin: Henschel, 2001), 309.
52. See introduction, note 39.
53. Konrad, "Die *Deutsche Motette*," 310.
54. Bryan Gilliam, " 'Friede im Innern': Strauss's Public and Private Worlds in the Mid 1930s," *Journal of the American Musicological Society* 57 (2005): 565–98; see also idem, *The Life of Richard Strauss*, 153.
55. Michael P. Steinberg, "Richard Strauss and the Question," in *Richard Strauss and His World*, 173.
56. Mahler to Alma Mahler, December 15, 1901. *Gustav/Alma*, 70.
57. Bauer-Lechner, 59.
58. Ibid., 37; *Memories and Letters*, 110, 238.
59. Bauer-Lechner, 37.
60. *La Grange I*, 85.
61. Ibid., 104.
62. On Mahler's reception of Dostoyevsky, see Constantin Floros, *Die geistige Welt Gustav Mahlers in systematischer Darstellung* (Wiesbaden: Breitkopf & Härtel, 1977), 65–66, and M. Wagner, "Mahlers Verhältnis zur zeitgenössischen Literatur," 307–9.

63. Inna Barsova, "Mahler and Russia," in *The Mahler Companion*, ed. Donald Mitchell and Andrew Nicholson (Oxford: Oxford University Press, 1999), 518.

64. *Chronicle*, 131, 151.

7. AUTOBIOGRAPHERS

1. In private sketches for the ostensibly confessional *Ein Heldenleben*, for example, we learn that the most dangerous antagonists are not the critics mentioned in the program, but "inner enemies" confronted in a private philosophical dilemma. See Youmans, *Richard Strauss's Orchestral Music*, 208–10.

2. Bauer-Lechner recalled that in his first rehearsal with the Vienna Court Opera, "he was afraid of one thing only: the speech which he had been told he must deliver to the musicians." *Bauer-Lechner*, 89.

3. Henry T. Finck, *Richard Strauss: The Man and His Works* (Boston: Little, Brown, and Company, 1917), 199.

4. Strauss prepared the Weimar Court Orchestra for the performance of the First conducted by Mahler on June 3, 1894, at the conference of the Allgemeiner Deutscher Musikverein. Strauss admired the work but suggested that Mahler consider a final ending at the first climax in the finale (m. 375, reh. 34), a moment the Mahler called a "false conclusion." The implication is that Strauss found the authentic conclusion (m. 636, five measures after reh. 53) redundant, though unfortunately only Mahler's side of the exchange survives. Needless to say, Mahler did not take kindly to the advice. Mahler to Strauss, May 15, 1894, May 17, 1894, July 19, 1894. *Mahler/Strauss*, 35–37.

For details of the speech against programmaticism that Mahler gave at a post-concert dinner in Munich after a 20 October 1900 performance of the Second Symphony, see Chapter 8, p. 169 and note 16. The source of the anecdote is Ludwig Schiedermair, *Gustav Mahler* (Leipzig: Seemann, 1900), 14.

5. In the recent formulation of Constantin Floros, Mahler "wanted to express himself, his inner being"—in contrast to Strauss, who typically diverted attention from himself with literary characters. Constantin Floros, "Exkurs II: Zur Relevanz der 'Programme' in Mahler's Symphonien," in *Gustav Mahler: Interpretationen seiner Werke*, ed. Peter Revers and Oliver Korte, vol. 1 (Laaber: Laaber-Verlag, 2011), 400.

6. That goes for the Sixth Symphony as well, notwithstanding the private meaning described below.

7. Seidl's word is "Verkappung," as when Socrates and Till Eulenspiegel don the "fool's cap" in order to delude their antagonists. Seidl, "Richard Strauss: Eine Charakter-Skizze," 54.

8. Adorno was already complaining in 1924 that "the emotional phenomena that Strauss portrays do not penetrate down to the deepest stratum of the problems of inner life." Adorno, "Richard Strauss at Sixty," 409.

9. A case study of this private level of reflection can be found in Youmans, "The Private Intellectual Context of Richard Strauss's *Also sprach Zarathustra*," 101–26. Various implications of the composer's methodical distinction between public and private meaning are explored in Youmans, *Richard Strauss's Orchestral Music*.

10. *La Grange IV*, 1489–90.

11. Stephen Hefling describes the latter as "a chronic, fluctuating mood disturbance involving numerous periods of hypomanic and depressive symptoms (which symptoms are, however, less numerous or severe than those of the bipolar disorders)." Stephen E. Hefling, *Mahler: "Das Lied von der Erde"* (Cambridge: Cambridge University Press, 2000), 16.

12. Ibid.

13. Adorno would praise Mahler and indict Strauss for their respective responses, but he had no doubt that these terms framed their creative work. Particularly in their treatment of form, Adorno saw a response to the plight of the individual. It is typical of his analyses that the same sorts of challenge to received forms are read differently for Mahler and for Strauss. Whereas in Strauss the "rationally planned irrationality" is a capitulation—"the life which celebrates itself in this music is death"—in Mahler "art omits to satisfy its norms" because it "takes up Nietzsche's insight that the system and its seamless unity, its appearance of reconciliation, is dishonest." It is tempting to read such contradictions as the belated attempts of a rejected member of the Second Viennese School to impress his elders. Adorno, "Richard Strauss. Born June 11, 1864," 28, 19; idem, *Mahler: A Musical Physiognomy*, 65, 64.

14. Mahler to Strauss, August 12, 1897. *Mahler/Strauss*, 46.

15. Natalie: "I have never seen such a whirlwind succession of mood-changes in anyone else." *Bauer-Lechner*, 54. Characteristically, Alma read this quality in terms of how it affected her: "What he said one day was not to hold good the next [...] I could never be sure of what he thought and felt." *Memories and Letters*, 76.

16. Hansen, *"Gustav Mahler's Symphonies"*; the quotation is from 131.

17. Ibid., 134.

18. Mahler to Friedrich (Fritz) Löhr, January 1, 1885. *Mahler Letters*, 81.

19. Freud described Mahler's hearing the old Viennese melody "Ach, du lieber Augustin" on the barrel organ in the streets of Iglau after witnessing a "violent

quarrel" between his father and mother. "This contrast after the dramatic scene of the father with the mother he reproduced all through his life in his music." *La Grange IV*, 894.

20. Mahler to Löhr, January 1, 1885. *Mahler Letters*, 81.

21. This description was included in the program for the performance of the First Symphony in Hamburg on October 27, 1893. *La Grange I*, figure 47, between 574 and 575.

22. Mahler to Strauss, February 2, 1894. *Mahler/Strauss*, 27.

23. See the reviews of the disastrous Munich premiere (November 16, 1895) in Franzpeter Messmer, *Kritiken zu den Uraufführungen der Bühnenwerke von Richard Strauss* (Pfaffenhoffen: W. Ludwig, 1989), 9–15. This was the first performance of the work in a major urban center, after four moderately successful performances in Weimar in May and June 1894.

24. On Ritter, see chapter 1, note 34.

25. Assorted documents relevant to the chronology are provided in the "*Guntram* Chronicle" in *Chronicle*, 271–93. Further documentary evidence is discussed in Youmans, *Richard Strauss's Orchestral Music*, 62–68 and 74–82.

26. In Strauss's diaries of 1892–93 one finds Strauss speculating on the philosophical implications of sexuality. For example: "the consciousness of eternal generation [and] of eternal being [is] the sublime happiness ensured by the enjoyment of the act of generation." Or, more explicitly, "is not the way to the redemption of the will to be sought here (in the condition of the receiving woman)! Not in the denial of the will, but in the '*consciousness*' of affirmation?" *Chronicle*, 309.

27. Seidl made the claim in the *Neue deutsche Rundschau* 5 (1894); see *Chronicle*, 297.

28. James Hepokoski has called *Till* "the first of several tone-poem manifestos." See Hepokoski, "Framing Till Eulenspiegel," 7.

29. The links among this postmetaphysical orientation and the program and musical structure of *Till* are painstakingly disentangled by Hepokoski in ibid., 4–42.

30. Strauss witnessed the spectacle of lusty booing at the performance of Mahler's First Symphony in Weimar on June 3, 1894, at the same festival of the Allgemeiner Deutscher Musikverein that saw the fourth performance of *Guntram*.

31. Assorted correspondences between the program and Mahler's own life are treated in Stephen E. Hefling, "Mahler's 'Todtenfeier' and the Problem of Program Music," *19th-Century Music* 12 (1988): 30, 38. Hefling speculates that

Mahler suppressed details that might have been embarrassing to his current love interest, Marion von Weber (wife of the grandson of Carl Maria von Weber).

32. Bauer-Lechner, 30.

33. Ibid., 53.

34. Ibid., 43.

35. Walter, *Gustav Mahler*, 107.

36. Mahler to Max Marschalk, March 26, 1896. *Mahler Letters*, 180.

37. The "outcry" appears in the program for a performance of the Second in Dresden on December 20, 1901. The program is reprinted in *Memories and Letters*, 213–14. See also the discussion in Floros, *Gustav Mahler: The Symphonies*, 63–65.

38. Bauer-Lechner, 30.

39. Karpath, *Begegnung mit dem Genius*, 90.

40. Josef Bohuslav Foerster, *Erinnerungen eines Musikers* (Prague: Artia, 1955), 456.

41. Early that fall, Mahler invited Strauss to conduct the work with the Vienna Philharmonic. Mahler to Strauss, late summer/early fall 1900 (dated by a letter from Strauss to his parents on October 14 mentioning the invitation). *Mahler/Strauss*, 49. Mahler himself first conducted it on January 17, 1911, in Carnegie Hall with the New York Philharmonic. Martner, *Gustav Mahler im Konzertsaal*, 145.

42. Charles Youmans, "The Role of Nietzsche in Richard Strauss's Artistic Development," *Journal of Musicology* 21 (2004): 309–42.

43. This section begins at m. 713 (reh. 87), with a brief foreshadowing at m. 676 (five measures after reh. 83). A catalogue of the citations is given in Del Mar, *Richard Strauss*, 177.

44. These preliminary notes were made during a trip to the Isle of Wight in May 1902. Werbeck, *Die Tondichtungen von Richard Strauss*, 173.

45. In the *Alpensinfonie*, the complex of family, art, and nature was central to the early version of the work, known as the "Künstlertragödie" ("artist's tragedy"), and to the several stages through which it evolved before reaching its final conception. See Werbeck, *Die Tondichtungen von Richard Strauss*, 183–207.

46. See chapter 8.

47. Bauer-Lechner, 52–53.

48. In Alma's words, the Sixth was "the most completely personal of his works," one in which "he anticipated his own life in music." *Memories and Letters*, 70.

49. Rudolf Stephan, *Gustav Mahler, Werk und Interpretation: Autographe, Partituren, Dokumente* (Cologne: Volk, 1979), 38–39; F. Kaplan, *Adagietto*, 20–24.

50. Constantin Floros has claimed that the Fifth's anomalies indicate an "inner program." He also extends the Berlioz connection, noting that the *Symphonie funèbre et triomphale* begins with a funeral march. See Floros, *Gustav Mahler: The Symphonies*, 141–42. Specht had proposed the idea of autobiographical programmaticism already in 1905, noting that the Fifth followed the same basic structural plan as the Second Symphony but ended with a more exuberant, and more worldly, form of triumph. Richard Specht, *Gustav Mahler*, 44.

51. Hansen, "Gustav Mahler's Symphonies," 461–64.

52. Bauer-Lechner, 172–73.

53. *Memories and Letters*, 47–48.

54. Not the least conspicuous sign of the work's autobiographical fidelity is its utter lack of erotic content. Julian Johnson has commented on the "studied avoidance" of sexuality across Mahler's oeuvre, a quality "curiously out of line" with Viennese artistic culture ca. 1900. See Johnson, *Mahler's Voices*, 229.

55. When Mahler conducted the work in Vienna on January 4, 1907, the label appeared on the program. See also Walter, *Gustav Mahler*, 137.

56. *Memories and Letters*, 100.

57. Ibid., 70.

58. See the discussion in Floros, *Gustav Mahler: The Symphonies*, 175–76.

59. Hansen, "Gustav Mahler's Symphonies," 492.

60. Floros, *Gustav Mahler: The Symphonies*, 163, 172, 176, 181.

61. Peter Franklin, "Mahler, Gustav," in *The New Grove Dictionary of Music and Musicians*, 2nd ed., ed. Stanley Sadie, vol. 15 (New York: Grove's Dictionaries, 2001), 620.

62. Ibid.

63. Richard Strauss, "Letzte Aufzeichnung," in *Recollections*, 182 (German edition; this document is not included in the translation). For further discussion of this document, especially regarding irony, see chapter 11.

64. Jackson, "The Metamorphosis of the *Metamorphosen*," 199–202; see also Gilliam, *The Life of Richard Strauss*, 173–74.

65. Hefling, *Mahler: "Das Lied von der Erde*," 5–27.

66. She spoke here of the first two symphonies. *Bauer-Lechner*, 30.

67. Kohler "Richard Strauss. Eine Alpensinfonie, op. 64," 43.

8. PROGRAMMMUSIKER

1. Carl Dahlhaus, *Nineteenth-Century Music*, trans. J. Bradford Robinson (Berkeley: University of California Press, 1989), 330.

2. Anonymous review, *Musikalisches Wochenblatt* 20 (November 21, 1889): 577 (first and third quotations); anonymous review, *Allgemeine Musik-Zeitung* 16 (November 15, 1889): 490; both reviews are quoted in Mark-Daniel Schmid, "The Tone Poems of Richard Strauss and Their Reception History from 1887–1908" (PhD diss., Northwestern University, 1997), 99–100. The Bülow quotation comes from *Chronicle*, 184–85. Though the first and second versions of *Macbeth* were composed before *Don Juan* (completed on January 9, 1888, and February 8, 1888, respectively, whereas *Don Juan* was finished on September 30, 1888), the latter was the first to be performed (November 11, 1889, at the Weimar Court Theater; the second version of *Macbeth* had its premiere on October 13, 1890, and the final version on February 29, 1892).

3. Herzfeld's words are "Bizarrien," "nichtssagende Tonfiguren," and "[ein] betäubende[s] Wirrwarr von schmerzhaften Mißklängen." V. von Herzfeld, *Neues Pester Journal*, November 21, 1889.

4. Ludwig Schiedermair, *Gustav Mahler: Eine biographisch-kritische Würdigung* (Leipzig: H. Seemann, 1900), 13–14. See below, note 16, for a fuller quotation and the German original.

5. Floros has articulated this view repeatedly, most recently in "Exkurs II: Zur Relevanz der 'Programme' in Mahler Symphonien," 400.

6. "From Beethoven on, there is no modern music that does not have its inner program." Mahler to Max Kalbeck, January 1902. *Mahler Letters*, 262, quoted in Floros, "Exkurs II: Zur Relevanz der 'Programme,'" 408, where it is dated as November 1900.

7. Liszt's phrase, "Erzählung innerer Vorgänge," from the 1855 essay "Berlioz und seine 'Harold-Symphonie,'" is quoted in Floros's useful consideration of the various meanings of "program music." See "Zur Konfusion um den Begriff 'Programmusik,'" in Floros, *Gustav Mahler, I*, 33–35; quotation on 34. Richard Wagner, "Über Franz Liszt's symphonische Dichtungen: Brief an M. W.," in *Gesammelte Schriften und Dichtungen von Richard Wagner*, vol. 5 (Leipzig: C. F. W. Siegel, n.d. [1907]), 182–98.

8. John Williamson, "The Earliest Complete Works: A Voyage towards the First Symphony," in *The Mahler Companion*, ed. Donald Mitchell and Andrew Nicholson (Oxford: Oxford University Press, 1999), 47.

9. Zoltan Roman, *Gustav Mahler's American Years, 1907–1911: A Documentary History* (Stuyvesant, NY: Pendragon Press, 1989), 421.

10. This incident was reported by Arthur Neisser; see *Gustav/Alma*, 365.

11. Leonard Bernstein, *The Unanswered Question* (Cambridge, MA: Harvard University Press, 1976), 317. See also Charles Amenta, "The Opening of the Mahler Ninth Symphony and the Bernstein 'Heart-Beat' Hypothesis," *Naturlaut* 4 (2005): 17–18.

12. Michael Tilson Thomas has produced a fascinating documentary on the First, filmed on location in Iglau and sharing insights on the work as a programmatic representation of the composer's life in the town. See *Gustav Mahler: Origins and Legacy*, prod. and dir. Joan Saffa and David Kennard (San Francisco: Independent Communications Associates, 2011).

13. Max Kalbeck, "Feuilleton: Gustav Mahler and His Fifth Symphony," trans. Karen Painter and Bettina Varwig, in *Mahler and His World*, ed. Karen Painter (Princeton: Princeton University Press, 2002), 309.

14. Ernst Otto Nodnagel, *Jenseits von Wagner und Liszt* (Königsberg: Ostpreußische Druckerei und Verlagsanstalt, 1902), 8; Specht, *Gustav Mahler*, 173.

15. Floros, "Exkurs II: Zur Relevanz der 'Programme,'" 400.

16. "'Fort mit den Programmen, die falsche Vorstellungen erzeugen. Man lasse dem Publikum seine eigenen Gedanken über das aufgeführte Werk, man zwinge es während der Wiedergabe nicht zum Lesen, man bringe ihm kein Vorurteil bei! Hat ein Komponist den Hörern von selbst die Empfindungen aufgedrängt, die ihn durchfluteten, dann ist sein Ziel erreicht. Die Tonsprache ist dann den Worten nahegekommen, hat aber unendlich mehr, als diese auszudrücken vermögen, kundgegeben . . .' Und Mahler ergriff sein Glas und leerte es mit einem 'Pereat den Programmen.'" Schiedermair, *Gustav Mahler*, 13–14.

17. This request was not honored, Schiedermair choosing instead to paraphrase it.

18. "Mahler perhorresziert aufs energischste jedes Programm"; "die Musik selbst Kern und Schale zugleich sein kann." Bruno Walter to Ludwig Schiedermair, December 5, 1901, Moldenhauer Archives, Bayerische Staatsbibliothek.

19. "Dieser Satz nicht komponirt worden, um eines dieser Bilder musikalisch zu schildern." Ibid.

20. "Sein unnerhört reifes und kompliziertes Empfindungsleben"; "da sie einer Sphäre entstammen, die nichts mit Zeit und Raum, der Form der einzelnen Erscheinungen, zu thun hat." Ibid.

21. "*Ihr Reich ist den "Göttern" eine Stufe näher als das der anderen Künste.*" Ibid.

22. "Sie sehen, daß jemand, der das Wesen der Musik so begriffen hat—als Gleichnis des tiefsten Wesens der Dinge, und deshalb ungeeignet, dessen

einzelne Erscheinungen wiederzugeben—niemals Musik zu einen Programm schreiben kann." Ibid.

23. "Dagegen wird er im Stande sein, eine ganze Anzahl von Bildern zu nennen, deren Wesen mit dem seines Werkes verwandt ist." Ibid.

24. "Ihr Herz recht anzuhören und hie und da der Intelligenz, welche die Schlagfertigkeit besitzt, Schweigen zu gebieten." Cosima Wagner to Strauss, February 25, 1890. Trenner, *Cosima Wagner, Richard Strauss: Ein Briefwechsel*, 26.

25. "Bezüglich des Überwiegens der Intelligenz über das Gefühl glaube ich (allgemein gesprochen), daß bei einer groß angelegten Künstlernatur das Unbewußtsein und die Unwillkür, die doch den Urgrund jedes wahren und intensiven Schaffensdranges, sei es nun beim produzierenden oder beim reproduzierenden Künstler, bilden, immer noch mächtiger sein werden als der Intellekt, sei er noch so hoch entwickelt." Strauss to Cosima Wagner, March 3, 1890. Ibid., 29.

26. "Der spielende Verstand" brings "die Unruhe," which interferes with the listener's perception of the "erschaute Gestalt," and the composer's ability "sie mit möglichster Prägnanz an das Licht zu bringen." Cosima Wagner to Strauss, March 6, 1890. Ibid., 31–32.

27. "Wir haben die Vollendung der Kunst erlebt, aber gerade diese Vollendung lehrt uns Einfachheit." To her it appeared "als wie daß die Personen selbst [of the Don Juan story] zu Ihnen gesprochen hätten. Das nenne ich eben das Spiel der Intelligenz gegen das Gefühl." Ibid.

28. "Unsere Kunst führt uns auf die ewigen Motive zurück." Ibid., 32.

29. Ibid.

30. Strauss to Cosima Wagner, March 22, 1890. Ibid., 36.

31. Ibid.

32. See chapter 6, note 52.

33. "The debate over program music," remarked Dahlhaus, "was waged under the banner of an aesthetic as natural and self-evident to composers of the time (from Strauss and Pfitzner to Mahler and Schönberg) as it was consigned to the ash heap of history by their successors: the aesthetic of Schopenhauer, elevated on Wagner's authority to a metaphysic of music in an age of positivism." Dahlhaus, *Nineteenth-Century Music*, 360.

34. Felix M. Gatz, *Musik-Ästhetik in ihren Hauptrichtungen: Ein Quellenbuch der deutschen Musik-Ästhetik von Kant und der Frühromantik bis zur Gegenwart mit Einführung und Erläuterungen* (Stuttgart: Ferdinand Enke, 1929), 22.

35. Juliane Wandel, *Die Rezeption der Symphonien Gustav Mahlers zu Lebzeiten des Komponisten* (Frankfurt am Main: Peter Lang, 1999), 272.

36. Franz Lösch, interview with Piero Rismondo published in unidentified Viennese journal, quoted in Norman Lebrecht, ed., *Mahler Remembered* (New York: Norton, 1998), 71.

37. Fredric Jameson, personal communication, January 5, 1993. In Jameson's view, Strauss came naturally to a form of rhetoric that allowed "this music illicitly to arouse passions in the public"; Mahler's inwardness meant that such a connection would always be a struggle for him, but one with which, at least in the Eighth, he could produce a public success.

38. Mahler to Alma Mahler, June 22, 1909 (date approximate). *Gustav/Alma*, 326–28.

39. Ibid., 326.

40. *Venezianische Epigramme*, 66: "Wenige sind mir jedoch wie Gift und Schlange zuwider; Viere: Rauch des Tabaks, Wanzen und Knoblauch und [the sign of the Cross]."

41. Constantin Floros, *Gustav Mahler, II: Mahler und die Symphonik des 19. Jahrhunderts in neuer Deutung* (Wiesbaden: Breitkopf & Härtel, 1977), 8.

42. See Jackson, "The Metamorphosis of the *Metamorphosen*," 199–202. The poem is translated in Gilliam, *The Life of Richard Strauss*, 174, as follows: "No one can know himself/Separate from his inner being,/Yet he tries to do it every day,/That which is clearly from the outside,/What he is and what he was,/What he can do and what he wants to do.//But what happens in the world,/No one actually understands,/And up to the present day,/No one wishes to understand,/Conduct yourself with reason,/As the day is at hand,/Always think: 'It's gone all right until now,/So it may well continue that way until the end.'"

9. IMPORTS

1. *La Grange IV*, 787.
2. Mahler to Alma Mahler, June 5, 1907. *Gustav/Alma*, 269.
3. Franz Strauss advised him not to accept this offer. "As inviting as it might be from a financial standpoint, just as strongly do I believe that *now* it is not right for you; let it be something for later, and moreover a temporary arrangement, not for longer." Strauss followed this advice to the letter. Franz Strauss to Richard Strauss, February 5, 1891. Franz Grasberger, ed., *Der Strom der Töne trug mich fort: Die Welt um Richard Strauss in Briefen*, with assistance from Franz Strauss and Alice Strauss (Tutzing: Hans Schneider, 1967), 61.
4. Mahler to Friedrich Löhr, February 1887. *Mahler Letters*, 107.
5. *La Grange IV*, 112.

6. Already in the autumn of 1906 Mahler was telling Mengelberg that he would not be able to tolerate the situation in Vienna much longer. Mahler to Willem Mengelberg, September 12, 1906. *Mahler Letters*, 196; see Hefling, *Mahler: "Das Lied von der Erde,"* 28.

7. *La Grange III*, 660–62.

8. These *Schreibkalender* are held at the RSA.

9. Mahler to Alma Mahler, June 5, 1907. *Gustav/Alma*, 268–69.

10. *Memories and Letters*, 135–36. To Justine and Arnold Rosé he would write in February 1908, "I endeavor to earn my salary with the least amount of work possible." McClatchie, *The Mahler Family Letters*, 390.

11. Strauss did in fact return to the United States once, touring the Northeast and Midwest with Elizabeth Schumann from October 26, 1921, through January 3, 1922. Here I restrict myself to a consideration of the first tour in order to facilitate comparison with Mahler's experiences.

12. *New York Times*, March 20, 1904.

13. Strauss to his parents, March 2, 1904. *Der Strom der Töne*, 152.

14. *New York Times*, February 28, 1904; *Boston Globe*, March 6, 1904.

15. Editorial in *Musical America*, June 22, 1907, quoted in Roman, *Gustav Mahler's American Years*, 33.

16. *La Grange IV*, 44.

17. Ibid., 28–31.

18. *Boston Journal*, March 19, 1904.

19. Henry Louis de La Grange has argued at length against the commonly held view that in his last years Mahler believed his death to be imminent. From the fall of 1908, "he realized how exaggerated his fears had been, and returned to conducting and concerts with undiminished energy." *La Grange IV*, xvi. Whatever the depth of Mahler's fears, the evidence marshaled by La Grange shows considerable planning for the future, and thus a degree of hope greater than has generally been acknowledged.

20. Two of his symphonies had been heard in the United States before his arrival. Walter Damrosch conducted the Fourth Symphony with the New York Symphony Orchestra on November 6, 1904. The Fifth Symphony had its US premiere on March 24, 1905, in Cincinnati, played by the Cincinnati Orchestra under Franz van der Stucken. The same work was heard in February 1906 in performances of the Boston Symphony conducted by Wilhelm Gericke in Boston, Philadelphia, and New York.

21. Alma called the end of the Fifth "hymnal and boring." *Memories and Letters*, 47. Adorno complained of "pomp" in the "vainly jubilant" finale of the

Seventh, declaring, "Mahler was a poor yea-sayer." Adorno, *Mahler: A Musical Physiognomy*, 137.

22. *Memories and Letters*, 100.

23. Edward R. Reilly, "Mahler in America," in *The Mahler Companion*, ed. Donald Mitchell and Andrew Nicholson (Oxford: Oxford University Press, 1999), 421; Hefling, "Mahler's 'Todtenfeier,'" 30, 38.

24. *Musical Courier*, March 21, 1904, quoted in Robert Breuer, "Richard Strauss in Amerika. Teil I: 1904," *Richard-Strauss Blätter* 8 [new series] (1976): 4.

25. *New York Times*, March 6, 1904.

26. Ibid., March 22, 1904.

27. Ibid., March 23, 1904.

28. *Musical* Courier, date unknown, quoted in Kennedy, *Richard Strauss*, 138.

29. *La Grange IV*, 68.

30. Ibid., 71.

31. *La Grange IV*, 305–11.

32. After the first US performance of the tone poem, in February 1895 with the Chicago Orchestra under Theodore Thomas, the critic for the *Chicago Tribune* praised the work's "extraordinary power." By 1900 it had been performed in New York, Boston, Philadelphia, Cincinnati, and Pittsburgh. Schmid, "The Tone Poems of Richard Strauss, 186–96.

33. *New York Times*, March 26, 1904.

34. *Boston Journal*, March 9, 1904.

35. *New York Tribune*, January 27, 1910, quoted in Roman, *Gustav Mahler's American Years*, 334.

36. *La Grange IV*, 653–54.

37. *New York Times*, February 28, 1904.

38. This critique was provided by one "Sharp" in "Musikalisches aus New York," *Neue Zeitschrift für Musik* 71 (June 29, 1904): 491, quoted in Schmid, "The Tone Poems of Richard Strauss," 414.

39. *New York Times*, February 28, 1904.

40. *Chicago Tribune*, April 4, 1904, quoted in Schmid, "The Tone Poems of Richard Strauss," 318. *New York Times*, March 4, 1904.

41. Kennedy, *Richard Strauss*, 139.

42. Ferruccio Busoni to Gerda Busoni, March 6, 1904. Rosamund Ley, ed. and trans., *Ferruccio Busoni: Letters to His Wife* (New York: Da Capo Press, 1975), 72.

43. Reilly, "Mahler in America," 423.

44. Aldrich: "It obviously has a 'programme' of some kind as a basis, and without a suggestion of what it is the music is not of itself wholly intelligible." *New York Times*, December 17, 1909. Krehbiel: "The symphony has no justification without a programme." *New York Tribune*, December 18, 1909, quoted in Roman, *Gustav Mahler's American Years*, 312, 314.

45. *New York World*, January 21, 1911, quoted in *La Grange IV*, 1129.

46. *New York Tribune*, January 18, 1911, quoted in Roman, *Gustav Mahler's American Years*, 437.

47. *New York Times*, January 18, 1911.

48. Adorno wrote of Mahler's predilection for discontinuities, "his fractures are the script of truth." Adorno, *Mahler*, 166. See also Peter Franklin, "'... his fractures are the script of truth.'—Adorno's Mahler," in *Mahler Studies*, ed. Stephen E. Hefling (Cambridge: Cambridge University Press, 1997), 271–94.

49. *New York Times*, December 6, 1908; Roman, *Gustav Mahler's American Years*, 179.

50. Hepokoski, "Framing Till Eulenspiegel," 4–5, 13.

51. Stephen E. Hefling, "Gustav Mahler und Arnold Schönberg," in *Gustav Mahler: Unbekannte Briefe*, ed. Herta Blaukopf (Vienna: Bibliothek der Internationalen Gustav Mahler Gesellschaft, 1983), 186.

52. *New York Times*, April 7, 1909.

53. Perhaps because taking multiple approaches to "ancient" repertoire was at least as old as Liszt, and retouching of the Ninth had begun with Wagner, critics declined to think more carefully about why an implicitly "ahistorical" performance of Beethoven would incorporate revisions to the musical text.

54. J. Machlis, *Introduction to Contemporary Music* (London, 1963), 75, quoted in Denis McCaldin, "Mahler and Beethoven's Ninth Symphony," *Proceedings of the Royal Musical Association* 107 (1980/81): 101.

55. *New York Times*, March 26, 1904.

56. Ibid., March 27, 1904.

57. Ibid.

10. ALLUSIONISTS

1. Constantin Floros compares mm. 273–80 of the Scherzo from the Sixth with mm. 218–25 of *Domestica*. Floros, *Gustav Mahler: The Symphonies*, 176. On reminiscences of the Sixth in the *Alpensinfonie*, see below.

2. These issues have been addressed in recent work on both composers. La Grange provides a useful classification in Henry-Louis de La Grange, "Music about Music in Mahler: Reminiscences, Allusions, or Quotations," in *Mahler*

Studies, ed. Stephen E. Hefling (Cambridge: Cambridge University Press, 1997), 122–68. For a study enumerating many specific instances of intertextuality in Strauss, with special focus on their dramatic and emotional impact, see Günter Brosche, "Musical Quotations and Allusions in the Works of Richard Strauss," in *The Cambridge Companion to Richard Strauss*, ed. Charles Youmans (Cambridge: Cambridge University Press, 2010), 213–25.

3. Scott Warfield, "Friedrich Wilhelm Meyer (1818–1893): Some Biographical Notes on Strauss' Composition Teacher," *Richard-Strauss Blätter* 37 [new series] (June 1997): 54–74.

4. A wealth of such instances are tracked in John Daverio, *Crossing Paths: Schubert, Schumann, Brahms* (Oxford: Oxford University Press, 2002).

5. Strauss's reworkings of Couperin, though not well know, form an instructive example in this vein. See Wayne Heisler Jr., *The Ballet Collaborations of Richard Strauss* (Rochester: University of Rochester Press, 2009), 171–216.

6. On the early history of the phrase "Musik über Musik," see Anette Unger, *Welt, Leben und Kunst als Themen der "Zarathustra-Kompositionen" von Richard Strauss und Gustav Mahler* (Frankfurt am Main: Peter Lang, 1992), 20–25.

7. Todd, "Strauss before Liszt and Wagner," 28.

8. When Mahler "would not leave the piano, even to eat," he found that "my father's cane got me to the table." *La Grange I*, 17.

9. La Grange, "Music about Music," 122.

10. Ibid., 144.

11. Ibid., 123.

12. The classic explication of Wagner's and Brahms's differing approaches to purging transitional material from their music, or to making every moment of the music "thematic," is Carl Dahlhaus, "Issues in Composition," trans. Mary Whittall in collaboration with Arnold Whittall, in *Between Romanticism and Modernism: Four Studies in the Music of the Late Nineteenth Century*, trans. Mary Whittall (Berkeley: University of California Press, 1980), 40–78.

13. On the interwoven programmatic threads in this movement, see Floros, *Gustav Mahler: The Symphonies*, 38–43.

14. I have discussed the often-overlooked idealistic dimension of Hanslick's aesthetics in *Richard Strauss's Orchestral Music and the German Intellectual Tradition*, 6–15, relying especially on Gatz's *Musik-Ästhetik in ihren Hauptrichtungen*, 21–50.

15. Adorno often expressed the impossible redemption sought by Mahler in terms of a union of subject and object: "Mahler's music is the individual's dream of the irresistible collective. But at the same time it expresses objectively the

impossibility of identification with it." The essential claim, however, is that the triumphs are illusory. Adorno, *Mahler: A Musical Physiognomy*, 33.

16. Floros, *Gustav Mahler*, 167.

17. Unger's approach is to read Mahler as providing a musical account of music history itself, in particular the gradual emancipation of musical form. See Unger, *Welt, Leben und Kunst*, 257.

18. Floros, *Gustav Mahler*, 175–76.

19. Ibid., 186.

20. Norman Del Mar, *Richard Strauss: A Critical Commentary on His Life and Works*, vol. 2 (London: Barrie and Rockliff, 1969), 109–12. Ashley also discusses echoes of the Second and Seventh; see Tim Ashley, *Richard Strauss* (London: Phaidon, 1999), 116–17.

21. "Ich bin Germane, dem der *Anblick* einer herrlichen Gebirgsnatur darüber der blaue Himmel, der strahlenden, wärmenden Sonne schon der Gipfel des Erreichbaren und Erstrebenswerten darstellt. Daran freue ich mich, dies hält mich gesund und gibt mir Freude zur *Arbeit*. Eine unproductive Rasse wie die der Juden mochten diese christliche, jüdische Metaphysik ersinnen, sie mögen die Spekulation an die Stelle der Produktion setzen [. . .] Wann wird die germanische Rasse endlich den furchtbaren Bacillus: Christentum d. h. Neojudentum aus seinem Blute ausgestossen haben?" November 22, 1915, "Brown Diary" ["braunes Tagebuch"], RSA.

22. Rainer Bayreuther, *Richard Strauss' Alpensinfonie: Entstehung, Analyse und Interpretation* (Hildesheim: G. Olms, 1997), 226.

23. La Grange, "Music about Music," 147.

24. Leon Botstein, "The Enigmas of Richard Strauss," in *Richard Strauss and His World*, ed. Bryan Gilliam (Princeton: Princeton University Press, 1992), 22.

11. IRONISTS

1. Stephen E. Hefling, "The Ninth Symphony," in *The Mahler Companion*, ed. Donald Mitchell and Andrew Nicholson (Oxford: Oxford University Press, 1999), 484.

2. Johnson, *Mahler's Voices*, 141.

3. Mahler cited the "the uncannily and ironically brooding sultriness of the death march." Mahler to Max Marschalk, March 20, 1896. *Mahler Letters*, 178.

4. Melissa Lane, "The Evolution of *Eironeia* in Classical Greek Texts: Why Socratic *Eironeia* Is Not Socratic Irony," in *Oxford Studies in Ancient Philosophy*, ed. David Sedley (Oxford: Oxford University Press, 2006), 53.

5. Hansen, "*Gustav Mahler's Symphonies*," 134.

6. Jeremy Barham, "Mahler's *Verkehrte Welt*: Fechner, 'Learned Satire' and the Third Movement of Symphony No. 3," in *Mahler im Kontext/Contextualizing Mahler*, ed. Erich Wolfgang Partsch and Morten Solvik (Vienna: Böhlau, 2011), 182.

7. Richard Strauss, "Introduction to *Die Musik* (A Collection of Illustrated Essays)," in *Recollections*, 9.

8. An alternative translation is "Of the Afterworldsmen," which captures more of the metaphysical intent while obscuring the pun (backwoodsmen/backworldsmen).

9. A description of Strauss's annotations in this source can be found in Charles Youmans, *Richard Strauss's Orchestral Music and the German Intellectual Tradition*, 103–104. Translations from Friedrich Nietzsche, *Thus Spoke Zarathustra*, trans. R. J. Hollingdale (New York: Penguin, 1969), 59, 61.

10. That includes the perceptive Hans Merian, whose *Richard Strauß' Tondichtung Also sprach Zarathustra: eine Studie über die moderne Programmsymphonie* (Leipzig: Meyers, 1899) was for decades the only serious attempt to come to grips with the complexities of music and program in Strauss's tone poems.

11. Max Graf, review of Mahler's First Symphony, *Wiener Rundschau*, December 1, 1900, quoted in "Mahler's German-Language Critics," ed. and trans. Karen Painter and Bettina Varwig, in Painter, ed., *Mahler and His World*, 286.

12. Ibid.

13. Eduard Hanslick, review of Mahler's First Symphony, *Neue freie Presse*, November 20, 1900, quoted in Painter, ed., *Mahler and His World*, 290.

14. Graf, review of Mahler's First, 287.

15. Pierre Boulez, "Gustav Mahler Up-to-Date?," in *Gustav Mahler in Vienna*, ed. Sigrid Wiesmann (London: Thames & Hudson, 1976), 14, quoted in Johnson, *Mahler's Voices*, 145.

16. Theodor Helm, review of Mahler's First Symphony, *Pester Lloyd*, November 27, 1900, quoted in *Mahler and His World*, 292–93.

17. Robert Hirschfeld, review of Mahler's First Symphony, *Wiener Abendpost*, November 20, 1900, quoted in *Mahler and His World*, 296.

18. See the discussion in chapter 8.

19. Richard Strauss, "Letzte Aufzeichnung [1949]," in *Recollections*, 182. (This source is not included in the translation.)

20. *Chronicle*, 479.

21. Strauss, "Letzte Aufzeichnung [1949]," 182.

22. Kristiansen, "Richard Strauss's *Feuersnot*," 402.

23. Ibid., 415–48.

24. Ibid., 413.

25. "Das Rätsel der Straussschen Natur zu lösen, die, obwohl Trägerin einer der erstaunlichsten Begabungen, dennoch nicht von ihr durchdrungen und besessen ist wie die anderer grosser [sic] Künstler, sondern sie in der Tat nur 'trägt' wie einen Anzug, den man ablegen kann—dies ist weder mir noch wohl irgend jemand anderem gelungen." Busch, *Aus dem Leben eines Musikers*, 169.

26. *Memories and Letters*, 47–48.

27. David Matthews, "The Sixth Symphony," in *The Mahler Companion*, ed. Donald Mitchell and Andrew Nicholson (Oxford: Oxford University Press, 1999), 372.

28. *Memories and Letters*, 100.

29. Quoted by Johnson alongside similar reactions of Hans Redlich and Robert Hirschfeld. Johnson, *Mahler's Voices*, 145–46.

30. Hansen, "Gustav Mahler's Symphonies," 430–31.

31. Kennedy, *Richard Strauss*, 192.

32. Richard Strauss, "On Melodic Inspiration," in *Recollections*, 112.

33. Ibid., 114.

34. Hefling, *Mahler: "Das Lied von der Erde,"* 20.

35. Mahler to Bruno Walter, July 18, 1908. *Mahler Letters*, 324.

36. Hansen, "Gustav Mahler's Symphonies," 798.

12. METAPHYSICIANS

1. "Es kommt aber leider auf die Rasse an." Mahler made this remark in reference to a possible appointment for Bruno Walter at the Vienna Court Opera, noting that Walter had long been a Protestant. Karpath, *Begegnung mit dem Genius*, 179.

2. An early history of the *alt-katholisch* faith can be found in Johann Friedrich Schulte, *Der Altkatholizismus. Geschichte seiner Entwicklung, inneren Gestaltung und rechtlichen Stellung in Deutschland*. (Gießen: Roth, 1887; reprint, Aalen: Scientia, 1965).

3. Breuer, "'My Brother, Richard Strauss,'" 33.

4. *La Grange I*, 2–3, 6; Mitchell, *Gustav Mahler*, vol. 1, 4.

5. *Memories and Letters*, 44.

6. Bauer-Lechner, 76, 182.

7. *La Grange I*, 15; Bauer-Lechner, 53.

8. *Chronicle*, 294. It was this "individualist" rejection of authority, rather than the Schopenhauerian tendencies described in chapter 5, that struck early reviewers of the work.

9. Werbeck, *Die Tondichtungen von Richard Strauss*, 540.

10. For this insight I am indebted to Bryan Gilliam.

11. See Youmans, *Richard Strauss's Orchestral Music and the German Intellectual Tradition*, 74–82.

12. Stephen E. Hefling, "Siegfried Lipiner's *On the Elements of a Renewal of Religious Ideas in the Present*," in *Mahler im Kontext/Contextualizing Mahler*, ed. Erich Wolfgang Partsch and Morten Solvik (Vienna: Böhlau, 2011), 110.

13. *Bauer-Lechner*, 67.

14. Mahler to Friedrich Löhr, August 29, 1895. *Mahler Letters*, 164.

15. Niekerk, *Reading Mahler*, 110–14; quotation on 113.

16. Floros, "Die Begriffe der '*ewigen Liebe*' und der '*Seligkeit*,'" in *Gustav Mahler, I: Die geistige Welt Gustav Mahlers in systematischer Darstellung*, 125–27.

17. Julian Johnson traces the expressive mode of this Adagio from the slow movements of the late Beethoven string quartets, through Mendelssohn and Schumann, to "*Parsifal*, whose predominant Adagio voice provided Mahler with a paradigm of a music that raises the subjective lyrical voice to the status of an absolute religiosity," and finally to Bruckner, where "he would have found that voice once again enshrined within the symphony." See Johnson, *Mahler's Voices*, 274.

18. Peter Franklin, *Mahler: Symphony No. 3* (Cambridge: Cambridge University Press, 1991), 76.

19. Henahan did qualify his characterization: "With the Mahler Third, however, the game is won or lost in the finale, which in prosaic hands can turn to sentimental slush." Donal Henahan, "Mahler's Third Symphony," *New York Times*, May 29, 1987.

20. Niekerk, *Reading Mahler*, 110–11.

21. "I'll call the whole thing 'My Joyful Science,'—for that's just what it is!" *Bauer-Lechner*, 41.

22. *Venezianische Epigramme*, 66: "Wenige sind mir jedoch wie Gift und Schlange zuwider; Viere: Rauch des Tabaks, Wanzen und Knoblauch und [the sign of the Cross]."

23. *Memories and Letters*, 101.

24. Ibid.

25. Ibid.

26. See chapter 3, note 29, and chapter 10, note 21.

27. Kennedy, *Richard Strauss*, 183.

28. Strauss to Hugo von Hofmannsthal, September 11, 1912. Strauss and Strauss, *The Correspondence between Richard Strauss and Hugo von Hofmannsthal*, 142.

29. Hofmannsthal to Strauss, September 13, 1912. Ibid., 144.

30. Bryan Gilliam, *Rounding Wagner's Mountain: Richard Strauss and Modern German Opera* (Cambridge: Cambridge University Press, 2014), 157.

31. Lipiner's *Über die Elemente einer Erneuerung religiöser Ideen in der Gegenwart*, given as a lecture to the Leseverein der deutschen Studenten Wiens on January 19, 1878, is reproduced in its entirety, with English translation, in *Mahler im Kontext/Contextualizing Mahler*, ed. Erich Wolfgang Partsch and Morten Solvik (Vienna: Böhlau, 2011), 115–51; quotation on 137. Hefling, "Siegfried Lipiner's *On the Elements of a Renewal of Religious Ideas in the Present*," 91–114, serves as introduction.

EPILOGUE

1. See chapter 1 on the eleven-year-old Strauss's performance of Weber's *Invitation to the Dance* at a children's concert. *Chronicle*, 25.

2. Ibid., 100.

3. Ibid., 94.

4. For an account of these brilliant and amusing pedagogical classes, see Richard Zimdars, *The Piano Master Classes of Hans von Bülow* (Bloomington: Indiana University Press, 1993). See also Walker, *Hans von Bülow*, 321–22.

5. Richard Strauss, "On Melodic Inspiration," in *Recollections*, 116.

6. *La Grange I*, 25–26.

7. This story is related in an unpublished portion of Natalie Bauer-Lechner's memoir. It comes from one of Mahler's student colleagues at the conservatory, Carl Schnürmann, who turned pages for him at the concert in question, in Iglau, on September 12, 1876. See *La Grange I*, 37–38.

8. Ibid., 14, 17.

9. *Rivalry*, 117–18.

10. *La Grange I*, 19.

11. Ibid., 17.

12. Ibid., 24.

13. Albrecht Joseph, Anna Mahler, Marina Mahler, and Donald Mitchell, "Mahler's Smile: A Memoir of His Daughter Anna Mahler (1904–1988)," in *The Mahler Companion*, ed. Donald Mitchell and Andrew Nicholson (Oxford: Oxford University Press, 1999), 590.

14. Richard Strauss, "On Melodic Inspiration," in *Recollections*, 114.

15. Mahler to Josephine Poisl, March 18, 1880; Mahler to Poisl's mother, March 29, 1880. Bayerische Staatsbibliothek, Ana 600, B, I, 2b.

16. Bauer-Lechner, 150.

17. Ibid., 149.

18. See introduction, note 39.

19. "Sittliche Reinigung aus eigener Kraft." Kohler, "Richard Strauss: *Eine Alpensinfonie*," 42.

20. Mahler to Strauss, October 20, 1893. *Mahler/Strauss*, 23.

21. Mahler to Arnold Berliner, January 31, 1895. *Mahler Letters*, 158.

22. Strauss to Mahler, December 10, 1895. *Mahler/Strauss*, 44–45.

23. Mahler to Alma Mahler, January 12, 1907; Mahler to Alma Mahler, August 16, 1906. *Gustav/Alma*, 257, 236. Mahler to Max Marschalk, December 4, 1896. *Mahler Letters*, 201.

24. Mahler to Strauss, July 19, 1894. Strauss to Mahler, March 5, 1905. *Mahler/Strauss*, 37, 75.

25. Mahler to Alma, December 18, 1901. *Gustav/Alma*, 76. The remark about sincerity is published only in the latest edition of Bauer-Lechner's memoir; see *Bauer-Lechner*, 170–71.

26. Mahler to Alma Mahler, May 22, 1906. *Gustav/Alma*, 233.

27. Mahler to Alma Mahler, November 8, 1905, January 31, 1902. Ibid., 222, 100.

28. Mahler to Alma Mahler, January 13, 1907, January 10, 1907. Ibid., 258, 255.

29. *Memories and Letters*, 41.

30. Quoted in Unger, *Welt, Leben und Kunst als Themen der "Zarathustra-Kompositionen,"* 93.

31. Strauss to Stefan Zweig, May 5, 1935. Knight, *A Confidential Matter*, 90. See also the discussion of Wagnerian grandiloquence in chapter 4.

32. This remark is related in an annotation by Alma Mahler of a letter from Mahler to Arnold Berliner of June 15, 1892. Alma Mahler, ed., *Gustav Mahler Briefe, 1879–1911* (Berlin: Paul Zsolnay, 1924), 126.

33. Mahler to Alma Mahler, January 12, 1907. *Gustav/Alma*, 257.

34. *La Grange IV*, xvi. La Grange's view, reflected in his book's subtitle ("A New Life Cut Short"), is that by the fall of 1908 Mahler "realized how exaggerated his fears had been, and returned to conducting operas and concerts with undiminished energy"—expecting, moreover, to have many more years of creative productivity.

35. Mahler to Alma Mahler, June 22, 1909 (date approximate). *Gustav/Alma*, 326–28.

36. Gilliam, *The Life of Richard Strauss*, 182.

37. It was the Hartmann from which he tore the pages one at a time, as described in chapter 6. *Memories and Letters*, 196–97, 200.

38. Gilbert Kaplan, ed., *The Mahler Album*, new, expanded edition (New York: Kaplan Foundation, 2011), item 77.

39. Ross, *The Rest Is Noise*, 3–4.

40. The location of the trip is given in Trenner, *Richard Strauss: Chronik zu Leben und Werk*, 277. Trenner records that the trip took place "in the auto of a factory owner."

41. *Memories and Letters*, 97.

42. That is, the party could not have left in the afternoon for a round trip of 280 miles. The photo was taken at the far-right entrance of the building's southwest side.

43. Here I use the now-familiar translation of "meine Zeit wird kommen, wenn die seine um ist." Mahler to Alma Mahler, January 31, 1902. *Gustav/Alma*, 100.

Bibliography

The sources listed in the Note on Translation are not included in this list.

Adamy, Bernhard. "Schopenhauer bei Richard Strauss." *Jahrbuch der Schopenhauer Gesellschaft* 61 (1980): 195–98.

Adorno, Theodor W. *Mahler: A Musical Physiognomy.* Translated by Edmund Jephcott. Chicago: University of Chicago Press, 1992.

———. "Richard Strauss at Sixty." Translated by Susan Gillespie. In *Richard Strauss and His World*, edited by Bryan Gilliam, 406–15. Princeton: Princeton University Press, 1992.

———. "Richard Strauss. Born June 11, 1864." Translated by Samuel Weber and Shierry Weber. *Perspectives of New Music* 4 (1965): 14–32, and 5 (1966): 113–29.

Amenta, Charles. "The Opening of the Mahler Ninth Symphony and the Bernstein 'Heart-Beat' Hypothesis." *Naturlaut* 4 (2005): 17–18.

Anderman, Walter Thomas. *Bis der Vorhang fiel: Berichtet nach Aufzeichnungen aus den Jahren 1940 bis 1945.* Dortmund: K. Schwalvenberg, 1947.

Anonymous. "Musikalisches aus New York." *Neue Zeitschrift für Musik* 71 (June 29, 1904): 491.

Aringer, Klaus. "Exkurs III: Orchesterbesetzungen und Instrumentation." In *Gustav Mahler: Interpretationen seiner Werke*, edited by Peter Revers and Oliver Korte, vol. 1, 416–34. Laaber: Laaber, 2011.

Ashley, Tim. *Richard Strauss*. London: Phaidon, 1999.
Bahr-Mildenburg, Anna. "Meine erste Proben mit Gustav Mahler." *Neue freie Presse*, May 26, 1912.
Barham, Jeremy. "Mahler's *Verkehrte Welt*: Fechner, 'Learned Satire' and the Third Movement of Symphony No. 3." In *Mahler im Kontext/Contextualizing Mahler*, edited by Erich Wolfgang Partsch and Morten Solvik, 177–206. Vienna: Böhlau, 2011.
Barsova, Inna. "Mahler and Russia." In *The Mahler Companion*, edited by Donald Mitchell and Andrew Nicholson, 517–30. Oxford: Oxford University Press, 1999.
Bayreuther, Rainer. *Richard Strauss' Alpensinfonie: Entstehung, Analyse und Interpretation*. Hildesheim: G. Olms, 1997.
Bekker, Paul. *Gustav Mahlers Sinfonien*. Berlin: Schuster & Loeffler, 1921.
Benedikt, Michael. "Friedrich Jodls *Kritik des Idealismus*." In *Wilhelm Bolin und Friedrich Jodl im Kampf um die Aufklärung: Festschrift für Juha Manninen*, edited by Georg Gimpl, 271–86. Frankfurt am Main: Peter Lang, 1996.
Berman, David. "Schopenhauer and Nietzsche: Honest Atheism, Dishonest Pessimism." In *Willing and Nothingness: Schopenhauer as Nietzsche's Educator*, edited by Christopher Janaway, 178–95. Oxford: Clarendon Press, 1998.
Bernstein, Leonard. *The Unanswered Question*. Cambridge, MA: Harvard University Press, 1976.
Bie, Oscar. *Das deutsche Lied*. Berlin: S. Fischer, [1926].
Birkin, Kenneth. "Richard Strauss in Weimar. Part 1: The Concert Hall." *Richard Strauss-Blätter* 33 [new series] (June 1995): 3–36.
———. "Richard Strauss in Weimar. Part 2: The Opera House." *Richard Strauss-Blätter* 34 [new series] (December 1995): 3–56.
"Blaues Tagebuch," Richard-Strauss-Archiv (RSA) quoted in *Rivalry*, 151.
Blaukopf, Herta. "*Bücher fresse ich immer mehr und mehr*. Gustav Mahler als Leser." In *Mahler Gespräche. Rezeptionsfragen—literarischer Horizont—musikalische Darstellung*, edited by Friedbert Aspetsberger and Erich Wolfgang Partsch, 96–116. Innsbruck: Studien Verlag, 2002.
———. "Mahler as Conductor in the Opera House and Concert Hall." In *The Cambridge Companion to Mahler*, edited by Jeremy Barham, 165–77. Cambridge: Cambridge University Press, 2007.
Blessin, Stefan. *Goethes Romane: Aufbruch der Modern*. Paderborn: Ferdinand Schöningh, 1996.

Böhm, Karl. *Ich erinnere mich ganz genau*. Edited by Hans Weigel. Zurich: Biogees, 1968.

Borchmeyer, Dieter. *Richard Wagner: Theory and Theater*. Translated by Stewart Spencer. Oxford: Clarendon Press, 1991.

Botstein, Leon. "The Enigmas of Richard Strauss: A Revisionist View." In *Richard Strauss and His World*, edited by Bryan Gilliam, 3–32. Princeton, NJ: Princeton University Press.

Boyle, Nicholas. *Goethe: The Poet and the Age*. 2 vols. Oxford: Clarendon Press, 1991–2000.

Brandmeyer, Rudolf. *Die Gedichte des jungen Goethe*. Göttingen: Vandenhoeck & Ruprecht, 1998.

Brecher, Gustav. *Richard Strauss: Eine monographische Skizze*. Leipzig: Hermann Seemann Nachfolger, [1900].

Breuer, Robert. "My Brother, Richard Strauss." *Saturday Review* (New York), December 27, 1958.

——. "Richard Strauss in Amerika. Teil I: 1904." *Richard-Strauss Blätter* 8 [new series] (1976): 1–17.

Brodbeck, David. "Brahms, the Third Symphony, and the New German School." In *Brahms and His World*, edited by Walter Frisch, 65–80. Princeton: Princeton University Press, 1990.

Brosche, Günter. "Musical Quotations and Allusions in the Works of Richard Strauss." In *The Cambridge Companion to Richard Strauss*, edited by Charles Youmans, 213–25. Cambridge: Cambridge University Press, 2010.

——. "Richard Strauss und Arnold Schoenberg." *Richard Strauss-Blätter* 2 [new series] (December 1979): 21–28.

Brown, A. Peter. "Brahms's Third Symphony and the New German School." *Journal of Musicology* 2 (1983): 434–52.

Bruford, W. H. *The German Tradition of Self-Cultivation: Bildung from Humboldt to Thomas Mann*. Cambridge: Cambridge University Press, 1975.

Bülow, Marie von, ed. *Hans von Bülows Leben, dargestellt aus seinen Briefen*. 2nd ed. Leipzig: Breitkopf & Härtel, 1921.

Busch, Fritz. *Aus dem Leben eines Musikers*. Zurich: Rascher, 1949.

Conrady, Karl Otto. *Goethe: Leben und Werk*. 2 vols. Königstein: Athenäum, 1982–85.

Dahlhaus, Carl. "Gustav Mahler und Richard Strauss. Die Geschichte einer problematischen Freundschaft in Briefen." *Frankfurter Allgemeine Zeitung*, November 8, 1980.

———. *The Idea of Absolute Music*. Translated by Roger Lustig. Chicago: University of Chicago Press, 1989.

———. "Issues in Composition." Translated by Mary Whittall in collaboration with Arnold Whittall. In *Between Romanticism and Modernism: Four Studies in the Music of the Later Nineteenth Century*, 40–78. Translated by Mary Whittall. Berkeley: University of California Press, 1980.

———. "Neo-romanticism." In *Between Romanticism and Modernism: Four Studies in the Music of the Later Nineteenth Century*, 1–18. Translated by Mary Whittall. Berkeley: University of California Press, 1980.

———. *Nineteenth-Century Music*. Translated by J. Bradford Robinson. Berkeley: University of California Press, 1989.

———. *Richard Wagner's Music Dramas*. Translated by Mary Whittall. Cambridge: Cambridge University Press, 1971.

Danz, Ernst-Joachim. *Die objektlose Kunst: Untersuchungen zur Musikästhetik Friedrich von Hauseggers*. Regensburg: Gustav Bosse, 1981.

Daverio, John. *Crossing Paths: Schubert, Schumann, Brahms*. Oxford: Oxford University Press, 2002.

Del Mar, Norman. *Richard Strauss: A Critical Commentary on His Life and Works*. Vol. 1. London: Barrie and Rockliff, 1962.

———. *Richard Strauss: A Critical Commentary on His Life and Works*. Vol. 2. London: Barrie and Rockliff, 1969.

Diener, Gottfried. *Goethes "Lila": Heilung eines "Wahnsinns" durch "psychische Kur."* Frankfurt am Main: Athenäum, 1971.

Edelmann, Bernd, Birgit Lodes, and Reinhold Schlötterer, eds. *Richard Strauss und die Moderne*. Berlin: Henschel, 2001.

Feder, Stuart. "Before Alma: Gustav Mahler and 'Das Ewig-Weibliche.'" In *Mahler Studies*, edited by Stephen E. Hefling, 78–109. Cambridge: Cambridge University Press, 1997.

———. *Gustav Mahler: A Life in Crisis*. New Haven: Yale University Press, 2004.

Finck, Henry T. *Richard Strauss: The Man and His Work*. Boston: Little, Brown, and Company, 1917.

Fischer, Jens Malte. *Gustav Mahler*. Translated by Stewart Spencer. New Haven: Yale University Press, 2011.

———. "Mahler. Leben und Welt." In *Mahler Handbuch*, edited by Bernd Sponheuer and Wolfram Steinbeck, 14–59. Stuttgart: Metzler, 2010.

Fischer, Theodor. "Aus Gustav Mahlers Jugendzeit." *Deutsche Heimat: Sudetendeutsche Monatsschrift für Kunst, Literatur, Heimat und Volkskunde* 7 (1931): 264–68.

Floros, Constantin. "Exkurs II: Zur Relevanz der 'Programme' in Mahlers Symphonien." In *Gustav Mahler: Interpretationen seiner Werke*, edited by Peter Revers and Oliver Korte, vol. 1, 398–415. Laaber: Laaber-Verlag, 2011.

———. *Gustav Mahler, I: Die geistige Welt Gustav Mahlers in systematischer Darstellung*. Wiesbaden: Breitkopf & Härtel, 1977.

———. *Gustav Mahler, II: Mahler und die Symphonik des 19. Jahrhunderts in neuer Deutung*. Wiesbaden: Breitkopf & Härtel, 1977.

———. *Gustav Mahler: The Symphonies*. Translated by Vernon Wicker and Jutta Wicker. Portland, OR: Amadeus Press, 1993.

———. "Mahlers intellektuelle Neugier." In *Mahler im Kontext/Contextualizing Mahler*, edited by Erich Wolfgang Partsch and Morten Solvik, 9–12. Vienna: Böhlau, 2011.

Foerster, Josef Bohuslav. *Erinnerungen eines Musikers*. Prague: Artia, 1955.

Frankenstein, Ludwig. *Arthur Seidl: Ein Lebensabriß*. Regensburg: Gustav Bosse, 1913.

Franklin, Peter. "'... his fractures are the script of truth.'—Adorno's Mahler." In *Mahler Studies*, edited by Stephen E. Hefling, 271–94. Cambridge: Cambridge University Press, 1997.

———. *The Life of Mahler*. Cambridge: Cambridge University Press, 1997.

———. "Mahler, Gustav." In *The New Grove Dictionary of Music and Musicians*, 2nd ed., edited by Stanley Sadie, vol. 15 (New York: Grove's Dictionaries, 2001).

———. *Mahler: Symphony No. 3*. Cambridge: Cambridge University Press, 1991.

———. "A Stranger's Story: Programmes, Politics, and Mahler's Third Symphony." In *The Mahler Companion*, edited Donald Mitchell and Andrew Nicholson, 171–86. Oxford: Oxford University Press, 1999.

———. "Strauss and His Contemporaries: Critical Perspectives." In *The Richard Strauss Companion*, edited by Mark-Daniel Schmid, 31–61. Westport, CT: Praeger, 2003.

Friedenthal, Richard. *Goethe: His Life and Times*. Cleveland: World Publishing Company, 1963.

Frisch, Walter. *German Modernism: Music and the Arts*. Berkeley: University of California Press, 2005.

Gatz, Felix M. *Musik-Ästhetik in ihren Hauptrichtungen: Ein Quellenbuch der deutschen Musik-Ästhetik von Kant und der Frühromantik bis zur Gegenwart mit Einführung und Erläuterungen.* Stuttgart: Ferdinand Enke, 1929.

Gerlach, Reinhard. "Die Orchesterkomposition als musikalisches Drama: Die Teil-Tonalitäten der 'Gestalten' und der bitonale Kontrapunkt in *Ein Heldenleben* von Richard Strauss." *MusikTheorie* 6 (1991): 55–78.

———. "Richard Strauss: Prinzipien seiner Kompositionstechnik." *Archiv für Musikwissenschaft* 23 (1966): 277–88.

Getz, Christine. "The Lieder of Richard Strauss." In *The Strauss Companion*, edited by Mark-Daniel Schmid, 335–81. Westport, CT: Praeger, 2003.

Gillespie, Susan, trans. "Selections from the Strauss-Thuille Correspondence: A Glimpse of Strauss During His Formative Years." In *Richard Strauss and His World*, edited by Bryan Gilliam, 193–236. Princeton, NJ: Princeton University Press, 1992.

Gilliam, Bryan. "'Friede im Innern': Strauss's Public and Private Worlds in the Mid 1930s." *Journal of the American Musicological Society* 57 (2005): 565–98

———. *The Life of Richard Strauss*. Cambridge: Cambridge University Press, 1999.

———, ed. *Richard Strauss and His World*. Princeton: Princeton University Press, 1992.

———, ed. *Richard Strauss: New Perspectives on the Composer and His Work*. Durham, NC: Duke University Press, 1992.

———. *Rounding Wagner's Mountain: Richard Strauss and Modern German Opera*. Cambridge: Cambridge University Press, 2014.

———. "Strauss's *Intermezzo*: Innovation and Tradition." In *Richard Strauss: New Perspectives on the Composer and His Work*, edited by Bryan Gilliam, 259–83. Durham, NC: Duke University Press, 1992.

———. "Strauss's Preliminary Opera Sketches: Thematic Fragments and Symphonic Continuity." *19th-Century Music* 9 (1986): 176–88.

Gimpl, Georg. *Wilhelm Bolin und Friedrich Jodl im Kampf um die Aufklärung: Festschrift für Juha Manninen*. Frankfurt am Main: Peter Lang, 1996.

Goethe, Johann Wolfgang von. *Lila (Ein Festspiel mit Gesang und Tanz)*. In *Sämtliche Werke nach Epochen seines Schaffens, Münchner Ausgabe*, edited by Karl Richter et al, vol. 2.1, *Erstes Weimarer Jarzehnt, 1775–1786, I*, edited by Hartmut Reinhardt, 131–60. Munich: Carl Hanser, 1987.

Gräner, Georg. *Anton Bruckner*. Leipzig: Fr. Kistner und C. F. W. S. Siegel, [1924].

Grasberger, Franz, ed. *Der Strom der Töne trug mich fort: Die Welt um Richard Strauss in Briefen.* With assistance from Franz Strauss and Alice Strauss. Tutzing: Hans Schneider, 1967.

Gregor-Dellin, Martin, and Dietrich Mack, eds. *Cosima Wagner's Diaries.* 2 vols. Translated by Geoffrey Skelton. New York: Harcourt Brace, 1976.

Gustav Mahler: Origins and Legacy. Produced and directed by Joan Saffa and David Kennard. DVD. San Francisco: Independent Communications Associates, 2011.

Haas, Frithjof. *Hans von Bülow. Leben und Wirken: Wegbereiter für Wagners Liszt und Brahms.* Wilhelmshaven: F. Noetzel, Heinrichshofen Bücher, 2002.

Hansen, Kelly Dean. "*Gustav Mahler's Symphonies* (*Gustav Mahlers Sinfonien*) by Paul Bekker (1921): A Translation with Commentary." PhD diss., University of Colorado, 2012.

Hanslick, Eduard. *Vom Musikalisch-Schönen.* Vol. 1, *Historisch-kritische Ausgabe.* Edited by Dietmar Strauß. Mainz: Schott, 1990.

———. "'Wanderers Sturmlied' von Richard Strauss" [1892]. In *Fünf Jahre Musik,* 202–204. Berlin: Allgemeiner Verein für Deutsche Litteratur, 1896. Reprint, Farborough: Gregg, 1971.

Harrison, Daniel. "Imagining *Tod und Verklärung.*" *Richard Strauss Blätter* 29 [new series] (1993): 22–52.

Hartmann, Rudolf. "The Last Visit with Richard Strauss." Translated by Susan Gillespie. In *Richard Strauss and His World,* edited by Bryan Gilliam, 295–301. Princeton: Princeton University Press, 1992.

Hausegger, Friedrich von. Review of *Vom Musikalisch-Erhabenen,* by Arthur Seidl. *Bayreuther Blätter* 11 (1888): 198–200.

Hausegger, Siegmund von. *Alexander Ritter: Ein Bild seines Charakters und Schaffens.* Berlin: Marquardt & Co., [1907].

Hefling, Stephen E. "Gustav Mahler und Arnold Schönberg." In *Gustav Mahler: Unbekannte Briefe,* edited by Herta Blaukopf, 173–87. Vienna: Bibliothek der Internationalen Gustav Mahler Gesellschaft, 1983.

———. "*Das Lied von der Erde.*" In *The Mahler Companion,* edited by Donald Mitchell and Andrew Nicholson, 438–66. Oxford: Oxford University Press, 1999.

———. *Mahler: "Das Lied von der Erde."* Cambridge: Cambridge University Press, 2000.

———. "Mahler's 'Todtenfeier' and the Problem of Program Music." *19th-Century Music* 12 (1988): 27–53.

———. "Miners Digging from Opposite Sides: Mahler, Strauss, and the Problem of Program Music." In *Richard Strauss: New Perspectives on the Composer and His Work*, edited by Bryan Gilliam, 41–53. Durham, NC: Duke University Press, 1992.

———. "The Ninth Symphony." In *The Mahler Companion*, edited by Donald Mitchell and Andrew Nicholson, 467–90. Oxford: Oxford University Press, 1999.

———. "The Rückert Lieder." In *The Mahler Companion*, edited by Donald Mitchell and Andrew Nicholson, 338–65. Oxford: Oxford University Press, 1999.

———. "Siegfried Lipiner's *On the Elements of a Renewal of Religious Ideas in the Present*." In *Mahler im Kontext/Contextualizing Mahler*, edited by Erich Wolfgang Partsch and Morten Solvik, 91–114. Vienna: Böhlau, 2011.

Hein, Hartmut. "Vierte Symphonie." In *Gustav Mahler: Interpretationen seiner Werke*, edited by Peter Revers and Oliver Korte, vol. 1, 355–97. Laaber: Laaber, 2011.

Heisler, Wayne, Jr. *The Ballet Collaborations of Richard Strauss*. Rochester: University of Rochester Press, 2009.

Heller, Erich. "Die Zweideutigkeit von Goethe's 'Faust.'" In *Aufsätze zu Goethes Faust I*, edited by Werner Keller, 64–85. Darmstadt: Wissenschaftliche Buchgesellschaft, 1974.

Henning, Hans. *Goethes "Götz von Berlichingen" in der zeitgenössischen Rezeption*. Leipzig: Zentralantiquariat der Deutschen Demokratischen Republik, 1988.

Hepokoski, James. "Fiery-Pulsed Libertine or Domestic Hero? Strauss's *Don Juan* Reinvestigated." In *Richard Strauss: New Perspectives on the Composer and His Work*, edited by Bryan Gilliam, 135–75. Durham, NC: Duke University Press, 1992.

———. "Framing Till Eulenspiegel." *19th-Century Music* 30 (2006): 4–42.

———. "Structure and Program in *Macbeth*: A Proposed Reading of Strauss's First Symphonic Poem." In *Richard Strauss and His World*, edited by Bryan Gilliam, 67–89. Princeton, NJ: Princeton University Press, 1992.

Hinrichsen, Hans-Joachim. *Musikalische Interpretation: Hans von Bülow*. Stuttgart: Franz Steiner, 1999.

Holden, Raymond. "Kapellmeister Strauss." In *The Cambridge Companion to Richard Strauss*, edited by Charles Youmans, 257–68. Cambridge: Cambridge University Press, 2010.

———. *Richard Strauss: A Musical Life*. New Haven: Yale University Press, 2011.
Houlgate, Stephen. *Hegel, Nietzsche and the Criticism of Metaphysics*. Cambridge: Cambridge University Press, 1986.
Hübscher, Arthur. *Denker gegen den Strom. Schopenhauer: Gestern-Heute-Morgen*. Bonn: Bouvier Verlag Herbert Grundmann, 1973.
Huneker, James. *Mezzotints in Modern Music*. New York: C. Scribner's Sons, 1899.
Jackson, Timothy L. "The Metamorphosis of the *Metamorphosen*: New Analytical and Source-Critical Discoveries." In *Richard Strauss: New Perspectives on the Composer and His Work*, edited by Bryan Gilliam, 193–241. Durham, NC: Duke University Press, 1992.
Jacob, Andreas. "Ein sachlicher Heiliger? Schönbergs Mahler." In *Gustav Mahler und die musikalische Moderne*, edited by Arnold Jacobshagen, 145–56. Stuttgart: Franz Steiner, 2011.
Janz, Curt Paul. "The Form-Content Problem in Friedrich Nietzsche's Conception of Music." In *Nietzsche's New Seas: Explorations in Philosophy, Aesthetics, and Politics*, edited by Michael Allen Gillespie and Tracy B. Strong, 97–116. Chicago: University of Chicago Press, 1988.
Johnson, Julian. *Mahler's Voices: Expression and Irony in the Songs and Symphonies*. Oxford: Oxford University Press, 2009.
Joseph, Albrecht, Anna Mahler, Marina Mahler, and Donald Mitchell. "Mahler's Smile: A Memoir of His Daughter Anna Mahler (1904–1988)." In *The Mahler Companion*, edited by Donald Mitchell and Andrew Nicholson, 580–96. Oxford: Oxford University Press, 1999.
Kalbeck, Max. "Feuilleton: Gustav Mahler and His Fifth Symphony." Translated by Karen Painter and Bettina Varwig. In *Mahler and His World*, edited by Karen Painter, 306–12. Princeton: Princeton University Press, 2002.
Kaplan, Gilbert E., ed. *Gustav Mahler, Adagietto: Facsimile, Documentation, Recording*. New York: Kaplan Foundation, 1992.
———, ed. *The Mahler Album*. New, expanded edition. New York: Kaplan Foundation, 2011.
———, ex. prod. *Mahler Plays Mahler: The Welte-Mignon Piano Rolls*. New York: Kaplan Foundation, GLRS 101, 1993, CD.
Karnes, Kevin. "Wagner, Klimt, and the Metaphysics of Creativity in fin-de-siècle Vienna." *Journal of the American Musicological Society* 62 (2009): 247–97.

Karpath, Ludwig. *Begegnung mit dem Genius*, 2nd ed. Vienna: Fiba, 1934.
Kater, Michael. *Composers of the Nazi Era*. New York: Oxford University Press, 2000.
Kennedy, Michael. *Richard Strauss: Man, Musician, Enigma*. Cambridge: Cambridge University Press, 1999.
Klatte, Wilhelm. "Aus Richard Strauss' Werkstatt." *Die Musik* 16 (1923–24): 636–41.
Knight, Max, ed. *A Confidential Matter: The Letters of Richard Strauss and Stefan Zweig, 1931–1935*. Translated by Max Knight. Berkeley: University of California Press, 1977.
Kohler, Stephan. "Richard Strauss: Eine Alpensinfonie, op. 64." *Neue Zeitschrift für Musik* 143, no. 11 (November 1982): 42–46.
Köhnke, Klaus Christian. *The Rise of Neo-Kantianism*. Translated by R. J. Hollingdale. Cambridge: Cambridge University Press, 1991.
Konrad, Ulrich. "Die *Deutsche Motette* op. 62 von Richard Strauss: Entstehung, Form, Gehalt." In *Richard Strauss und die Moderne*, edited by Bernd Edelmann, Birgit Lodes, and Reinhold Schlötterer, 283–310. Berlin: Henschel, 2001.
Korngold, Julius. *Die Korngolds in Wien: Der Musikkritiker und das Wunderkind: Aufzeichnungen*. Zurich: Edition Musik & Theater, 1991.
Krause, Ernst. *Richard Strauss: Der letzte Romantiker*. Munich: Wilhelm Heyne, 1963.
Kristiansen, Morten. "Richard Strauss's *Feuersnot* in Its Aesthetic and Cultural Context: A Modernist Critique of Musical Idealism." PhD diss., Yale University, 2000.
La Grange, Henry-Louis de. "Mahler and France." In *The Mahler Companion*, edited by Donald Mitchell and Andrew Nicholson, 138–52. Oxford: Oxford University Press, 1999.
———. "Music about Music in Mahler: Reminiscences, Allusions, or Quotations." In *Mahler Studies*, edited by Stephen E. Hefling, 122–68. Cambridge: Cambridge University Press, 1997.
Lane, Melissa. "The Evolution of *Eironeia* in Classical Greek Texts: Why Socratic *Eironeia* Is Not Socratic Irony." In *Oxford Studies in Ancient Philosophy*, edited by David Sedley, 49–83. Oxford: Oxford University Press, 2006.
Lebrecht, Norman, ed. *Mahler Remembered*. New York: Norton, 1998.
Lemmel, Monika. *Poetologie in Goethes west-östlichem Divan*. Heidelberg: Carl Winter, 1987.

Lessmann, Otto. "Die XXX. Tonkünstler-Versammlung des Allgemeinen Musikvereins. Weimar 31. Mai–6. Juni." *Allgemeine Musik-Zeitung* 24 (1894): 336.

Ley, Rosamund, ed. and trans. *Ferruccio Busoni: Letters to His Wife*. New York: Da Capo Press, 1975.

Liebscher, Julia. *Richard Strauss, Also sprach Zarathustra. Tondichtung (frei nach Friedr. Nietzsche) für grosses Orchester op. 30*. Munich: W. Fink, 1994.

———. "Richard Strauss und Friedrich Nietzsche." *Richard Strauss-Blätter* 27 [new series] (June 1992): 10–38.

Lipiner, Siegfried. "Über die Elemente einer Erneuerung religiöser Ideen in der Gegenwart/On the Elements of a Renewal of Religious Ideas in the Present." In *Mahler im Kontext/Contextualizing Mahler*, edited by Erich Wolfgang Partsch and Morten Solvik, 115–51. Vienna: Böhlau, 2011.

Litterschied, Frank, Helmuth Kreysing, and Maja Loehr, eds. *Hans Rott: der Begründer der neuen Symphonie*. Munich: Text+Kritik, 1999.

Lockwood, Lewis. "The Element of Time in *Der Rosenkavalier*." In *Richard Strauss: New Perspectives on the Composer and His Work*, edited by Bryan Gilliam, 248–55. Durham, NC: Duke University Press, 1992.

Louis, Rudolf. *Die Deutsche Musik der Gegenwart*, rev. ed. Munich: Georg Müller, 1912.

Magee, Bryan. *The Philosophy of Schopenhauer*. Oxford: Clarendon Press, 1997.

Mahler, Alma. *Diaries 1898–1902*. Selected and translated by Antony Beaumont. Ithaca, NY: Cornell University Press, 1999.

———, ed., *Gustav Mahler Briefe, 1879–1911*. Berlin: Paul Zsolnay, 1924.

———. *Mein Leben*. Frankfurt am Main: Fischer, 1960.

Mann, Thomas. "Goethes 'Werther.'" In *Goethes "Werther": Kritik und Forschung*, edited by Hans Peter Hermann, 88–101. Darmstadt: Wissenschaftliche Buchgesellschaft, 1994.

Marschalk, Max. "Frei nach Nietzsche." *Die Zukunft* 17 (1896): 617.

Martner, Knud. *Gustav Mahler im Konzertsaal: Eine Dokumentation seiner Konzerttätigket 1870–1911*. Copenhagen: private publication, 1985.

Matthews, David. "The Sixth Symphony." In *The Mahler Companion*, edited by Donald Mitchell and Andrew Nicholson, 366–75. Oxford: Oxford University Press, 1999.

———. "Wagner, Lipiner, and the 'Purgatorio.'" In *The Mahler Companion*, edited by Donald Mitchell and Andrew Nicholson, 508–16. Oxford: Oxford University Press, 1999.

McCaldin, Denis. "Mahler and Beethoven's Ninth Symphony." *Proceedings of the Royal Musical Association* 107 (1980/81): 101–10.
McClatchie, Stephen, ed. *The Mahler Family Letters*. Oxford: Oxford University Press, 2006.
———. "Mahler's Wagner." In *Mahler im Kontext/Contextualizing Mahler*, edited by Erich Wolfgang Partsch and Morten Solvik, 407–36. Vienna: Böhlau, 2011.
McGrath, William J. *Dionysian Art and Populist Politics in Austria*. New Haven, CT: Yale University Press, 1974.
Merian, Hans. *Richard Strauß' Tondichtung Also sprach Zarathustra: eine Studie über die moderne Programmsymphonie*. Leipzig: Meyers, 1899.
Messmer, Franzpeter. *Kritiken zu den Uraufführungen der Bühnenwerke von Richard Strauss*. Pfaffenhoffen: W. Ludwig, 1989.
Mitchell, Donald. *Gustav Mahler*. Vol. 1, *The Early Years*. Revised and edited by Paul Banks and David Matthews. Berkeley: University of California Press, 1995.
———. *Gustav Mahler: Songs and Symphonies of Life and Death*. Berkeley: University of California Press, 1985.
Monahan, Seth. "'I have tried to capture you . . .': Rethinking the 'Alma' Theme from Mahler's Sixth Symphony." *Journal of the American Musicological Society* 64 (2011): 119–78.
da Motta, José Vianna. *Nachtrag zu Studien bei Hans von Bülow*. Berlin: Friedrich Luckhardt, 1896.
Munter, Friedrich. *Ludwig Thuille: Ein erster Versuch*. Munich: Drei Masken, 1923.
Newman, Ernest. *Richard Strauss*. London: J. Lane 1908. Reprint, Freeport, NY: Books for Libraries Press, 1969.
Niekerk, Carl. *Reading Mahler: German Culture and Jewish Identity in Fin-de-Siècle Vienna*. Rochester: Camden House, 2010.
Niemann, Walter. *Die Musik der Gegenwart*. Berlin: Schuster & Loeffler, 1921.
Nietzsche, Friedrich. *Also sprach Zarathustra: Ein Buch für Alle und Keinen*. Part 6, vol. 1 of *Nietzsche Werke*. Edited by Giorgio Colli and Mazzino Montinari. Berlin: de Gruyter, 1968.
———. *Jenseits von Gut und Böse*. Part 6, vol. 2 of *Nietzsche Werke*. Edited by Giorgio Colli and Mazzino Montinari. Berlin: de Gruyter, 1968.
———. *Menschliches, Allzumenschliches*. Part 6, vol. 1 of *Nietzsche Werke*. Edited by Giorgio Colli and Mazzino Montinari. Berlin: de Gruyter, 1968.

———. *Werke und Briefe: Historisch-kritische Gesamtausgabe*, R. I, vol. 2, *Briefe der Leipziger und ersten Basler Zeit, 1868–1869*. Munich: Beck, 1940.

Nodnagel, Ernst Otto. *Jenseits von Wagner und Liszt*. Königsberg: Ostpreußische Druckerei und Verlagsanstalt, 1902.

Painter, Karen, ed. *Mahler and His World*. Princeton: Princeton University Press, 2002.

Petersen, Barbara A. "Die Händler und die Kunst: Richard Strauss as Composers' Advocate." In *Richard Strauss: New Perspectives on the Composer and His Work*, edited by Bryan Gilliam, 115–32. Durham, NC: Duke University Press, 1992.

Pfeiffer, Theodor. *Studien bei Hans von Bülow*. Berlin: Friedrich Luckhardt, 1894.

Pickett, David. "Arrangements and *Retuschen*: Mahler and *Werktreue*," in *The Cambridge Companion to Mahler*, edited by Jeremy Barham, 178–99. Cambridge: Cambridge University Press, 2007.

Pretzsch, Paul, ed. *Cosima Wagner und Houston Stewart Chamberlain im Briefwechsel 1888–1908*. Leipzig: Philipp Reclam jun., 1934.

Publig, Maria. *Richard Strauss: Bürger, Künstler, Rebell. Eine historische Annäherung*. Graz: Styria, 1999.

Puffett, Derrick. "'Lass Er die Musi, wo sie ist': Pitch Specificity in Strauss." In *Richard Strauss: New Perspectives on the Composer and His Work*, edited by Bryan Gilliam, 138–63. Durham, NC: Duke University Press, 1992.

———. "*Salome* as Music Drama." In *Richard Strauss: "Salome,"* edited by Derrick Puffett, 58–87. Cambridge: Cambridge University Press, 1989.

Rauchenberger-Strauss, Johanna von. "Jugenderinnerungen." In *Richard Strauss Jahrbuch 1959/60*, edited by Willi Schuh, 7–30. Bonn: Boosey & Hawkes, 1960.

Reilly, Edward R. "Mahler in America" In *The Mahler Companion*, edited by Donald Mitchell and Andrew Nicholson, 422–37. Oxford: Oxford University Press, 1999.

Richard, August. "Alexander Ritter und seine Tafelrunde." *Zeitschrift für Musik* 100 (1933): 817–18.

Ritter, Alexander. "Drei Kapitel: von Franz Liszt, von der 'heiligen Elizabeth' in Karlsruhe, und von unserm ethischen Defekt." *Bayreuther Blätter* 13 (1890): 380–88.

———. "Vom Spanisch-Schönen." *Allgemeine Musikzeitung* 18/10 (1891): 128–29.

———. "Was lehrt uns das Festspieljahr 1891?" *Bayreuther Blätter* 15 (1892): 1–20.

Rolland, Romain. "French Music and German Music." In *Richard Strauss and Romain Rolland: Correspondence*, edited and translated by Rollo Myers, 197–215. London: Calder and Boyars, 1968.

Roman, Zoltan. *Gustav Mahler's American Years, 1907–1911: A Documentary History*. Stuyvesant, NY: Pendragon Press, 1989.

Ross, Alex. *The Rest Is Noise: Listening to the Twentieth Century*. New York: Farrar, Straus and Giroux, 2007.

Safranski, Rüdiger. *Schopenhauer and the Wild Years of Philosophy*. Translated by Ewald Osers. Cambridge, MA: Harvard University Press, 1990.

Schäfer, Theo. "Richard Strauss als Symphoniker." In *Richard Strauss Woche Muenchen. 23–28 Juni*. Munich: F. Bruckmann, 1910.

Schiedermair, Ludwig. *Gustav Mahler: Eine biographisch-kritische Würdigung*. Leipzig: H. Seemann, 1900.

Schlötterer, Roswitha. "Richard Strauss uns sein Münchner Kreis." In *Jugendstilmusik? Münchner Musikleben 1890–1918*, edited by Robert Münster and Hellmut Hell, 13–24. Wiesbaden: Dr. Ludwig Reichert, 1987.

Schmid, Mark-Daniel. "The Tone Poems of Richard Strauss and Their Reception History from 1887–1908." PhD diss., Northwestern University, 1997.

Schoenberg, Arnold. "Brahms the Progressive" [1947]. In *Style and Idea*, edited by Leonard Stein, 398–441. New York: St. Martin's Press, 1975.

———. "New Music" [1923]. In *Style and Idea*, edited by Leonard Stein, translated by Leo Black, 137–38. New York: St. Martin's Press, 1975.

———. *Style and Idea: Selected Writings of Arnold Schoenberg*. Translated by Leo Black. Berkeley: University of California Press, 1984.

Schopenhauer, Arthur. *Die Welt als Wille und Vorstellung*, vol. 1. Stuttgart: Philipp Reclam jun., 1987.

———. *Die Welt als Wille und Vorstellung*. Vol. 2 of *Arthur Schopenhauer's sämmtliche Werke*. Leipzig: Brockhaus, 1888.

———. *The World as Will and Representation*, vol. 1. Translated by E. F. J. Payne. New York: Dover, 1969.

Schüler, Winfried. *Der Bayreuther Kreis von seiner Entstehung bis zum Ausgang der wilhelminischen Ära*. Münster: Aschendorrf, 1971.

———, ed. *Richard Strauss: Briefe an die Eltern, 1882–1906*. Zurich: Atlantis, 1954.

Schulte, Johann Friedrich. *Der Altkatholizismus. Geschichte seiner Entwicklung, inneren Gestaltung und rechtlichen Stellung in Deutschland.* Gießen: Roth, 1887. Reprint, Aalen: Scientia, 1965.

Seidl, Arthur. *Moderner Geist in der deutschen Tonkunst: Gedanken eines Kulturpsychologen zur Wende des Jahrhunderts.* Regensburg, Gustave Bosse, [1913].

———. "Richard Strauss: Eine Charakter-Skizze." In *Straussiana: Ausätze zur Richard Strauß-Frage aus drei Jahrzehnten,* 11–66. Regensburg: Gustave Bosse, [1913].

———. *Die Wagner-Nachfolge im Musikdrama.* Vol. 3 of *Wagneriana.* Berlin: Schuster, 1901.

Sengle, Friedrich. *Kontinuität und Wandlung: Einführung in Goethes Leben und Werk.* Edited by Marianne Tilch. Heidelberg: C. Winter, 1999.

Solvik, Morten. "Mahler and Germany." In *The Mahler Companion,* edited by Donald Mitchell and Andrew Nicholson, 126–37. Oxford: Oxford University Press, 1999.

Solvik, Morten, and Stephen E. Hefling. "Natalie Bauer-Lechner on Mahler and Women: A Newly Discovered Document." *Musical Quarterly* 97 (2014): 12–65.

Specht, Richard. *Gustav Mahler.* Berlin: Gose & Tetzlaff, 1905.

———. *Gustav Mahler's VIII. Symphonie. Thematische Analyse.* Vienna: Universal, 1912.

———. *Richard Strauss und sein Werk.* Vol. 1, *Der Künstler und sein Weg; Der Instrumentalkomponist.* Leipzig: E. P. Tal & Co., 1921.

Spotts, Frederic. *Bayreuth: A History of the Wagner Festival.* New Haven: Yale University Press, 1994.

Steinberg, Michael. "Richard Strauss and the Question." In *Richard Strauss and His World,* edited by Bryan Gilliam, 164–89. Princeton: Princeton University Press, 1992.

Steinitzer, Max. *Richard Strauss.* Berlin: Schuster & Loeffler, 1911.

———. *Richard Strauss.* 4th–8th eds. Berlin: Schuster & Loeffler, 1914.

Stephan, Rudolf. *Gustav Mahler, Werk und Interpretation: Autographe, Partituren, Dokumente.* Cologne: Volk, 1979.

Strauss, Franz, and Alice Strauss, eds. *The Correspondence between Richard Strauss and Hugo von Hofmannsthal.* Translated by Hanns Hammelmann and Ewald Osers, arranged by Willi Schuh. Cambridge: Cambridge University Press, 1980.

Strauss, Gabriele, ed. *Lieber Collega! Richard Strauss im Briefwechsel mit zeitgenössischen Komponisten und Dirigenten.* Berlin: Henschel, 1996.

Streller, Friedbert. "Der junge Strauss und die Renaissance der Stirnerschen Anarchismus." In *Richard Strauss: Leben, Werk, Interpretation, Rezeption. Internationales Gewandhaus-Symposium 1989*, 62–65. Leipzig: C. F. Peters, 1991.

Suder, Alexander L., ed. *Ludwig Thuille*. Tutzing: Hans Schneider, 1993.

Thuille, Ludwig, and Rudolf Louis. *Grundriss der Harmonielehre*. Stuttgart: C. Grüninger, 1907.

Todd, R. Larry. "Strauss before Liszt and Wagner: Some Observations." In *Richard Strauss: New Perspectives on the Composer and His Work*, edited by Bryan Gilliam, 3–40. Durham, NC: Duke University Press, 1992.

Trenner, Franz. *Richard Strauss: Chronik zu Leben und Werk*. Edited by Florian Trenner. Vienna: Verlag Dr. Richard Strauss, 2003.

———. *Richard Strauss: Dokumente seines Lebens und Schaffens*. Munich: C. H. Beck, 1954.

———, ed. *Richard Strauss, Ludwig Thuille: Ein Briefwechsel*. Tutzing: Hans Schneider, 1980.

———. *Richard Strauss Werkverzeichnis*. 2nd ed. Vienna: Verlag Dr. Richard Strauss, 1999.

———, ed. *Cosima Wagner, Richard Strauss: Ein Briefwechsel*. With the assistance of Gabriele Strauss. Tutzing: Hans Schneider, 1978.

Turner, J. Rigbie. "Richard Strauss to Cäcilie Wenzel: Twelve Unpublished Letters." *19th-Century Music* 9 (1986): 163–75.

Unger, Anette. *Welt, Leben und Kunst als Themen der "Zarathustra-Kompositionen" von Richard Strauss und Gustav Mahler*. Frankfurt am Main: Peter Lang, 1992.

Urban, Erich. *Richard Strauss*. Berlin: Gose & Tetzlaff, 1901.

———. *Strauss contra Wagner*. Berlin: Schuster & Loeffler, 1902.

Wagner, Margarete. "Mahlers Verhältnis zur zeitgenössischen Literatur." In *Mahler im Kontext/Contextualizing Mahler*, edited by Erich Wolfgang Partsch and Morten Solvik, 291–335. Vienna: Böhlau, 2011.

Wagner, Richard. "Über Franz Liszt's symphonische Dichtungen: Brief an M. W." In *Gesammelte Schriften und Dichtungen von Richard Wagner*, vol. 5, 182–98. Leipzig: C. F. W. Siegel, [1907].

Walden, Herwarth, ed. *Richard Strauss: Symphonien und Tondichtungen*. Berlin: Schlesinger, [1908].

Walker, Alan. *Hans von Bülow: A Life and Times*. Oxford: Oxford University Press, 2010.

Walter, Bruno. *Gustav Mahler*. Translated by Lotte Walter Lindt. New York: Knopf, 1958.

Wandel, Juliane. *Die Rezeption der Symphonien Gustav Mahlers zu Lebzeiten des Komponisten*. Frankfurt am Main: Peter Lang, 1999.

Warfield, Scott. "Friedrich Wilhelm Meyer (1818–1893): Some Biographical Notes on Strauss' Composition Teacher." *Richard-Strauss-Blätter* 37 [new series] 37 (June 1997): 54–74.

———. "The Genesis of Richard Strauss's *Macbeth*." PhD diss., University of North Carolina at Chapel Hill, 1995.

———. "'Reveal Nothing to Him of His Market Value': The Publication of Strauss's First Three Tone Poems." Unpublished manuscript.

Werbeck, Walter. *Die Tondichtungen von Richard Strauss*. Tutzing: Hans Schneider, 1996.

Wilhelm, Kurt. *Richard Strauss: An Intimate Portrait*. Translated by Mary Whittall. New York: Rizzoli, 1989.

Williamson, John. "The Earliest Complete Works: A Voyage towards the First Symphony." In *The Mahler Companion*, edited by Donald Mitchell and Andrew Nicholson, 39–61. Oxford: Oxford University Press, 1999.

Willnauer, Franz, ed. *Gustav Mahler, "Mein lieber Trotzkopf, meine süße Mohnblume": Briefe an Anna von Mildenburg*. Vienna: Paul Zsolnay, 2006.

Wolzogen, Hans von. "Gedenkwort." In *Zum Andenken Alexander Ritters*, 19. Mannheim: Neue Musikalische Rundschau, 1897.

———. *Lebensbilder*. Regensburg: Gustav Bosse, 1923.

Youens, Susan. "Actually, I like my songs best": Strauss's Lieder." In *The Cambridge Companion to Richard Strauss*, edited by Charles Youmans, 151–77. Cambridge: Cambridge University Press, 2010.

Youmans, Charles. *The Cambridge Companion to Richard Strauss*. Cambridge: Cambridge University Press, 2010.

———. "The Private Intellectual Context of Richard Strauss's *Also sprach Zarathustra*." *19th-Century Music* 22 (1998): 101–26.

———. "Richard Strauss's *Guntram* and the Dismantling of Wagnerian Musical Metaphysics." PhD diss., Duke University, 1996.

———. *Richard Strauss's Orchestral Music and the German Intellectual Tradition*. Bloomington: Indiana University Press, 2005.

———. "The Role of Nietzsche in Richard Strauss's Artistic Development." *Journal of Musicology* 21 (2004): 309–42.

———. "Ten Letters from Alexander to Richard Strauss, 1887–1894." *Richard Strauss Blätter* 35 [new series] (1996): 3–24.

———. "The Twentieth-Century Symphonies of Richard Strauss." *Musical Quarterly* 84 (2000): 238–58.

Zimdars, Richard. *The Piano Master Classes of Hans von Bülow*. Bloomington: Indiana University Press, 1993.

Zweig, Stefan. *The World of Yesterday* [1942]. Translated by Anthea Bell. London: Pushkin Press, 2009.

Zychowicz, James. *Mahler's Fourth Symphony*. Oxford: Oxford University Press, 2000.

Index

For topics to which a chapter is devoted, page numbers are given only for the other chapters. Page numbers in italics refer to figures.

absolute music, 26–27, 56, 117, 123, 129–30, 133, 159, 165, 177–79
Adler, Guido, 69
Adorno, Theodor W., 1, 14, 29, 76, 90, 104, 108, 150, 161, 166, 203, 212n4, 239n13
Aldrich, Richard, 141, 144, 146, 149, 151
Allgemeiner deutscher Musikverein (General German Music Association), 2, 7–8, 80, 127
alt-katholisch theology, 30, 183–84
Aristotle, 168

Bach, Johann Sebastian, 12, 15, 64
Bahr, Hermann, 50, 97
Bauer-Lechner, Natalie, 39, 49, 51, 53, 55, 69–70, 76, 96, 99, 103–4, 109–10, 120, 125, 135, 181, 185–86, 189–90, 201, 203
Bayreuth, 8, 84–85
Beer, August, 126

Beethoven, Ludwig van, 5, 12, 17, 40–41, 43, 45–46, 66, 158, 165, 174, 178; *Christus am Ölberge*, 186; *Coriolan* Overture, 47; Piano Concerto No. 5, *Emperor*, 26; String Quartet, op. 132, 177; Symphony No. 3, *Eroica*, 40, 47; Symphony No. 5, 109, 126, 143, 156; Symphony No. 6, *Pastoral*, 125–26; Symphony No. 9, 44, 46, 69, 146, 151
Bekker, Paul, 110, 117, 119, 168, 177–78, 181
Bellini, Vincenzo, 179
Berg, Alban, 17–18, 91
Berliner, Arnold, 203
Berlioz, Hector, 4, 122, 131, 178, 221; *Symphonie fantastique*, 117, 126
Bernstein, Leonard, 156
Bierbaum, Otto Julius, 96, 100
Bildung, 6, 24–25, 74, 93, 108
Bismarck, Otto von, 184

277

Blaukopf, Herta, ix, 1–3, 7, 40, 85, 199
Blumenberg, Marc, 146
Boulez, Pierre, 172
Brahms, Johannes, 64, 95, 114, 154, 156, 158, 178; Symphony No. 3, 64, 165
Brecher, Gustav, 142
Bronsart, Hans von, 8, 67
Bruch, Max, Violin Concerto, 163–64
Bruckner, Anton, 15, 27–30, 64, 159, 167, 172, 176, 189; Symphony No. 3, 28; Symphony No. 7, 28; *Te deum*, 28–29
Bülow, Hans von, 2–5, 8, 26, 29–30, 36–42, 38, 44, 67, 77, 81–82, 84, 122–23, 156, 198, 202
Busch, Fritz, 13, 176
Busoni, Ferruccio, 149
Busse, Carl, 100

Callot, Jacques, 125, 127
Caruso, Enrico, 139
Casals, Pablo, 149
Cervantes, Miguel de, 104–5
Chopin, Frédéric, 81
Christianity, 19, 54, 57, 70, 121, 134–35, 162, 183–88, 190–94, 204
conducting, 3–5, 55, 65, 69, 75, 83–86, 123–25, 137–39, 141, 145–46, 148–52, 163–64, 199–200, 205–6
Conrat, Erica, 97
Conried, Heinrich, 137, 139, 141
Cornelius, Peter, 208
Cuvilliés, François de, 43

Dahlhaus, Carl, 2, 98, 122, 133, 161, 245n33, 250n12
Damrosch, Walter, 140, 149
D'Annunzio, Gabriele, 107
Dante, 127
De Koven, Reginald, 149
Dehmel, Ida, 73, 90
Dehmel, Richard, 74, 100, 102

Döllinger, Johann Joseph Ignaz von, 183–84
Donizetti, Gaetano, 179
Dostoyevsky, Fyodor, 93, 105; *The Brothers Karamazov*, 105; *Crime and Punishment*, 105

Eckermann, Johann Peter, 96
Epstein, Julius, 26, 65, 83, 157

Fechner, Gustav Theodor, 98, 102, 168
Finck, Henry T., 107, 146
Fischer, Franz, 67
Franklin, Peter, 11, 119, 189, 206
Freud, Sigmund, 49, 54, 64, 158, 183, 239–40n19

Gatz, Felix M., 133
Genossenschaft deutscher Tonsetzer (German Composers' Cooperative), 80, 91
Georg II, Duke of Meiningen, 198
Gewandhaus Orchestra, 3
Gilliam, Bryan, xiv, 100, 102, 179, 193, 229n39
Gilm, Hermann von, 25
Gilman, Lawrence, 146
Goethe, Johann Wolfgang von, 5, 17, 50, 53–54, 58, 77, 92–94, 182, 190, 192, 205, 207; *Farbenlehre*, 93; *Faust*, Part I, 58, 96, 99, 104; *Faust*, Part II, 53–54, 57, 96–98, 104, 134–35, 183; *Lila*, 95, 98–99; "Niemand wird sich selber kennen," 94, 120, 136; *The Sorrows of Young Werther*, 95; *Wandrers Sturmlied*, 95, 98; *West-Östliche Divan*, 97; *Wilhelm Meisters Wanderjahre*, 94–96
Graf, Max, 171–72
Grimm, Jacob and Wilhelm, 31
Gropius, Walter, 34, 53
Grünfeld, Alfred and Heinrich, 22, 27, 199

Hammerstein, Oscar, 141
Handel, George Frideric, 125
Hanslick, Eduard, 48, 98, 128–29, 160, 171
Hartmann, Eduard von, 208
Hartmann, Rudolf, 207
Hausegger, Friedrich von, 98, 173, 201
Haydn, Joseph, 77, 98, 149, 155–56, 186, 207
Hefling, Stephen E., xiv, 97, 101, 108, 120, 143, 167, 188, 228n26
Heidegger, Martin, 104
Hellmesberger, Josef, Sr., 28
Helm, Theodor, 172
Henckell, Karl, 100
Henderson, William, 146
Hirschfeld, Robert, 151, 172
Hoffmann, E. T. A., 75–76, 104–5, 150, 160
Hofmannsthal, Hugo von, 13, 93–94, 100, 163, 178, 193–94, 214n21
Hölderlin, Friedrich, 103–4; *Der Rhein*, 103
Homer, 104
Horn, Richard, 96
Huneker, James, 107

Jameson, Fredric, 246
Johnson, Julian, 50, 167
Judaism, 19, 22, 28, 30, 57, 79, 113, 121, 162, 182, 185–86, 191–92, 204

Kalbeck, Max, 123, 126
Kant, Immanuel, 54, 96–97, 109
Karajan, Herbert von, 47–48
Karpath, Ludwig, 91
Kienzl, Wilhelm, 9
Klemperer, Otto, 41
Klimt, Gustav, 74
Klopstock, Friedrich Gottlieb, 104
Des Knaben Wunderhorn, 9, 101–2, 104, 113–14, 123, 158, 178
Krauss, Clemens, 46, 179

Krehbiel, Henry, 146–47, 149
Krenn, Franz, 27
Krzyzanowski, Rudolf, 27–28, 218–19n27

La Grange, Henry-Louis de, xiii, 20, 22, 52, 157–58, 164, 206, 247n19
Lachner, Franz, 81
Lange, Friedrich Albert, 74
Levi, Hermann, 7, 67, 77–78, 81, 84–85, 123
Lipiner, Siegfried, 69, 71, 93, 97–98, 188, 194
Liszt, Franz, 4–5, 12, 26, 64–66, 122, 124, 126, 129, 130–31, 133, 156, 221; *Faust Symphony*, 66; *Dante* Symphony, 125
Löhr, Friedrich, 74, 92, 189
Luther, Martin, 187

Mackay, John Henry, 25, 100
Maeterlinck, Maurice, 96
Mahler, Alma Maria (*née* Schindler), 2–3, 15–17, 34, 69, 74–75, 85–88, 93, 96–97, 100–101, 104, 109–10, 118–19, 134, 137, 139, 181, 185–86, 191, 194, 195, 203, 205–10, 214–15n26, 226n5
Mahler, Anna Justine, 194, 195
Mahler, Bernhard, 22, 83–84, 157, 185
Mahler, Ernst, 26, 34
Mahler, Gustav: "Blumine," 126; *Die drei Pintos*, 3, 83; "Ich bin von der Welt abhanden gekommen," 55, 101, 180; "Das irdische Leben," 34; *Kindertotenlieder*, 31, 33–34, 101, 147; *Das klagende Lied*, 31; *Das Lied von der Erde*, 16, 75, 77, 86, 102, 120, 139, 159–60, 180–81, 189; *Lieder und Gesänge*, 124, 206; *Songs of a Wayfarer*, 4, 55, 110, 125–26, 159; Symphony No. 1, 2, 4–5, 7–8, 34, 55, 75, 86, 104, 107, 110–13, 122–23, 125–28, 130, 135, 142, 149, 151, 159–60, 168, 171–72, 188, 203, 213n10,

Mahler, Gustav (*cont.*)
    238n4; Symphony No. 2, 9, *10*, 12, 14, 17, 39, 41–42, 86, 112–13, 123, 127–28, 142–44, 146, 166, 178, 188, 191, 203; Symphony No. 3, 9, 11, 14, 18, 31, 70–71, 73, 75, 86–88, 103, 114, 117, 127–28, 143, 178, 186, 188–90, 201, 204–6; Symphony No. 4, 14, 17–18, 31–33, 75, 86, 114, 128, 145, 149, 158, 176, 178, 206; Symphony No. 5, 2, 4, 14–15, 50, 55, 75, 114, 117–18, 123, 126, 135, 143, 145, 159–60, 167, 176, 203; Symphony No. 6, 2, 14, 16–17, 50, 55, 58, 86, 118–19, 135, 143, 153, 161–62, 176–77, 203, 241n48; Symphony No. 7, 75, 109, 135, 143, 166, 178; Symphony No. 8, 2, 17–18, 50, 53, 57, 75, 96, 99, 104–5, 120, 134–35, 190–91, 193, 206–7; Symphony No. 9, 125, 135, 167, 181, 189, 206; Symphony No. 10, 75, 135
Mahler, Maria (Marie) (*née* Hermann) (mother), 22, 49, 83–84, 206–7
Mahler, Maria Anna (daughter), 34, 194, *195*
Mahler, Otto, 91, 105
Mann, Thomas, 24, 26
marketing, 5, 11–12, 15, 36, 58, 141
Marschalk, Max, 11, 24, 168
Massenet, Jules, 96
Maximilian Joseph, Duke in Bavaria, 81
Mendelssohn, Felix, 26–27, 156, 160; *Venetianisches Gondellied*, op. 19b, no. 6, 132; Overture to *A Midsummer Night's Dream*, 155
Mengelberg, Willem, 55
Merian, Hans, 252n10
metaphysics, 9, 11, 19, 30, 50, 53–59, 69–78, 95–98, 102–4, 111–16, 123–24, 129, 132–36, 150–51, 160–62, 170–71, 174–75, 179, 187, 192, 202, 204
Meyer, Friedrich Wilhelm, 29, 154–55

Meyerbeer, Giacomo, 65; *Robert le diable*, 68, 81
Mildenburg, Anna von, 40, 42, 50–53, 55, 69, 225n3
Mitchell, Donald, 22, 33
modernism, 3, 8, 11, 14, 16–18, 25, 41, 77, 93, 95–97, 99–100, 107, 114, 122, 125, 149, 151, 154, 160, 171, 179–80, 192–93
Moll, Karl, 137
Moser, Koloman, 74
Mottl, Felix, 85, 123
Mozart, Wolfgang Amadeus, 12, 36, 41–43, 45, 65, 77, 98, 152, 155–56, 168, 179, 208; *Così fan tutte*, 42–43; *Don Giovanni*, 42–43; *Die Entführung aus dem Serail*, 42–43; *Le nozze di Figaro*, 42; *Die Zauberflöte*, 42–43; Piano Concerto, K. 491, 26, 198; *Requiem*, 186; Symphony No. 40, K. 550, 47; Symphony No. 41, *Jupiter*, K. 551, 152
Muck, Carl, 9
Müller, Wilhelm, 200

Niekerk, Carl, 16, 189–90, 215n33
Niest, Carl, 29
Nietzsche, Friedrich, 9, 11, 19, 26, 32, 53, 58, 60, 70, 96–97, 99–100, 102–5, 107–8, 114–16, 133, 136, 159–60, 163, 170, 174, 182, 188–90, 194, 202, 205; *Also sprach Zarathustra*, 9, 11, 115, 148, 169–70, 190; *The Birth of Tragedy*, 74, 103, 202
Nijinsky, Vaslav, 192
Nikisch, Arthur, 2, 11, 37, 39, 83–85
Nodnagel, Ernst Otto, 127

Panofsky, Walter, 204
Paul, Jean, 104, 126–27
Pfitzner, Hans, 75, 245
Poisl, Josephine, 51–52, 200
Pollini, Bernhard (Baruch Pohl), 8, 53, 85

INDEX

programmaticism, 4–9, 11, 33–34, 49, 56–57, 70, 86, 94, 103–4, 107–8, 115–17, 120, 122, 143–44, 146–47, 149, 151, 156, 158–59, 163, 169, 174, 177–78, 188, 201
Pschorr, Georg, 21, 198

Ranke, Leopold, 19
Rauchenberger-Strauss, Johanna von, 21, 50, 184
Reger, Max, 214
Richter, Hans, 67, 123
Richter, Johanna, 110
Ritter, Alexander, 29, 66–67, 72, 77, 79, 105, 112, 133, 173, 186–87, 219–20n34
Rodin, Auguste, 107
Roller, Alfred, 42, 74
romanticism, 63, 95, 109, 116, 119, 150, 168, 179, 200
Rösch, Friedrich, 25, 27, 29, 72, 188, 218
Rosé, Justine (*née* Mahler), 49, 51, 55, 91, 101, 225n2
Ross, Alex, 16, 208
Rossini, Giaochino: *Stabat mater*, 186
Rott, Hans, 27–28, 79
Rückert, Friedrich, 101–3, 180

Saint-Saëns, Camille, *Danse macabre*, 161
Scheerbart, Paul, 89
Schiedermair, Ludwig, 123, 127–29, 142
Schiller, Friedrich, 180
Schindler, Emil, 96
Schnitzler, Arthur, 30
Schoenberg, Arnold, 1, 5, 15, 17–18, 59, 63, 91, 151, 156, 160
Schopenhauer, Arthur, 9, 19, 58, 69–73, 88, 98, 102–3, 105, 121, 129, 132–33, 160, 187–90, 205
Schubert, Franz, 155, 179; Fantasy in C Major, D. 760, 199; *Winterreise*, 201
Schuh, Willi, 85

Schumann, Robert, 150, 154, 156; "Mondnacht," op. 39, no. 5, 155
Seidl, Anton, 85, 146
Seidl, Arthur, 25, 27, 29, 71–72, 100, 108, 112, 203, 218
sexuality, 50, 58, 60, 73, 76, 93, 100, 112, 122, 130, 132, 186, 193, 240n26
Shakespeare, William, 93, 104
Slansky, Ludwig, 84
Smith, Max, 148
Socrates, 168
sonata form, 66, 118, 172, 174, 219n34
Sophocles, 92
Specht, Richard, 25, 127, 142
Spitzweg, Eugen, 81–82
Staegemann, Max, 83–84
Stanton, Edmund C., 83
Steinitzer, Max, 29, 81
Strauss, Alice (*née* von Grab), 207–8
Strauss, Franz (father), 21, 26, 37, 39, 43, 50, 80–81, 156–57, 184, 187, 246n3
Strauss, Franz (son), 31
Strauss, Josepha (Josephine) (*née* Pschorr), 21–22, 26, 28, 50, 184, 217n10
Strauss, Pauline (*née* de Ahna), 33, 62, 90, 145, 184, 194, 200, 207
Strauss, Richard: *Eine Alpensinfonie*, 116, 133, 163, 193, 201–3, 241n45; *Also sprach Zarathustra*, 11, 58–59, 71, 73, 94, 99, 115–16, 133, 138, 142, 151, 153, 163–64, 169–73, 180, 187–88; "Anbetung," op. 36, no. 4, 163; *Ariadne auf Naxos*, 94–95, 166, 178–80; *Aus Italien*, 156, 201; "Befreit," op. 39, no. 4, 100; *Burleske*, 64, 156, 166; *Capriccio*, 119, 154, 166, 179–80; Concert Overture in C Minor, o.op. 80, 81; *Deutsche Motette*, 102; *Don Juan*, 4–5, 45, 50, 58, 82, 100, 112, 115, 122, 124, 127, 130, 147, 172, 178; *Don Quixote*, 50, 59, 73, 105, 115–16, 124, 132–33, 142, 148, 173; *Drei Hymnen*,

Strauss, Richard (*cont.*)
op. 71, 103; Duett-Concertino, o.op. 147, 120; *Elektra*, 18, 48, 164; *Feuersnot*, 2, 13, 15–16, 60, 76, 86–87, 120, 166, 173–75, 178; *Four Last Songs*, 77, 103, 120, 165, 180; *Die Frau ohne Schatten*, 31, 76, 94, 180, 192–93; *Fünf Klavierstücke*, op. 3, 81; *Guntram*, 5, 8–9, 15, 58, 65–66, 71–72, 86, 105, 111–12, 115, 133, 163, 174, 186–88, 205, 213n12; *Ein Heldenleben*, 50, 59–60, 108–9, 114–15, 118–19, 133, 139, 142–43, 148, 154, 162–62, 173–74, 176–77, 205; Horn Concerto No. 1, op. 11, 82; *Intermezzo*, 63, 108, 119, 163; "Introduction to *Die Musik* (A Collection of Illustrated Essays)" (essay), 169; "Is There an Avant-Garde in Music?" (essay), 45; *Josephs Legende*, 192–93; "Letzte Aufzeichnung" (essay), 120, 173; *Die Liebe der Danae*, 180; "Das Lied des Steinklopfers," op. 49, no. 4, 100; *Lila* (unfinished Singspiel), 95, 98; *Macbeth*, 82, 178; *Metamorphosen*, 77, 94–95, 120, 133, 136, 165, 180; "Morgen," op. 27, no. 4, 100; "Die Nacht," op. 10, no. 3, 155; "On Melodic Inspiration" (essay), 95, 179, 198, 200; "On the Production of 'Tannhäuser' in Bayreuth" (essay), 40; Piano Sonata, op. 5, 156; "Recollections of My Youth and Years of Apprenticeship" (essay), 34; "Reminiscences of Hans von Bülow" (essay), 36–37; "Reminiscences of My Father" (essay), 66; *Der Rosenkavalier*, 14, 18, 59, 94, 100, 167; "Ruhe, meine Seele!," op. 27, no. 1, 100; *Salome*, 2, 7, 15–17, 30, 48, 60–61, 73, 87, 178, 192–93, 204, 208; *Die schweigsame Frau*, 166; Serenade, op. 7, 82; Suite, op. 4, 37; *Symphonia domestica*, 31–34, 50, 58–61, 100, 108, 116, 118–19, 132–33, 141, 143–44, 146, 148, 153, 161–63, 166–67, 194; Symphony No. 1, o.op. 69, 29, 81; Symphony No. 2, op. 12, 3–4, 37, 81, 163, 202; *Till Eulenspiegels lustige Streiche*, 9, 45, 49, 71, 73, 86, 95, 112, 116, 124, 132–33, 142, 147, 150–51, 187–88; "Timely Remarks on Music Education" (essay), 48; *Tod und Verklärung*, 32, 77, 82, 112, 119, 122, 124–25, 127, 131, 147, 162, 166, 178, 208, 248n32; "Traum durch die Dämmerung," op. 29, no. 1, 100; Violin Sonata, op. 18, 64, 156; *Wandrers Sturmlied*, 95, 98; "Wenn," op. 31, no. 2, 99

Strauss, Richard (grandson), 24, 93
Stuck, Franz, 107
subjectivity, 110–15, 119–20, 135–36, 142–43, 146, 150, 159–61, 164, 174–76, 180–81, 201, 207

Thalberg, Sigismond, 26, 65
Thomas, Theodore, 81
Thuille, Ludwig, 27, 29, 65–66, 72, 188
Tolstoy, Leo, 107
Toscanini, Arturo, 35, 78, 139, 233n58

Urban, Erich, 142

Vienna Academic Wagner Society, 27, 67
Virgil, 104

Wackenroder, Wilhelm Heinrich, 160
Wagner, Cosima, 30, 43–44, 65, 67, 72–73, 84, 98, 124, 130–32, 136, 172–73, 188, 191
Wagner, Richard, 3–5, 8–9, 12, 15, 19, 26, 29, 31, 36, 41, 43–45, 47, 98, 107, 121–22, 126, 130, 133, 136, 139, 145, 156–58, 160, 163, 169, 175, 177, 179–80, 190, 200, 205, 230n19; "Beethoven" (essay), 69; *Der fliegende Holländer*, 84;

Götterdämmerung, 27; *Lohengrin*, 47, 75, 84, 130; *Die Meistersinger von Nürnberg*, 72, 75, 84; *Oper und Drama* (treatise), 69; *Parsifal*, 72, 74–75, 125, 163, 177, 186–87, 190; *Das Rheingold*, 12; *Rienzi*, 84; *Der Ring des Nibelungen*, 44, 75, 77; *Siegfried*, 84; *Tannhäuser*, 44, 62, 72, 85; *Tristan und Isolde*, 41–42, 45, 56, 66, 70, 72–77, 114, 130, 132, 151; "Über Franz Liszt's symphonische Dichtungen: Brief an M. W." (essay), 124, 129, 131, 133; *Die Walküre*, 52
Wagner, Siegfried, 44
Walter, Bruno, 44–45, 48, 70, 73–77, 105, 113, 123, 126, 128–29, 133, 181
Weber, Carl Maria von: *Die drei Pintos*, 3; *Invitation to the Dance*, 26
Webern, Anton, 17–18, 91, 101

Weingartner, Felix, 85
Wenzel, Cäcilie, 50
Werbeck, Walter, xiv
Wetzler, Hermann Hans, 141, 144, 148
Whitman, Walt, 107
Wihan-Weis, Dora, 50
Wilde, Oscar, 100
Wilhelm II, Emperor of Germany and King of Prussia, 100
Wolf, Hugo, 27–28, 67, 79
Wolff, Hermann, 198
Wolzogen, Ernst von, 76
Wolzogen, Hans von, 76
Wüllner, Franz, 123

Zemlinsky, Alexander, 158
Ziegler, Edward, 148
Zweig, Stefan, 24–25

CHARLES YOUMANS, Professor of Musicology at Penn State University, is the author of *Richard Strauss's Orchestral Music and the German Intellectual Tradition: The Philosophical Roots of Musical Modernism* (IUP 2005) and the editor of *The Cambridge Companion to Richard Strauss* (Cambridge 2010).

Lightning Source UK Ltd.
Milton Keynes UK
UKOW05n1134250517
302000UK00008B/34/P